FIGHTER AND BOMBER
SQUADRONS AT WAR

FIGHTER AND BOMBER
SQUADRONS AT WAR

ANDREW BROOKES

Contents

It has been a conscious decision to include in this volume photographs of historic interest which might, in other circumstances, have been excluded on the grounds of quality. It is hoped that readers will accept the consequent reduction in production standards of some plates.

Right: Mosquito NF 30s. The NF 30 was a development of the NF XIX with two-stage Merlin engines.

This title first published by Ian Allan
as **2** separate volumes
Fighter Squadron at War © Andrew J. Brookes 1980
Bomber Squadron at War © Andrew J. Brookes 1983

This edition published 1995 by The Promotional Reprint Company Ltd, exclusively for Bookmart Limited, Desford Road, Enderby, Leicester LE9 5AD, Chris Beckett Ltd in New Zealand, Coles in Canada, Reed Editions in Australia and Booksales in New York.

ISBN 1 85648 246 4

Printed and bound in China

Preface

It is an interesting observation on modern society that as the years of peace increase from 1945, so popular interest in the happenings of World War 2 grows rather than diminishes. Perhaps this is due to the increasing number of young people who know nothing of war and want to learn, or perhaps it is an indictment of future prospects that people need to seek inspiration in the great deeds of the past, but there is no denying that histories of war grow ever more numerous and popular with each passing year. This is particularly true of the history of wartime aircraft, and the Ian Allan series on 'Aircraft at War' is foremost in this field, but we all know that the finest technology can be as nothing if the right men (and women) are not available to put it to good use. The heart of an aeroplane is undoubtedly its engine, but the people who maintain and fly it are its soul.

This book therefore is not so much a history of machinery as an attempt to round off the Ian Allan 'at War' series by underlining the human dimension of World War 2. This I have tried to do by illustrating what it is like to serve on an RAF fighter squadron between 1939 and 1945. The unit I have chosen had a particularly varied and exciting combat history, but I have made no attempt to put together a complete 'official' history of one particular unit — rather this is more of a kaleidoscope of life in the wartime as seen through the medium of the official reports, letters, diaries and mementoes that the members of one squadron left behind. This is how they saw themselves, and how others saw them; the words are theirs, the pictures are theirs, the emphasis is theirs, and if this book reinforces some points and neglects others it is only a measure of what the Squadron personnel regarded as important and, by implication, what they deemed of less consequence.

Fighter Squadron at War therefore should be regarded as a scrapbook of an age, and as such it attempts to portray how men and women in RAF uniform worked and played, fought and died. This is the story of a perfectly ordinary generation which was plucked from its studies and civilian jobs to take part in a conflict which was not of its making, which was often beyond its understanding, and which promised not ripe old age but rather death on the morrow. This story therefore is dedicated to everyone everywhere who served in the RAF, and in particular to those who fought for a peace they did not live to see.

Acknowledgements

Most of the material in this book comes from past members of 85 Squadron and their families, and I must say how grateful I am for all their generous and unstinting help. I also wish to record my gratitude to the many authors from whose works I have taken quotations and inspiration — Peter Townsend's *Duel of Eagles*, and C. F. Rawnsley and R. Wright's *Night Fighter* were particularly valuable. Finally, I must pay tribute to the help and assistance I have received from the staff of the Public Record Office, Kew, and I gratefully acknowledge permission to reproduce Crown Copyright material and photographs.

Left: Scout Experimental (SE) 5As of 85 Squadron at St Omer, France in 1918. *IWM*

Below: Second Lieutenant Stuart Elliott in an 85 Squadron Scout Experimental (SE) 5A. Notice the hexagon insignia on the fuselage. *IWM*

Right: Major W. A. 'Billy' Bishop VC.

In the Beginning

No 85 Squadron was formed at Upavon, Wiltshire, on 1 August 1917. It was equipped initially with single-seat SE 5A aircraft and after a period of training at Norwich the Squadron moved to Hounslow where, in March 1918, Major W. A. 'Billy' Bishop VC took command. William Avery Bishop was born in Ontario in 1894 and he transferred from the Canadian Cavalry to the Royal Flying Corps in July 1915 to see more action. As a fighter pilot he was a great 'loner' — he won the VC on 2 June 1917 after single-handedly attacking a German airfield at dawn. After a period as chief instructor at the Aerial Gunnery School he was given command of 85 Squadron, which he led to Marquise in France on 22 May 1918. Although he had been ordered to do very little operational flying, Bishop returned to the Western Front in a spectacular fashion, shooting down 25 enemy aircraft during 36½ flying hours spread over twelve days, and despatching 12 of them in the last three days. A combat report signed by Bishop and dated 19 June 1918 told higher authority in 14 laconic sentences that he shot down five aircraft in the space of 12 minutes as though it were an everyday occurrence. Higher authority was horrified, for Bishop was far too valuable to risk unnecessarily, and he was ordered back to England and an appointment in the Air Ministry straight away.

On 5 July the Squadron acquired another 'ace' as its CO, Major 'Mick' Mannock. Mannock was different from Bishop in that he did not work best alone but was probably the greatest fighter leader on any side in World War 1. He arrived on 85 with 61 victims to his name, but he had recently been stricken by the death of his great friend, Major James McCudden VC. Mannock vowed vengeance against the enemy, but he was living on his nerves. At dawn on 26 July he entered the Mess at St Omer and played his favourite gramophone record, *Londonderry Air*. He then took off to give Lieutenant D. C. Inglis, a newcomer to the Squadron, the benefit of his experience in the air. Mannock picked out a German two-seater from nowhere, got a burst in at close

10

Far left: A group of 85 Squadron aircrew in France in 1918. Major 'Billy' Bishop VC is standing fourth from the right. *IWM*

Left: 'Mick' Mannock VC.

Below left: Squadron aircraft, personnel and four-legged friends at St Omer, France, on 21 June 1918. *IWM*

Below: The old and the new in the Squadron hangar at Debden in 1938. The Gladiator (right) was the RAF's last biplane fighter and, although it introduced an enclosed cockpit, the Gladiator had a top speed of only 253mph. In addition it carried only four .303 Browning guns, which was not much of an improvement over the two .303 Vickers guns which had been the standard armament of the RAF when it was formed in 1918.

range, and shot him down. Then he did the very thing he had always warned others never to do — he followed the blazing aircraft down until it crashed. At 200 feet a German infantryman's random bullet pierced his fuel tank and Inglis could only watch helplessly as the RFC's greatest ace went into a slow dive and crashed in flames. When the news of Mannock's death reached 85 the pilots were stunned and they went to their huts and wept. The mechanics were similarly affected, although he had only been on the Squadron for three weeks. Later Mannock was to be awarded a posthumous VC, the original citation for which was to hang in the 85 Squadron dispersal for many years.

It was in France that 85 Squadron aircraft first displayed their famous 'Hexagon'. In order to differentiate between units in the heat of battle, it was decreed that squadrons should display distinctive geometric symbols on their aircraft, and 85 Squadron chose the hexagon — it was said that this was the shape of the font in the church at St Omer where the Squadron was based at the time.

Major C. M. Crowe took over the Squadron on 28 August and by the Armistice they had shot down a total of 99 enemy air-

craft. In February 1919 85 Squadron returned to England, and at Lopcombe Corner on 3 July 1919 the Squadron that had been led by the top two British aces of the war disbanded, its pilots mostly demobilised, and its aircraft sold for scrap.

It took a renewed threat from Germany to bring 85 Squadron back to life again 19 years later. Fighter Command was formed on 14 July 1936 but it only had eleven squadrons and seven airfields to its name; consequently, in an effort to give the new Command more teeth, an expansion programme was undertaken which resulted in 85 Squadron re-forming from 'A' Flight of 87 Squadron at Debden, Essex, on 1 June 1938. Debden had become an airfield by accident. In 1934 a Bulldog biplane had crashed into a cornfield near Saffron Walden and experts investigating the crash reported that the area would make an ideal airfield, so it was bought for £4,000. Thus it came about, in response to the growing might of the Luftwaffe in Germany, that 85 Squadron came back into being in an ex-cornfield under the command of Flight Lieutenant D. E. Turner.

However, it was one thing to form a squadron — it was another matter altogether

to give them the wherewithal to counter the most powerful airforce in the world, and for the next few months 85 Squadron never grew beyond the strength of one Flight and had only Gloster Gladiators to fly.

On 4 September 1938, 85 Squadron entered the monoplane age when it received its first Hawker Hurricane Is and expanded into 'A' and 'B' Flights plus a Headquarters Flight. The transition from the biplane Gladiator age to the Hurricane era was not without incident.

On returning from annual gun firing training in Northern Ireland at the end of October, the Squadron found itself with a new CO, Squadron Leader D. F. W. Atcherley. David Francis William Atcherley was born in 1904 at York. He was educated at Oundle and Sandhurst where he fenced for the College before being seconded from the Army to the RAF in 1927. He liked the new service so much that he obtained a permanent commission in it two years later and, along with his twin brother Richard, David Atcherley became a by-word in the RAF for panache and derring-do.

Above: Squadron Hurricanes in the winter of 1938. 'NO' were the Squadron code letters in 1938 and early 1939 — thereafter they changed to 'VY' for the duration of the war.

Left: Looking more at home in the spring sunlight of 1939.

The stories told about the Atcherley twins are legion, ranging from the time one stood in for the other at an annual medical examination to the occasion when one brother inspected a parade by flying upside down along the front rank. My favourite story however is the one told by Air Chief Marshal Sir Christopher Foxley-Norris:[*]

'On one occasion in 1943, David Atcherley was flying home from North Africa for an important operational conference. The weather over Southern England was very bad, and he had to be diverted to the only airfield that was still open, Portreath in Cornwall. As was, and remains mandatory during flying, an ambulance and a fire tender were standing by the Air Traffic Control Tower. David, now going to be very late for his meeting, taxied in at break-neck speed, leapt out of the aircraft and into the ambulance whose engine was running, and disappeared in a cloud of dust toward the nearest main line railway station, Redruth.

'The Station Commander was naturally furious. He addressed an indignant letter to Group HQ who ... despatched a stern rebuke in writing but unfortunately it was addressed in error to the other twin. Richard hastened to reply:

'Sir,

"I have the honour to acknowledge your letter of 23 November, whose sentiments I entirely endorse. To remove, without

[*]*A Lighter Shade of Blue*; Ian Allan Ltd, 1978.

12

Left: Squadron Hurricanes at Debden in 1939.

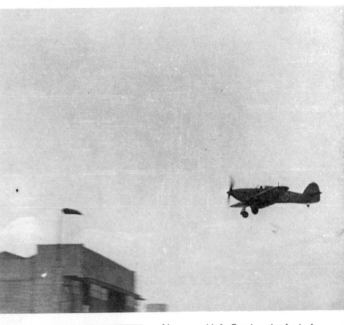

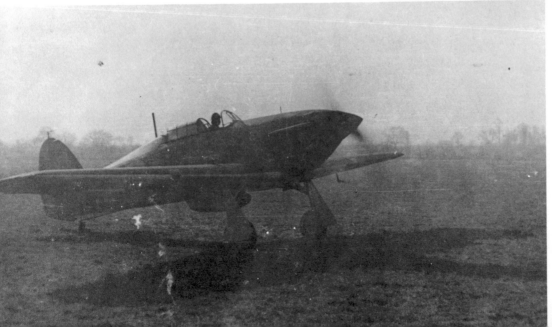

Above and left: Getting the feel of the new aircraft. The Hurricane was the first monoplane fighter to enter RAF service, and with its top speed of 316mph, not to mention a host of revolutionary new features including a retractable undercarriage, (it was amazing how many pilots forgot to put it down for landing after being used to fixed undercarriages), conversion to the new aeroplane could be a tricky business.

Above right: In comes a prospective 'prang'.

Right, far right and below: Squadron Hurricanes that bit the Debden dust.

Bottom right: David Atcherley in his own Comper Swift. He was the bane of 'Met' men and he became known as the man who raved, 'Well, where the blazes can we fly?'

14

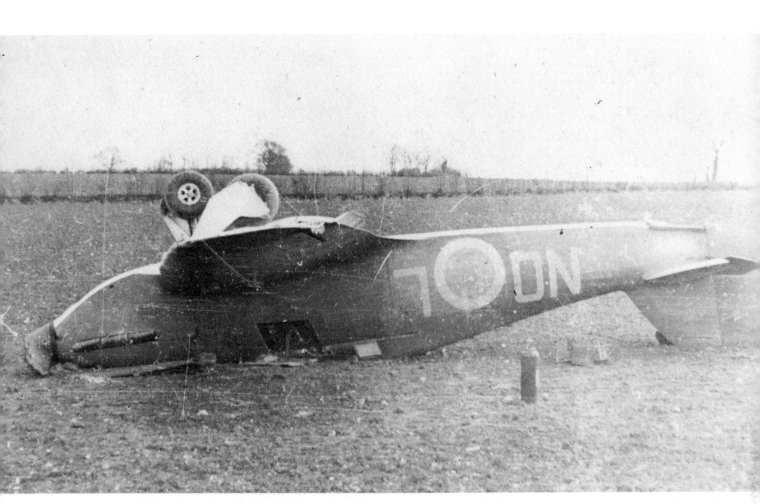

authority or permission, the emergency ambulance from an operating station, thus hampering the flying programme and imperilling the lives of crews already airborne is quite unforgiveable, and fully merits the tone and content of your communication.

"I have to inform you however, that I personally was in no way involved in this incident. I can only presume the officer concerned may have been my brother, D. Atcherley.

> I have the honour to be, Sir,
> Your obedient servant
> etc etc

PS   Personally, I always take the fire engine on these occasions." '

In pursuance of such high jinks, David Atcherley typified the 'officer class' in the prewar RAF. The principal method of obtaining a permanent commission in those days was either through a university or via the RAF College, Cranwell. Entry through either of these doors was theoretically open to all, but although there were scholarships available to those of limited means there were no university grants in those days and the fees for the two years' training course at Cranwell were £300 in 1938. To enter Cranwell a boy had to be between $17\frac{1}{2}$ and $19\frac{1}{2}$ years of age, of proven academic ability,

Other Squadron Hurricanes that came to grief at Debden.

and impress a board of officers as to his 'Interview and Record'. The 'Interview and Record' gave information as to mentality, character, and athletic prowess. The size and type of candidate's school would be taken into consideration, and whether he was a house or school prefect ... The report of his headmaster would carry much influence, whilst distinction in sport, especially in games involving severe physical strain, is an obvious indication of a high degree of physical stamina. Rowing, boxing, football, water-polo and long-distance running all require powers of endurance, and marked ability in fast-moving ball games (tennis, fives etc) indicates a good co-ordination of hand and eye.*

Such talk of 'type of school, rowing and fives' even put most grammar school lads out of the running, and add to this the fact that an RAF officer in 1938 had to maintain a social standard alongside brother officers who might not only keep a private horse in the Mess stables but also a private aeroplane in the hangar, and it becomes apparent that 'background' counted for a great deal. This is not to say that the average prewar RAF officer on a permanent commission was a chinless blockhead — in fact much of the Service's success in World War 2 was undoubtedly due to the standard of leadership and example set by men taken into Cranwell during the thirties. Rather, it was more a question of glamour and challenge.

*The Royal Air Force; Monk & Winter, Blackie & Son Ltd, 1938.

Top left: The Squadron Miles Magister and *(centre left)* Tiger Moth which were used for communications work and for generally enjoying life in the prewar skies.

Right, below left and below: The Debden Hunt, early 1939. Hunting and riding were very much part of the social life of the RAF before the war. The blemish on the photograph below is the result of light leaking on to the film during development.

Neither the Army nor Navy had come out of the First World War with overmuch glory, and to sons of men who had suffered at the hands of uninspiring admirals and generals, the RAF in the thirties often promised a brighter and less conservative prospect than the other two services. As a result the RAF was able to select the elite of the elite because it could afford to pick and choose from the best youth in the land.

A newly commissioned and unmarried Pilot Officer fresh out of Cranwell was paid £381 14s 7d a year in 1938, and the operational world of the squadron was then open to him. The Cranwell men were the 'career' stream, those who would eventually fill such prime executive posts on the squadron as commanding officer and flight commanders.

No 85 Squadron was divided into two operational Flights and OC 'A' Flight and OC 'B' Flight were flight lieutenants each responsible for eight pilots, their aircraft and their groundcrew. Of the pilots, those holding the King's commission were either young

Top left: Squadron aircrew outside their Headquarters in the winter of 1938/39. Left to right: Pilot Officer Woods-Scawen, Pilot Officer Blair, Pilot Officer Hemingway, Pilot Officer Aven, Pilot Officer Lecky, Pilot Officer Mawhood, Pilot Officer Gowers.

Above: The whole Squadron looking their best — Easter 1939.

Left: Squadron aircrew at the same time (notice the two-bladed fixed-pitch wooden propellers of the Hurricane Is trying to capture the limelight). Left to right: Pilot Officer Woods-Scawen, Pilot Officer Stevenson, Pilot Officer Rawlinson, Pilot Officer Hemingway, Pilot Officer Mawhood, Pilot Officer Mitchell, Sergeant Goodman, Pilot Officer Lecky, Flying Officer Boothby, Flying Officer Lorimer, Squadron Leader Atcherley, Pilot Officer Aven, Flying Officer Lee, Flight Lieutenant Carver, Pilot Officer Gowers, Pilot Officer Blair, Sergeant Hampshire, Sergeant Jowitt, Sergeant Lenton.

Cranwell men or officers who could not gain, or did not aspire to, a permanent commission. The latter served on short-service commissions, which were available to 'those between 18 and 22, unmarried, and of pure European descent' and which allowed a man to serve for four years followed by six in the Reserve. A £100 gratuity was paid for each year served, though those of proven worth were allowed to transfer to a permanent commission if they so desired.

The NCO pilots were drawn from men who had worked their way up from direct entry into the ranks or from aircraft apprenticeships. In *The Mint*, T. E. Lawrence praised the aircraft mechanics as more important in their way than the pilots themselves since, but for their conscientious work, the pilots could not carry out their tasks. This was a very sound attitude and one that was certainly reflected in the pilots' approach to the groundcrews of 85.

Direct entrants to the ranks swelled in number with the RAF Expansion Scheme and they were initially paid between 2s and 3s 6d a day depending on their trade group. At the end of the training course, say for a Flight Rigger at No 2 School of Technical Training, Henlow, there came the great day of the Control Test Board. 'A senior NCO took each trainee on the oral part of the subject. There were practical jobs to be done, a built-up riveting and a splicing exercise. There was also a written paper to complete. The results were collated from each part and the average of all was the final result. Below 40% was a fail, 40-60% made one an Aircraftman 2nd class, with 60-80% one became 1st class, and 80% and over elevated one to the dizzy heights of Leading Aircraftman. It was a good man indeed who passed out LAC with the high standard demanded.*

The longest serving engagements in those trades most directly associated with aircraft maintenance were reserved for those who undertook an RAF apprenticeship. Introduced by Lord Trenchard, the apprentice scheme was designed to provide the service with a nucleus of highly skilled technicians at the end of an intensive three-year course, and from this cadre were to come the engineering officers and NCOs of the future. Boys between the ages of 15 and 17¼ could sign on for 12 years from their 18th birthday if they were accepted for apprenticeships, but like the permanent commission, an apprenticeship was a coveted prize only awarded to the elite.

A skilled LAC on 85 Squadron in 1938 earned 35s a week less 7s for food and accom-

*'Memoirs of an Aircraftman', F. J. Adkin, *Aeroplane*, February 1979.

22

Showing the new and expanding RAF to the public on Empire Day 1939. Empire Air Days were held on a Saturday in May each year from 1934 to 1939 and it was a measure of public interest in aviation that nearly a million people visited the 62 RAF stations and 15 civil airfields open to the public in 1939.

Left: Shiny Squadron Hurricanes on parade. Notice the Fairey Battle at the far right. 85 Squadron would soon be allocated to the Air Component of the British Expeditionary Force earmarked to go to France, and part of their job there would be to protect the bases occupied by the ten squadrons of Battle and Blenheim bombers assigned to the Advanced Air Striking Force.

Below, far left: Some £30,000 was raised for RAF Charities at all the Empire Air Days held in 1939, and here 85 Squadron aircrew are making their contribution with 'Lorrie' Lorrimer dressed up as 'Old Mother Riley' in preparation for some crazy flying.

Below left: Old Mother Lorrimer being wheeled out to his aircraft.

Right: The Squadron car.

Left: In more serious vein, Squadron aircrew await the call to 'Scramble' . . .

Below left: . . . and they're off.

Above: Pilot Officer Aven

Above right: Pilot Officer Stevenson

Above, far right: Pilot Officer Lecky

Right: Flight Lieutenant Carver

Centre, far right: An airman riding the range.

Bottom, far right: But war was coming and here Sergeant Geoffrey 'Sammy' Allard is digging a trench. Like his CO, Allard was born in York but of a totally different background. He joined the RAF as an apprentice at Halton in September 1929 and graduated as a metal rigger with the top grade of Leading Aircraftman three years later. A tallish, slim boy with a shock of sandy-coloured hair, Allard excelled on the hockey field and for four years as a rigger his overriding ambition was to fly. In 1936 he was accepted for pilot training and went to the Bristol Flying School at Filton for elementary training before progressing to Thornaby and then Hullavington. He finally graduated as a Sergeant Pilot on 23 October 1937, with an above-average grading, and he soon proved to be a 'natural' pilot on 85 becoming one of the Squadron's foremost exponents of aerobatics.

modation. Good conduct badges were worth an extra 3d a day, these being awarded after 5, 8, and 13 years. 'There was a tremendous esprit de corps, and comradeship was the operative word. Help was given quite unsolicited, and it was quite normal, when working late after tea, to have a couple of friends arrive and put on their overalls to lend a hand. If one inadvertently left one's money around, it was soon put in a safe place or left under the pillow. At week-ends, when most of the lads had gone home, those remaining always went round making the beds in readiness for those returning. Obviously it was the men that set the standard, and . . . we had the type of men of which the RAF could be proud.'

To the 'erks', 'COs before the war were almost God-like in their approachability' but the Warrant Officer who was in charge of the Squadron engineering establishment* was held in nearly as much awe and certainly greater fear. Each Hurricane had its own engine fitter and airframe rigger who nursed their individual charges with jealous pride, but each Flight also had its specialists in wireless, electrics etc who assisted whenever necessary, and it was from men such as these that the RAF got its NCO aircrew.

'You will have an opportunity', quoted the appropriate Air Ministry Pamphlet to apprentices, 'if you so desire, of volunteering for training as an airman pilot. One month

*There were some 87 airmen and NCOs (excluding aircrew) in the Squadron in 1939.

24

before the end of the course, your commanding officer will call for volunteers, and during your third year at a Service unit the final selection will be made subject to physical fitness.

'If you are selected you will receive practical and theoretical training, during which an allowance (at present 2s a day) will be payable. But no airman lower than leading aircraftman will be recommended for this distinction.'

The same opportunities were also open to direct entrants and all successful airmen pilots became Sergeants employed on full flying duties. However they did not lose touch with their technical trades, and on completion of six years' flying service they normally reverted to their technical duties, retaining their rank and being paid accordingly. This arrangement tended to disappear with the war, for the RAF could ill-afford to lose proven aircrew, and many airmen pilots were subsequently elevated into the commissioned ranks.

Having thus built up a pool of highly trained and highly motivated officers, NCOs, and airmen, 85 Squadron found itself allocated to the Air Component of the British Expeditionary Force on 27 June 1939. This Force was earmarked to cross over to France should war be declared, and the Squadron's brief was to help support the Battle and Blenheim bombers of the Advanced Air Striking Force and defend its bases around Rheims.

No 85 received a signal ordering the mobilisation of all units of the Component Force at 2359 hours on 23 August 1939. At 1115 hours the following day, 85 was ordered to disperse all aircraft around the airfield boundary and to bring both operational Flights to readiness. By 26 August the Squadron hangar had been camouflaged and 72 'E' class Reservists* had been posted in from Personnel Transit Centres together with six extra MT vehicles. 'Mobilisation brought many problems in its wake, not the least of which, as far as we were concerned, being accommodation. Whereas Expansion recruitment had gradually increased room accommodation to 30 to a room, another eight or ten men were pushed into each barrack block and the space between the beds shrank literally to inches, just enough to undress. In addition, an efficient blackout was fitted to all windows and doors which, on a hot summer's night, generated a fug atmosphere that could be carved out.'

'A' Flight and 'B' Flight took it in turns to keep Hurricanes at constant readiness during day and night, and by 1 September the Squadron had completed mobilisation. Two days later they heard the news that war had been declared on Germany.

*The Reserve of all airmen in all trades with and without previous service in the RAF. In fact, many of the old lads were ex-RFC who, though full of gen on Gnome, Bentley, Le Rhône, and Monosoupape rotaries, were sadly bewildered by Merlin engines, stressed skin, hydraulics, pneumatics and electrics. To their great credit they knuckled down and soon became Squadron stalwarts.

Left: The first day of the war. As yet, few seem aware of what the next six years will bring.

Below: Relaxing after practising operations 'in the field'. 'One aspect of flying which seldom receives publicity', wrote an 'Erk' in his diary 'is the work of the firetender and "blood tub" (ambulance) crews. These were the boys in the old Crossley fire wagons who saw the horrors of day and night crashes at close quarters. With the standard of equipment then in use, the chances of extinguishing the fierce fires caused by large-capacity tanks were practically nil. After a crash, the smell of burnt flesh lingered in the hangars for a long time after the wreckage had been brought in. The crews of the airfield vehicles were to face this kind of thing to an ever-increasing degree as the war progressed, with its attendant high casualty rates and horrific sights.'

Below: King George VI, together with the Duke of Gloucester and the Commander-in-Chief of the British Expeditionary Force, Viscount Lord Gort, inspecting the Squadron at Lille. Hurricane VY-R was 'Dicky' Lee's aircraft.

Passage to France

'4/9/39. 0700 hours. Squadron Leader J. H. Hill, who had been posted to the Squadron for Operations Room Duties, left by Magister for Rouen, France, as air advance party.

'0800 hours. Advance party, consisting of 150 airmen under the command of Pilot Officer Rawlinson, left by rail.'*

The Advance Party arrived at Boos near Rouen on 5 September and prepared to receive the aircraft. Two days later the Squadron aircrew were released from operational readiness duties for 48 hours 'stand-down' before David Atcherley led the whole strength of sixteen Hurricanes to France via Thorney Island on 9 September. They were declared operational at Boos at 0900 hours the following day.

The Squadron began by protecting cross-Channel convoys and on 22 September it was moved up to Merville to the west of Lille.

'Throughout October the two Flights were maintained at the following states of readiness in rotation together with 87 Squadron (which had accompanied 85 Squadron to France from Debden).
Readiness — 1 day
Available at 15 minutes notice — 1 day.
Available at 30 minutes notice — 1 day.
Released — 1 day.'

On 1 November the Squadron moved again, this time to Lille/Seclin aerodrome. General Mobilisation of civilians had been ordered on 1 September 1939 and it was at Lille that the first of these new men arrived on the Squadron after completion of their hurried training. One such man was Pilot Officer T. J. Molony who joined 85 as Adjutant. Tim Molony was 'a massive and dignified man, urbane and very conscious of the niceties of decorum,' wrote a member of the Squadron. 'In civilian life he was a director of Ladbroke's, the turf accountant ... He also laid

*This, and many subsequent quotations, are taken from the Squadron Operations Record Book (RAF Form 540). 'The object of the Operations Record Book,' declared *Kings Regulations for the RAF*, 'is to furnish a complete historical record of the unit from the time of its formation ... During major operations, or when a unit is placed on a war footing, the Operations Record Book is to be compiled from day to day.'

27

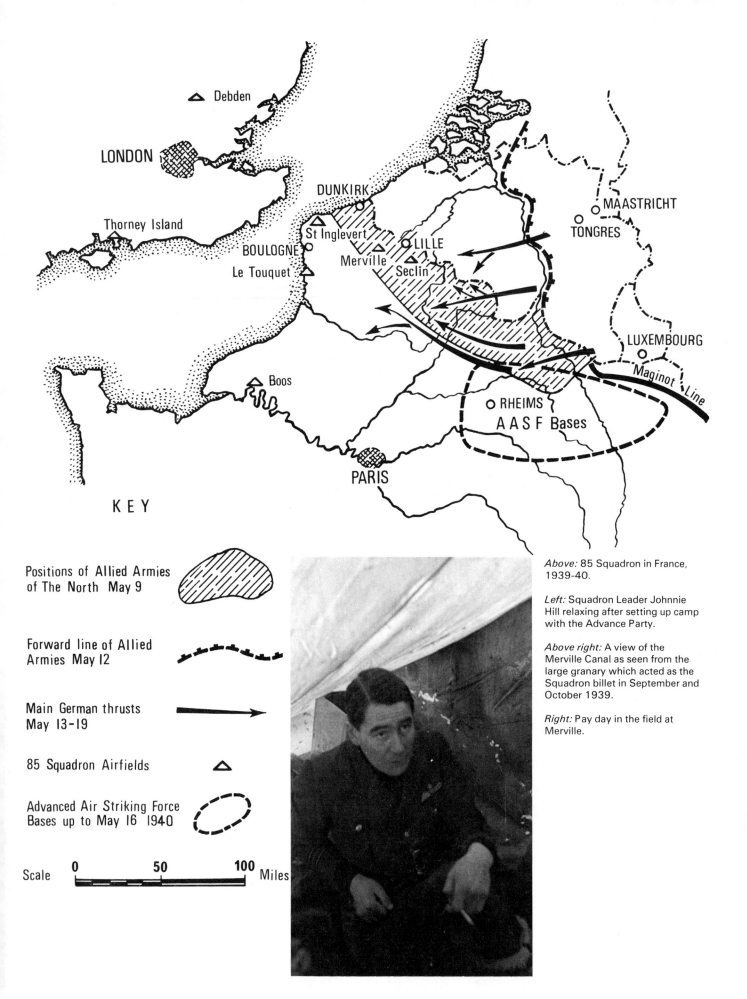

△ Debden

LONDON

Thorney Island

DUNKIRK

St Inglevert
BOULOGNE
Merville
Le Touquet
LILLE
Seclin

MAASTRICHT
TONGRES

LUXEMBOURG
Maginot Line

Boos

RHEIMS
A A S F Bases

PARIS

KEY

Positions of Allied Armies
of The North May 9

Forward line of Allied
Armies May 12

Main German thrusts
May 13-19

85 Squadron Airfields   △

Advanced Air Striking Force
Bases up to May 16 1940

Scale   0   50   100 Miles

Above: 85 Squadron in France,
1939-40.

Left: Squadron Leader Johnnie
Hill relaxing after setting up camp
with the Advance Party.

Above right: A view of the
Merville Canal as seen from the
large granary which acted as the
Squadron billet in September and
October 1939.

Right: Pay day in the field at
Merville.

claim to being the last man to bowl underarm in first-class cricket, playing for Surrey.'

As the Squadron effort centred on patrols over the Channel to protect shipping from possible air attack, 85 had Sections detached to Le Touquet (north of Boulogne) and St Inglevert near Calais.

'21/11/39. Whilst on search patrol over Boulogne, Flight Lieutenant R. H. A. Lee attacked an He 111 which crashed into the Channel and burst into flames. It was the Squadron's first victory in the present war.'

Those aircraft and crews that remained at Lille reinforced the coastal detachments and hopefully deterred possible German bomber raids inland, but it was really shadow-boxing against an elusive enemy and the only Squadron losses were a couple of Hurricanes which crashed on take-off. In spite of Dicky Lee's success therefore, Squadron personnel relied on visiting personalities to sustain morale during the Phoney War.

'6/12/39. Visit by His Majesty the King, in company with the Duke of Gloucester and Viscount Lord Gort. His Majesty inspected aircraft on tarmac and visited the Operations Room. Whilst in the Ops Room, orders were given to a Section of aircraft, which were then at readiness, to intercept an enemy raid over Calais.' But as usual, the Luftwaffe had only been probing the defences and there was no enemy to engage when the Hurricanes got there.

Left: Preparing for all eventualities. Gas warfare was considered a grave possibility at the time, and here a member of the Squadron groundcrew on exercise labours to wheel a Hurricane into position while wearing a tin helmet, gas mask, gas cape and rifle. *IWM*

Below left: He awaits the pilot's thumbs up by the starter trolley. The old days of hand-swinging had long since gone — all the aircraftman had to do was press a switch and the batteries in the starter trolley would do the rest electrically. *IWM*

Bottom left: Off goes a smoke cannister behind the Hurricane to simulate a gas attack. *IWM*

Right: Tim Molony, the Squadron Adjutant, in nonchalent pose.

Far right: Flight Lieutenant 'Dicky' Lee who scored the first Squadron 'kill' in World War 2.

Below: Squadron Hurricanes at Merville.

'8/12/39. Leslie Henson and his concert party visited the station to give a very fine performance in the Airmen's Sleeping Quarters under difficult circumstances.'

'16/12/39. Visit by the Prime Minister, the Rt Hon N. Chamberlain, the Duke of Gloucester and Lord Gort. PM inspected aircraft on tarmac and officers and airmen in hangar. Afterwards he inspected Airmen's Sleeping Quarters and Airmen's Dining Hall.'

On 8 January 1940, Squadron Leader J. O. W. Oliver took over from David Atcherley but he did not bring the sun with him.

'Throughout January all Squadron aircraft were at "Super Readiness" but the weather conditions made flying impossible except in emergency. Snow cover of sundry mole hills took their toll of tail-wheels due to freezing earth. Sometimes the temperature was down to -10° of frost in the Airmen's Sleeping Quarters and no amount of fires would keep the place warm. Colds, 'flu, bronchitis etc took many valuable members of the Squadron to their beds — illness prevalent.'

The snows started to melt in February but this only led to slush and soggy conditions on the grass airfield.

'24/2/40. 0900 hours — plot received on E/A (enemy aircraft) approaching aerodrome at 20,000 feet. Three aircraft ordered to protect Lille/Seclin at 20,000ft but when they

Above: Building roads at Lille/Seclin. Administrative difficulties with the French over the allocation of airfields and supplies led to the RAF having to undertake most of the airfield development work themselves on a 'self-help' basis. The Sergeant on the right *(top)* starts off in a supervisory capacity but he soon despairs of this and has to start digging himself *(above)* to lead by example.

Left: 'Pay attention at the back there.' Instruction in the use of Brownings on a tripod which the Squadron armourers put together to provide at least some semblance of airfield defence. Unfortunately, such unofficial initiative had its drawbacks. When the Blitzkrieg started, there were rumours that the Germans were using some captured Blenheim bombers, so when two bona fida RAF Blenheims flew low over Lille on their way to attack the enemy, they were shot at.

Below left: Squadron Hurricane outside the control tower at Lille. The RAF always referred to control towers as 'Watch Towers'.

Above right: King George VI leaves the tarmac at Lille looking well pleased with what he has seen.

Right: 85 Squadron personnel at Lille in formal pose. Squadron Leader Oliver is third from the left, and Warrant Officer Newton, in charge of the groundcrews, is far right. Mr Newton joined 85 as a Sergeant rigger when it reformed in 1938 and he rose to become Squadron Engineering Officer by 1940. Several times after that he refused further promotion in order to stay with the Squadron.

Above right: Aircrew at Lille in more ebullient mood.

Right: Sergeant Cole posing in front of a Lysander which dropped in to visit the Squadron. There were five squadrons of Lysanders in France responsible for reconnaissance over the BEF front.

Below: The winter of 1939/40 at Lille. Flight Lieutenant Boothby discussing technical matters with the NCO in charge of 'A' Flight groundcrews, Flight Sergeant Howard.

Dressed for the winter weather. *(below right)* Pilot Officer Stevenson *(below far right)* Sergeant Allard.

attempted to take-off, one aircraft stood up on its nose and the two others sank up to their axles. The Ops Room abandoned any further attempts to get aircraft off. E/A turned about in the meantime and made for home. Aerodrome placed U/S (unserviceable — the RAF abounded in abbreviations) once more.'

'8/3/40. First award of the war. Flight Lieutenant Lee awarded DFC for outstanding brilliance and efficiency ... in operating as Flight Commander terminating in his despatch of He 111 aircraft.'

'10/4/40. Squadron moved south to Mons-En-Chaussee near Peronne. Advance Party proceeded by road in the morning and took over billets from 13 Squadron. Aircraft arrived at 1700 hours and main party by road at 2300 hours. One Section left behind at Lille/Seclin for operational flying.'

Mons-En-Chaussee made a welcome change from the bleak countryside around Lille. On 23 April Squadron personnel helped extinguish a large fire in the village during which LAC Fletcher fell off a roof and broke his arm. Nothing much else happened there though and 85 Squadron moved back to Lille three days later where they set up the Orderly Room in an adjacent Chateau.

These moves, and the associated packing and unpackings of lock, stock and barrel, reminded some of the perambulations of the Grand Old Duke of York, but if men tired of the Phoney War few relished the action when it finally arrived.

The Squadron strength on 10 May 1940 was the CO, an adjutant, a medical officer, an equipment officer, and an intelligence officer, together with 20 aircrew and some 80 groundcrew. The following record of their achievements in the Battle of France was completed from memory after the event because all original documents were destroyed before evacuation.

Above left: The Squadron car looking somewhat forlorn.

Above: Flight Lieutenant Boothby arrives to keep it company.

Left: Pilot Officer Lecky comes to grief on a makeshift toboggan.

Below left: David Mawhood relaxing in the snow. He was to lose an eye in action on the first day of the Blitzkrieg.

'10/5/40. 0410 hours. At the marginally noted hour the Blitzkrieg started, and the first intimation the Squadron received was the sound of innumerable Hun aircraft overhead and the sound of anti-aircraft fire both light and heavy. Within a few minutes one section of "A" Flight and one of "B" Flight were in the air after the Hun, and inside 40 minutes the two Sections had landed to refuel and re-arm. Three Henschels and one He 111K were brought down in this first sortie,* our casualties being Pilot Officer

*The Air Ministry defined enemy casualties as follows:

'Destroyed
(a) Aircraft must be seen on the ground or in the air destroyed by a member of the crew or formation, or confirmed from other sources, eg ships at sea, local authorities, etc.
(b) Aircraft must be seen to descend with flames issuing. It is not sufficient if only smoke is seen.
(c) Aircraft must be seen to break up in the air.

'Probables
(a) When the pilot of a single-engined aircraft is seen to bale out.
(b) The aircraft must be seen to break off the combat in circumstances which lead the pilot to believe it will be a loss.

'Damaged
Aircraft must be seen to be considerably damaged as a result of attack, eg under-carriage dropped, engine stopped, aircraft parts shot away, or volumes of smoke issuing.'

All Squadron claims therefore had to undergo scrutiny before they were officially accepted. However, postwar research reveals that some claims were exaggerated even though they were made in good faith and apparently verified at the time.

Above and left: But winter had its more serious side. Pilot Officer Mawhood's aircraft after it 'nosed over' when the wheels got bogged down in soggy ground on take-off.

Below left: David Mawhood's replacement aircraft.

'A Book of Verse underneath the Bough,
A Jug of Wine, a Loaf of Bread — and Thou
Beside me singing in the Wilderness —
Oh, Wilderness were paradise enow!'

Left: The calm before the storm. Whether or not they were reading *Omar Khayyam* or *The Sporting Life,* Allard and Boothby *(above left)* and other members of the Squadron *(left)* enjoy bottles of 'plonk' and a chat beneath the spring foliage. Few appreciated that the 'Phoney War' was about to end.

Below: The hot war is getting closer. A Hurricane carried 333 rounds of .303 ammunition for each of its eight guns and armourers are seen here loading the belts. *IWM*

D. V. G. Mawhood who was wounded in one eye, and one machine rendered temporarily unserviceable. Intermittently throughout the day, as each Section and Flight landed, the pilots and aircraft were on the ground only long enough to allow re-arming and refuelling and so it went on from dawn till dusk; by the end of the day the Squadron had a total bag of 17 E/A to their credit with the loss of two more of our aircraft which were rendered unserviceable. Two bombing attacks were made on the aerodrome which proved inaccurate, the bombs dropping to the north and south-east of the Squadron head-quarters.'

'11/5/40. Eight E/A were shot down today. Flight Lieutenant R. H. A. Lee failed to return from an offensive patrol covering the advance of the British Expeditionary Force over the Tongres-Maastricht Section — he was reported last seen on a Dornier's tail at about 2,000ft. The Hun made a successful raid on the aerodrome at 1220 hours and registered five 50 kilo bombs on the Officers' Quarters and Mess. Fortunately the casualties were few — the Adjutant's driver, AC 1 Bolton, W. J., was killed and his car written-off. One of the cooks in the Officers' Mess was slightly wounded. In the evening the Squadron moved to Lesquin village where billets were found to house Squadron personnel.'

'12/5/40. Seven E/A accounted for. The Hun made another raid at approximately 1350 hours; the bombs dropped about 400 feet to the north of the Chateau. Of the seven E/A shot down, five were He 111Ks, one Dornier, and one Ju 88. Flight Lieutenant R. H. A. Lee reported back to the Squadron. He had been shot down and had to bale out — he was only slightly wounded. He descended by parachute in or near a village in Belgium which was in the process of being reoccupied by German mechanised forces. He borrowed a peasant's smock and walked through the German lines and reported all he had seen to the first English unit he met; the information proved to be of the greatest value.'

'13/5/40. Squadron Leader Oliver decided that Lesquin was unhealthy due to the fact that there was a munitions factory in the village, and he ordered a move to Fretin and Ennetierre villages. The officers and Squadron headquarters took up residence in a chateau in the former village, and the NCOs and men and transport were quartered at Ennetierre. 'A' Flight moved into a wood one mile west of their dispersal point, but 'B' Flight remained in the farm house behind their dispersal point. As a matter of interest it ought to be stated here that the chateau at Fretin occupied by the officers was at one time (1708) the property of the Duke of Marl-borough.

'Squadron Leader Oliver failed to return from an offensive patrol and was reported to have been shot down after having disposed of

Top: Armourers loading ammunition for Hurricane guns. *IWM*

Above: Checking a Squadron Hurricane's gunsight. In aerial warfare, a fighter pilot usually had to aim at a target that was moving relative to himself, and consequently he was only likely to hit it if he aimed ahead of the target. This was known as the 'deflection angle' and the ring on the Hurricane rear sight corresponded to the amount of 'aim-off' necessary to hit a target with a 50mph crossing speed. Thus when the target intersected the ring-sight, the pilot fired, and hopefully the enemy and the bullets found themselves in the same piece of airspace. However this 'ring and bead' sight was a crude system, being aligned for only one crossing speed, and until more sophisticated reflector sights became available, the ability to calculate deflection angles accurately became the hall-mark of the fighter 'ace'.

two E/A, one to the north of Lille and the other on the suburbs of Hazelbrook. A total of 13 E/A were accounted for today. Squadron Leader Oliver returned to the Squadron in the afternoon. His aircraft had been hit by a cannon shell and he had to bale out. On the way down he was shot at by Belgians who mistook him for a Hun parachutist. The Hun made two bombing attacks on the aerodrome but without success.'

'14/5/40. Five E/A shot down today. Flying Officer A. B. Angus accounted for two of them. Again the Hun made two attempts to bomb the aerodrome with slightly better results.'

'15/5/40. Four E/A shot down today. Sergeant Pilot Allard shot down an He 111K within 1½ miles of the aerodrome — nothing of interest could be found except six unexploded 50 kilo bombs as the occupants and the plane were a smouldering mass of ruins. Flying Officer D. H. Allen, Flying Officer T. G. Pace and Pilot Officer J. H. Ashton failed to return from a patrol over Belgium.'

'16/5/40. Eight E/A shot down today. Flying Officer Allen and Pilot Officer Ashton returned, the former having had to bale out due to his machine being set on fire as a result of a combat against unequal odds. Today it was learnt that Flying Officer Pace crashed his machine while on fire and he was seriously wounded and burnt — he is in

hospital in England. The Hun, for the first time since the Blitzkrieg started, failed to bomb the aerodrome. Flying Officer A. B. Angus and Pilot Officer M. H. G. Rawlinson were shot down fighting against odds — both accounted for two E/A each in this fight before they met their end. It is estimated that 75 E/A were encountered in this action. Sergeant Pilot Crozier was reported missing.'

'17/5/40. Sergeant Pilot Crozier reported safe. Only four E/A shot down today. The roads through Fretin and Ennetierre villages were crammed with refugees from Belgium. The Hun bombed the area between Fretin village and the 'drome and registered a direct hit on the old windmill immediately to the south. Pilot Officer A.B. Angus buried in Fretin cemetery. Flight Lieutenant Lee, Flying Officer Blair, Pilot Officer Ashton and Sergeant Pilot Allard flew over to England for a short rest.'

This last observation underlined the strain involved in flying all day, every day, in combat again superior odds. Sergeant 'Sammy' Allard for instance destroyed ten enemy aircraft in a week but only by flying four and five times a day with little or no rest in between. This had to take its toll of mind and body and on 16 May, after only an hour and a half's sleep the previous night, Allard took-off on the first of four sorties that day. Bombs were bursting on the aerodrome as he and his section took-off on their second patrol and on the third patrol Allard fell

Above: The Chateau at Fretin, once owned by the Duke of Marlborough, to which the Squadron HQ and Officers' Mess moved after the Blitzkrieg on 13 May 1940.

Above: Sergeant Allard showing Flight Lieutenant Boothby how he shot down two German aircraft. Not that Boothby needed much instruction for he shot down three enemy aircraft in one day during the Battle of France. *IWM*

asleep three times over German-occupied territory. As he taxied in from his last patrol of the day, the groundcrew were surprised not to see him jump out after the aircraft shut down. A mechanic opened the canopy only to find that Allard had finally succumbed to sheer weariness and fallen asleep where he sat. He was still unconscious when the groundcrew lifted him out and it was decided to let him sleep on until the dawn patrol the next day. But at dawn they still could not wake him, so Allard was sent off to hospital in England. In all he slept for 30 hours.

That evening, American war correspondent William H. Stoneman dined in the Lion d'Or at Lille with Flying Officers Noel Lepine and Derek Allen. 'Both boys were red-eyed from the lack of sleep,' he recounted to his readers, 'and dozed over their meal that night.' 'The last meal of ours must have been pretty miserable for you,' wrote 'Piney' Lepine later; 'Derek and I were both very tired.'

In such an exhausted state it was no wonder that Lepine and Allen were no match for the superior numbers of the Luftwaffe on the following day.

'18/5/40. Seven E/A shot down today. Pilot Officer J. W. Lecky reported killed in road accident and Flight Lieutenant Boothby injured returning from 48 hours leave at Le Touquet. Pilot Officers A. H. Wiens, Pilot Officer L. W. Chambers, Flying Officer W. N. Lepine, and Flying Officer D. H. Allen for the second time, failed to return from an offensive patrol over the Le Chateau quadrant. Squadron Leader J. O. W. Oliver took over command of HQ No 60 Wing vice Wing Commander J. A. Borot MC, AFC.'

Allen died but Lepine was more fortunate and he ended up as a slightly wounded prisoner of war.

Thus, in spite of everything that the Allied forces in France tried to do, the Germans rolled inexorably forward, and on 19 May instructions were given to retire the remaining RAF units from France to continue the fight from southern England. That day therefore Squadron Leader Oliver at 60 Wing HQ sent the following order to his old Squadron:

'To judge from our patrol lines the Huns are close to Douai. I have received nine extra lorries and am sending four down to Lille/Marcq who I believe are very short. I want you (Molony) and Martin (the Intelligence Officer) to supervise the packing up of the *whole* Squadron except Flight personnel who must remain to start aircraft. Draw the convoy up in the village of Ennetierre amongst the by-roads at the back. All airmen are to keep in vicinity of lorries but under cover until I send word to move. Move NW to Merville and report to 63 Wing. Report to me by Hillman Van on completion of preparations to move.'

While this was going on, the Squadron aircrew carried out offensive patrols and shot down 16 aircraft. Pilot Officer A. G. Lewis accounted for five E/A before being shot down himself and having to bale out over Lille, and Sergeant Pilot Little disposed of two more before being shot down in flames. At 1600 hours the aerodrome was bombed and one Hurricane damaged; one airman was slightly wounded. At 1830 hours the Squadron transport moved off for Merville where it arrived at 2130 hours.

'20/5/40. Squadron Leader Peacock reported to take over command from Squadron Leader Oliver, who left for England* with Pilot Officer Woods-Scawen and Sergeant Pilot Deacon by air transport. At noon, eight enemy bombers arrived over the aerodrome and proceeded to unload — no casualties except for one Hurricane at the dispersal point. What was left of the Squadron carried out offensive patrols throughout the day. Sergeant Pilot Howes missing believed forced-landed at Abbeville.

*The contribution Squadron Leader Oliver made to the Battle of France was recorded in his DSO citation dated 28 May 1940. 'This officer commanded a Squadron in France until he was invalided to England on 20 May 1940. Over 50 enemy aircraft have been brought down by the Squadron, of which Squadron Leader Oliver himself accounted for at least eight. Although ill from the effects of glycol when his engine was damaged, he did not allow his condition to handicap his flying or administration. He was an incomparable fighter commander and his personal example in the air and on the ground was a very great inspiration to his pilots. It was, in fact, necessary to restrain him from flying again after his aircraft had been shot down and he had landed by parachute.'

Above: Allard walks away from his aircraft with his brother pilots. Gone were the smart white flying overalls of the Empire Air Day mainly because a pilot shot down in them might be mistaken for, and executed as, a spy. Instead the dress in war was optional so long as it involved some semblance of official RAF uniform and generally men worked and flew in whatever was most comfortable.

Squadron Leader Peacock, Pilot Officer Burton and Pilot Officer Shrewsbury failed to return from offensive patrols and ground straffing. At 1330 hours the Adjutant received orders to destroy all Squadron files, records and cyphers etc; the Squadron was to jettison all kit belonging to airmen and officers and to move off in 30 minutes time by road to Boulogne. The ground staff remaining behind to service the remaining Hurricanes left by transport aircraft at 1800 hours escorted by four Hurricanes.* The road party, commanded by the Adjutant, arrived at Boulogne at 1830 hours, the roads being congested with refugees and their transport. The air transport and four Hurricanes landed at Hendon at 1930 hours. The ground party stayed at Boulogne for the night and were subjected throughout the night to bombing by the Huns.'

'21/5/40. The ground party went on board ship at 1100 hours. They left Boulogne at approximately 1300 hours and arrived at Dover at 1500 hours; from there they proceeded to Tidworth Camp.'

'22/5/40. The Adjutant and ground personnel reported to Debden together with the returning aircrew.'

In the 11 short days between 10 May 1940, when the Germans first invaded Holland, Belgium and Luxembourg, and 20 May when von Kleist's tanks broke through to the Channel at Abbeville thereby cutting off Allied forces in the north, 85 Squadron shot down no fewer than 90 confirmed enemy aircraft and many unconfirmed others. For this

*'The last thing we saw', recorded a wireless mechanic, 'was a French soldier shaking his fist at us.'

reason, the London Gazette of 30 May 1940 announced that the King 'has been graciously pleased to approve the under mentioned awards in recognition of gallantry displayed in flying operations against the enemy:

Squadron Leader J. L. W. Oliver	DSO and DFC
Flight Lieutenant R. H. A. Lee	DSO
Flight Lieutenant J. R. M. Boothby	DFC
Flying Officer K. H. Blair	DFC
Flying Officer D. H. Allen	DFC
Flying Officer A. B. Angus	DFC
Sergeant G. Allard	DFM'

But 85 Squadron had been devastated in the process. It returned from France with only three aircraft but these could be replaced; what was more important was the loss of valuable and experienced men. Angus and Lecky had died, Mawhood, Pace, Boothby, Clark, Brown and Crozier had been wounded, and Peacock, Lepine, Allen, Rawlinson, Burton, Shrewsbury, Chambers, Wiens and Little were missing. In other words, the Battle of France had taken seventeen front-line pilots out of 85 Squadron and, although some of these casualties had been posted in after the Blitzkrieg started, only half the pilots available on 10 May were still in a position to fight less than a fortnight later. Moreover the Squadron had lost its new CO the day after he arrived; thus, on 23 May, 'Squadron Leader P. W. Townsend DFC reported to take command of No 85 Squadron at Debden, and he proceeded with the task of re-forming the Squadron and bringing it up to operational efficiency.'

The Battle of Britain

Below: The CO being strapped into his Hurricane by Corporal Spilsby at Debden.

Below right: Squadron Leader Peter Townsend. In the middle of 1940, Captain Cuthbert Orde was commissioned to draw a series of portraits of fighter pilots, and he subsequently recorded in *Pilots of Fighter Command* (Harrap, 1942), 'It doesn't seem to me to be right that a chap with a face like Peter Townsend's should be so successful as a Fighter Pilot! But that is the fact. If you changed the muffler and uniform to a bow-tie and a sloppy coat you would, I swear, take him for a poet or musician, or even an artist! Sold again! For in civilian life he is, or wishes to be — I can't remember which — a farmer. Anyway, whatever he may be able to do, he is clearly sensitive, highly strung, intelligent and amusing. I found him very entertaining to talk to, and, of course, interesting to draw (with his qualities of) humour, vitality, and bouyancy. He's "got what it takes".'

'At Debden', wrote Peter Townsend,* 'we never even smelt the smoke of Dunkirk. 85 Squadron was non-operational. With a dozen boys not long out of school and about the same number of new Hurricanes, my job was to reform it into a fighting unit. . .

'The new boys were a varied group — an Air Marshal's son, a couple of undergraduates, an ex-insurance clerk, and among them two New Zealanders. They were boys of twenty and sometimes less with only ten hours' Hurricane experience. This was the major problem. In a single-seater you have to do it all yourself. No one can help you. It had taken me years to gain what experience I had and even then my chances of survival were not high. Theirs were infinitely less.'

It was to the survivors from France — Dickie Lee, 'Paddy' Hemingway, 'Nigger' Marshall, Patrick Woods-Scawen, A. G. Lewis, 'Sammy' Allard and Geoff Goodman — that Townsend turned to provide the fund of experience on which the inexperienced could draw. 'We taught them to search the sky, and watch their tails. They jousted with us in the sky to learn the tricks of air combat

*Duel of Eagles; Weidenfeld and Nicholson Ltd, 1970.

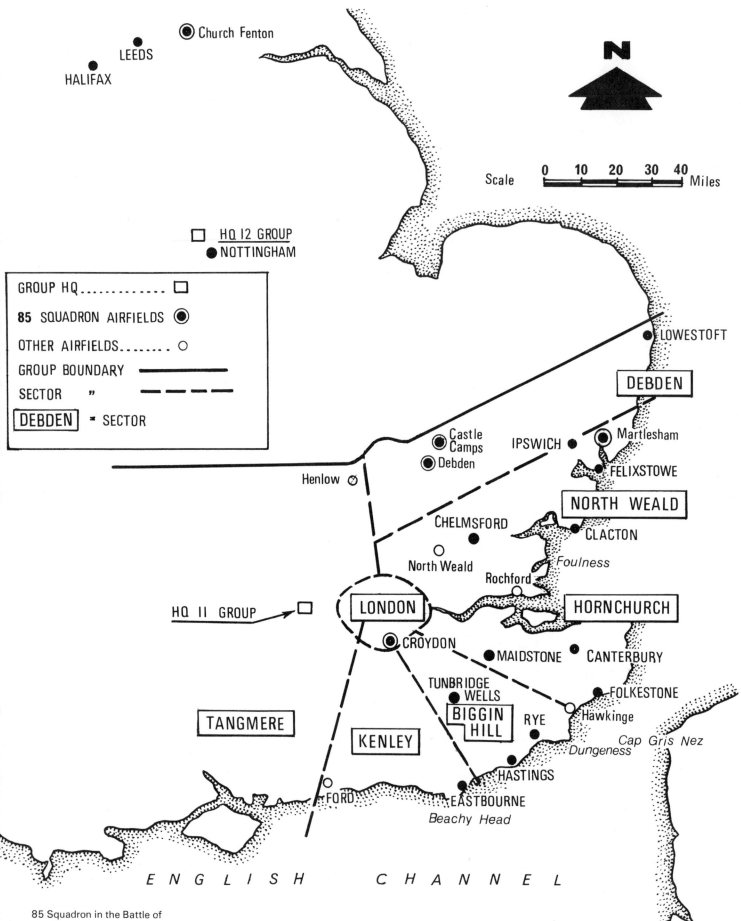

N

Church Fenton

LEEDS
HALIFAX

Scale 0 10 20 30 40 Miles

HQ 12 GROUP
NOTTINGHAM

GROUP HQ . . . . ☐

85 SQUADRON AIRFIELDS ◉

OTHER AIRFIELDS . . . . ○

GROUP BOUNDARY ——————

SECTOR   „   — — —

DEBDEN = SECTOR

LOWESTOFT

DEBDEN

Castle
Camps   IPSWICH   Martlesham
Debden   FELIXSTOWE

Henlow ⊘   NORTH WEALD

CHELMSFORD   CLACTON
North Weald   Foulness

Rochford

HQ II GROUP → ☐   LONDON   HORNCHURCH

CROYDON   MAIDSTONE   CANTERBURY

TUNBRIDGE
WELLS   FOLKESTONE
TANGMERE   BIGGIN   Hawkinge
HILL   RYE
KENLEY   Cap Gris Nez
Dungeness
HASTINGS
FORD   EASTBOURNE
Beachy Head

E N G L I S H   C H A N N E L

85 Squadron in the Battle of
Britain.

— above all never climb or dive in front of an Me 109, but turn and turn again since it was here that the Hurricanes outclassed the Me 109. We led them up to Sutton Bridge to fire their guns. And as they progressed, I sent them out over the East Coast convoys to learn discipline, loyalty and vigilance..

'Day by day 85 grew strong again, watching and waiting with growing impatience.'

On 10 July, 85 was ordered to disperse its satellite landing grounds at Martlesham Heath, Suffolk, and Castle Camps (a few miles north-east of Debden). The Flights rotated to Martlesham because its proximity to the coast made it ideal for the early interception of raiders, and from here the Hurricanes maintained almost continuous patrols from dawn to dusk over convoys with marvellous codenames like 'Agent' and 'Booty'. They were full and busy days.

'11/7/40. Morning of low cloud and drizzle. Squadron Leader Townsend on lone patrol at 0530 hours intercepted a Dornier; the latter turned for home and safety, and having the height over the interceptor drew away. Squadron Leader Townsend gave up the idea of trying to manoeuvre for a favourable position to attack and attacked from astern. He got in a couple of bursts when he stopped a cannon shell in his glycol tank and inside the cockpit.'

Powerless, Townsend could only glide down through the rain clouds. 'I called Kiwi One, the ground station: "Wagon leader calling. Am hit and bailing out in sea. One, two, three, four, five. Take a fix if you can." Then I was clear of cloud and the sea opened up below — twenty miles to England, 200 to the other side. Not a ship in sight. Now only two things mattered, life and death. The next few moments would decide. Meanwhile, I was far more concerned about trying to spot

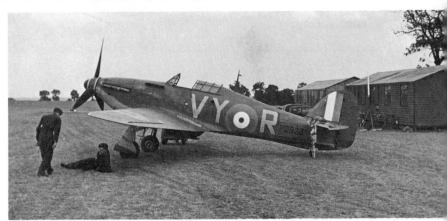

a ship, and peering below I banked my aeroplane steeply to left and to right. Then below my right wing a little ship appeared ... It looked like a toy, as if someone had put it there at the last moment ...

'I crossed my arms in front of me, my right hand firmly on the vital ring. Then I dived out head first, and down to the sea. I was falling on my back, in total silence, my feet pointing at the sky, when I pulled the ripcord. The parachute canopy clacked open and the harness wrenched my body violently from its headlong fall. Far below I could see Hurricane VY-K diving vertically towards the sea to disappear in an eruption of spume and spray ...

'When the big splash came I hit the harness release knob and sank... When at last I broke the surface I saw the little ship lying less than a mile away. Luckily they had seen me and were lowering a boat. I kicked off my boots and feeling tiny and impotent in that immense sea swam around rather relaxed, supported by my Mae West...

'When the little boat, rowed by four stalwart sailors, approached, a fifth stood up in the stern brandishing a boat-hook and shouted, "Blimey, if he ain't a f...... Hun."

Above: Castle Camps dispersal, June 1940. 'The pilot's life on the ground depends to a great extent on the state of the Blitz at the moment', recorded Cuthbert Orde. 'Let us suppose that there is an average day on. Generally speaking, some of the squadrons at each aerodrome are said to be at readiness, and when a squadron is at readiness it has to spend possibly the whole day on the aerodrome within a few yards of its aircraft, which are dispersed around the perimeter so that if it were attacked by the enemy no one bomb could wreck more than one machine. Near the dispersal point is a hut, and inside that hut, or outside it according to the weather, the pilots spend their day, always wearing their Mae West life-saving jackets and ready at any moment to go into the air. The engine of each aeroplane is kept warmed up. By each aeroplane are three mechanics: one is sitting in the cockpit, one is standing by the self-starter battery wagon, and the third is waiting to help the pilot into his parachute when the word "Scramble" is given.'

Only one answer was possible: "I'm not, I'm a f...... Englishman"...'

Townsend had to live with being shot down by a Dornier but he was Mentioned in Dispatches that day and he was on patrol again that evening in a new Hurricane.

'12/7/40. From 0600 to 1800 hours and later, both Flights carried out continuous patrols, both local and convoy. During a protective patrol over a convoy enemy bombers were encountered, and Pilot Officer Bickerdyke, Sergeant Pilot Rust and Sergeant Pilot Jowitt went into action. Pilot Officer Bickerdyke delivered two attacks on an He 111, the first from quarter starboard which accounted for the rear gunner, and the second from quarter port which put paid to the E/A and it crashed into the sea; a conclusive victory. Sergeant Pilot Rust attacked another E/A which made for home as he put in one attack from the three-quarter astern which silenced the rear gunner; the E/A escaped in a dive through clouds. Sergeant Pilot Jowitt was shot down and crashed into the sea off Felixstowe. Reported missing and believed killed.'

The pilots of 85 Squadron and the ground-crews who kept them flying, clocked up more hours in policing Britain's maritime lifelines in July than they would have amassed in three months of normal peacetime flying, a fact that was readily appreciated by Air Vice-Marshal Trafford Leigh-Mallory when the Squadron was transferred from his 12 Group to 11 Group.

'Telegrams: Airgroup, Hucknall
Telephone: Hucknall 411-415
HEADQUARTERS
NO 12 GROUP
ROYAL AIR FORCE
HUCKNALL
NOTTINGHAMSHIRE
9 August 1940

Dear Townsend

1. I am very pleased to see what an excellent month's flying No 85 Squadron put in during July.
2. I should like to congratulate you on the performance of your Squadron, both in attacking the enemy and in your training. I much admire the spirit of keenness shown by you and the other members of the Squadron.
3. I am very sorry to be losing you from No. 12 Group and wish you all the best of luck.

Leigh-Mallory'

Top: The alarm has gone and Flying Officer Lewis has doubled over to his aircraft at Castle Camps which is already ticking over. All he has to do now is don his helmet and strap in. The whole Squadron of 12 aircraft could be airborne within three minutes of hearing the word 'Scramble'.

Above: Dicky Lee makes a low pass over Castle Camps. Lee's prowess in the air was legendary and when some action film was required for a George Formby comedy film, Dicky Lee duly obliged by flying his aircraft *through* No 3 Hangar at Debden for the benefit of the cameras.

Now in 11 Group, 85 returned to Debden on 13 August to prepare for the big battle that was already heating up in the south:

'18/8/40. At 1724 hours the Squadron, comprising 13 aircraft, was ordered to patrol Debden home base at 10,000 feet. At 1730 hours they were airborne and immediately ordered to patrol Canterbury at 20,000 feet. At 1735 they were ordered to intercept Raid 51* which was crossing coast in vicinity of Folkestone, and at 1739 hours when eight miles NE of Chelmsford, Squadron Leader Townsend sighted E/A approximately 15 miles east of him. The Squadron set a course east to deliver attack. The enemy raid consisted of a number of aircraft estimated at between 150 and 250 machines approaching in a very rough Vic formation stepped up from 10,000 to 18,000 feet. The lower advanced tier comprised Ju 87s, followed by He 111s 2,000 feet higher, and higher were Ju 88s and Me 110s at approximately 15,000 feet with Me 109s at approximately 17,000 feet.

'The enemy, on sighting the Squadron, employed the following tactics: (A) The two lower tiers comprising Ju 87s and He 111s immediately turned seawards. (B) The three higher formations of Ju 88s, Me 110s, and Me 109s, started climbing steeply while turning sharply from left to right con-

*This raid was aimed at North Weald airfield as part of the Luftwaffe's all-out attempt to destroy Fighter Command.

Above: Relaxing at Debden in August 1940. Left to right: Pilot Officer Bickerdyke (from Tasmania), Flying Officer Woods-Scawen, Pilot Officer Lockhart, Flight Lieutenant Lee, Sergeant Jowitt (complete with shorn head as a result of a bet taken during a particularly boisterous party), Flight Lieutenant Bieber (Medical Officer) and Sergeant Webster. 'The most striking thing about Fighter pilots,' thought Cuthbert Orde, 'is their ordinariness. Just "You, I, Us and Co," ordinary sons of ordinary parents from ordinary homes. So when you wonder where they come from, dear reader, whoever you may be, contemplate your own home, your family, your profession, and your background, and you have the answer. You have everything in common with them . . . they are not a race apart.' The Hurricane behind has a deflector fitted below the canopy to protect the pilot from being dazzled by his own exhaust on night patrols.

Left: Pilot Officer Hemingway watching and waiting.

47

tinuously, eventually forming two circles; the Ju 88s which were numerically small combined with the Me 110s and formed one circle turning anti-clockwise at approximately 18,000 feet, while the Me 109s flew their anti-clockwise circle at 20,000 feet.

'Owing to the numerical superiority of the enemy the Squadron was unable to deliver any set method of attack and the battle developed into individual 'dog-fights'. The main action took place approximately 8 to 12 miles east of Foulness Point.

'Squadron Leader Townsend attacked an Me 110 with a full deflection three second burst while doing a left-hand turn, and the E/A keeled over spiralling vertically downwards out of control from 10,000 feet. Pilot Officer English and Sergeant Howes saw it go down and corroborate the opinion that the pilot must have been killed.

'He (Townsend) then attacked an Me 109 and the E/A caught fire after a three second burst and spun down in flames. He was then attacked by another Me 109 but without difficulty manoeuvred on its tail, the pilot bailed out, and the machine broke up in the air.

'He then attacked another Me 109 ineffectively and with ammunition exhausted returned to Debden.

'Pilot Officer English (Red 2) followed Squadron Leader Townsend in the attack on 20 Me 110s. He attacked an Me 110 which dived ahead of him — he gave one long burst, saw tracer entering the wing, and silenced the rear gunner.

'Sergeant Howes (Red 3), while Red 1 and 2 were attacking, climbed to 9,000 feet and attacked an Me 110 and saw it crash into the water. He then climbed and made a second attack on one of several Me 110s circling which burst into flames. He then climbed to 15,000 feet and tackled a straggling Do 17 which went down out of sight with thick smoke trailing from it.

'Flight Lieutenant Hamilton (Yellow 1) attacked an He 111 with a five-second burst, and on breaking away it dropped its under-carriage, smoke poured from the fuselage and two engines, and it went gliding slowly down into the sea. He then attacked an Me 110 which dived down with both engines on fire.

'Pilot Officer J. E. Marshall (Yellow 2) followed Yellow 1 in pursuit of the Me 110 but broke away to engage an He 111 three miles away. He opened fire at 250 yards, pieces broke away from the aircraft which was in a cloud of white smoke, and on flying into this Pilot Officer Marshall's starboard wingtip was cut off by the tail of the E/A. Despite a damaged aircraft minus wing tip he landed safely at Debden.

'Sergeant Ellis (Yellow 3) destroyed an Me 109 and damaged one Me 110. He used

his cine-gun camera throughout the combat.

'Sergeant Walker-Smith (Blue 3) delivered a frontal attack on an Me 110 from 150 yards above it. The E/A glided down from 8,000 feet to hit the sea 40 miles out. After firing several ineffective bursts at another aircraft he made a similar frontal attack. This time the Me 110 broke up, one of the crew baling out into the sea.

'Pilot Officer W. H. Hodgson (Blue 4) during the dog-fight climbed to 12,000 feet and dived on a Do 17 which went diving down, white smoke pouring from its engines. He then turned on the tail of an Me 109 and after a short burst the E/A dived vertically down to the sea. He then climbed to 20,000 feet to a circle of Me 110s, made a snap shot at one, and then dived at another making the enemy starboard engine smoke.

'Pilot Officer Gowers (Green 1) attacked a Ju 87 from dead astern with a five-second burst, followed by a seven second burst, and the E/A was almost completely blotted out by black smoke and dived towards the sea.

'Pilot Officer J. Lockhart (Green 2) attacked an Me 110 and silenced the rear gunner.

'Pilot Officer A. G. Lewis (Green 3) encountered 12 Me 110s circling at 18,000 feet, one of which proceeded to dive at a Hurricane down below and in so doing presented a plain view in the sights at 150 yards. Two short bursts caused it to smoke and dive at a steep angle.

'Pilot Officer Hemingway (Blue 2) followed Flight Lieutenant Lee (Blue 1) who chased a lone Ju 88 but (Hemingway) broke away to attack a circling formation of Ju 88s. He attacked a Ju 88 but was himself attacked by two Ju 88s in close formation. His engine was hit, his cockpit filled with oil and glycol, and his aircraft went into a spin. Hemingway pulled out at 7,000 feet and set course for land but his engine stopped and he had to bale out. After being in the sea for 1½ hours he was picked up by Lightship 81's boat, 12 miles east of Clacton. He was then landed at Felixstowe by Motor Torpedo Boat and returned to Debden the next day.

'Flight Lieutenant Lee (Blue 1) was last seen by Squadron Leader Townsend and Flying Officer Gowers ten miles NE of Foulness Point chasing three Me 109s well ahead of him. He failed to return to Debden and was reported missing.'

The total Squadron claim for 18 August was six Me 110s, three Me 109s, and one He 111 destroyed, one He 111, one Me 119 one Ju 87 and one Me 109 probably destroyed, and four Me 110s and two Do 17s damaged. 'All pilots agreed', concluded the Operational Record, 'that the enemy was disinclined to make combat and that in this action the Me 110 and Me 109 proved

extremely easy to overcome.' To balance this, the Squadron lost two Hurricanes and another damaged, but even more importantly it lost Flight Lieutenant Dicky Lee DSO DFC. Then aged 23, Richard Hugh Anthony Lee was outwardly a rather shy and timid man but in the air he was absolutely fearless. 'He had such precision too,' wrote a mechanic. 'Today he flew upside down over Castle Camps and when he landed there was grass on his aerials.' He must have bitten off more than he could chew in chasing three Me 109s however and so Dicky Lee, 'B' Flight Commander and Lord Trenchard's godson, as well as the man who opened 85's account in World War 2, was never seen again.

The following day the Chief of Air Staff, Sir Cyril Newall, sent a signal to Debden: 'Well done 85 Squadron in all your hard fighting. This is the right spirit for dealing with the enemy.' The reply was not slow in coming: '85 Squadron respectfully thank the Chief of Air Staff for his kind message and will strive to their utmost to carry on the good work.'

Also on 19 August, at 0630 hours, 85 Squadron moved to Croydon to take over from 111 Squadron which moved in turn to Debden. '85 Squadron was now in the forefront of the battle, which was about to enter its most crucial phase,' wrote Townsend. 'Of the 18 pilots I led to Croydon, 14 were to be shot down (two twice) within the next two weeks.'

Not that this was to be immediately

apparent, for five days of cloudy weather came after the move — 'It was as if a referee had blown the whistle for half time.' This lull was very much appreciated — 'Although 85 Squadron had been north of London in the more quiet Debden sector,' wrote Townsend, 'two months of convoy patrols, (day in, day out, dawn to dusk) had worn us down more than we cared to admit. . .

'Our dispersal point, with ground crews and pilots' rest rooms, was in a row of villas on the airfield's western boundary. Invariably I slept there half-clothed to be on the spot if

Above: Sammy Allard prepares for a flight. By now the Squadron Hurricanes had exchanged their two-blade, fixed-pitch wooden airscrews for de Havilland two-position, three-blade propellers to improve performance.

anything happened. In the small hours of 24 August it did. The shrill scream and the deafening crash of bombs shattered my sleep. In the doorway young Pyers Worrall, a new arrival, was yelling something and waving his arms. Normally as frightened as anyone, not even bombs could move me then. I placed my pillow reverently over my head and waited for the rest. Worrall still had the energy to be frightened. I was past caring. It was a bad sign; I was more exhausted than I realised. . .'

When the raid finished, Townsend got up. 'I stuck my toothbrush in my left breast pocket, took my spongebag, and made for the bathroom. The Duke of Kent, brother of the King, was expected at 10.00am. Halfway to the bathroom, the alarm went. 85 Squadron, Scramble!'

Twelve Squadron Hurricanes took off at 0758 hours to patrol Dover and intercept enemy bombers. 'Four landed at 0825 hours having lost contact with their leader resulting from R/T interference apparently due to Green 2's (Pilot Officer Worrall) switch being reversed and the transmitter being on,' reported the Operational Record.

'At 0830 hours Pilot Officer Allard (he was commissioned on 17 August) sighted a lone Me 109, 1,000 feet below him when flying at 15,000 feet near Ramsgate. The Me 109 was climbing to join a formation of 20-30 Me 109s flying above and Allard turned to the right, dived, and pulled up under the E/A. He fired two short bursts at about 250yds range and saw a cloud of white smoke come from E/A. The Me 109 then dived out of control with black smoke emitting and it was finally seen to crash into the sea three miles from Ramsgate. Pilot Officer Allard dived after the E/A, witnessing the crash, as he was pursued by some of the other Me 109s. He landed at Croydon at 0908 hours.

'Pilot Officer Lockhart's Hurricane was hit by what he believed to be anti-aircraft fire when near Dover. He force-landed at Hawkinge and over-ran the aerodrome owing to his flaps being out of order. Aircraft damaged and Pilot Officer Lockhart was slightly wounded in the ankle.'

Back at Croydon, Tim Molony hurried Peter Townsend from his debriefing to meet the Duke of Kent. "Flight Lieutenant Hamilton from Canada," I introduced Hammy, who to my consternation seemed to be squinting at me and doing his best not to laugh. I retreated a pace and glanced down at the front of my tunic. On my left breast, beside my wings and a solitary DFC ribbon a gleaming white toothbrush stuck out of my pocket. I had taken it into battle with me.'

On 26 August, 12 Hurricanes took off at 1449 hours to patrol overhead base before being vectored to the Maidstone area. 'At 1520 hours near Eastchurch, fifteen Dornier 215s were sighted flying in stepped up Vic formation at 15,000 feet and escorted by approximately 30 Me 109s which were flying 5-10,000 feet higher.' To Townsend there was only one way to get at the bombers without mixing it with the fighter escort first. 'I brought the squadron round steadily in a wide turn, moving it into echelon as we levelled out about two miles ahead on a collision course. Ease the throttle to reduce the closing speed ... Get a bead on them right away, hold it, and never mind the streams of tracer darting overhead. Just keep pressing on the button until you think you're going to collide — then stick hard forward. Under the shock of 'negative G' your stomach jumps into your mouth, dust and muck fly up from the cockpit floor into your eyes and your head cracks on the roof as you break away below.'

This head-on attack forced the leading section of the enemy bomber wave to break formation. 'This section was followed by several Hurricanes, the remainder of the E/A having turned back in SE direction.

'The engagement became general, and three Do 215s were definitely destroyed by the Squadron as a whole for nearly all contributed. One Do 215, after a series of astern and quarter attacks, was seen to go down in low diving left-hand turns with the starboard engine stopped. It was followed down by Pilot Officer Allard and Pilot Officer Worrall and it force-landed at Rochford aerodrome.

'The second Dornier broke away after repeated attacks and made out to sea on port motor only, but he then apparently thought better of it as pieces were falling off because the Dornier turned back and pancaked 1-2 miles E of Eastchurch.

'The third Dornier was seen to disappear in clouds losing height. It was then encountered by Sergeant Howes who finished it off with the remainder of his ammunition — he saw it crash into the sea 10-15 miles E of Foulness. The crash was witnessed by Pilot Officer Allard.

'Pilot Officer Hemingway, after the general engagement with the Dorniers, was climbing to engage some Me 109s when he was hit behind the cockpit and in the engine by cannon shell.' He had to bale out over Pitsea Marshes.

The RAF was now well into the crucial phase of the Battle of Britain, but 27 August was a quiet day. 'We sat around at dispersal,' wrote Townsend, 'talking of trivial things, waiting. Sam Allard said he preferred metal propellers to wooden because they would chop through the trees better when flying low. Little Sargeant Ellis told me, "If I go, it will be in the sea; my second name is Mortimer, Mort-i-mer." But we never thought it would happen. Ceaselessly the gramophone churned out some well-known tunes: *Tuxedo Junction, I'm in the mood for love, Don't you every cry.* They were the favourites.

"Don't you ever cry, don't ever shed a tear Don't you every cry after I'm gone . . .".'

It was inevitable that some would die in the next few days. Day combats were exhausting enough; night patrols pushed everyone to the limits of their resistance.

Above: 85 Squadron over Kent on its way to meet the Luftwaffe. Peter Townsend is in the lead in the third aircraft from the left. 'This is how we fought,' he wrote, 'independently in squadrons of twelve aircraft. We had often discussed among ourselves how to go about it . . . I led 85 in four sections of three, each section in line astern, my own in the centre, one on each side, one behind, and each at a comfortable distance. The Squadron had a narrow front and was easy to manoeuvre. Each pilot was able to search. The Germans laughed at our serried formations. Their real weakness lay in the section of three, which was later abandoned for the German *Rotte* of two!' *IWM*

Landing at 0300 hours on the morning of the 28th after two hours on patrol, Townsend had a short 'kip'. Just after dawn he led the squadron off on the first of four sorties that day.

At 1602 hours, ten Hurricanes took-off to patrol Tenterden before being ordered to intercept Raid 15. At 18,000 feet, Townsend's Section was in the being ordered to intercept Raid 15. At 18,000 feet, Townsend's Section was in the lead with Hamilton's Red Section on his right, Allard's on the left, and Woods-Scawen's Green Section under his tail; from these positions the eyes searching the skies discovered some twenty Me 109s and one Me 110 around Dungeness. Townsend's orders were to attack bombers and avoid fighters but the opportunity was too good to miss. 'The Squadron approached from the sun, but were spotted at the last moment by E/A who appeared not to be anxious to engage and they broke formation in all directions. Squadron Leader Townsend gave a two to three second burst and E/A rolled over and dived steeply; it was seen going down by Flight Lieutenant Hamilton and Pilot Officer Gowers both of whom saw black and white smoke coming out of the E/A. Squadron Leader Townsend estimated his position as about 12 miles NW of Lympne and this was confirmed by Maidstone Observer Corps who received a report at 1646 that an Me 109 had crash-landed, the pilot being taken prisoner.

'Pilot Officer Allard attacked E/A at 200 yards closing to 20 yards and it caught fire and dived vertically into the sea two to three miles outside Folkestone harbour. Witnessed by Pilot Officer English. Allard then fired several short bursts from 250 yards at another Me 109 which was making for France. E/A dived and flew at 20 feet over the sea but engine failed with black smoke coming out, position then was about five miles N of St Inglevert. This kill was confirmed by 11 Group signal.

'Pilot Officer Hodgson chased E/A from 17,000 feet down across the Channel to 20 feet above sea level. He fired several bursts and saw pieces falling off and only one-third of rudder left. E/A was going very slowly when last seen and emitting much black smoke. Pilot Officer Hodgson had to turn back when five miles NW of Cap Gris Nez owing to lack of ammunition but he was certain that E/A was finished. This was confirmed by 11 Group signal.

'Flying Officer Woods-Scawen attacked E/A from quarter round to astern and gave two long bursts. Black smoke and what appeared to be petrol from the wing tanks poured out of E/A and it dived down vertically. He followed it down for several thousand feet and left it when it was obviously out of

52

Left: Quick turn-round in between patrols. Squadron Leader Townsend leaps out to report to the Intelligence Officer while two airmen start to replenish the Hurricane and carry out minor repairs if necessary. The airman at the front is refuelling from the bowser; the Hurricane carried its fuel in three tanks, one each side of the centre section and a gravity tank in the fuselage, and the bowser could refuel at a rate of 150 gallons per minute. The airman at the back of the wing is about to remove the panel at the base of the code letter 'V' in order to check the oxygen contents.

Below: Giving the Hurricane its teeth. Armourers in the RAF were known as 'plumbers' and the two men on the wing are loading the magazines. Leading Aircraftman Knell on the right is demonstrating the most efficient way of carrying a belt of .303 ammunition to the aircraft.

control. It was believed to have crashed near Dungeness and this was confirmed by Maidstone Observer Corps who reported an Me 109 in the sea off Dymchurch at 1640 hrs.

'Sergeant Walker-Smith attacked Me 109 and the port petrol tank was seen to explode and then the aircraft went into steep dive. At that moment Sergeant Walker-Smith was fired at and had to take evasive action but immediately afterwards dived and saw a large explosion on the sea and black smoke. Pilot Officer Hodgson confirmed having seen an Me 109 dive into the sea at this point.

'Pilot Officer Gowers attacked Me 110 from astern and saw bullets entering but it went into a shallow dive towards French coast and got away. Pilot Officer Gowers used all his ammunition and definitely damaged E/A.

Enemy Casualties 6 Me 109s destroyed, 1 Me 110 damaged.

Our Casualties Nil

'This action was witnessed by the Prime Minister during a visit to the SE coast defences.'

The next day was even busier. Twelve Hurricanes battled it out at 1530 hours over Hastings and Beachy Head with an enemy force estimated at 'between 200 and 300 aircraft', and at 1816 hours 11 of the Squadron pilots and aircraft were ordered off again to patrol Maidstone before being vectored towards Dungeness. 'They climbed to 24,000 feet and were then joined by a Spitfire and a Hurricane which both began weaving behind the flank sections. Warned of the presence of E/A some miles to the north, the Squadron wheeled to attempt interception. While circling, Red 3 (Pilot Officer Hodgdon) suddenly shouted a warning that E/A were behind. These turned out to be three Me 109s, the leader of which was not identified until he was within range on account of the previous

presence of the Spitfire and the strong resemblance at a certain distance of a Spitfire and an Me 109 from front view. On receipt of warning, the Squadron circled steeply left. Red 3 saw tracer ammunition passing close above him and he saw a cannon shell explode on Red 1's tail unit blowing most of it off. Red 1, (Flight Lieutenant Hamilton), was also seen to lose his starboard wing tip.

'Pilot Officer Marshall attacked one Me 109 as it was doing a right hand climbing turn. Enemy then dived followed by Pilot Officer Marshall who fired again. Engagement commenced at 22,000 feet and was broken off at 5,000 feet when E/A was last seen diving vertically out of control towards the sea ten miles from Dungeness. This was confirmed by Pilot Officer English and although the E/A was not actually seen to hit the sea on account of the thick haze and bad visibility, it was claimed as destroyed in view of the circumstances of the combat.

Top left: 85 Squadron over Kent on its way to meet the enemy. *IWM*

Centre left: The Squadron sections in line astern. *IWM*

Below left: Alone in the clear blue sky. According to the 1938 RAF Manual of Air Tactics, the aim of each fighter pilot was to get into a firing position behind an enemy bomber where 'he stays until either he has exhausted his ammunition, the target aircraft has been shot down, or he himself has been shot down or his engine put out of action.' *IWM*

Right: 'Nigger' Marshall in the cockpit.

Far right: Marshall smoking a quick cigarette to cool his nerves.

Below: Flying Officer Lewis displaying all the casual enthusiasm of operational life which characterised Fighter Command during the Battle of Britain. Many pilots preferred to wear jerseys or mufflers instead of collars and ties because they were more comfortable and less chaffing on necks that were forever turning as eyes searched the skies.

'Ten Hurricanes landed at Croydon between 1916 and 1955 hours.
Enemy Casualties 1 Me 109 destroyed
Our Casualties 1 Hurricane (Flight Lieutenant Hamilton killed).'

Yet despite all that had taken place over the previous two days, the morning of Friday 30 August saw the beginning of the fiercest 48 hours of fighting in the whole Battle:
'Eleven Hurricanes took off at 1036 hours and vectored on a course of 105 degrees to intercept various raids approaching coast. At 1110 hours approximately 50 He 111s were sighted at 16,000 feet near Bethenden flying in sections of three in general mass. Above these were large numbers of Me 109s in support. Estimated total of E/A about 150-200.

'The Squadron went inland until well in front of Heinkels and then executed a head-on attack on them, diving from the sun in waves of three. This had the desired effect and the bomber formation was effectively dispersed, although in view of the nature of the attack and the rapidity with which it was carried out, it was quite impossible to see the extent of the damage inflicted at the time.

'A general dog-fight then ensued and numerous individual combats took place. It was noticed that the firing from E/A, in particular the Me 110s, was erratic and indiscriminate. The Me 110 showed in this combat, and in preceeding ones, a marked disinclination to go down lower than about 16,000 — 18,000 feet. It was further noticed that the He 111 did not stand up to the head-on attack at all well, and that this form of attack was far more successful against them than against the Dorniers a few days previously.

'Squadron Leader Townsend attacked an Me 110. Gave burst at 200 yards range and E/A last seen 20 miles S. of Beachy Head with black and white smoke coming from port engine but aircraft still in control.

'Pilot Officer Hodgson attacked an Me 110, fired long burst from beam to line astern. E/A dived out of sight with both engines stopped and white glycol smoke pouring out from underneath. He repeated the dose at another Me 110 five miles E of Ramsgate with exactly the same result. He then attacked another Me 110. Fired burst into belly of E/A from 100 yards closing to 50 yards and E/A rolled over with smoke pouring from underneath. He went down in a controlled glide but Pilot Officer Hodgson had to break off combat due to lack of ammunition and because he was being chased by seven Me 110s. Previous to these encounters he damaged an He 111 during the head-on attack.

'Sergeant Goodman fired long burst into Me 110 which was forced to break formation and when last seen had port engine on fire and was losing height out to sea. He then attacked another Me 110 from astern, set it on fire, and saw it pancake on sea four to five miles S of Sandgate.

'Pilot Officer Allard destroyed two He 111s. The first one had both engines set on fire and was seen to crash on land by Pilot Officer English. The second one he attacked from above and beam and E/A burst into flames and dived straight down. It was believed to have crashed in a field about 30 miles SW of Croydon.

'Pilot Officer English damaged one He 111 and destroyed one Me 110 which was last seen diving steeply crab-fashion with both engines on fire.

'Flying Officer Gowers fired two bursts of five seconds into Me 110 from astern and white smoke was seen coming from both engines. E/A was followed down to within 2,000 feet of sea. He was diving slowly with one engine out of action, used no evasive tactics or answering fire and probably crashed 15 miles out to sea off Dungeness.

'Flying Officer Woods-Scawen fired several bursts into Me 110 stopping starboard engine and setting port engine on fire. E/A dived steeply into cloud and was lost to sight, but columns of smoke seen on ground shortly afterwards. This was near Dover.

'Sergeant Booth attacked and damaged one Me 110.

'Pilot Officer Marshall was badly shot up and obliged to bale out. He landed safely near Ashford.

COMBAT REPORT.

Sector Serial No. _____ (A) _____

Serial No. of Order detailing Flight or Squadron to Patrol _____ (B) _____

Date _____ (C) 30. 8. 40.

Flight, Squadron _____ (D) Flight: A Sqdn.: 85.

Number of Enemy Aircraft _____ (E) 150 - 200.

Type of Enemy Aircraft _____ (F) HE. 111 ME. 109s ME. 110.

Time Attack was delivered _____ (G) 11. 10.

Place Attack was delivered _____ (H) BETHENDEN AREA.

Height of Enemy _____ (J) 15000' - 20000'

Enemy Casualties _____ (K) TWO HE 111 DESTROYED.

Our Casualties   Aircraft _____ (L) NIL

     Personnel _____ (M) NIL.

GENERAL REPORT _____ (R)

I was leading red Section in Squadron Formation. Tally ho was given and HYDRO LEADER manoeuvred the squadron into position for a head on attack on a formation of approx 95 HE.111. I attacked a formation of three on the left of the enemy formation. This a/c fell out of the formation and I turned quickly and gave a few seconds burst from line-astern. Both engines went up in smoke and a/c rolled onto its back and went down to the ground. I saw he was out of control so broke off attack - this was confirmed by RED. 2. Hotspur. I then climbed to 19000' into sun and carried out an attack from sun on leading E.A. from above and beam, this time I hit the LEADERS engines and he burst into flames and went straight down.

Signature Samard PO

O.C. { Section RED
Flight A
Squadron 85. Squadron No.

The enemy aircraft then began to turn for the coast, so I continued climbing into the sun and hacking away at these formations until my ammunition was expended - two or three of these E.A. seemed to lose speed and fall behind. The latter a/c seemed to crash in a field approx 30 mile SW. Worran

(3567—1611) Wt. 27885—2553 860 Pads 9/39 T.S. 700 FORM 1151

'Ten Hurricanes landed at Croydon between 1133 and 1201 hours.
Enemy casualties 6 Me 110 destroyed, 2 He 111 destroyed, 2 Me 110 probable, 2 Me 110 damaged, 2 He 111 damaged.
Our Losses 1 Hurricane destroyed — pilot unhurt.'

No 85 Squadron was due to come back to readiness at 1300 hours on 31 August but lunch had to wait because the Luftwaffe raided Croydon and bombs started to fall on the east side of the airfield just as 12 Hurricanes got airborne at 1255. Townsend was irate to say the least. 'I had just moved the lever to raise the undercarriage, when my engine faltered, faded, and picked up again. Blast had struck the motor like a punch in the wind. Turning in the cockpit, I saw the rest of the squadron emerging from a vast eruption of smoke and debris. Then I looked up;

thousands of feet above, Me 110s were wheeling in the blue, with Me 109s swarming above. I thought the Me 110s had bombed. Yet some say a dozen Dorniers had attacked from lower down. If so, I never saw them. I was mad with rage at the Me 110s. 'After them, but look out for the 109s,' I called and the furious chase began.'

Townsend made contact with the enemy over Tunbridge Wells and the Luftwaffe strength was assessed at about fifty. By then the enemy was withdrawing and when the Squadron reached the same level, 'Squadron Leader Townsend fired a three second burst into an Me 109 which caused it to give out black and white smoke. It then slowed up and dived down, obviously out of control, in a left-hand spiral. He then gave a three second burst to another Me 109 from quarter, which rolled over and went down.' Then came another from just below, so close that Townsend could see the pilot. 'An intimate shot — but beyond was an Me 110, guns winking. So intent was I aiming at the Me 109 sitting just below, I never realised the Me 110 was aiming at me.

'My thumb was on the firing button, but I never fired. A blast of shot suddenly splattered my Hurricane, my left foot was kicked off the rudder-bar, petrol gushed into the cockpit. The shock was so terrific that for a few instants I had lost control and went into a steep dive... Over to the right a Hurricane was going down vertically, etching a black line of smoke across the sky.'

Fortunately the CO's aircraft did not burst into flames and he decided to force-land, 'but finding he was over a densely wooded area he baled out from 1,400 feet and landed near Hawkhurst, the aircraft crashing $\frac{1}{2}$ mile away. He was taken by Hawkhurst police to the cottage hospital where his wound was dressed, and he was subsequently transferred

to Croydon General Hospital. The nose cap of cannon shell was extracted from his left foot and his big toe amputated.

'The Hawkhurst police put Squadron Leader Townsend's pulled parachute on view and raised £3 for a Spitfire fund.

'Pilot Officer Worrall attacked an Me 110 at 25,000 feet SE of Tunbridge Wells. E/A wheeled down and over to the left apparently out of control but exact damage could not be seen owing to oiled goggles and windscreen. However Pilot Officer Worrall had his rudder bar and elevator controls blown away by cannon shell almost immediately afterwards and he was obliged to bale out. He landed at Benenden, where a member of the Field Ambulance which picked him up confirmed that he had seen the Me 110 go down on fire. Pilot Officer Worrall was slightly wounded in the leg and was transferred to Croydon General Hospital.

'Flying Officer Gowers attacked on Me 109 east of Biggin Hill which was firing at a Hurricane. He delivered two three second bursts and saw much black smoke appear followed by white smoke from E/A. It dived away into the haze and was lost to view.

'Sergeant Howes fired long bursts into a Do 215 and saw it roll over on its back with black and white smoke coming from it as it fell. End of E/A not seen as pilot had to adopt evasive tactics to get away from Me 109.

'Pilot Officer Hemingway fired a burst into an Me 109 and saw much white smoke issuing from E/A.

'Ten Hurricanes landed at Croydon between 1340 and 1400 hours.'

With the CO out of action and having lost both Flight Commanders, Patrick Woods-Scawen took over the Squadron temporarily. At 1710 hours that same evening, he led the 10 remaining Hurricanes into the air to intercept an enemy raid making for the Thames Estuary. About thirty Do 125s were sighted at 1740 hours flying at 16,000 to 17,000 feet accompanied by approximately 100 mixed Me 109 and Me 110s.

'The Squadron attack opened about 20 miles south of Purfleet and they effectively broke up the enemy formation and separated bombers from fighters by diving on his sections in line astern.

'Pilot Officer Hodgson did a head-on attack on a Do 215 and saw pieces fall off nose and starboard wing. He then engaged an Me 109 with a long burst, followed by a short burst at 200 yards, and E/A rolled over and went down with engine on fire near Thames Haven oil storage tanks.'

At this juncture, Hodgson's Hurricane was hit by a cannon shell which blew up his oil lines and glycol tank and set fire to his engine. Mutilation by fire was probably the greatest fear of any fighter pilot and in the time it took for a Hurricane to fall from 20,000 feet a man could roast alive; thus Pilot Officer Hodgson's subsequent actions were deemed so commendable that his example was held up to all other pilots in 11 Group Intelligence Brief No 50. 'He prepared to bale out and was actually half out of his aircraft when he realised that he was over a thickly populated area and near some oil storage tanks. Fully appreciating the danger, he decided to remain with his aircraft and endeavour to force land, and thus avoid the serious risk of a Hurricane on fire crashing in the area mentioned. By skilful side-slipping he managed to keep the fire under control and finally succeeded in making a wheels-up landing in a field near Shotgate, Essex, narrowly missing wires and other obstacles erected with a view to preventing the landing of hostile aircraft.'

Eight Hurricanes landed at Croydon between 1815 and 1855 hours, but there was little respite because the aircraft were ordered off again at 1917 hours to patrol Hawkinge and then to intercept Raid 18C. 'The first indication of position of E/A was given by AA fire from Dover and then nine Me 109s were seen flying at about 15,000 feet. The Squadron circled out to sea as E/A passed on left, then wheeled in and caught them by surprise when individual combats ensued.

'Pilot Officer Allard opened fire on E/A from 150 yards astern and parts of the wing appeared to break off. E/A dived down and crashed near Folkestone either on land or just out to sea.

'Flying Officer Woods-Scawen carried out beam attack causing E/A to dive steeply, then gave a further burst from astern and E/A went down on fire with wing-tank burning — confirmed by Pilot Officer Lewis.

'Pilot Officer Lewis fired a four second burst at E/A from 150 yards on the beam and from slightly below. Black smoke billowed out and E/A dived steeply. Pilot Officer Lewis followed it down to 5,000 feet making sure it was done for and then rejoined Squadron — position then above sea near Folkestone.

'Flying Officer Gowers fired two bursts of five seconds and seven seconds causing a large piece to blow out of port wing of E/A — petrol streamed out as E/A dived vertically and when Flying Officer Gowers left him at 4,000 feet he was still diving straight down and by then was in flames. Confirmed by Pilot Officer Lewis.

'Nine Hurricanes landed at Croydon between 2005 hours and 2022 hours.'

During August 1940, the 85 Squadron 'bag' was 44 E/A destroyed, 15 probably destroyed and 15 damaged for the loss of eight Hurricanes destroyed and three

Top left: 'Scramble!' 'Though I have watched so many "scrambles" and waited for many returns,' wrote Cuthbert Orde, 'I still find it difficult to remember that there are chaps in the aeroplanes. One knows it, but doesn't remember it. One cannot recognise them as they taxy along the tarmac because the oxygen masks and goggles completely cover their faces. They look like robots, and the moment they leave the ground they cease even to be that and become just aeroplanes. "Yellow Section! Scramble!" — not "Smith, Jones and Robinson, get into your Hurricanes." So you don't see Smith, Jones and Robinson in the sky — just Yellow Section. And 'Yellow Section" soon becomes "some Hurricanes". It is just as well perhaps. It is less hard on the mind to be told, "Two of our fighters are missing," than "Smith and Jones have not returned".'

Bottom left: Flying Officer Patrick Woods-Scawen DFC who took over temporary command of the Squadron after Peter Townsend was shot down on 31 August. Woods-Scawen's DFC citation read: 'During May 1940, this officer destroyed six enemy aircraft and assisted in the destruction of others. On one occasion, although heavily outnumbered, he attacked without hesitation a large formation of enemy aircraft, shooting down two of them. His own aircraft was hit by cannon shell and he was slightly wounded, but he succeeded in escaping by parachute and rejoined his unit. He has displayed great courage, endurance, and leadership.'

damaged. Most of the Squadron pilots involved were only slightly wounded but Flight Lieutenant 'Hammy' Hamilton, the Canadian Flight Commander who was shot down on 29 August was among the unlucky ones. Here was the other side of the coin — success in the Battle of Britain meant public acclaim and accolades, but it was left to the Recovery Inspector to write the epitaph on the dead:

REPORT TO SQUADRON LEADER GOODMAN
R.A.F. DEPOT. 27.9.40

HURRICANE V 6640   Nr. Rye. Clearing instructions dated 17.9.40

         I ascertained the location of this machine from the
Police at Rye as having crashed on the foreshore near the
Old Castle ruins, immediately in front of the Town.
I inspected the site of the crash. This aircraft is
completely burnt out, both fuselage and engine. Inspecting
the remains I discovered a piece of the fuselage bearing
the following number - V 6623. Amongst the wreckage were
burnt pieces of the Pilot's uniform from which I salved a
piece of the pocket with a linen tab bearing the following -
Gieves Ltd., L/5/38. 40/16207 H.R. Hamilton. I have
instructed a gang to clear the wreckage to-morrow
Saturday the 28th inst:.

Signed ...

But those that survived flew on.

'1/9/40. 12 Hurricanes of 85 Squadron took-off from Croydon at 1105 hours to patrol home base, and were then vectored to Hawkinge area to intercept Raid 23. Nine Me 109s were sighted at 1130 hours flying at 17,000 feet believed to be attacking Dover Barrage balloons.

'Pilot Officer Allard led Squadron above E/A and dived on them from the sun. He chased last aircraft in formation out to sea but found it impossible to gain on him so he opened fire at 300 yards — he continued firing in one second bursts and as white smoke came from E/A Allard was able to close to 100 yards. He gave a long burst and E/A dived into sea 10 miles from Cap Gris Nez.

'Sergeant Goodman dived on four Me 109s from 22,000 feet and attacked rear E/A with only port guns firing. A large piece fell away from port wing of E/A and it immediately started to fall over and over sideways after a sharp pull upwards. It must have fallen down either in sea or on land near Dungeness but visibility was bad owing to haze and Sergeant Goodman had to break off combat at this point as his aircraft was badly shot up by another E/A and was U/S on landing.'

The Squadron landed back at Croydon around noon but eleven aircraft were up again at 1350 hours to intercept a raid heading for the Tunbridge Wells/Kenley area. This time things were not to go so well.

'At about 1355 hours an estimated 150-200 E/A were sighted near Biggin Hill flying at about 15,000 feet. E/A consisted of Dornier 17s and 215s, and Me 109s and 110s. When sighted, the Squadron was about 5,000 feet below the enemy and while climbing to intercept bombers they were attacked continuously by Me 109s and 110s.'

Thus the element of surprise was gone and the Hurricanes were at a height disadvantage before they started. 'Pilot Officer Allard attacked Do 17 which was flying apart from the main formation. E/A turned away towards Dungeness and Pilot Officer Allard climbed above and carried out three successive attacks from quarter developing to line astern. Both engines of E/A began to belch oil and smoke, and port engine burst into flames — pilot attempted a forced landing and rear gunner baled out. E/A landed near railway line at Lydd.

'Oil pressure on Pilot Officer Allard's aircraft dropped so he landed at Lympne with engine dead. Shortly afterwards while the aircraft was being repaired, the aerodrome was bombed and the aircraft damaged, one mechanic being killed and another seriously injured.

'Pilot Officer English attacked Do 215 twice from the quarter with bursts of five and seven seconds and put starboard engine out of action. E/A dived then circled slowly down, finally pancaking in a field — two of the crew were seen to emerge.

'Sergeant Evans gave a burst of about seven seconds to an Me 109 from astern — white glycol smoke issued from underneath E/A and he lurched to starboard and dived straight down, obviously finished. Actual point of crash not seen as Sergeant Evans was attacked by more Me 109s immediately afterwards. He then attacked last aircraft in formation of Me 110s and gave it a five second burst from beneath and converging from the beam — both engines were set on fire and E/A was staggering out of control when Sergeant Evans was again attacked by fighters and had to break away.

'Sergeant Howes attacked last member of Do 215 formation from quarter to full astern and E/A went down with black and white smoke coming out — shortly afterwards two parachutes were seen descending in the same area and a large column of black smoke seen coming from the ground where E/A crashed — position a little south of Tunbridge Wells.

'He then fired a good burst into an Me 109 from above and behind while E/A was attacking a Hurricane — E/A broke away to the right with much white smoke coming out. Combat then had to be abandoned as Sergeant Howes had another Me 109 on his tail.

'Flying Officer Gowers was shot up by cannon shell and forced to bale out. His Hurricane crashed near Oxted. He landed safely but was severely burnt on hands and had slight wounds in hand and foot. He was taken to LCC Mental Hospital, Caterham.

'Sergeant Booth's aircraft was badly hit by cannon shell and he baled out near Purley, his aircraft crashing in Sanderstead in a wood. Sergeant Booth's parachute was partially damaged causing him to descend too rapidly, and as a result he fractured a leg and an arm and a vertebrae of the spine. He was taken to Purley hospital.

'Flying Officer P. P. Woods-Scawen DFC was missing from this patrol and his body was subsequently found on 6 September near Kenley. His parachute was unopened but it was impossible to establish in what manner he was killed.

'Sergeant Ellis was also missing from this patrol and up to date no trace of him or his machine has been found. He is therefore believed killed.

'Six Hurricanes landed at Croydon between 1427 and 1500 hours.'

Despite accounting for six of the enemy, disaster had at last overtaken 85. Patrick Woods-Scawen was dead. The tall, quiet Sergeant Booth who jumped with his parachute on fire endured months of agony before dying, and 'Cock-sparrow' Mortimer Ellis probably died in the sea just as he predicted. To cap it all, Sergeant Goodman brought his aircraft back from Henlow on 3 September to report that the Maintenance Unit had discovered the reason for the failure of his four starboard guns during the penultimate engagement — a German sympathiser had blocked the air pressure lines with matchsticks.

Flesh and blood could only stand so much, and that applied as much to the groundcrew who sweated round the clock patching and repairing while dodging the bombs as it did to the aircrew. Moreover, 85 was now completely leaderless, and so the Squadron was moved out of the immediate front-line on 5 September and sent to the relative tranquility of Church Fenton in Yorkshire to rest and re-equip within 12 Group.

The Squadron 'bag' since it returned from France was 54 enemy aircraft destroyed, 16 probables and 17 damaged, and for leading 85 to such good effect, Peter Townsend received a bar to his DFC. Tim Molony spoke for the whole Squadron when he invoked his C.O. to 'Hurry up and get well. If you're not back in three weeks, they'll give us a new squadron commander.' Townsend obliged by returning to his Squadron on 21 September, but he still had to prove that he was fit to lead it from the front, so to the amazement of all onlookers he immediately hobbled out to his aircraft, took-off, and executed an aerobatics sequence. 'When I reported to the doctor, he told me gravely: "It will be some time before you can fly again." "But I've just been flying," I replied and he said no more.'

On 30 September, six of the best remaining pilots on 85, Townsend, Allard, Marshall, Hemingway, Hodgson and Goodman, flew in formation over Halifax to raise subscriptions of the local Spitfire fund. This sextet accounted for 24 of the 85 Squadron 'bag' in the Battle of Britain, but even more importantly three of these survived the Battle of France as well. Perhaps survivors survived if they lived long enough to learn all the tricks, but fate could be a fickle mistress. On the afternoon of 13 March 1941 'Sammy'

Above: Most of the Squadron pilots during the Battle of Britain were very young and not long out of school as this picture of Sergeant Ellis illustrates. Sergeant Deacon, an ex-flying instructor, was one of the old hands at the age of 23 and he saw at first hand the results of throwing inexperienced teenagers into the fray with only their new pilots' wings and a mere 150 flying hours to their credit. 'Most of them didn't last long,' he recorded. It took time to convince a man that if he was flying at 240mph, and the enemy crossed his nose also doing 240mph, then he had to aim ahead to shoot him down. We tried to put old heads on to young shoulders but in most cases you just couldn't do it.'

Allard, now a Flight Lieutenant and Flight Commander, decided to pilot two of his officers from Debden to Ford aerodrome in a Douglas Havoc. It was a very simple ferry trip for one so experienced, but as he arrived at the dispersal Allard found a rigger struggling to fasten a metal nose plate on the aeroplane. Being an ex-Halton apprentice rigger, Allard took the screwdriver from the airman and completed the fastening himself. Then he climbed into the Havoc and took-off. But the obstinate nose panel was still not secure and it worked loose, flew back over the cockpit and jammed the aircraft's rudder. The Havoc flicked over on its side and spun straight into the ground near Wimbush. All three men on board were killed.

Allard had been with 85 Squadron since its re-formation in 1938. He was its highest scoring 'ace' with 21 enemy aircraft and a share in two others to his name, and he had been awarded the DFC, DFM and bar for his undoubted skill and bravery, yet in the end he died not in action but as a result of something as stupid as a loose panel. The heroic war films never showed this futile side of death. 'Deeply regret to hear of Allard's death which is a great loss to the Service.' signalled the AOC. Allard's body lies in the Service Plot of the Saffron Walden Borough Cemetery in Essex.

60

Sector Intelligence Officer, R.A.F., Debden.

Officer Commanding, R. A. F., Debden.

1st September 1940.

536359 Pilot Officer Geoffrey Allard, D.F.M. of No. 85 Sqdn.

Up to the 6th August P/O Allard, D.F.M. had destroyed ten enemy aircraft, apart from others he shared in downing.

About 14 days ago he received his commission. With his squadron he moved to Croydon on the 19th August.

On the 24th August he destroyed a Me.109. Two days later with his squadron he made repeated attacks on three Do.215's, and finally all these were destroyed. On the 28th he destroyed two Me.109's.

No details have been received of combats, but it is known from his Squadron Intelligence Officer that on the 30th and 31st August up to noon today he has destroyed two Me.109's, and also two Me.111's and probably destroyed two Do.215's.

In all therefore, he has without any doubt destroyed seventeen enemy aircraft in individual combat, and probably destroyed two others, and has shared in the destruction of several enemy aircraft

(Signed)   F/Lt.

Sector Intelligence Officer.

Above left: Peter Townsend returns to his Squadron at Church Fenton with a damaged foot. Allard (far left) was now an Acting Flight Lieutenant and Flight Commander of 'A' Flight. Among the personnel now on the Squadron are French, Polish and New Zealand pilots plus an airman from Nigeria.

Left: The report which helped secure a DFC for Allard on 8 October 1940.

Above: Allard receiving the DFC from King George VI. Sammy Allard also met the King and Queen under less formal circumstances when they visited Debden on 28 January 1941. 'On arrival at No 2 Hangar, Their Majesties proceeded to the Pilots' Room and after the pilots of 242 Squadron, who had flown from Martlesham, had been presented to them, the pilots of 85 were each in turn presented to the King by Squadron Leader Townsend.

'The King noticed that all our pilots had their top tunic button undone and he asked Flight Lieutenant Allard the reason for this. Flight Lieutenant Allard explained to him that it was a tradition among fighter squadrons. His Majesty then asked why the pilots of the other Squadron had not got their's undone, to which Flight Lieutenant Allard replied: "I don't know, Sir. I expect they're a bit too shy." '

Right: Flight Lieutenant G. Allard DFC, DFM and bar — the ace of 85 and the Squadron's highest scoring member of the war.

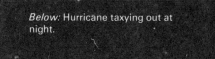

Below: Hurricane taxying out at night.

Day into Night

Between 3 September 1939 and 3 September 1940, 85 Squadron accounted for 144 enemy aircraft definitely destroyed, and another 61 probably destroyed or damaged, and this feat brought fame in its wake.

'*What Victories Take — Gallant RAF Fighters Give Their Lives*. By William H. Stoneman, Special Correspondent to the *Chicago Daily News*. *Somewhere in Yorkshire*, 19 September 1940 — British Hurricanes faced the Luftwaffe in Belgium and Holland for 10 solid days last May.

'On one memorable day five of these Hurricanes picked a fight with a hundred Germans and sent them scuttling back over Maastricht.

'On 18 August, 13 Hurricanes fought it out with 250 German planes. They destroyed 10 and probably got another eight. One Hurricane was lost.

'I knew the men who fought in all those battles. I used to while away long rainy mornings last fall in the officer's mess of "X" squadron, near Lille. Later, during the battle of Flanders, I saw them in the thick of their gallant struggle.

'So today I came up to Yorkshire to see those who were left and, of course, I found what the casualty lists had told me I would find . . . What has happened to "B" Flight since last October deserves to be recorded if only as a reminder that gallantry has its price and that all of the British victories which have been making headlines day after day have been purchased with the lives of a number of very human and fine young men.'

Not a few hearts fluttered around the world on reading words such as these.

20-1-1941

'Dear Mr Townsend,
As an admirer of RAF pilots I like to have your photograph with your signature.

By chance I read your name in the newspaper at the foot of your photograph. But this photograph is too indistinctly.

Please be so kind as to send me your photograph.

Sincerely
Miss Lenie van der Zwaan
Blimbing by Malang
East Java'

The records don't reveal whether or not she got her photograph.

Although some of the stories of RAF prowess during the Battle of Britain were undoubtedly exaggerated by the propagandists, there was no denying that the Luftwaffe had suffered a bloody nose by attacking en masse in daylight. The lesson having been learned, the Germans thereupon began to seek sanctuary for their bombing missions under cover of darkness and on 10 October Squadron Leader Townsend received the following signal from HQ 12 Group:

'85 Squadron and 151 Squadron have been selected to specialise in Night Fighting forthwith. Night Flying Training is to be concentrated on immediately. It is intended to bring the Squadrons at once up to strength of 12 operationally trained night pilots by posting volunteers to fill vacancies.'

Night flying at that time was a primitive business with the landing strip on the grass being marked by oil burning gooseneck flares. In fact such was the novelty of the art of night fighting that 85 was left to decide on how best to go about it, and the Squadron's recommendations are reproduced below.

SECRET
From:— No 85 Squadron, RAF.
To:— Headquarters, RAF Station, KIRTON-IN-LINDSEY.
Date:— 1 November, 1940.
Ref:— 85S/6/1/Air.

NIGHT FLYING — HURRICANE AIR-CRAFT

Consequent upon a conference on Night Flying held on the afternoon of 31 October,

1940, at Headquarters, No 12 Group, I wish to reiterate briefly the requests I then made, and ask that they might be confirmed and attended to as expeditiously as possible.

2. I and my pilots are pleased and enthusiastic about our new role, as, apart from the sentimental feelings we have about destroying Germans by night and allaying the night onslaught upon the British Public, Industry and so on, we appreciate that there is great scope for developing night fighting technique. Consequently, we are immediately aware of the unsuitability of the Hurricane for serious night fighting owing to:

(1) Its inherent instability and the absence of controllable rudder bias.
(2) Its short endurance.
(3) The lack of space in the cockpit which causes acute discomfort of the pilot and renders movement in the cockpit difficult, especially if he is of more than average stature, or if he is heavily clothed as he has to be on cold nights.
(4) Absence of cockpit heating.
(5) Badly designed cockpit lighting.
(6) Indifferent view of instrument panel, owing to obstruction by reflector sight.
(7) Absence of VHF radio.
(8) Absence of airborne intercept radar.
(9) Absence of anti-glare device on exhaust manifold.
(10) Commitment to line-astern attack, owing to fixed .303 machine guns. These are considered inferior to a well-handled cannon gun as mounted in many enemy aircraft, owing to the greater effective range of the cannon.
(11) Absence of 'Black-out' paint for bottom surface of wings.

Such a lengthy list of disadvantages may give the impression that the difficulties of night fighting in a Hurricane are insuperable. Not at all. My intention is to show that the Hurricane is by no means an ideal night fighter and that it is of paramount importance to equip it with some extra devices in order that we might execute our night fighting role with efficiency and some hope of success. On the other hand, the Hurricane is generally considered a pleasant machine to fly on a good night, and while I am given to understand that the Hurricane will not in the near future be superseded by a new type, I am confident of operating it successfully for some time to come, provided that my squadron (and, of course, other Night-Hurricane squadrons) are given first consideration in the matter of additional equipment.

3. I have, therefore, to ask that my unit be re-equipped with Hurricane II aircraft, before day-fighting squadrons. The Hurricane II is obviously superior in performance to the Hurricane I and has the very important feature of controllable rudder-bias. (It is noted here that while the Hurricane can be trimmed to fly hands off, straight and level, once a climb or dive is started, the rudder trim alters completely. Controllable rudder-bias would, of course, obviate this difficulty, which is most noticeable in instrument flying.)

4. Pending the arrival of the Hurricane II (which I suggest, might be fitted with the necessary modifications before delivery and known as a 'Night Hurricane'), I ask that urgent attention and action may be given to the following:

(1) The removal from this unit of the obsolescent models of Hurricane I (ie with curved windscreen, non-automatic selector box etc) and replacement with modern Rotol Hurricanes, see this unit's postagram 85S/2301/Eng dated 1/11/40.
(2) Improved cockpit lighting (W/Cmdr Stephen Hardy has already (am 1/11/40 sent to obtain drawings of improved scheme from W/Cmdr Broadhurst, OC Wittering.
(3) Installation of VHF radio.
(4) Fitting of Rolls-Royce design of anti-glare shields for exhaust manifolds (see this unit's postagram 85S/2301/Eng dated 30/10/40).
(5) The issue of 'black-out' paint for covering under surface of wings.
(6) Fitting of the Prismatic gun-sight to allow a better view of the instrument panel.
(7) Improvement of armament either by installation of cannons (if successful) or by installation of the Browning 0.5in machine-gun (which I understand is being developed).

5. In conclusion, I would say that even the smallest consideration to the above-mentioned details would react favourably on the morale of my pilots who have responded keenly to their new role, and who would appreciate the act of their Hurricanes being fitted with special equipment for a specialised job.

P. W. TOWNSEND
Squadron Leader, Commanding
No 85 Squadron, RAF.

Nevertheless, Peter Townsend was able to keep his promise to the AOC 12 Group that all 85 Squadron pilots would be night operational by the full moon in November 1940.

Appropriately, it fell to Peter Townsend to notch up the first Squadron victory at night when he shot down a Do 217 on 25 February 1941, but the fact that the Dornier had left its lights on helped considerably and 85 soon

Centre left: Squadron Leader James Wheeler gets into the cockpit at Debden. By now the Squadron Hurricanes were painted black.

Bottom left: Squadron Leader Wheeler discusses a patrol with Wing Commander Harvey, the Hunsdon Station Commander. James Wheeler MC joined 85 as a Pilot Officer, soon became a Flying Officer, and then because of his age and previous military service, was promoted from Flying Officer straight to Acting Squadron Leader on 11 April 1941. The reason for this rapid elevation was that the Squadron establishment was to be increased and henceforward, it was to be commanded by a Wing Commander. This left a vacancy for a Squadron Leader Flight Commander, and James Wheeler was the ideal man to fill the post. He was awarded the DFC on 26 September 1941.

Far right: Boulton Paul Defiant making a low pass. 85 received notice on 28 December 1940 that its Hurricanes were to be replaced and the first Defiant arrived on 2 January 1941.

Right: Howitt, Wheeler and Hemingway relaxing in the crew-room after night flying.

Below: Hemingway, Howitt, Marshall, Townsend and Kim with Carnaby who is holding the Squadron propeller-blade scoreboard. Peter Townsend was promoted to Acting Wing Commander on 3 March 1941.

found that the single-seat Hurricane was unsuited to the night fighter task. The work load involved in flying and navigating accurately in darkness, while finding and manoeuvring into position to shoot down an intruder, demanded a two-man crew, and so Boulton Paul Defiants were given to the Squadron at the beginning of 1941. This single-engined fighter carried an air gunner, the first of whom, Sergeant W. J. Cox, joined the Squadron on 5 January, and initially the German night bomber crews were rudely surprised by the Defiant's rearward-firing guns. Unfortunately a Defiant crew could only find a night intruder in bright moonlight: what the night interceptor squadrons really needed was a device that could tell them, in pitch darkness, how far away a target was, whether it was above or below the fighter, and whether it was horizontally to port or starboard. This need was filled by the Airborne Interception (AI) radar but such a bulky device necessitated a larger and more powerful aircraft than the Defiant to get the best out of it, plus a new breed of aircrew to operate the radar. The latter were christened Radio Observers (ROs) and they came to 85 when the Squadron re-equipped with Douglas DB-7 Havocs which carried the AI Mk IV. The first of these aircraft, which were modifications of the American built Boston bomber fitted with eight Browning .303in machine guns in the nose, arrived on the Squadron on 15 February 1941.

The Ground Control Interception (GCI) radar stations on the ground pointed night fighter crews towards incoming bombers, but it was the AI radar which would hopefully bring the night fighter in close enough behind the intruder for the pilot to see the enemy,

Above: Douglas Havoc I in Squadron colours. This aircraft was a trainer version.

identify it and shoot it down. The early rudimentary AI radar could give a very confused or blurred picture and the amount of information that an operator could extract from it was often limited. 'Climbing to 8,000 feet,' wrote one RO* under training, 'we followed visually the aircraft which was to act as our target. The operator adjusted the AI set, and made way for me. This was the big moment!

Night Fighter; Rawnsley and Wright, Collins, 1957.

Mark IV AI Radar Display

Interception information was presented to the Mosquito radar operator on two cathode ray tubes — one for azimuth and one for elevation. Running across the centre of each tube was a luminous green line known as the time base — attached to this was a triangular shape looking like a Christmas tree which was formed by returns from the ground. An enemy aircraft echo appeared as a diamond shape sitting astride the time base line (the stem of the Christmas tree); the distance of this blip from the root end of the stem indicated range from the fighter.

On the azimuth tube the blip always remained astride the base line but it could move from one side to the other as the target altered course. The elevation tube was turned on its side to ease interpretation but otherwise it worked on the same principle — a target that was above the fighter would produce a blip with most of the diamond above the time base.

ELEVATION TUBE   AZIMUTH TUBE

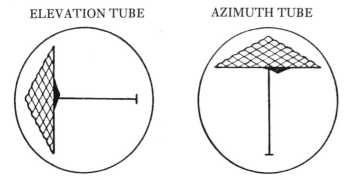

Fighter flying at 14,000 feet. Target just emerging from ground returns — its range is about three miles, above and to starboard.

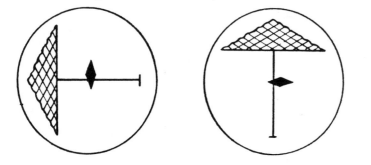

Target range now decreased to just under two miles, position about 15° above and 20° starboard.

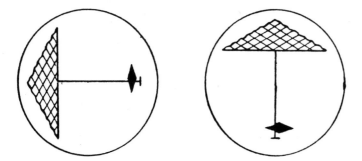

The fighter has now closed to within about 1,000 feet of the target, which is now 10° above and 10° starboard. This was minimum radar range and at this stage the Mosquito pilot should soon be able to see the quarry visually and shoot it down.

'I peered into the visor, trying to accustom my eyes to the dim light. Slowly there came into view not the clear-cut picture I had seen in the ground trainer but instead a shivery confusion of waving lines. An enormous Christmas tree blotted out more than half of the cathode ray tubes, and on both sides of the wobbling traces there was a wavering, choppy fringe. Horrified at the indistinct picture I was seeing, I turned to the operator.

' "What's all that stuff?" I asked.

' "Grass," he replied off handedly. "It's like the background noise of a wireless set."

'We were closing in on the target aircraft. A faint, spidery blip slid down out of the Christmas tree, wobbled drunkenly from side to side, and then faded coyly into the grass.

' "Any joy yet?" the pilot asked. He sounded bored, a little impatient. I swallowed hard, and then found myself making non-committal noises.

' "Well . . . come on . . . Where is it?" the pilot demanded.

' "It's not very good today."

'There was a snort of disgust from the front as the pilot complained·

"Is it ever any good? Leave it . . . we'd better act as target for a bit." '

This specialised training in AI operations reflected the change that had taken place in RAF aircrew recruiting during the first two years of war. Before 1939, the RAF aircrew selection procedure could be loosely termed 'survival selection' under which candidates for aircrew training were both selected and classified solely on the basis of the impression they made at a personal interview with a board of officers. Be they Cranwell men, university graduates or exceptional airmen like Geoffrey Allard, they were nevertheless the elite, and many other men, who might be just as capable of fighting an aerial war, were often excluded for no better reason than they lacked the right sporting or social background.

After 1939 this had to change. The numerical demands of war, and the growing number of new specialisations such as RO which demanded an educational standard capable of coping with rapid technological advances, meant that the RAF could no longer afford to reject any men of aptitude. Consequently the Service replaced the prewar system of 'survival selection' with a scientific system of 'quality selection' whereby marks were given during a series of practical and psychological tests. From this it was hoped to determine flying aptitude with reasonable accuracy, and all who gained sufficient marks were welcomed in so long as they were medically fit.

During the war the normal method of providing flying personnel for the RAF was through the RAF Volunteer Reserve (RAFVR).

'Sir,

1. I am commanded by the Air Council to inform you that they have approved your application for a commission in the General Duties (Flying) Branch of the Royal Air Force Volunteer Reserve and you will be appointed in the rank of Pilot Officer on Probation with effect from the date on which you report for duty. The appointment will be for the duration of hostilities.

2. Memoranda dealing with the uniform and outfit required, and the issue of pay, allowances and outfit grant are enclosed herewith. It will be necessary for you to provide yourself with uniform and other necessaries in accordance with the particulars stated in the memorandum, before you actually report.

3. Please take your civilian pattern respirator with you.

I am, Sir,
Your obedient Servant

for Under Secretary of State'

However although 'past or present members of University Air Squadrons who hold proficiency certificates will be eligible for consideration for appointment to commissions on entry'* (together with certain specialists in the ground branches), 'direct appointments to commissions for flying duties are only made in exceptional circumstances. Entry into the General Duties (Flying) Branch is normally through the ranks ... As vacancies occur for commissions, they are filled by promotion from the ranks, either on completion of flying training or subsequently.'

The age limits for acceptance for flying training for operational duties were 18-29 and a School Certificate† was the minimum requirement.

Prospective aircrew then went to an Initial Training Wing where, for the most part, they were instructed in physical training and drill. After eight weeks of this, pilots went to an Elementary Flying Training School and observers to an Air Observer's Navigation School. At EFTS an embryo pilot received 50 hours of flying on Tiger Moths or Magisters before progressing to a Service Flying Training School for a further 110 hours on Masters, Oxfords, or Harvards.*

In April 1940 the flying syllabus at the Air Observer Navigation Schools was increased to 67 hours but night flying instruction was abolished because of the difficulty of carrying it out without wireless aids. Only if and when they had completed their basic flying training were pilots and navigators considered for commissions.

A newly commissioned officer received an Outfit Allowance of £40 in 1940 and if he was suitable for immediate posting to a service unit he was paid 14 shillings and 6 pence a day as a Pilot Officer. He was provided with free accommodation and rations and if he was separated from his family 'by the exigencies of the service', he received an extra 4 shillings and 6 pence per day to put a roof over their head. He also knew that if he was 'invalided in consequence of wound, injury or disease directly attributable to the conditions of service, he may be granted disability retired pay or other award calculated according to his rank and the degree of disablement. Disability retired pay will not be granted or continued if the degree of disablement is assessed at less than 20 per cent.'

Having therefore received their wings, and been commissioned or confirmed as NCO aircrew, prospective night fighter pilots and observers joined up to learn their new specialisations. Conversion training before the war had been left to the squadrons, but after 3 September 1939 the operational squadrons had little time or opportunity for this so Operational Training Units (OTUs) were established to do the job.† By the time 85 Squadron moved to Hunsdon in Hertfordshire in May 1941 to work in North Weald sector, which guarded London from anything crossing from the east across the Essex marshes or up the Thames Estuary, most of the old single-engined men had gone. In their place, wrote one officer, 'the Squadron became composed mainly of crews drawn from No 54 OTU, then stationed at Church Fenton under the command of Wing Commander Richard "Batchy" Atcherley (David's brother). Known as "Batchy's Air Force,"

---

*Air Ministry Pamphlet 101, 5th Edition, July 1940.

† Roughly equivalent to five O Levels today, including Maths and English, *and all subjects passed at the same sitting.*

* At the end of April 1940, the supply of pilots for the RAF came from 12 Flying Training Schools in the UK, each dealing with 160 pupils. This was woefully insufficient, so the Empire Air Training Scheme was introduced whereby thousands of aircrew members could be trained in safety around the Empire. In similar vein, No 85 Squadron became a typically cosmopolitan RAF unit with personnel from all corners of the Empire and occupied Europe.

† Fighter Command established one OTU for every ten fighter squadrons.

this was the first organised night fighter OTU in the country and the crews trained there were of the keenest. These crews began to arrive on 85 Squadron in March 1941, the first two being Pilot Officers Bunting and Babington. These new crews arrived at regular intervals until by the beginning of 1942 all the junior officers were ex-54 OTU.'

'One of the cynics with us,' wrote an RO, 'once likened a night fighter sortie to the affairs of a married couple: once the door had slammed behind them no one quite knew what went on except that one of the partners had a virtual monopoly of speech and the other of action.' Teamwork between pilot and RO therefore was the key to success in night fighting. 'Usually these pairings had been made after careful consideration and it was only rarely that changes were needed. The job we were now engaged on demanded keenness and initiative equally from the pilot and the navigator. A brilliant pilot could expect little success if he was flying with a navigator who could not get the best out of AI; the same held true for first-class navigator with a poor pilot.'

A Squadron crew managed to convert an AI contact into a visual attack within three nights of 85 becoming operational again on 6 April, and thereafter the crews at Hudson were not slow to demonstrate that night fighting had become much more of an individual and scientific battle of wits than the mass dog-fighting days of the Battle of Britain.

Right: Wing Commander Peter Townsend DSO, DFC portrayed by Eric Kennington.

Below: Peter and Rosemary Townsend after their wedding on 17 July 1941. Tim Molony was best man and Squadron Leader Wheeler, Flight Lieutenant Marshall and Flight Lieutenant Hemingway acted as ushers. The reception was held in 'The Lordships' at Much Hadham (near Bishops Stortford) after which the couple were given 'a rousing send-off' by the Squadron.

'13/7/41. Flight Lieutenant Raphael and his RO, Sergeant Addison, took-off at 0100 hours and after being controlled by North Weald they were taken over by Waldringfield Radar. Havoc was at 12,000 feet about 15 miles ESE of Clacton when AI contact was obtained of an E/A flying E. A visual was soon obtained of an He 111 about 200 yards distant and 200 feet below.

'Havoc closed in to 50 yards range and fired a short burst into the starboard engine, strikes being observed. At the same time return fire was experienced from the top rear gunner of the E/A but Havoc was not hit. The E/A now commenced a slight dive and the Havoc fired three more bursts into the fuselage which caused a fire to break out. The Heinkel now went into a steep dive and was seen to strike the sea in flames. Havoc returned to base and landed 0305 hours. This was the Squadron's 153rd confirmed victory and the 9th at night.'

Not that the new night fighting system was infallible.

'24/10/41. 1950 hours. Wing Commander Sanders and Pilot Officer Reed took-off and landed 21.35 hours. Under CHL (Chain Home Low — the low level part of the

national radar early warning system), contact was made on an aircraft given as a Bandit. Contact was at 2045 hours at 12,000feet at maximum range below and to port. After a 15 minute chase a visual was obtained and Wing Commander Sanders identified the aircraft as a Hampden. Reference was made to the Controller who insisted that it was a Bandit. Accordingly a second approach was made and a visual from below confirmed the Wing Commander's opinion that it was a Hampden and he abandoned the chase. Subsequently, the so-called Bandit landed in England and proved the Wing Commander correct.'

This problem of differentiating between RAF and Luftwaffe should have been solved by the introduction of IFF — 'Identification Friend or Foe' - which allowed a friendly aircraft to superimpose a distinctive mark over the radar blip it made on the screen, but the trouble was that this mark was sometimes not clearly seen and there was no way of ensuring that a radar blip without IFF was not just a friendly aircraft whose crew had forgotten to turn it on. Thus aerial combat, especially at night, was rarely as clear-cut and straightforward as romanticised fiction led many to believe.

'31/10/41. Wing Commander Sanders and his operator, Pilot Officer Austin, took-off at 1900 hours and were taken over by Waldringfield Radar at 1930 hours. The Controller reported as follows:

' "Rainbow 14 was patrolling 12-15 miles off shore between Orfordness and Harwich at 1930 hours. An aircraft was plotted coming up from SE but as it showed IFF, Waldringfield took it to be a Beaufighter. Bawdsey Radar plotted this aircraft as hostile because they had no IFF indication.

' "Rainbow 14 next reported AA fire from the ground. Actually a convoy was firing at either R 14 or the unidentified aircraft which were only $\frac{3}{4}$ mile apart. Both were at 10,000feet. Next bombs were reported at (map reference) NO7, and Bawdsey confirmed that a ship was on fire. Unidentified aircraft then proved hostile and R 14 was vectored after it. After a five minute chase, contact was made at 1945 hours. After another 7 minutes R 14 asked how long he could keep on his vector which was 170°. Told to come back soon. At 2005 R 14 very agitated said, 'Put me over land. I will have to bale out ... have been rather badly hit.' Their position was then about 20 miles NE of Deal.

' "Given vectors 270° and 290° which he acknowledged at 2006 hours. R 14 next said, 'I'm going over ... I can't make it ... I can't make land.' Told to call Bantam for fix but no reply. Bawdsey report that just before R 14 asked to be put over land he had overshot the E/A.

Above: Squadron Leader James Wheeler with Wing Commander A. D. T. 'Scruffy' Sanders who took over command of 85 from Peter Townsend.

' "The Air Sea Rescue Service was put into operation at once and search was carried out throughout the night without result. The weather was fine with bright moonlight but the sea was very rough.

' "At dawn, Squadron Leader J. F. Maffett (Pilot) and Sergeant Waldeck and Pilot Officer Reeves (crew), took-off in a Havoc to continue the search. They were escorted by six hurricanes of No 3 Squadron. A thorough search was carried out over the sea at low altitude but nothing was seen. The sea was very rough. There is now very little hope of Wing Commander Sanders and Pilot Officer Austin being alive." '

The Times carried the obituary of Wing Commander A. T. D. Sanders DFC, known to Squadron personnel as 'Scruffy'.

' "Scruffy" in an age and in a service of splendid youth, was always different from all his fellows, whether it was in his unexpected enthusiasms — few could extract greater thrill than he from the discovery of a whitethroat or a willow wren's nest, or in his original and quaint nomenclature for the everyday things around him — distinctive yet never aloof, his fine clear brain — his passion for his job, his deep, selfless courage

Above: Tim Moloney and Kim outside the Mess at Hunsdon. Flight Lieutenant Molony was summoned for an interview at the Air Ministry after being Squadron Adjutant for 21 months and offered promotion to Squadron Leader if he took up a post in the Isle of Man. This move was in keeping with RAF philosphy because the Service has always believed in moving men on at regular intervals to broaden their individual experience and to stop them getting into ruts: however, such was Molony's loyalty to 85 that he declined the promotion and persuaded the powers-that-be to allow him to stay with the Squadron for a bit longer. But he could not delay the fateful day for long, and in September 1941, Tim Molony gave farewell parties to all at the Piebald Inn, Stanstead Abbots, prior to a new posting in the USA. The new Adjutant arrived on 17 September but he was immediately admitted to Ely hospital and on 28 September a delighted Tim Molony resumed the duties of Squadron Adjutant, his posting to America having been cancelled.

added to his picturesque almost d'Artagnanesque personality — all combined to make him loved by his squadron as few men are loved.'

'3/11/41. Wing Commander R. K. Hamblin arrived from Tangmere and took over command of the Squadron.'

However it would be misleading to imply that life on 85 by the end of 1941 was wholly devoted to the task of destroying large numbers of German bombers every night. The demands made on the Luftwaffe by the invasion of Russia steadily reduced their bomber force in the west, and consequently a new pattern of attacks emerged. The massed daily forays of the Battle of Britain were replaced by a night fighter war which was largely one of attrition against individual German intruders such as minelayers, or small groups of 'Baedeker' bombers that periodically tried to creep through to attack the smaller, less well-defended cities of Britain. Most of these raids lasted about half an hour but they were certainly not mounted every night and as many pairs of Havocs were launched on quiet nights to practice interception techniques between themselves or to fly fruitless search patrols as were scrambled to take on the enemy. In fact, operations had become much more ordered and less hectic and, for the first time since 3 September 1939, the Squadron found time to resurrect some of the pleasures and pastimes of pre-war Service life.

'14/12/41. Boxing contests held in Entertainments Hangar. Pilot Officer Len Harvey refereed. No flying at night.'

'24/12/41. Seven night patrols by "A" Flight. In the morning Sergeant Pilots and Operators and Flight Sergeants were invited to Officers' Mess to drink with Officers of the Squadron. At the Airmen's Mess, officers assisted in serving the main Christmas Dinner.'

'25/12/41. Three night patrols by "B" Flight. Christmas Night and "The Emptiness of the Operations Board" were celebrated in "B" Flight dispersal by a select company. The climax of the proceedings was reached when an officer (who shall remain nameless) offered himself for a supreme high flying test and retired to his wigwam wrapped in a blanket.'

'29/12/41. No flying at night. At 1530 hours, a Children's Party was held in the Officers' Mess. There was a tree, presents, plenty to eat and comic drawings by Pilot Officer David Langdon.* A large number of the next generation of 85 attended.'

*David Langdon, later to become well-known as a newspaper and magazine cartoonist, was then the Squadron Intelligence Officer. Such was his affinity with No 85 that he regularly returned after being posted away to draw cartoons and decorative murals.

There were no lack of recreations to while away the adverse winter weather.

'2/3/42. 10/10 cloud and frost. Bad vertical visibility improving in afternoon. Heavy ground mist and an eclipse of the moon at 2330 hours made flying impossible. Cecil Beaton visited the Station and made some sketches.'

'19/3/42. 10/10 cloud and heavy rain in morning. In the afternoon, the final of the AOC's Cup was played at Hunsdon as the pitches were not fit at North Weald. Results as follows:

Rugby: Hunsdon 8 West Malling 3
Soccer: Hunsdon 5 West Malling 0
Hockey: Hunsdon 7 West Malling 0

The Cup was presented on the field by Air Vice-Marshal Leigh-Mallory to the three captains. The AOC said that he was pleased that the two night flying stations in the Group, which had got leave to play as separate units, had reached the final. On the other hand, he said, he had heard that the Night Fighters had nothing to do but play games all day and sleep all night!'

If that were true, 85 deserved a rest by virtue of their position in the league table of operational successes published in the 11 Group Intelligence Summary for March 1942:

'Following is a list of the first 12 Squadrons who, according to the records of HQ Fighter Command, have to their credit the most enemy aircraft destroyed since the beginning of the war, in France and the British Isles. The figures are as at 31/12/41:

Squadron	Total
92	$176\frac{1}{2}$
303	$160\frac{1}{2}$
234	156
1	$155\frac{1}{2}$
85	153
609	137
54	$136\frac{1}{2}$
87	128
41 } 603	$127\frac{1}{2}$
74 } 242	123'

As the tally increased, so the old names either moved on, came back, or fell by the wayside.

'18/4/42. Squadron Leader "Nigger" Marshall on returning to West Malling with two passengers crashed at Widford in the field next door to Mr Pawle's house. All were killed. Squadron Leader Marshall had served with 85 Squadron from before the war to June 1941.'

'19/4/42. Flying Officer G. Goodman

Above: Wing Commander Gordon Learmonth Raphael, who assumed command of 85 in May 1942. Born at Brantford, Ontario, in 1915, Gordon Raphael was educated at Quebec High School and the College of Aeronautical Engineers, Chelsea, before enlisting as an aircraftman in 1935. He was commissioned on 20 January 1936 and served on bombers until 1940, receiving a DFC in May of that year. He then transferred to fighters, joining 85 as a Flight Lieutenant in June 1941 and receiving a bar to his DFC the following month. He was promoted to Squadron Leader and became a Flight Commander on 16 August, shortly before Wing Commander Hamblin was posted in to command the Squadron following the death of 'Scruffy' Sanders. Raphael was detached to the Air Ministry for six weeks on 18 May 1942 to tour round aircraft and armaments factories and give morale boosting lectures to the production workers, but eight days later Hamblin was promoted and moved on. As a result, Gordon Raphael found himself promoted and recalled to take command of the Squadron.

posted to 51 OTU* for instructor duties. He had served with the Squadron since its formation in 1938 with the exception of three months (April-June 1940) when he was "hors de combat" as a result of a flying accident in France. He was therefore overdue for a rest from operational duties. Flight Lieutenant G. L. Howitt DFC returned to the Squadron from 51 OTU and was posted to "A" Flight.'

Nor was life any less hectic or dangerous for the men on the ground.

'3/5/42. During the night, Aircraftman Cooke was accidentally killed by running into a propeller of a Havoc which had been started up prior to taking off. Two Dusk Patrols. No enemy activity.'

By May 1942, 85 had been at Hunsdon for a year, the longest stay it had had in any one place since the war started. Even so, it had now become apparent that the Havoc had severe limitations when it came to taking on enemy bomber crews who were now prepared for it and who generally flew much faster aircraft.

'8/5/42. Squadron Leader Maude and Flight Sergeant Cairns up at 2230 hours and made two contacts. While on Silent Patrol (North) flying north at 10,000 feet, contact

*No 51 Operational Training Unit was formed as another night fighter OTU on 7 August 1941 with Blenheims and Beaufighters.

was made above and to starboard at 0015 hours. Bandit was chased on approximate 330° weaving course. E/A was followed for 10 minutes. Climbing and diving at 270mph, Squadron Leader Maude was unable to overtake at this speed and every time he tried to climb E/A appeared to draw away so that he could not get closer than 4,000 feet. When 1,000 feet below. Havoc attempted to climb again; E/A turned hard to starboard and was followed but the blip was lost. Sector was called but vectors were not understood. At 0115 hours while orbiting at 9,000 feet 40 miles out to sea off Orfordness, Squadron Leader Maude received a chance contact which lasted only 30 seconds. E/A was coming head on and well below: Havoc turned hard on reciprocal but E/A was lost. Havoc landed at Bradwell to refuel and returned to base.

'Flight Lieutenant Howitt and Flying Officer McInnes up at 2325 hours and down at 0210 hours had five contacts. While on Silent Patrol at 11,000 feet on course 350°, contact was made at 0110 hours below and to starboard at maximum range. E/A was below and already taking evasive action, gently weaving. Havoc followed at maximum speed but E/A dived to starboard and drew away. A second brief contact was made below and to starboard. It was lost in 30 seconds. Three contacts were obtained at once, two to starboard and one to port all below. Port target was selected but IFF was shown.'

What was needed was an aircraft that could fly much higher and faster than the Havoc, and 85 personnel bent Leigh-Mallory's ear as far back as December 1941 in an effort to secure the de Havilland Mosquito. By May there were rumours of better things to come but in the meantime 85 had to make do as best they could.

'2/6/42. No cloud, moon and good visibility. 25 E/A attacked Canterbury between 0130 and 0300 hours. It was ascertained that they were approaching the target on course 280° at heights around 10,000 feet. Thirteen fighters (seven from "A" Flight and six from "B" Flight) were put in the air. Two of these were already on patrol (Ground Control Interception practice), five took-off between 0130 and 0150 hours, and a further six between 0225 and 0245 hours. They were ordered by Squadron Leader Maude (Officer in Charge of Night Flying) to fly at 12,000 feet and approximately 160mph along the main incoming stream gradually losing height, then to turn off to starboard at North Foreland and fly in a wide circuit increasing speed as they approached a point about 30-40 miles NE of the Foreland before recommencing the slow approach along the incoming lane. The object of this was to com-

73

Above: Wing Commander Raphael and some of his aircrews at Hunsdon, 1942. From left to right: back row — Flying Officer Townsin (Nav), Flying Officer House (Pilot), Flight Lieutenant Snell (Pilot), Flight Lieutenant Bunting (Pilot), Raphael, Sergeant Mold (Nav), Unknown (Nav), Flying Officer Hall (Pilot), Flight Lieutenant Reed (Nav), Unknown (Pilot), Flying Officer Skelton (Nav). Front row — Sergeant Bray (Nav), Flying Officer King (Pilot). Remainder unknown.

Centre right: Two of the Squadron Mosquito NF IIs which replaced the Havocs. Note the AI Mk IV aerials on the nose.

Bottom right: The same photograph as issued to the press — notice that the censor's paint brush has been at work.

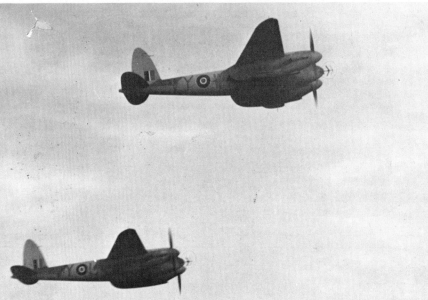

74

pensate for the Havocs' speed disadvantage by seeking contacts behind and below, putting the nose down and getting into firing range before the E/A could pull away.

'Squadron Leader Maude and Flight Sergeant Cairns on Silent Patrol on course 280° made contact at 0230 hours to port and slightly above. Fighter was brought in dead astern as target began to lose height. After a three minute chase, target was brought to minimum range and visually identified as a Do 217. Havoc was doing 260mph with nose down. Squadron Leader Maude gave a short burst at 200 yards range as E/A put his port wing down to make a diving run on the target. When the Squadron Leader recovered from the flash of his guns he saw the E/A flying level and on fire. Suddenly it burst into flames and crashed into the sea where it burned on the surface.

'Flight Sergeant Gibbs and Sergeant Waller while on course 300° at 12,500 feet at 150mph were pursued and shot down between 0235 and 0242 hours by an aircraft which Flight Sergeant Gibbs presumed to be friendly as his Operator reported getting IFF. Havoc crashed in the sea approximately five miles E of Foulness Point.

'At 0530 hours approximately, a Walrus of Air Sea Rescue Services picked up Flight Sergeant Gibbs who had succeeded in baling out by standing up in the cockpit, opening the cover and rolling down the fuselage. He had inflated his dinghy and climbed in, but being doubtful of his position he allowed two rescue launches to pass without signalling lest they were German. When picked up he was very exhausted and suffering from cuts and bruises on the head.

'At 0730 hours approx the body of Sergeant Waller was picked up in the sea at the mouth of the River Crouch.'

Improvements were fortunately close at hand and on 29 July 85 Squadron received its first dual control Mosquito T.III. Not that it did them much good initially:
'29/7/42. Squadron Leader S. N. L. Maude DFC (pilot) and Flight Lieutenant G. L. Howitt DFC took-off in the Mosquito and on landing the aircraft swung and ground looped damaging the port propeller, nacelle and undercarriage.' Such was the price the RAF paid for expecting crews to convert themselves on to a new type at the drop of a hat.

More Mosquitos arrived during August — 'not before time', wrote the Squadron record, 'because on 23/8/42 Flight Lieutenant Bunting could not catch a Do 217 even though "clocking" 300/310mph on his Havoc.'

'During September, Havocs returned by ATA (Air Transport Auxiliary) to 12 Maintenance Unit. About time — on

night of 16/9/42, Pilot Officer Medhurst about to engage E/A when gunsight fell off.'

'19/10/42. The first combats since the Squadron re-equipped with Mosquitos took place in the morning. "Sneak" raiders were reported coming in over East Anglia and Flight Lieutenant Bunting with his Op (Flying Officer Reed) and Sergeant Clunes with his Op (Pilot Officer Jones) took-off at 1005 hours and 1040 hours respectively.

'At 1050 Flight Lieutenant Bunting when about 45 miles NW of Foreness at 7/8,000 feet obtained a visual on a Ju 88 NW at 3,000 feet. He dived out of the sun and opening fire at 400 yards closed to 250 yards. Hits were seen on the port wing and port engine from which came a bright flash followed by black smoke. E/A dived steeply into cloud — Bunting followed down through cloud but could find no trace of E/A in the poor visibility. Two further contacts were made but E/A disappeared into cloud. Bunting landed at base at 1315 hours. One Ju 88 claimed as damaged.

'Sergeant Clunes obtained a visual of a Do 217 flying at 1,500 feet E of Clacton. He closed in to attack from 250 yards and fired three bursts. Bits were seen to fall off the port engine of the E/A which dived steeply to

Below: The World War I ace, Air Marshall 'Billy' Bishop VC, DSO, MC, DFC, drops in to Hunsdon to see his old Squadron on 5 October 1942. Fellow Canadians Raphael and Bishop (far right) together with Colonel Laurence K. Callaghan (USAAF), Callaghan was another First War member of 85 Squadron.

Bottom: Inside the Squadron HQ inspecting souvenirs. Squadron Leader W. P. Green ('A' Flight Commander) is on Bishop's left. A slightly built, deceptively mild-mannered man, Peter Green was plagued with a nervous stammer which, as with most aircrew, disappeared the moment he left the ground. There was certainly no nervousness about his flying. Also in the picture: Back — Pilot Officer George 'Ginger' Irving, Flight Sergeant Waldeck. Left — Sergeant Fisher, Flight Sergeant Grimstone (who flew with Peter Green). Right — Squadron Leader Green, Flying Officer Maguire, Flying Officer Skelton, Pilot Officer Jones.

Above: Bishop talking to Flight Lieutenant C. P. Reed (wearing Mae West) 'You don't know what a thrill it gives me to visit this Squadron again,' said Bishop to the crews. Under his First War leadership, 85 had been known as the 'Dawn Patrol' Squadron and, 'I can say with truth that it was a very happy Squadron. However, I can see here among you the signs that it is still a very happy Squadron.' When asked if he had any advice to give his successors Bishop replied, 'All I can say is, and I have said this countless times before but it's still true — get good and close before you open fire. Then let him have it.' Looking at the cluster of cannon and machine guns around the Squadron he exclaimed, 'My God, I'd like to have a Hun in front of me with that lot!'

Above right: Leaving 'B' Flight dispersal. Front — Wing Commander D. de B. Clark (Station Commander), Air Marshal Bishop, Squadron Leader Green. Behind — (left to right) Flying Officer 'Chuck' Medhurst, Flight Lieutenant Geoff Howitt DFC, Flying Officer Hugh 'Nausea' Norsworthy, Flight Lieutenant Nigel Bunting, Pilot Officer George 'Ginger' Irving, Sergeant Fisher.

port with black smoke pouring from the engine. Sergeant Clunes followed down through cloud and almost hit the sea but owing to the poor visibility could find no further trace of E/A.

'Returning to patrol at Bradwell at 4,000 ft he was vectored on to an E/A which he identified as a Ju 88. Several momentary visuals were obtained but E/A disappeared into cloud. A further chase after a supposed Bandit turned out to be a Mosquito. Clunes landed at base at 1340 hours. One Do 217 claimed as probably destroyed.'

Having grown accustomed to the limitations of the Havoc, the Germans were taken aback by the appearance of the night fighter Mosquito.

'Night Pilots Surprise Nazis
First Admission
Germany last night admitted the appearance of a new menace to her raiders — the British night fighter. Berlin radio gave the following account of a clash between a bomber and a British fighter, said to have been received from an eye-witness:

' "On our way towards our targets, the rear-gunner suddenly shouts, 'night-fighter!' The Englishman races on to us. He is in one of those new and extremely fast night-fighters.

' "He gives us a first burst, disappears before our gunners can reply. He is an excellent pilot. Then he comes at us again. Another burst. His bullets tear holes in our fuselage. Then a third attack.

' "Everything seems blown to pieces inside out cabin. We turn towards the sea. The Englishman turns too, it is impossible to shake him off. We go down until we are just above the water. We want to force him to attack us from above. Even this move does not make him change his mind. He is still after us. He is on our tail.

' "We return to our base with only one motor working, and our landing gear smashed and with 107 holes in our fuselage. What a lucky escape!" '

Nevertheless, there were teething troubles with the Mosquito. The first batch of Mozzies carried 'a wretched new Mark of AI', said one RO. 'This was the Mark V AI, which has all the faults of the early Mk IV plus many of its own. It was a retrograde step even when compared with Mk IV and it was rather like going back to a divining rod. There were times in the next few months when I thought that if I took a hazel twig, persuaded a Dachshund to lift a leg against it and then took that twig into the Mozzie with me, it would lead me to a German more readily than would Mk V AI.'

The Mosquito also gave its pilots much greater problems when things went wrong. '28/11/42. Fair weather, visibility good. Squadron Leader Green and his Operator* Flight Sergeant Grimstone, took-off at 1700 hours from the E-W runway for a Ground

Above: The Squadron aircrew at Hunsdon, November 1942.

Left: The official party leaving the Mess. Left to right: Kim, Tim Moloney, Bishop, Callaghan, Raphael, Bunting, Green, Unknown. On his way out of the Squadron, Billy Bishop saw a card hanging on Raphael's door with the inscription 'Commanding Officer, 85 Squadron.' 'May I have that for my trophy room?' inquired the Air Marshal. Raphael autographed the card and Bishop carried it triumphantly away.

*By now the ROs on night fighters had become known as NRs — Navigators Radio.

Control Interception practice when their port engine cut. They just cleared the first road narrowly missing a lorry, just missed the Direction Finding tender in the adjoining field, jumped the second road and in doing so hit a lorry which caused one fatal casualty, and finally knocked down a corner of the Sergeants Mess and the ablutions where they came to rest. Squadron Leader Green got out through the emergency exit in the roof and Flight Sergeant Grimstone escaped through the main door. There was a nasty moment when Flight Sergeant Grimstone got caught in the door and the port engine caught fire. However he was quickly hauled out by the NCOs on the spot and the fire was extinguished by the prompt action of some of the Sergeants. The aircraft was completely wrecked.

'Flying Officer Maguire also experienced trouble with his engines soon after take-off and successfully landed downwind. The trouble appears to have been caused by coolant getting into the fuel system — an investigation is taking place. All aircraft grounded for a day.'

But in the midst of such crises there was always gaiety. 'The whole social life of the Squadron seemed to revolve around the junior officers,' commented an observer. 'As Hunsdon was within easy reach of London, it gave the Squadron plenty of scope in that direction with the "Suivi" and the "Embassy" clubs being the most usual "Last ports of call". In January 1941, a Watch Office Log Book was borrowed from the Air Ministry and installed at Bobby's Bar in "Oddenios" where any member of the Squadron at a loose end in London could write his name, place he arrived from and his destination for the evening or weekend. From this source and a liberal supply of Bobby's lager, many impromptu and unexpected parties began. George Black's young ladies became great favourites with the Squadron and made up many large parties at "Grosvenor House" and the "Embassy". '

For those with less expensive and less exotic tastes, there was never any lack of social life back at base, especially around Christmas time.

'4/12/42. Day, fine. Wing Commander Raphael and Flight Lieutenant Molony visited RAF Comforts, Berkeley Square, London,* and came back with various comforts for the airmen.

'6/12/42. Night. Mist prevented flying — several officers and airmen went to a special performance of *The Importance of Being Earnest* in London.

'25/12/42. Weather dull. No flying. Usual Xmas festivities. Flight Lieutenant Bunting read lesson in Church. The Sergeants were entertained at the Officers' Mess before the airmen's dinner — all officers and SNCOs waited on airmen who had an excellent dinner.

'In the evening the officers and their wives and lady friends sat down to their dinner which was a great success. After dinner there was an impromptu dance to the radio-gram. Flying Officer Farrell dressed up as a WAAF causing great amusement. Squadron Leader Bradshaw-Jones rode his motor cycle through the Mess without causing any damage to himself or cycle. This happened in the early hours after the ladies had left. A very successful party eventually broke up very late.'

*Helped by the public and various voluntary organisations, the RAF Comforts Committee distributed over 10 million woollen garments, 61,667 dartboards, 18,628 shovehalfpenny boards, 21,067 chess sets, 438 pianos, 27,129 musical instruments, 8,335 gramophones, 611,594 books and over 160 million cigarettes to the RAF between October 1939 and June 1946.

Below: Night Ops List.

```
                 NIGHT   OPERATIONS.
                No. 85 Squadron, R.A.F.
                                        4th November, 1942
 Officer i/c Night Flying :-       S/Ldr. W.P. Green.
 ================================================================

      Pilot.              Crew.            Call Sign.

 W/Cdr. Raphael.      W.O. Addison.            23.

 F/O. Burbridge.      F/Sgt. Webster.          16.
 F/O. Mould.          Sgt. Vane.               17.
 F/Lt. Howitt.        P/O. Jones.              18.
 F/O. House.          P/O. Mold.               31.
 Sgt. Shaw.           Sgt. Wyman.              27.
 P/O. McBride.        Sgt. Carr.               33.
 P/O. Sutcliffe.      W.O. Medworth.           20.
 P/O. Harris.         F/Sgt. Waldeck.          19.
 S/Ldr. Green.        F/Sgt. Grimstone.        26.
      Available at 2 hours notice. :-
 S/Ldr. Hatton.       F/O. Reeves.             41.
 Sgt. McCormick.      Sgt. Nixon.              35.
 F/Sgt. Tinkler.      Sgt. Fisher.             22.
 F/Sgt. Sullivan.     Sgt. Skeel.              24.

      Duty Intelligence Officer -- F/O. E.A. Robertson.
      N.C.O. i/c Duty Flight.   -  Sgt. Baines.
 ================================================================

                  for, Wing Commander, Commanding,
                      No. 85 Squadron, R.A.F.

 DISTRIBUTION :-
 Officer Commanding, R.A.F. Station, Hunsdon.  - 1 Copy.
 Officer Commanding, No. 85 Squadron.          - 1 Copy.
 Station Intelligence Officer, Hunsdon.        - 1 Copy.
 Intelligence Officer, No. 85 Squadron.        - 1 Copy.
 Medical Officer, R.A.F. Station, Hunsdon.     - 1 Copy.
 Signals. R.D.F. Officer, No. 85 Squadron.     - 1 Copy.
 N.C.O. i/c "A" Flight.                        - 1 Copy.
 N.C.O. i/c "B" Flight.                        - 1 Copy.
 Operations.                                   - 1 Copy.
 Aerodrome Control Officer.                    - 1 Copy.
 Officers' Mess.                               - 1 Copy.
 Sergeants' Mess.                              - 1 Copy.
 File.                    =====o0o=====        - 1 Copy.
```

THE DE HAVILLAND AIRCRAFT COMPANY LIMITED

TELEPHONE: HATFIELD 2345
CABLES: HAVILLAND, HATFIELD

HATFIELD, ENGLAND

FEN StB/CM

Wing Commander G.L. Raphael, D.F.C.,   3rd
No. 85 Squadron,   Nov.
Royal Air Force,   1942
Hunsdon,
Nr. Ware, Herts.

Dear Sir,

My fellow directors and I would like to thank
you for the excellent fly-past which your squadron
executed yesterday over our Hatfield factory and
some of our dispersed units in the St. Albans and
Welwyn Garden City areas. This was the first time
any of us had seen so many Mosquitoes in formation and
it was a heartening and enjoyable sight which we all
greatly appreciated.

We were naturally sorry about the unexpected
change of the weather which prevented you from passing
over our many depots in the north-west London area
but we are hoping that some further opportunity
may arise on a really clear day.

May I take this opportunity to wish 85 squadron
very good success in its most important work.

Yours faithfully,
for THE DE HAVILLAND AIRCRAFT CO. LTD.

Director.

Above: Wing Commander
Raphael leads a Squadron 'Balbo'
of 12 aircraft over de Havilland's
factory at Hatfield on
2 November 1942 during the
lunch break to inspire the war
effort.

Left: Letter of appreciation.

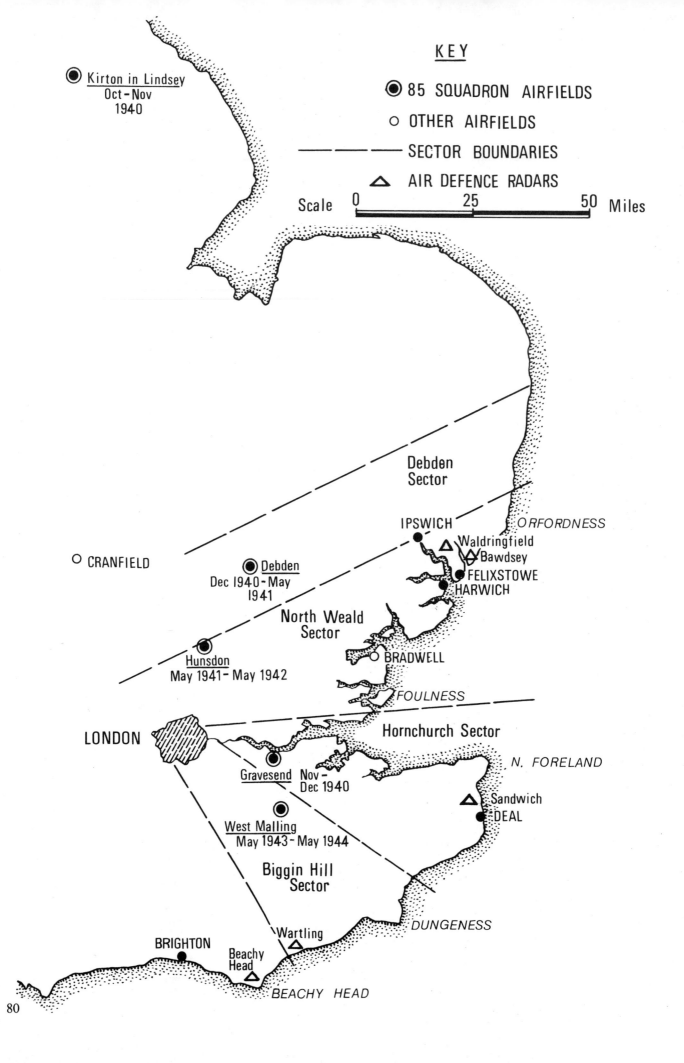

KEY

◉ 85 SQUADRON AIRFIELDS
○ OTHER AIRFIELDS
— — — SECTOR BOUNDARIES
△ AIR DEFENCE RADARS

Scale

0   25   50 Miles

Kirton in Lindsey
Oct-Nov
1940

Debden
Sector

IPSWICH   ORFORDNESS

○ CRANFIELD   Waldringfield
△ Bawdsey
Debden   FELIXSTOWE
Dec 1940-May   HARWICH
1941

North Weald
Sector

Hunsdon
May 1941- May 1942

○ BRADWELL

FOULNESS

Hornchurch Sector

LONDON   N. FORELAND

Gravesend Nov-
Dec 1940   Sandwich
△
DEAL

West Malling
May 1943- May 1944

Biggin Hill
Sector

DUNGENESS

Wartling
△

BRIGHTON
Beachy
Head
△

BEACHY HEAD

Middle of the Night

During the summer of 1942, the numbers of German bombers involved in the 'Baedeker' raids declined steadily, for such was the effectiveness of the night fighter Mosquito working in close co-operation with the early warning radar stations that Britain became a perilous place for night raiders. Thus the end of 1942 saw 85 somewhat dispirited by the lack of opposition. 'There are rumours that the Squadron is shortly to be employed as day intruders,' quoted the Record Book with enthusiasm, 'which has bucked the boys up as they are getting browned off with no Huns to play with.' Certainly the Squadron did diversify, setting up a third Flight ('C' Flight) for a time with special pressurised Mosquitos XVs to try to eliminate the hitherto elusive Ju 86P reconnaissance aircraft that photographed Britain unhindered around 50,000 feet. On 31 March 1943. 'Flight Lieutenant Bunting carried out climb to 43,800 feet,'* while at less rarefied levels the Squadron mounted some intruder sorties to try to intercept enemy bombers taking-off and landing at their French airfields when they were most vulnerable. Unfortunately, neither the high flying nor the few intruder forays mounted were crowned with much success.

'2/4/43. 1035 hours. Squadron Leader K. R. Sutton DFC and Pilot Officer S. R. Streeter DFM took-off for a special intruder patrol over France. On their return to the English coast they endeavoured to make landfall at Beachy Head but the weather was bad there and to the east. Pilot turned west for a bit and then turned in at about 900 feet, which was the height of the cloud base, between Brighton and Shoreham.

'Guns started firing at the Mosquito and Squadron Leader Sutton told Pilot Officer Streeter to fire off the colours of the day which he did. In spite of this the guns continued to fire and the Mosquito was badly shot up and Pilot Officer Streeter seriously wounded.

'Squadron Leader Sutton was unable to keep control and told Pilot Officer Streeter to jump but he was unable to do so and Squadron Leader Sutton stayed with the aircraft down to 500 feet endeavouring to help him and then leapt himself and just managed to open parachute before hitting the ground. He landed at Hove with a badly shattered left arm and left ankle. The aircraft, which had caught fire, crashed nearby on the railway embankment on the Shoreham-Hove line. Pilot Officer Streeter was killed.

'The Hove ARP Wardens rendered invaluable first aid assistance to Squadron Leader Sutton whilst waiting for the ambulance to arrive, which it did not do for 20 minutes. He was then taken to Hove General Hospital, Squadron Leader Sutton had his left foot and left arm amputated during the night.

'A Court of Inquiry is being convened to inquire into this very regrettable occurrence. It appears that unless something is done about it, all intruder aircraft returning to this country from operational patrols in bad weather are in danger of being shot down.'

Consequently, night fighting still remained the most efficient course of action for 85 and they were given improved Mosquitos and AI radars for the purpose. By now, 85 had a new 'Boss', Wing Commander John Cunningham. Born in 1917, Cunningham was the first night fighter pilot to be awarded a DFC and together with his radar operator, C. F.

*Bunting's Mosquito XV reached 40,000ft in 18½ minutes — 'not bad going'.

Left: 85 Squadron in the night fighter role 1940-44.

Below: John Cunningham (right) and Jimmy Rawnsley (left). Born in 1917 at South Croydon, Surrey, John Cunningham was educated at Whitgift School where rugger was his favourite game. He spent three years in de Havilland's Technical School and learned to fly with the County of Middlesex Auxiliary Squadron where he crewed up with Jimmy Rawnsley in 1937. Thereafter they worked very closely together as a team despite the difference in the ages; in 1943 when Cunningham took over 85 he was still only 26 while Rawnsley was 39.

'Jimmy'* Rawnsley, he shot down eight He 111s in April 1941 and received the DSO for destroying three aircraft in one night. For security reasons, no public mention could ever be made of the fact that Cunningham and Rawnsley owed their success to AI radar, so Cunningham was credited with remarkable night vision in a 'cover story' released to the newspapers.

Back in 1940, when Fighter Command was considering ways of locating enemy aircraft in darkness, someone sent in the following suggestion: 'Take a cat in night fighter and aim guns where cat is looking.' In similar vein, John Cunningham became dogged with the alliterative nickname 'Cat's Eyes', and officialdom fuelled the popular theory that men like him ate copious quantities of carrots because the Vitamin C therein was supposed to improve night vision. 'Nuvver victory for Carrots' — 'nuvver victory for Carrots!' cried the news-vendors of London when John Cunningham shot down another victim, but he ate no more carrots than anyone else and, had he done so, they would not have done him much good. The mythical ocular qualities of carrots have persisted long after the secret they were meant to hide.

'His great success as a night-fighter,' wrote Cuthbert Orde, who got to know John Cunningham during portrait sittings, 'is due to skill, knowledge, determination and the most complete imperturbability — I've never met anyone more calm. Before the war he was a civilian test pilot, so his skill comes of experience. He is the sort of chap who will find out everything there is to be known about the job he is doing, the machine he is flying and the gadgets he is using; he leaves nothing to chance. Once he is on the trail of a Hun nothing but impossible conditions can stop him getting it, and nothing in the world could make him lose his head. He has, I've no doubt, unusually good night vision and does everything he can to make it even better, but it is his other gifts that really get the Hun.'

Nevertheless, Cunningham was stuck with the nickname 'Cat's Eyes' even though he detested it, because he personified night fighting in the public mind: moreover, his reputation increased once he left his desk job to take over 85 Squadron on 28 January 1943,* teaming up once more with Jimmy Rawnsley as his navigator leader.

Cunningham's arrived on 85 was somewhat propitious because the Luftwaffe bomber force in the west was revitalised early in 1943 in order to strike more effectively against major British cities in retaliation for Bomber Command raids on the Reich.

'14/15 April 1943. A very busy night. Twelve operational patrols flown starting at 2050 hours and finishing at 0600 hours. Some Huns appeared over the estuary and east

*Such nicknames were common in the RAF because, as Rawnsley appreciated from an early date, 'the Christian names Cecil Frederick . . . were not the sort that would go down with a swing among my comrades.'

*Gordon Raphael was awarded a DSO in January 1943 for his service in command of 85. Group Captain Raphael was later killed on active service.

Below: Four Commanding Officers of 85 Squadron outside the Officers' Mess at Hunsdon on 6 February 1943; from left to right: Wing Commander Townsend, Group Captain Oliver, Wing Commander Raphael and Wing Commander Cunningham.

Above: The Squadron executives in 1943. Left to right: Wing Commander John Cunningham, Flight Lieutenant Tim Molony, Squadron Leader Peter Green (OC 'A' Flight), Squadron Leader Edward Crew (OC 'B' Flight) and Kim.

Tim Molony remained a stalwart of the Squadron, only very occasionally taking a day off, as on 12 May 1942 'to witness the 2000 Guineas at Newmarket.' The Air Ministry kept trying to move him, and on 13 June 1942 he was posted to 605 Squadron for Adjutant duties, but Molony always seemed to wangle his way back. His worth to the Squadron was tremendous, and not always on the administrative side. '29/9/43. Several officers went over to Grafty Green in the morning to attend an auction at Flight Lieutenant Molony's sister's house. An ancient Jowett car was bought by a local farmer for ten guineas and presented to the Squadron.'

Left: 'Will it start?'

83

coast about midnight and two Do 217s were destroyed by Squadron Leader Green and Flight Lieutenant Howitt. This was a happy augury for the new equipment — Mosquito XII fitted with AI Mk VIII.'

On 17 January 1943, the Luftwaffe launched 118 bomber missions against London, the largest assault on the capital since 10 May 1941. On 3 March they returned with over a hundred bombers and although the damage caused by these two raids was relatively small, there were a large number of deaths which had a considerable effect on public and political opinion. As a result, it was decided to put 85 into the famous Biggin Hill sector to strengthen the night fighter defences on the short and direct south-east approach to London known as 'Bomb Alley'.

The news of the pending move was first given by the AOC 11 Group, Air Vice-Marshal H. W. L. 'Dingbat' Saunders, when he came to Hunsdon on 5 May to present 85

Left: The Squadron Crest which was presented on 5 May 1943 by the AOC 11 Group, Air Vice-Marshal H. W. L. Saunders CBE, MC, DFC, MM. The badge is described as a 'Hexagon Voided upon an Ogress' and the motto means 'We hunt by day and by night.' Badges and mottoes had long been used in the RAF but they were only recognised officially in 1936 when a standard scheme was laid down. All Squadron crests had to be designed by the Chester Herald of the Royal College of Heralds and submitted to the King for his approval and signature. Officially these crests 'stand for tradition and foster an esprit de corps and this promotes the very necessary efforts of the individual'.

Bottom, far left; Wing Commander John Cunningham, the Hunsdon Station Commander (Station Commanders were irreverently referred to as 'Station Masters') and Air Vice-Marshal Saunders.

Left: Falling in for the Parade.

Below: The Squadron on the Parade Ground as the Crest is presented. Note the Mosquito NF XII in the hangar entrance. The NF XII did not sport any external AI aerials as its new bulbous nose housed the scanner of the Mk VIII AI radar. However, the phantom pen of the censor struck again on the press release.

Right: Marching off past the saluting dais.

Below: Hunsdon Officers' Mess Dining-In Night menu.

Cafe Keep Fit.

Menu

Potage Prang.

Scotch (I don't mind if I do) Salmon.
Mayonaise Bomphoon.
Cucumber Zulu.

Roast Turkey. Quatre Vingt Cinq.
Mosquito Stuffing- Rolled Bacon.
Night Ops.
Chips De Boomer- Pommes Homing.
Haricots Duff Gen.

Flan Cunningham.

Asparagrass Travail Blue.

Cafe Cent Octane.

Vin v Ordinaire.

Toast

HIS MAJESTY THE KING.

Above: John Cunningham admires the new crest with Flying Officer E. A. Robertson, the Squadron Intelligence Officer. 'Robbie', a dry old Scot, left his fishery business in Hull and volunteered to join the RAFVR in 1940. His Intelligence Hut was a mine of information and it 'was always filled with cigarette smoke and navigators eager to discover the latest "gen" '. Robbie had such a thick Scottish accent that he was once mistaken for a Pole, but he was held in much esteem by the Squadron personnel even though the younger members would sometimes rag him unmercilessly. 'It was the wonderful, unselfish backing of coves like yourself,' wrote Jimmy Rawnsley in 1946, 'which enabled us to make the Squadron such a success.'

with its official badge. The Squadron was formed upon three sides of a square outside the Bellman hangar for, as Rawnsley recalled, 'we made quite an event of the proceedings. But we had not counted on the other squadron — No. 3 — who shared Hunsdon with us. They waited until we were all drawn up and the AOC had started to speak. Then with a crack of its Kaufmann starter — a rather startling noise even when one was ready for it — the first of their Typhoon fighter-bombers started up and taxied out. Their timing was perfect, and now we understood why they had made such careful inquiries about how and when we were going to do things. One by one the whole squadron of Typhoons took-off, climbing low in the line astern slap over our parade.'

Most of the men on parade therefore could only see the AOC's mouth opening and closing as the fiendish din of the Typhoon engines blotted out his every word, but those in the front rank managed to hear the great man's announcement that the Squadron would shortly be moving south where he expected it would be much more actively engaged and wished it the best of luck.

This news was confirmed by secret cipher signal on 10 May. 'The Squadron has now been at Hunsdon for over two years and is delighted at the prospect of the move, principally because there should be many more chances of getting Huns at West Malling.'

'13/5/43. Soon after 0930 hours the Mosquitos took-off for West Malling, and Hunsdon was treated to a most spectacular farewell. Each aircraft swooped low over the Watch Tower several times before leaving. For half an hour the roar of engines was terrific and then complete silence reigned and there were many heavy hearts at Hunsdon especially among the Flying Control Officers.

'Shortly after the departure of the Mosquitoes, the Harrows took-off conveying some of the airmen and equipment. The special train with the main party left St Margaret's Station at 1045 hours.

'1030 hours. All the Mosquitoes landed safely at West Malling and took over the 29 Squadron dispersals. They are not nearly so comfortable as the Hunsdon dispersals but no doubt the Squadron will improve them in a very short time.

'The special train arrived about 1530 hours with the main party who were met by the Station Commander (Wing Commander P. W. Townsend DSO DFC). By nightfall, most of the unloading of the equipment has been completed and the airmen billeted in widely dispersed places. They should be very comfortable. "A" Flight are housed at "The Retreat" and "Guest House" in West Malling, and "B" Flight in a large mansion (called "Hamptons") standing in a park about six miles from the aerodrome. The journey to and from the aerodrome on bicycles is well compensated the comfort and beautiful surroundings of Hamptons.

'The NCO aircrew live in the Sergeants' Mess on the Station while the officers have their own Squadron Mess in an attractive house called the "Manor House" which stands high up about half a mile from Malling and about $1\frac{1}{2}$ miles from the aerodrome (up hill all the way). There is also accom-

Right: John Cunningham relaxing on the steps of the Manor House. Squadron mess accommodation varied throughout the war from tents at Castle Camps to the Sergeants' Mess at Debden which for a time was situated in a very lovely house near Haverhill once owned by Sir Cedric Hardwick. This house, like the Manor House, complied with official policy which was to billet personnel away from the airfield they served in order to minimise the consequences of any enemy bombing. However whether personnel lived in a requisitioned stately hall or a barrack block, they always managed to stamp their own personality on their temporary 'home'.

'A few days later I was at the operation station of a night flying squadron,' wrote Sir William Rothenstein. 'On the evening I arrived the weather was too bad for flying, and I spent it therefore in the Mess . . . It consisted of a dining-room, a room for games with tables for billiards and ping-pong, and a sort of general sitting-room, called the ante-room. The writing-tables, the piles of newspapers and magazines, the roomy leather chairs, in which people lounge about with glasses at their elbows, give the place a club-like air. But it is a surprisingly youthful club. One of the features of the RAF world is that everyone in it looks young. My own thirty-nine years have never seemed to me a great age, in civil life; but in an air station I felt positively elderly. Wing-Commanders and Group Captains whom I looked at with veneration, so dignified did they seem to me from the responsibilities of their position, turned out generally to have been still at preparatory schools when I was at the University. This impression of youth is agreeable. It is pleasant to find that heroes are flushed with youth, in fact as well as in fiction. But it adds to the general strangeness.

'As a matter of fact there are always some older men in the Mess, a sprinkling of Intelligence Officers, Medical Officers, etc. But their grey hairs and lined cheeks show up as an exception amid the crowd of smooth pink faces. And even these older men seem touched by the prevailing spirit of youth. Ardently and on equal terms, they discuss the latest films and the best place to dance, with their boyish companions . . .

'Everyone was so friendly. The atmosphere was eminently lively, hospitable and convivial. People sat about the ante-room talking and drinking, now and again moving into the other room for a game of ping-pong. The conversation roved easily about from films to games, from games to matrimony, its advantages and disadvantages, from matrimony to flying. It was interspersed with a great deal of banter and outbursts of laughter at some approved and established joke. In so far as the atmosphere was not like a club, it was like a sixth-form room. People has the unthinking cheerfulness of boys just out of class; the established jokes seemed as splendidly and unfailingly amusing as the established jokes of school life.

'The war seemed far away. It was with a start of surprise that I remembered that these people risked their lives night after night. If the physical circumstances had been harsher, it mightn't have been so difficult to keep it in mind; but the comfortable warm room, the pleasant tap of the ping-pong balls and the homely schoolboyish atmosphere seemed fantastically unwarlike. One realised the war only when flying was mentioned. Then the faces grew keen and voices more serious, then the intent purposeful look came back.'

modation for officers at a small house called the "Old Parsonage" near the entrance to one of the drives to the "Manor House".

'The Orderly Room is tucked away in an orchard just behind "A" Flight dispersal.'

The Manor House was a mellow, creeper-covered Georgian house with a beautifully kept walled garden at the back and a long, reed-banked lake with ducks and swans at the front. 'The Manor House had formerly been used, we were told, as some sort of convalescent home for elderly ladies. We found a list of rules for the patients, one of which stated that ladies could not be accepted unless they were capable of walking upstairs without assistance. This was naturally preserved, with that particular rule heavily underlined, and was smartly produced at parties whenever anyone started showing signs of falling by the wayside.'

The Operations Record Book also mentioned the Flying Control Officers at Hunsdon and it paid tribute to 'an exceptional team lead by Squadron Leader Bradshaw-Jones' and the 'close liaison that existed between it and the pilots of the Squadron'. 'Brad' was in charge of aerodrome air traffic control and this 'tallish, gaunt, piratical figure of a man' typified the dedicated breed of often forgotten chaps on

Right: All the Squadron aircrew autographs on a Mosquito photograph.

Below: The Squadron, now much enlarged in numbers from 1938, sits for the official photograph.

the ground who helped to keep the aircraft flying. Before the war Brad had been in manufacturing and wholesaling of fine silverware and in antiques, and he had been a keen amateur yachtsman who also raced in cars and on motor-cycles. When war broke out he tried to join the RAF; five times he was turned down on medical grounds but he succeeded at the sixth attempt and went into Air-Sea Rescue on high-speed launches. During the Battle of Britain he was badly injured during a dive-bomber attack at Gosport and his spine was stretched. Later he was shot up on the launches during the bombing of a convoy and eventually he ended up in charge of 'a set of Flying Control Officers at Hunsdon in whom the pilots had absolute confidence and who never failed when off duty to join the squadron boys in their lighter moments in the bar or in London. So strong were their ties with the Squadron that it took them less than a month after 85 left for West Malling for them all to get themselves there as well.'

The airfield at West Malling was a grass one with a strip at Somerfield track — wire mesh pinned down on the turf — to act as the main runway. Surrounding this was a concrete perimeter track with brick crew-rooms and Squadron offices dispersed around the fringe in among the plum trees of a half cleared orchard. 'The mental atmosphere of an RAF station is in harmony with its setting,' wrote Sir William Rothenstein, another member of that band of artists who went around drawing pictures of aircrew for posterity. 'It is not so sensational as might be expected, considering the violent nature of its work. On the contrary, compared with the jolting uncertain confusion of civilian England in wartime, it seems almost peaceful. The dominating impression is of a monastic segregation, undisturbed by the outside world, almost unaware of it. The visitor feels as if he had entered a self-contained universe, revolving upon its own centre and absorbed by its own task. Everyone has something to do; everyone knows what it is and everyone is aware that it is vital that it should be done properly . . .

'The visitor feels himself an outsider, so strong is this impression of the corporate spirit. But equally he notices the individual character of air warfare. The community is a small one. Everyone, from the Squadron Leader, down to the mechanics, whose job it is to keep the planes in readiness, feels himself part of a unit. And each part is of extreme importance. For this reason distinction of rank seem less rigid in the RAF than

in any other services. Working every day on the aircraft, flying at night, officers and non-commissioned officers get to know each other very well. All alike are welded together by this strange life, that alternates between air station and sky.'*

By now though, the number of people on the ground who kept the RAF in the air had grown considerably both in number and specialisations.

A Guide for Airmen on joining the RAF† — October 1941

Daily Routine Orders as printed from day to day are for your information — READ THEM.

Don't play cards for money. Gambling is forbidden.

Don't bring food or intoxicating liquor into the barrack hut.

Don't light the stove before 1600 hours unless permission IS FIRST GIVEN by the Medical Authorities.

Don't make down your bed before 1200 hours unless you are ordered to do so.

You must have a bath at least once each week and must sign the bath-book if one is kept by NCO i/c Hut.

Airmen leaving camp must always be properly dressed and must carry both respirator and steel helmet.

The practice of airmen assembling at main road junctions and signalling motorists, is forbidden.

Normally you will not be granted any leave while you are under training, but exceptionally compassionate cases will receive sympathetic consideration. When you have completed your training you may be granted seven days' leave every three months if you can be spared from your duties. You may, in addition to your ordinary leave, be allowed a pass up to forty-eight hours from time to time at the discretion of your unit or station commander.

NAAFI facilities are provided at nearly all stations and contain a restaurant, a games room, a reading room and a writing room. Conduct yourself as you would in any restaurant or club. This is your club.

Facilities exist on most stations for practically all games, and airmen are encouraged to make use of these facilities as often as possible.

Have one object always in view: to make yourself the best airman in the hut.

GOOD LUCK, and a safe return as soon as possible to your ordinary life.

Trade Groups in the Royal Air Force

The RAF trades and the groups in which they are placed for purposes of pay are as follows:

GROUP I

Blacksmith and welder	Fitter (MT)
Coppersmith and sheet metal worker	Fitter (torpedo)
Draughtsman	Instrument maker
Electrician, grade I	Instrument repairer, grade I
Engine driver (fitter)	Link trainer instructor
Fitter, grade I	Machine tool setter and operator
Fitter, grade II (airframe)	Metal worker
Fitter, grade II (engine)	Radio mechanic
Fitter (armourer)	Wireless mechanic
Fitter (armourer) (bombs)	Wireless operator mechanic
Fitter (armourer) (guns)	
Fitter (marine)	

GROUP II

Acetylene welder	Armourer (bombs)
Armoured car crew	Armourer (guns)
Armourer	Balloon operator
Blacksmith	Miller
Bricklayer	M.T. mechanic
Carpenter	Photographer
Coppersmith	Plumber
Electrician, grade II	Radio operator
Electrician (wireman)	Sheet metal worker
Flight mechanic (engine)	Steel erector
Grinder	Turner
Instrument repairer, grade II	Wireless operator

Men of the RAF; Oxford University Press, 1942.

† Extracts from *Air Ministry Pamphlet No 130*.

GROUP III

Balloon rigger
Balloon fabric worker
Concreter
Cook and butcher
Drainlayer
Driver (winch) (balloon)
Fabric worker
Hydrogen worker
Motor boat crew
PAC operator
Shoemaker
Tailor

GROUP IV

Clerk (accounting)
Clerk, equipment accounting
Clerk, pay accounting
Clerk (general duties)
Clerk (special duties)
Equipment assistant
Teleprinter operator
Radio telephony operator

GROUP V

Aircrafthand
Aircrafthand (under trade training)
Batman
Driver (MT)
Ground gunner
Ground observer
Groundsman
Machine-gun instructor
Maintenance assistant
Messing duties
Armament assistant
Barber
Musician
Motor cyclist
Parachute packer
Pigeon keeper
PT instructor
Service police
Telephone operator
Torpedoman

GROUP M

Dispenser
Laboratory assistant
Masseur
Medical orderly under training
Mental nursing orderly
Nursing orderly
Operating-room assistant
Radiographer
Sanitary assistant
Special treatment orderly
Trained nurse
Dental clerk orderly
Dental mechanic
Dental orderly under training

On completion of training, radio operators are placed in Group IV and after six months satisfactory service therein are placed in Group II.

The minimum daily rates of pay, ie for Aircraftmen, 2nd class, to the maximum, ie Warrant Officer, are as follows:

Group I, 3s 9d to 16s 6d
Group II, 3s 6d to 15s
Group III, 3s to 13s 6d
Group IV, 3s to 14s
Group V, 2s to 13s 6d
Group M, 2s to 13s 6d

War pay of 6d per day is issued to all, in addition to the above. Additional payments are made when good conduct badges, etc, are awarded. These badges are awarded for very good conduct after three, eight and 13 years' qualifying service rendered after the age of 18 has been reached. Good conduct pay of 3d per day is awarded for each badge. Airmen are eligible for an allowance of 2s a day while under instruction as pilots. Airmen while under instruction as air observers are eligible for an allowance of 1s 6d a day.

Age limits may vary from time to time, but, roughly, the minimum age for all Groups or trades is 18 and the maximum for any one is 50.[*]

It is obvious from this 'pecking order' that the most highly trained and skilled personnel, and consequently the best paid, were those most closely associated with servicing aeroplanes. For the first year of the war ground crews in Fighter Command formed an integral part of the Squadron they served, but early in 1941 it was decided to try to improve the distribution and efficient employment of skilled manpower by transferring the bulk of squadron engineering personnel to the station maintenance party which was then organised so that it could throw off 'echelons' to each Squadron in residence. Then, on 14 November 1941, Air Ministry Organisation Memorandum No 1001/41 was issued which stated that, 'In order to facilitate the mobility of Fighter Squadrons, their servicing echelons have been borne on the strength of the Sector Station concerned. It has now been decided that the servicing echelons will be treated as separately numbered and

[*]*The Royal Air Force*, E. Sargent, Sampson Low, 1942.

91

Below: The interior of a Mosquito night fighter cockpit showing the Mk VIII AI radar tube. This made AI operations much easier for the Nav Radar compared with the Mk IV for now there was only one tube to worry about and it showed range, azimuth and elevation information in a very simple form without all the Christmas tree effect. 'Taking the centre of the tube to represent his own aircraft, the blip of the target aircraft would show as a circle, or part of a circle, of light. An aircraft dead ahead and absolutely level with the fighter would show as a complete circle, the range being assessed by the distance of the circle from the centre of the tube. If the target was slightly to one side, the circle would break, and when the target had gone out to ten degrees it would show as a half circle on that side. At fifteen degrees there would be an arc which would gradually get smaller the further the target went over. At forty degrees the arc was very small, and at forty-five degrees the target would be outside the coverage of the transmitter's cone of search.

'Elevation was read in exactly the same way . . . Thus, if one imagined the tube to be a clockface, the target's position could be read straight off the tube to the pilot. He in turn could look upon his windscreen as a clockface, and when the navigator told him a target was two o'clock twenty degrees he would know exactly where to look for it. This method of clockface references for interception purposes became standardised soon after the introduction of Mk VIII AI to squadron service. (Rawnsley and Wright). *IWM*

established units'. Thus when 85 Squadron moved from Hunsdon to West Malling, No 3006 Servicing Echelon went with them.

The Engineer Officer with 85 Squadron was now Flight Lieutenant J. Hoile, 'a good-natured, hard-working old sweat of a Regular who knew his job thoroughly and in every detail from spinner to tail wheel.' Suffice to say that he was known affectionately as 'Castor' to all the aircrew.

Despite all the new echelon nomenclature, the ground personnel still regarded themselves as part of 85 Squadron; similarly, the aircrew went out of their way to cement links with all the trade groups on whose efforts their lives depended. Thus endowed with excellent support from around the station, 85 settled in at West Malling to counter whatever bomber raids the Luftwaffe endeavoured to mount.

'13/5/43. Eight sorties flown consisting of Ground Control Interception patrols under Sandwich, Wartling, and Beachy Head, and searchlight co-operation. No activity in this area. There was some activity in our old area, the Huns bombing Chelmsford. They must have known that 85 had left!'

But the Luftwaffe was to prove more of a match from now on. Having finally dispaired of getting their orthodox bombers through the British night fighter defences, the Germans took their latest single-engine fighter, the Fw190, and gave it a mixture of long-range auxiliary fuel tanks and bombs in the hope that it would get through by sheer turn of speed. 85 knew that even a heavy Fw190 would be very hard to catch — 'Because of the shortness of the run they had to make, and the closeness of the enemy coast, a lively vigilance and lightning scrambles were essential if we were to do our job properly. These factors, added to the high

speed of the fighter-bombers, called for big changes in the tactics we had been using in the past.' No sooner had the Squadron arrived at West Malling than the fighter-bombers came over.

'16/17/5/43. A red letter day. Higher Command had doubted the ability of the Mosquito to catch the Fw 190 and had ordered Typhoons to deal with them much against the advice of the CO and other night fighting experts.

'A few Fw 190s started to come over shortly after 2300 hours and the Typhoons took to the air. After an hour or so it was clearly seen that the Typhoons were unable to cope, so the 11 Group Controller risked his bowler hat and grounded them, thus enabling the 85 Mosquitos to go in and deal with the 190s which they did in no uncertain manner.

'Between 2309 and 0425 hours, seventeen Fw 190s operated over area of Kent, Essex, Hertfordshire, Bucks, Surrey and Sussex. Bombs were dropped in several places inflicting some damage and casualties.

'Squadron Leader Green and Flight Sergeant Grimstone were the first to get to work. Under the control of Sandwich Radar they patrolled the Channel for some time at 10,000 feet, and then having got a vector of 040° increased height to 18,000 feet. Pilot got a contact* at three miles range and closing in rapidly, got a visual at 1,000 feet

*The new Mk VIII AI radar not only combined everything on one screen unlike two as before, but the pilot also had an indicator as well. It showed roughly whether the other aircraft was up or down, right or left, and when approaching minimum range. The navigator therefore controlled the interception in the early stages until the pilot took over and the navigator simply called out the ranges. When they were close enough to hope for a visual sighting, the navigator would take over the full commentary again to free his pilot from having to watch his tube.

range on an Fw 190 with long-range tanks and a bomb under the fuselage. Pilot opened fire with a short burst from dead astern at 100 yards range whereupon E/A blew up with a large red flash, the Mosquito having to dive sharply to port to avoid the burning debris. Remains of burnt-out aircraft found on Mosquito after landing.

'Squadron Leader Green and Flight Sergeant Grimstone landed base at 0025 hours. They have the honour of being the first night fighters to shoot down an Fw 190 over this country at night. They also landed the prizes offered for the first Fw 190 which were as follows:

'£5 from Flight Lieutenant Molony, a bottle of gin from Wing Commander Cunningham, a bottle of champagne from Squadron Leader Crew and a bottle of whisky from Squadron Leader Green. Also a silver model of a Mosquito (for the Squadron) from Squadron Leader Bradshaw-Jones.

'Flight Lieutenant Howitt and Flying Officer Irving were the next to get to work. Following the searchlights they got a contact at two and a half miles range, dead ahead at 8,000 feet over the sea near Hastings. Losing height down to 4,000 feet, pilot got a visual of an Fw 190 which had been taking evasive action. Pilot got in a long burst from dead astern at 600 feet. Strikes and vivid flashes were observed and pieces of burning debris flew off the E/A which fell away to port. Pilot followed down and gave E/A another long burst whereupon it caught fire and dived into the sea. Pilot pulled out at zero feet. Landed base at 0230 hours.

'Flying Officer Thwaites and Flying Officer Clemo took-off at 0005 hours. Controlled by Sandwich Radar, they chased an E/A across the sea but were called off when approaching the French coast. Pilot then got a contact below and crossing below and crossing from starboard to port at three miles range. After obtaining a visual of an Fw 190, pilot closed to 50 yards range and opened fire, whereupon the E/A blew up and went down in flames where it was seen blazing in the sea. Some of the debris was found in the air intake on landing.

'Pilot, having been given a vector of 350°, obtained another visual of an Fw 190 and opened fire at 200 yards range. A vivid flash was seen. The E/A lost height with pilot following it down giving it three more bursts and vivid flashes were again seen. E/A now appeared to be going down and a large object was seen to come away from the top of it. Pilot then overshot and was unable to see if the E/A crashed, and therefore this Fw 190 was claimed as probably destroyed.

Left: Flight Lieutenant Bernard Thwaites, a native of Gillingham and later South Africa, who flew with Will Clemo. Clemo, who hailed from Liverpool, was a thoughtful man who took his pleasures in smoking an enormous pipe and going on solitary nature study rambles. He was also one of several schoolmasters-turned-Nav Radar on 85 Squadron.

Below: A Fw 190 A-4/U8 fighter-bomber which landed in error at West Malling on 16 July 1943. This aircraft belonged to SKG (High-speed Battle Group) 10 which operated against British targets from the Amiens area. *IWM*

'Flying Officer Shaw and Flying Officer Lowton took-off at 0125 hours. A contact was obtained at two miles range slightly below and to port. The Mosquito was then caught in the searchlights which held it for about five minutes in spite of continuous flashing of the letter of the period, and it prevented pilot from obtaining a visual. Contact, however, was maintained and eventually a beam of the searchlight illuminated the target which pilot identified as an Fw 190 with the long range tanks and a bomb under the fuselage.

'Pilot closed in underneath and opened fire at about 100 yards range. E/A exploded with a huge orange flash and went down in flames, crashing near Gravesend. (This Fw 190 could be seen coming down in flames from the Squadron dispersal.) Flying Officer Shaw was unable to avoid flying through the burning debris which covered his windscreen and perspex with soot so he returned to base, landing at 0220 hours.

'As can be imagined, there was great jubilation in "A" Flight disperal at these successes and before turning into bed at 0600 hours, Squadron Leader Green and some of the aircrews singing "Yip, Addy 85" invaded the Adjutant's bedroom in the "Old Parsonage" and claimed the £5 which needless to say he was delighted to disgorge.'

Thus 85 debunked the menace of the Fw 190 in one night. 'My heartiest congratulations to 85 Squadron on their fine work last night,' signalled 'Dingbat' Saunders from 11 Group HQ. 'Congratulations also to Biggin Hill and Sandwich Controllers for their good work which enabled the Squadron to inflict such high losses on the enemy.'

Jimmy Rawnsley vividly described operational life at West Malling in the summer of 1943.* 'At all times two standing patrols were maintained throughout the night. The only thing that would stop that was if the weather became so bad that it was impossible to fly. We had two Ground Control Interception stations — "Skyblue" and "Recess" — with which we worked, each one controlling one of the patrolling aircraft. While they were waiting, the aircraft would make practice interceptions on each other. As soon as the indications on the cathode ray tubes showed that the enemy was forming up over France for another swoop, the standing patrols would be sent out across the Strait almost to the coast of France and made ready to pounce. At the same time the telephone back in the crewroom at the aerodrome would start ringing.

'We sat around in various stages of flying kit, depending on our position in the pre-

Night Fighter, Rawnsley and Wright, Collins 1957.

arranged order of patrol, talking or reading or listening to the radio. Always in the background there was the chatter of the inveterate card players which rose and fell with the fortunes of the game.

'A scramble late at night usually produced something in the nature of a well ordered stampede similar to that of a fire station turning out. At the sudden ring of the telephone down would go all the books and cards, and the radio set would be quickly silenced. The next crews to take off would be on their feet as the Flight Commander reached for the phone, and there would be a tense hush as he listened to the voice rattling in the earpiece. Then he would nod at the waiting crews and they would start for the door. He wasted no words on the telephone, merely answering: "OK. We'll be off."

'Picking up his own helmet he would call to the Flight Sergeant in charge of the ground crews that the next four aircraft were to go off, and at the door he would turn back for a word of explanation to the others.

' "Fifteen plus forming up over the Somme, you had better stand by."

'Outside in the darkness the Flight Sergeant would be calling to the airmen already on the alert. "Crews for C, M, L and Q."

'There would be the sound of running feet, and torches would flash. "Where's Arthur got to?" a voice would shout. Another would call out: "Bring another trolley-acc" [starter trolley].

'In quick succession the engines would come to life, raising their voices in a deafening pandemonium of crackling exhausts. Navigation lights would whirl and there would be clouds of dust, and the aircraft would be on their way around the perimeter track. For a moment the lights would disappear behind a corner of the orchard. Then, one by one, the green starboard lights would flit along the runway, lift, sway, and then flick out as the aircraft were airborne into the darkness, and the drone of the engines would fade away to the south-east. Already the sirens would be wailing along the Medway, and the thunder of the Dover guns would be shaking the air with the heavy pulsing that could be felt rather than heard.'

On the night of 13 June, Cunningham and Rawnsley missed all this familiar excitement because they were one of the fortunate crews already in the air when the raid started.

'13/14 June 43. Wing Commander Cunningham and Flight Lieutenant Rawnsley took-off at 2355 hours. When about 10 miles E of Dungeness under the control of Sandwich Radar at 23,000 feet, Mosquito was vectored on to 330° and a contact obtained at 4 o'clock and one and a half miles range. E/A was losing height gently and at

Group Captain A. G. Malan, D.S.O., D.F.C.,
and the Officers of the Biggin Hill Sector

request the pleasure of the Company of

Flight Lieutenant Nolany and Lady

to a Dance at Grosvenor House, Park Lane, London, W. 1.,

on Wednesday, the 9th of June, 1943,

to commemorate the shooting down of the 1,000th Hun Aircraft
by Pilots of the Sector.

9 p.m. - 3 a.m.

This invitation must be produced
to gain admission.

Biggin Hill - Gravesend - West Malling - Hawkinge - Lympne.

219

270mph with maximum boost obtainable and 2,850 revs the pilot was just able to close in. Losing height to 18,500 feet he got a visual against 10/10 cloud at 1,500 feet range 20° above. At 1,000 feet range the E/A was identified as an Fw 190 and at 600 feet the exhausts were visible, the E/As speed being about 250mph. Pilot eased up to slightly below and fired a short burst into the fuselage whereupon the E/A burst into flames and crashed to the ground near Wrotham. The bomb went off when the E/A hit the ground and the explosion could be heard for miles around. The Hun pilot found himself catapulted into mid-air and somehow or other managed to pull the ripcord. He landed near Wrotham suffering from burns and was taken prisoner.

'Wing Commander Cunningham and Flight Lieutenant Rawnsley landed base at 0155 hours. Everybody on the Squadron was delighted at the CO's success, his first with 85 Squadron. His bag is now 17 destroyed (16 at night).'

Having therefore become fully appreciative of the prowess of the Mosquito, the Germans endeavoured to build a version of their own called the Me 410. 'Nigel Bunting, a Flight Lieutenant, and one of the old guard in the Squadron,' wrote Jimmy Rawnsley, 'was the first to make closer acquaintance with the 410. Freddie French was flying as his navigator, and they were at 20,000 feet over the Straits of Dover when the Radar put them on to a raider heading up the East

95

"Distinguished Gathering"

by

JAMES PARISH

Characters in order of their appearance :—

Felix Montague	-	RICHARD MANSBRIDGE
Judith Montague	-	SYBIL BRADLEY
Sir Brian Howet	-	JAMES ELWIG
Lady Thalia Wilmer	-	LYNNE BATES
"Lesley Guest"	-	MAVIS LUCAS
Caroline Beckwith	-	RITA DENTON
C. D. Williams	-	ARTHUR BILLCLIFF
Major "Runty" Pearson		OWEN DOVE
Dorinda Caswell	-	ZENA GATES
Eliot Richard Vines	-	PETER COLEMAN
Blair	-	TOM COOPER
Detective-Inspector Rutherford		GEORGE BLOCK
Detective-Sergeant Ferris		EDMUND HENDERSON
Detective-Sergeant Ramage		DICK DICKENSON

Produced by - JOAN GURNEY

Act I. The drawing-room of Felix Montague's house at Hampstead; evening.

Act II. The same; after dinner.

Act III. The same; half-an-hour later.

Set by Cape of Chiswick

Lighting by Ronnie Weakley

Costumes by Charles Fox, High Holborn and Morris Angel, Shaftesbury Avenue

Properties by Robinson Bros., London, W.

Stage Management } Jessie Husk
Ronnie Weakley

Programmes by Rita Denton

Above: Captain Johan Rad. Rad and Lovestad were the first Norwegian crew to join 85 in April 1943.

Above left: 'A' Flight in 1943. From left to right: Back row — Pilot Officer Lowton (Nav), Unknown (Nav), Lieutenant Lovestad (Nav), Unknown (Nav), Flight Sergeant Misselbrook (Pilot), Unknown (Nav), Unknown (Pilot), Flying Officer Sutcliffe (Pilot), Unknown (Nav), Unknown (Nav), Flying Officer Shaw (Pilot), Flying Officer Clemo (Nav), Flight Lieutenant Robb (Pilot). Middle row — Flight Lieutenant Thwaites (Pilot), Squadron Leader Green (Pilot and Flight Commander), Flight Lieutenant Maguire (Pilot), Captain Rad (Pilot).

Front row — Flying Officer Bray (Nav), Flight Sergeant Grimstone (Nav), Flying Officer Jones (Nav), Flying Officer Thomas (Pilot).

Left: Programme from a performance at the West Malling theatre.

Coast. Within a few minutes, Freddie suddenly got two contacts on the AI, both at a range of three miles, one well below and the other above. Looking down, Nigel saw a red light, but he was too experienced a hand to be drawn. That red light looked altogether too much like bait, and he decided to have a go at the higher, unlighted contact.

'Climbing at full power, Nigel began to close in, and when they were still seven thousand feet behind he spotted two bright exhaust flames ahead. They had been at it for fifteen minutes and had climbed to twenty-five thousand feet before they were close enough for Nigel to get a really good look at the outline, now clearly silhouetted against the bright glow of the northern sky. There was no mistake about it: there were the two engines trailing bright yellow exhaust flames, with the narrow fuselage and the twin bar-bettes bulging on either side.

'Nigel closed in until he was two hundred yards astern, and he worked his gun sight on to the target. Then he hit the slipstream and he was put completely off his aim. He dived to recover, and began to ease up into position again. The Messerschmitt flew on as evenly and steadily as an air liner, and the German gunner had missed his last chance. Nigel's second aim was true: and with flames streaming from the fuselage the enemy raider rolled over on its back and dived vertically into the sea five miles east of Felixstowe.'

Thus on the night of 13/14 July 85 shot down the first Me 410 over the British Isles. Two nights later they got another one off Dunkirk: it was opportune that the Squadron had its eye in because that autumn the Luftwaffe mounted the biggest series of raids for many a night.

'7/8 October 43. 1st Phase (2002-2130 hours) about 15 E/A flew NW from the direction of Vitry. The first overland appeared at Maidstone at 2030 hours. Thereafter some 15 E/A flew over Kent and Surrey between 12,000-20,000 feet. One aircraft crossed the river at Tilbury and flew to Chelmsford. Another flew as far westward as Oxford and Newbury. Approximately six E/A penetrated the London area.

'2nd Phase (2030-2130 hours) about 30 E/A first shown flying towards Yarmouth at 9,000 feet. The first overland was at 2050 hours near Lowestoft and subsequently some 30 E/A operated from 10,000-15,000 feet mainly over Norfolk, Suffolk, Cambridge and Huntingdonshire. One flew as far westward as Woburn and Bedford and it is possible some left the country over London and Kent.

'3rd Phase (2135-2245 hours) about 12 E/A flying from Lille made landfall via the Estuary at heights between 9,000-20,000 feet and approximately eight penetrated the London area. After operating over Kent,

Surrey and Sussex, E/A left the country over the South Coast.

'Eight sorties were flown by "A" Flight and the two stand-by aircraft from "B" Flight also flew. Squadron Leader Maguire had a terrific dog-fight with an Me 410 which was carrying lights. Taking off at 1910 hours with Captain Lovestad as his operator, Squadron Leader Maguire was under the control of Wartling and was ordered up to 25,000 feet before being vectored on to a Bandit flying NW at 16,000 feet. Losing height rapidly, Squadron Leader Maguire obtained a visual of airborne lights well below on the starboard quarter. Controller warned him that there were two bandits a mile apart in line astern. Pilot lost more height and steadied up behind at about 2,000 feet range when the E/A took very violent evasive action. The E/A which was an Me 410, was carrying a red light and yellow light on the port and starboard wing tips respectively, and a very bright white light on the tail.

'A violent dog-fight now ensued with the E/A appearing to make repeated attempts to get on the tail of the Mosquito. After several minutes Maguire managed to get in 2 bursts and observed strikes on the port side of the fuselage and on the port wing. The E/A now turned and dived on to a southerly course followed by the Mosquito at about 300mph. Pilot managed to close the range again to about 250-300 yards and fired another burst as the E/A steadied up and was about to enter cloud at a height of 3,500 feet — further strikes were observed. The time was now 2055 hours and estimated position about 10-15 miles south of Hastings. Nothing further was seen of the E/A. Squadron Leader Maguire and Captain Lovestad landed base at 2155 hours and at first only claimed a damaged. Pilot Officer Shaw and Flight Sergeant Wyman however, who were up at the same time, had seen a burning mass fall through cloud and burn on the water south of Hastings and as this was undoubtedly the same E/A, Fighter Command stepped up the claim to destroyed.

'Captain Bugge and Lieutenant Bjorn took-off at 2050 hours and landed base 2355. Pilot's report is as follows:

'I took off and was told to go to orbit Beacon "J" at 15,000 feet. Arriving there I was taken over by Wartling Radar who told me to go after searchlight interceptions in the vicinity. Five targets were engaged and intercepted, all being identified visually as friendly bombers. Returning to orbit I saw a target nearby on the coast moving north and went towards it. Wartling told me to investigate with caution as it might be friendly.

'Contact was obtained at two and a half miles range, head on, at 20,000 feet. Turning

'Lieutenant Weisteen and Flying Officer French took-off 2120 hours. Pilot was crossing the coast near Dungeness under the control of Sandwich when he was instructed to vector 060° on to a Bandit travelling NW at 25,000 feet, range 27 miles. Contact was obtained at four miles range and 4 o'clock, target weaving gently and at 18,000 feet. Both aircraft were illuminated by searchlights and the E/A obviously saw the fighter for he immediately took evasive action. The chase went in a southerly direction from the Eastchurch area and at 1,500 feet range the pilot got a visual of the target against the moon and recognised it as an Me 410.

'The height was now 16,000 feet and with the target diving hard, pilot fired a one second burst from about 1,000 feet astern. Hits were seen on the tail unit and the E/A disappeared down to port. Contact was lost momentarily but regained at 4,000 feet range. Pilot now closed in again at 1,000 feet and gave another burst causing flashes and a stream of sparks from the starboard engine. E/A half turned over and went down vertically to starboard. Pilot's speed was 340mph and he was unable to turn quickly enough to follow.

'Lieutenant Weisteen and Flying Officer French landed base at 0025 hours. An Me 410 was claimed as damaged but Sandwich Radar received information that an aircraft was seen to go down into the sea in flames in the Dungeness area where the combat was broken off and the claim was stepped up to destroyed. Subsequently the AA claimed to have shot down an aircraft from 500 feet and in the end Lieutenant Weisteen was only credited with a half.*

'Wing Commander Cunningham and Flight Lieutenant Rawnsley took-off 2030 hours. Shortly afterwards their weapon (the AI radar) became unserviceable and they were on their way back to base when suddenly they obtained a chance visual on an E/A which the Wing Commander at once chased (he was not called "Cat's Eyes" for nothing). Closing in, neither the Wing Commander nor Flight Lieutenant Rawnsley was at first able to identify the E/A and so did not immediately attack. It appeared to be a Ju 88 type with long pointed wings.

'Having decided that it was a Ju 188, the Wing Commander closed in to attack and was just about to open fire when the rear gunner of the E/A opened up and smashed the Wing Commander's windscreen. The Wing Commander fired a burst but was

Top: Second Lieutenant Per Bugge, who flew with Claus Bjorn 'These doughty Norwegians,' wrote Rawnsley, 'Like many of our own crews, did not believe in going on a rest, and they usually arranged that they merely had a change of scene.' Bugge died on 8 February 1944 when his Mosquito collided with a Wellington target during a night training exercise.

Above: Freddie French and Tarald Weisteen. Tarald eventually became 'A' Flight Commander on 6 October 1944, a measure not only of his own prowess but also of the number of Norwegians who served on 85.

after target I closed in slowly going at full throttle and descending down to 18,000 feet. Target was going straight but dived and climbed steeply. Exhaust flames were seen at 2,000 feet range. Closing in further from underneath, the target dived in front of me and at 800 feet the silhouette was seen and recognised as an Me 410. Fire was opened at 100 yards range with a short burst and strikes and a bright flash were seen in the middle of the fuselage. The E/A went straight forward into a nearly vertical dive and was firing red tracers which went completely wide. Visual and radar contact was lost in the dive and Watling, when asked, could give no help so I returned to orbit beacon.

'60 rounds were fired. One Me 410 claimed as damaged.

*'Fahn!' exclaimed Tarald Weinsteen when told of the revised score. 'Those bloody guns. Which half did they shoot down, I'd like to know?'

unable to observe result. He then returned to base and landed 2125.

'On coming into the crew-room it was discovered that the Wing Commander's face was slightly cut and he was taken off to Sick Quarters by the MO (Flight Lieutenant E. Mortimer)* who removed many tiny splinters from his left eye, forehead and head. Wing Commander Cunningham and Flight Lieutenant Rawnsley had had a very narrow escape.'

The British press described the night's work in typically good-humoured fashion:

'Scalded Cat Raider Down

Three of the dozen raiders that flew over East Anglia and South-East England in the night were destroyed.

'One of the raiders shot down was an Me 410, a new twin-engined fighter-bomber mentioned by the Air Minister when he described the "scalded cat" raids on London.

'This was the seventh successive "propaganda raid" on Britain. Ten raiders have been shot down this month.

'Only a few of the night's raiders penetrated to the London area. Bombs dropped caused a little damage and a small number of casualties. A woman was killed and another person injured when a bungalow in East Anglia was demolished.'

'Saved by Bus Girl

When a bomb fell near a bus that was travelling between two London suburbs the girl conductor stopped the bus, threw her money on the seat and said: "Look after that. Don't pinch it."

'With Mr Richard Hornsey, a local warden, she climbed over the debris of a house adjoining a school, calling out to see whether anyone was trapped. In the wreckage she found Mr Jack Buckman, his wife, his daughter and 12 year old son. They were not hurt, and the boy greeted her by saying: "I shan't have to go to school tomorrow."

'After seeing that the Buckman family was all right, the conductress went back to her bus which drove on.'

'Bagged by Mosquito

A Fighter Command Mosquito sent an Me 410 crashing in flames in the south of England. 'The Mosquito pilot, Squadron Leader W. H. Maguire, who lives at Ware, Herts, caught sight of the Me nearly half a mile away in the moonlight, chased it, and closed to 200 yards before opening fire. He hit it first time and then, as he closed again, fired once more.

* Known to all on 85 as 'Rigor' Mortimer for obvious reasons.

Above: Cunningham's windscreen after it had been shattered by the rear-gunner of a Ju 188 on 7/8 October 1943.

Left: A jovial Squadron Leader W. H. Maguire in front of his Mosquito. Bill Maguire had been in the millinery business before the war and he joined up to become a fine pilot and flying instructor. He crewed up on 85 with Flying Officer W. D. Jones, a Welsh schoolmaster.

'The Me was now on fire, and burning pieces of it flew back past the Mosquito before it finally dived into the ground. It was the fifth night raider to be destroyed by the Squadron Leader in less than five months.'

The following night was just as eventful.

'8/9 Oct 43. Hun activity started early. Of 12 E/A which flew from the direction of Holland, six operated over coastal areas of Kent and Essex. Two penetrated to the outskirts of Greater London and four were suspected of mine-laying in the Barrow Deep area. Bombs were dropped on E Horndon, Berwick, Great Worley, Hockley, Elmstead and Sutton-at-Home.

'Two of the E/A were destroyed by the Squadron. Flying Officer Holloway shot down a Ju 88 south of Bradwell and Flight Lieutenant Bunting shot down a Ju 88 type, believed to be a Ju 188, SE of Dover. The night however was marred by the failure of Lieutenant Thoren and his operator, Pilot Officer Benge, to return from their patrol. They were chasing an intruder SE towards Dover when the intruder, together with the Mosquito close on its tail, were shot down by the Dover AA guns.

'10/10/43. The following signal was received from HQ 11 Group:

"His Majesty the King on the recommendation of the AOC-in-C has been graciously pleased to award the Distinguished Service Order to Flight Lieutenant C. F. Rawnsley, a Bar to the Distinguished Flying Cross to Acting Squadron Leader G. L. Howitt, and the Distinguished Flying Cross to Flight Lieutenant B. J. Thwaites and Flying Officer W. P. Clemo. Please convey AOC's congratulations."

'Flight Lieutenant Rawnsley is the first Navigator Radio and Observer with a night fighter squadron to have received the DSO. A party was held to celebrate in which Flight Lieutenant Rawnsley's fireworks and Pilot Officer Medworth's juggling tricks were the main features. Lieutenant Carruthers (Searchlight Liaison Officer) returned from the aerodrome to find that his motor-cycle had walked upstairs and parked itself in his bedroom at the top of the "Manor House".'

Lacking nothing if not perseverance, the Luftwaffe continued to mount their 'scalded cat' raids, and in so doing they gave 85 an insight into the working life of their opponents.

'15/16 Oct 43. Fine night. A total of some 17 E/A operated in two phases. Of these only eight crossed the coast making shallow penetrations over coastal areas of Suffolk, Essex and Kent. Minor bombing incidents were reported from scattered districts. Damage and casualties only on a very small scale. Three of the E/A were destroyed by the Squadron and a fourth crashed near Kirton from unknown causes.

'Squadron Leader Maguire and Flying Officer Jones took-off 2215 hours. Under Sandwich Radar whilst on patrol off Foreland at 15,000 feet they were instructed to climb to 20,000 feet for a Bandit at 20 miles range. Contact obtained at two and a half miles range, height 18,000 feet, when E/A took violent evasive action. E/A did a hard diving port turn but Mosquito turned inside it and the pilot, recognising it as a Ju 188, closed to 150 yards and opened fire. Strikes were observed on the port engine which burst into flames. A second burst increased the fire and the E/A went down in flames and crashed near Ipswich at 2258 hours.

'Pilot checked his machine after the combat and was immediately given another Bandit, range eight miles, travelling west at 23,000 feet. Climbing up in steps, pilot closed in an obtained a visual of an Me 410 which also saw Mosquito and did steep diving port turn. Pilot followed and closed in firing three bursts which set the starboard engine and central section on fire. E/A went down in flames and crashed just off Clacton at 2310 hours.'

Maguire and Jones landed back at base at 2335 hours having expended 382 rounds and disposed of a Ju 188 and Me 410 in the space of 12 minutes. This was the first Ju 188 to be brought down over land and if it all sounded incredibly straightforward, a transcript of Squadron Leader Maguire's R/T log shows differently:

'2246½hrs   Sandwich Controller (SC): "Starboard 080°, Bandit 20 miles."
Squadron Leader Maguire (F15): "Starboard 080. What Angels?" [How high?]

2247   SC: "060° ten miles. I think it's below you but stay where you are."
F15: "Say again."

2248   SC: "Stand by. It's Angels 19½ [19,500 feet] but stay where you are."
F15: "OK."
SC: "040°."
F15: "040°."

2249   F15: "Range?"
SC: "Six miles at 2 o'clock."
SC: "Now five miles at 10 o'clock."
F15: "OK."
SC: "Starboard on to 100°."
F15: "100°."

2250   SC: "Starboard 280°, Angels 20."
F15: "Say again."

SC: "Turn hard starboard on to 280. Angels 20."

F15: "280."

SC: "Range two miles now."

F15: "OK."

2251 SC: "Canary please." [Switch on IFF identification — this enabled the ground controller to positively identify the fighter when the blips were close together.]

SC: "Canary thank you. Range two miles, Angels 20½."

SC: "Range one mile."

SC: "Any joy?"

2252 F15: " ? ? ? ?" [distorted]

SC: "Canary please."

SC: "Canary thank you."

2252½ SC: "Hard port 270°. Range three."

F15: "270."

SC: "240°."

F15: "240."

2253 SC: "Starboard 280°, two miles."

F15: "280."

SC: "Angels 19½."

F15: "OK Thank you." [He was obviously looking frantically at this stage.]

SC: "OK Good work."

2254 SC: "There's a friend but the bandit is straight ahead of you."

F15: "Are you sure he's a friend?"

SC: "Yes, I think so."

2255½ SC: "Canary please. Any joy?"

F15: "Make sure that it is a friend."

SC: "Yes. He's gone away below you. Any joy?"

F15: " ? ? ? ?" [distorted]

2256 SC: "Do you want any more help?"

F15: "No thank you."

2259 F15: "We've got him."

SC: "Good show."

2259½ F15: "He's going down, curse him."

SC: "Congratulations. I've another for you when you're ready."

2300½ F15: "I'm just checking up on my machine and orbiting."

SC: "OK."

F15: "Canary."

SC: "Canary. Thank you, I have your position."

2301 F15: "OK Was that overland?"

SC: "You bet it was."

F15: "Is there anything doing?"

SC: "Two friends. One bandit, vector 160°."

2302 F15: "160."

SC: "Port 060°. I think I've got a bandit."

F15: "OK 060."

SC: "No, that's a friend. Vector 100°."

F15: "100."

SC: "Canary please."

F15: "Canary".

2303 SC: 'I have another one for you. 12 miles, westerly course, 160°."

F15: "What range?"

SC: "12 miles."

2303½ F15: "What Angels?"

SC: "Angels 17½. He may be going up."

F15: "OK."

2304½ SC: "Speed up turn on to 160°. He has turned."

F15: "OK."

SC: "Range eight miles. He's flying west now at three o'clock."

F15: "OK."

2305½ SC: "Range four, Angels 18."

2306 F15: "OK."

SC: "Port 195°, Crossing port to starboard. Starboard 220°."

F15: "Sorry. More help."

SC: "Starboard 220°."

2306½ SC: "Starboard 280°. Speed 240. Four miles."

F15: "OK."

F15: "Are there any more near us?"

SC: "No. I don't think there's anyone there."

2313½ F15: "He's gone. We've got him."

SC: "Good show."

F15: "He's nicely on fire, thank you."

2314 SC: "Canary, thank you."

F15: "Bit short of ammunition."

SC: "I think you had better come back then. Vector 190°."

F15: "OK."

While all this was going on, Flying Officer Thomas and Warrant Officer Hamilton took-off at 2245. Under the control of Sandwich at 6,000 feet, 'Pilot was instructed to climb on a vector of 060° and was then informed of a Bandit at 20 miles range. Contact was obtained at four miles range nearly head-on and well above on a vector of 100°.

'Pilot climbed to 21,000 feet where a visual was obtained well above. E/A started to take evasive action and dived steeply away to port with the Mosquito about a mile behind. E/A was recognised as a Ju 188. Eventually pilot closed in to 300 yards and fired four bursts. From the first burst, strikes were seen on the port engine and on the starboard engine from the second burst. From the fourth burst large pieces fell off the port engine and wing and the E/A fell away to starboard with both engines well on fire, eventually crashing about two miles SW of Birchington. The blazing Hun was seen descending by Squadron Leader Maguire and personnel from Manston, Sandwich and Gravesend at 2315 hours. It was Flying Officer Thomas' first victory and everyone was delighted at his success.'

On this one occasion, the Squadron received extracts from the interrogation reports of the prisoners of war captured from the Ju 188s shot down that night.

'1) *Type and Marks* Ju 188 3E+HH (shot down by Flying Officer Thomas)
Unit 1st Staffeln, KG 6
Crew Pilot — Leutnant Karl Geyr — born 27 April 1924 — PoW
Observer — Feldwebel (Sergeant) Flossner — dead
W/T — Obergefreiter (Leading Aircraftman) Dietram Kretzchmar — born 1 January 1924 — dead
Air Gunner — Name and rank unknown. Missing, assumed dead.
Morale Extremely high. The W/T operator carried Belgian money and had a receipt from a shop in the village of Ath, which is close to Chièvres airfield.

Details of last flight

'During the afternoon of the 15th October, a total of seven aircraft of I Gruppe, KG 6* (three from 1st Staffel and four from 3rd Staffel) took-off from their base at Chièvres and flew direct to Münster/Handorf whence they were to refuel preparatory to an attack on London. It was understood by the crews that the sortie was a reprisal attack on London and was to be in the nature of a nuisance raid.

'All the aircraft were bombed up at Chièvres with identical loads of one 1,000kg plus ten 50kg bombs.

'It was found that insufficient petrol was available at Münster/Handorf for all the aircraft involved, and some of them were sent to Rheine to refuel. These aircraft and crews were to return to Münster/Handorf after refuelling and to circle the airfield until the remaining aircraft took-off. However the aircraft from Münster took-off without waiting for those from Rheine and the latter were consequently 10 minutes behind the others

---

*The basic Luftwaffe flying unit was the Gruppe, similar to an RAF Wing with about 30 aircraft. Such Gruppen were combined into Geschwader of about 90 aircraft equivalent to an RAF Group — KG 6 was a Kampfgeschwader (Bomber Group) with I Gruppe at Chièvres and, according to the PoW, II was in Greece, III at Istres and IV at Brétigny. Each Gruppe was sub-divided into Staffeln, each Staffel of 9-10 aircraft being equivalent to an RAF squadron. The commander of the Staffel was known as the Staffelkapitän.

on the operation. This unforeseen complication interfered with the timing of the raid and, in the opinion of PoW, prejudiced its success.

'The crews were briefed to return to Münster/Handorf after the attack. PoW believed that the Gruppe was to remain there for the next three to four days and to continue operations.

'3E+HH was the second aircraft to take-off from Rheine. The pilot flew a zig-zag course over the sea, intending to make landfall north of the Thames Estuary and approach London from the East. The crews were informed at briefing that the Knickebein transmitters at Den Helder and Boulogne were to be laid on for operations and that their beams would intersect at a point over NW London. The observer on 3E+HH succeeded in picking up the beam of the Den Helder Knickebein and upon reaching the intersect point of the two beams the pilot made a left hand turn and the bombs were released from 20,000 feet according to plan. Something must have gone wrong with the calculation however as it is believed that the bombs were actually dropped over the outer Thames Estuary.

'Shortly after turning for home, the aircraft was attacked by a night fighter and set on fire. The crew baled out and the pilot was taken PoW. The body of the W/T operator was found on the beach near Birchington, and that of the observer has since been found. The gunner presumably came down in the sea and has not yet been traced. The aircraft crashed on land south of Birchington and the wreckage was strewn over a wide area.'

'2) *Type and Marks* Ju 188 — 3E+FL (shot down by Squadron Leader Maguire).
Unit 3rd Staffel, KG 6.
Crew Pilot — Hauptmann Helmuth Waldecker — born 13 September 1914 — Staffelkapitän of the 3rd Staffel — PoW.
Observer — Obergefreiter Waldemar Haupt — born 31 March 1921 — slightly wounded.
W/T — Unteroffizier (Corporal) Karl Heinz — dead.
Air Gunner — Oberfeldwebel (Flight Sergeant) Julius Hohmann — born 19 September 1918 — dead.
Morale Very high. The pilot and observer wore the Iron Cross First Class, and the W/T and gunner had the Iron Cross Second Class.

Details of Last Flight

'3E+FL was piloted by the Staffelkapitän of the 3rd Staffel and because the aircraft had to make an intermediate landing with bombs on board, only experienced crews were chosen. However, because the Staffelkapitän's regular observer was sick in hospital, he flew with an observer who was a newcomer to the crew and who was on his first operational flight.

'This aircraft was a quarter of an hour late in take-off due to refuelling difficulties mentioned above and it eventually crossed the Dutch coast at about 2200 hours. The intention was to start climbing immediately after leaving the coast so as to attain a height of 26,000 feet on arrival over the English coast. It was then planned to continue at this height until over the target, release the bombs, go into a dive to gain speed and fly back to Münster/Handorf.

'The crews were told that there would be considerable ground fog over SE England and that in consequence they would be immune from night fighter attack. Whilst over the sea and still below 20,000 feet, the aircraft was attacked by a night fighter but took successful evasive action and then continued to climb. Some 6 to 10 minutes later, when flying over 20,000 feet, the aircraft was attacked simultaneously by several night fighters ! ! ! — the pilot thought three ! ! ! — with the result that the port engine was disabled and the controls severely damaged. Soon afterwards the pilot lost control of the aircraft and gave orders to bale out.

'It was then found that the gunner was unconscious with very severe leg injuries and that the W/T operator had one arm shot away. After some difficulty in opening the escape hatch, the gunner was pushed out and the other three members of the crew baled out at about 7,000 feet. The pilot and observer were captured but the W/T operator and gunner were killed. The aircraft crashed into the ground and was completely destroyed.

'The observer commented that the transmissions of the Den Helder Knickebein were almost inaudible throughout the flight owing, he thought, to British interference.

I Gruppe of KG 6

'The three Staffeln of I/Kg 6 moved individually from Italy to Chièvres during August 1943 and the whole Gruppe was still based there when the present aircraft were shot down on 15 Oct.

'The first Staffel reached Chièvres on or about 1 August. Ju 188 E-1s awaited their arrival and the Erprobungsstaffel (Test Squadron) of KG 6, which had already converted to Ju 188s at Rechlin, proceeded to retrain the crews on to new aircraft.

'At about the end of August, when the training of the first Staffel was nearing completion, the 2nd and 3rd Staffeln arrived at Chièvres from Italy to find sufficient Ju 188s awaiting them. The crews of the 1st Staffel were detailed to act as instructors while the 2nd and 3rd Staffeln converted to the new

aircraft because the Erprobungsstaffel transferred to Brussels/Melsbroek, presumably to supervise the conversion course of Gruppe III.

Ju 188

'PoW seemed to be very pleased with the Ju 188. It has a much roomier cockpit than the Ju 88, visibility is greatly improved, and the instrument panels can be seen more easily.

'As regards performance, the Ju 188 has better flying qualities than the Ju 88. It is faster, has a better rate of climb, does not tend to swing off to port during take-off, and is steadier in flight at low speed. According to the PoW, the optimum height of the Ju 188 is 6,000 metres. Pilots had orders not to exceed 8,000 metres.

'The dorsal turret of the Ju 188 protrudes about 25cm above the fuselage. The MG 131 gun with which it is provided can be operated either by the observer or the W/T operator and has an arc of fire of 360°.

Radar and Window

'When crews of the Gruppe took over their new Ju 188s, no form of night fighter detector was provided. Then aircraft were flown to Reims and there fitted with "Neptun Gerät". In the Ju 188, the presentation part of the Neptun rearward-looking radar is mounted in front of the pilot in such a way that the screen can be seen by both the pilot and the observer at the same time. The Neptun Gerät is stated by the PoW to scan an arc of 20° to either side of the longitudinal axis of the aircraft, 30° upwards and 50/60° downwards. It scans rearwards only, with two settings, fine and coarse, the maximum range with the coarse setting being 5km.

'It is stated that by 15 October almost all the aircraft of the Gruppe were equipped. In the case of 3E+HH however, although the Neptun aerials and leads were fitted, the presentation unit was not carried on the last flight as it was u/s.

'The pilot of 3E+HH had seen the equivalent of 'Window'* and although it had not been used by his Gruppe up to the time when he was shot down, he gleaned a little information as to its use.

'The German cover-name for "Window" is "Duppel", a simple strip of foil being termed "der Duppel". PoW stated that the strips were made up into small packets about 3cm thick. From hearsay he understood that aircraft using Duppel from France would fly at a lower height than the main bomber force and would begin to release the strips when about

*'Window' was the British codename for tinfoil strips dropped from aircraft to simulate aircraft echoes and confuse ground search radars.

Above: Pilot Officer G. G. Gilling-Lax. After a first-class career at Marlborough and Cambridge, Gilling-Lax was a housemaster at Stowe before joining the RAF as a navigator.

Gilling-Lax flew with Flight Lieutenant J. P. M. Lintott, a 22-year old pilot from Surrey. On 9 July 1943 they were scrambled at 1700 hours to be 'taken over by Wartling Radar. At 1719 hours, Lintott was put on to a raid at 6,000 feet and contact was made at $1719\frac{3}{4}$ and held. Wartling watched the two aircraft merge together at 1720 hours and the Radar continued watching them until 1727 hours when both indications faded together. Soon after at 1730 hours it was reported that two aircraft had crashed near Detling.

'It transpired that the Mosquito had crashed at Boxley near Maidstone, both Flight Lieutenant Lintott and Pilot Officer Gilling-Lax being killed, and that a Do 217 had crashed about two miles away, the German crew and aircraft being blown to smithereens.

'On investigation of the wreckage of the Mosquito it immediately became apparent that it had broken up in the air before the impact with the ground. It appears likely that Lintott shot the Do 217 down and either a bit flew off the E/A and hit the Mosquito causing it to crash, or more likely, after shooting the aircraft down a structural failure occurred in the Mosquito.

'Flight Lieutenant Lintott and Pilot Officer Gilling-Lax were a brilliant crew and they are a severe loss to the Squadron. They had already shot down three E/A in 12 weeks and both had been recommended for the DFC.'

half way across the English Channel, continuing until over the English coast.

Crest

'I Gruppe of KG 6 continues to use as its crest a golden duck carrying a small bomb slung from its beak.

Quarters at Chièvres Airfield

'At Chièvres, the officers of I Gruppe of KG 6 had their Mess and quarters in the Chateau de Bauffe off the SE corner of the airfield. It will be remembered that the Chateau was used for the same purpose by the Italians during their short time at the Channel front in 1940. The remaining flying personnel were accommodated in the Convent de Brugelette which is situated a few hundred yards NE of the northern boundary.

Precautions Against Intruders

'When returning to Chièvres from night flights, aircraft of KG 6 homed on to the dummy airfield five miles to the West. The lighting on the dummy airfield was kept on and when aircraft arrived over it, they reported their presence to ground control by R/T using code phrases. A different phrase was used for every operation. When intruders were in the vicinity of the airfield, returning aircraft were as a rule instructed by R/T to proceed to a waiting area.

Personalities

'The Kommodore of KG 6, the famous Storp, known as "Senior", was promoted from Oberstleutnant to Oberst in August of this year.

'The following are some of the senior officers of the Geschwader:

Kommandeur I — Major Fuhrhopp
Kommandeur II — Major Schreiner
Kommandeur IV — Major Schallmeyer
Staffelkapitän 1 — Hauptmann Manowarda
Staffelkapitän 2 — Leutnant Barz
Staffelkapitän 3 — Hauptmann Waldecker
(now PoW)
Staffelkapitän 5 — Hauptmann Schmidt
Staffelkapitän 10 — Oberleutnant Bertram

'Hauptmann Manowarda is a nephew of the famous Manowarda. He is of Viennese origin but is stated to be "More Prussian than the Prussians". He is a capable pilot and holds the Silver War-Flights Badge (awarded for 60 operational flights).

'Hauptmann Waldecker, the Staffelkapitän of the third Staffel, has acted as Gruppenkommandeur in the absence of Major Fuhrhopp. The operation on 15 October was the first sortie to be made by the third Staffel since its re-equipment and its return from the Mediterranean in August. Now that Waldecker is a PoW, his successor no doubt will be Leutnant Diermann who has

acted in the past as Deputy Staffelkapitän. Diermann was in Gruppe II before being posted to the third Staffel and has over 20 war-flights to his credit.

Careers

'3E+FL — The pilot of 3E+FL, a Hauptmann born 13 September 1914, transferred to the Luftwaffe in 1937 from the German Navy. He operated on the Western Front and in the Greece and Crete campaigns and was promoted from Oberleutnant to Hauptmann in the autumn of 1941. He has 150 war-flights to his credit, holds the Deutsches Kreuz in Gold, and expected shortly to receive the Ritterkreuz.

'The observer, an Obergefreiter born 31 March 1921, joined the Luftwaffe on 1 May 1941. On 15 January 1942 he reached the Observers' School at Bug-auf-Rugen where he made his first training flight in June 1942. In August 1942, he and 29 other observers who had completed their training were posted to the Observers' School at Tutow for further training as observers for the Russian front. Three months later however, 10 of them, including PoW, were transferred at short notice to IV Gruppe of KG 6 at Brétigny where they arrived on 15 November.

'On 1 February he was posted to V Gruppe but shortly afterwards sustained an injury and spent some months in hospital. In June 1943 he returned to IV Gruppe and on 1 September was posted as supernumerary to III/KG 6 at Chièvres. He was on his first war-flight when shot down.

3E+HH

'The pilot of 3E+HH, a Leutnant born 27 April 1924, joined the Luftwaffe early 1941 as an officer cadet and was sent to FlAR (Recruit Depot) at Salzwedel. Six months later he was posted to a Luftkriegsschule at Dresden/Klotsche for basic training and after a year there proceeded to Neuruppin. After four months training at this school he did two months blind flying at Brandis and was then posted to IV Gruppe of KG 6 at Brétigny in March 1943.

'In July he was sent from Brétigny by train to Istres and flew from there in a Ju 88 to join I Gruppe at Foggia. A day after his arrival in Foggia he was attached to the first Staffel with which he left by train for Chièvres on the same day. He had made only two war-flights when shot down and holds no decorations.'

'So much for the night of 15/16 October 1943' concluded the Operations Record Book with relish. Did it prove anything? Certainly the men on both sides were very similar in their backgrounds and high morale, but the levels of experience on the German bomber

force had undoubtedly diminished due to the demands of the Eastern Front and training standards had also been lowered. The crews on 85 Squadron were experienced night fighter specialists who had the best equipment science could produce, who had perfected their techniques to a fine art, and who knew that they were an integral part of the most sophisticated and comprehensive air defence system in the world. On the other hand, the men of I/KG 6 lacked many of the defence and penetration aids they should have had, they had only recently arrived from the sunny skies of Italy, and at a time when Bomber Command could send 653 heavy bombers over Hamburg within the space of 43 minutes, the Germans apparently could not pre-position seven aircraft together over Münster in preparation for a co-ordinated raid.

The Germans were not unimaginative in their approach to raids on Britain — their bombers often hugged the waves for as long as possible to creep in under the early warning radar screen or operated in pairs, the first aircraft acting as bait while the other tagged along behind waiting to jump a night fighter once he was busy with the interception — but such individual subterfuges could not disguise the fact that, at the end of the day, the RAF was better organised in defence than the Luftwaffe was in attack. Therefore, during October 1943 when the Luftwaffe attacked on 21 nights and sent some 210 aircraft into the 11 Group area, 85 disposed of five Ju 188s, three and a half Me 410s, and one Ju 88, plus two Me 410s damaged. This brought their night 'bag' to 49½ and the wartime Squadron total to 193½ destroyed and 104 'probables' and 'damaged'.

Nor were any men braver than those who served on 85.

'6/7 Nov 43. Squadron Leader Selway shot down an Fw 190 and was shortly afterwards hit in the stomach by rear gunner of a Ju 188. Pilot momentarily blacked out and Mosquito entered a dive but quickly recovered control. Although seriously wounded and without airspeed indicator or altimeter he brought aircraft safely back to base.

'After landing he walked into "B" Flight crew-room unconcerned and started to discuss his 190. Nobody knew that he had been wounded and when he started to undress, everyone was startled to see a mass of blood. The MO (Flight Lieutenant Mortimer) was sent for and Squadron Leader Selway was immediately taken off to Preston Hall hospital where it was found that the bullet had lodged in his stomach. A major operation was immediatly performed and the bullet extracted — Squadron Leader Selway stood the operation well but was on the danger list.'

Fortunately he subsequently recovered, and received the DFC on 19 December.

Above: Some of the Squadron at the end of 1943. From left to right: Back row — Flying Officer Symon (Nav), Flying Officer Cleaver (Pilot), Flight Lieutenant Molony (Adjutant), Flying Officer Skelton (Nav), Flight Lieutenant Burbridge (Pilot), Squadron Leader Gonsalves (Pilot), Squadron Leader Davison (Pilot), Wing Commander Cunningham, Captain Weisteen (Pilot), Unknown, Unknown, Flying Officer Farrell (Pilot), Flying Officer Thomas (Pilot). Front row — Flying Officer Custance (Taking over from Molony as Adjutant), Unknown (Nav), Unknown (Nav), Squadron Leader Rawnsley (Nav Leader), Unknown (Nav).

Below: '24/25 March 1944. Flight Lieutenant Nowell took off at 1950 hours to fly the dusk patrol and Flight Sergeant Rogers did Practice Intercepts. Soon indication of hostile activity became strong and Rogers returned. Flying Officer Hedgecoe scrambled but returned with U/S exhausts. The picture was still very confused, some enemy aircraft penetrating inland at great speed and going out, but a large concentration of aircraft remained mixed up with "Window" south of Beachy Head. To counter these, four aircraft were scrambled at intervals from 2200 to 2300 hours. Finally, at about 2330 hours, the Hun began to set course for London but coming in right to the west of our Sector. Flying Officer Hedgecoe however, was given an interception by Wartling. Contact obtained at 8 miles at 19,000 feet on Hun vectoring 320°. Closing in to 1,000 feet, Hedgecoe recognised it as a Ju 188 in good visibility, although a dark night. First burst at 700 feet produced no results so Flying Officer Hedgecoe closed to 300 feet and fired a second burst which produced a great explosion and the Mosquito flew through the middle of it. The fabric caught fire and the aircraft appeared to be enveloped in flames. Having ordered the Radar Operator (Flying Officer Bamford) to bale out, the flames went out so Flying Officer Bamford was hauled back. Finding that the aircraft was quite stable, Flying Officer Hedgecoe flew back to base and landed safely. The aircraft was bereft of all madapaulin [A fabric, similar to linen, which covered the wooden aircraft structure], there was a hole in the port wing from which a piece of Ju 188 was later removed, and the rudder afforded no control at all because all the fabric was burnt off. The combat was described by the press as "Blazing Fighter Gets Raider" and aircraft O for Orange as "a soot-blackened and charred Mosquito"!

'Edward Hedgecoe, who came from Brookmans Park, started off life in the service as an Accountant Officer before remustering to aircrew. He was then 34 year of age and, like Norman Bamford, who came from Sevenoaks, was awarded the DFC after this incident. Hedgecoe was to shoot down eight enemy aircraft in all, and Bamford to take part in the destruction of 10, before they were both killed in flying accidents.'

Bomber Support

'2/3 Jan 44. The Squadron's first victory and the first British night victory of 1944 was achieved by Wing Commander Cunningham at 2359 hours when he shot down an Me 410 in flames in the region of Le Touquet. Scrambled at 2310 hours and subsequently chased a raider back to French coast under Sandwich Radar control.'

The following month John Cunningham was promoted, given a second bar to his DSO, and posted to 11 Group as Group Captain Night Operations. 'This terminated a 14 month period of command of 85 Squadron during which his brilliant leadership had produced a very high standard of efficiency in all the crews and each new tactical development of the Hun bomber had been met and dealt with by his determination and tireless research. During his command, 46 E/A have been destroyed by 85 Squadron.

'Command of 85 Squadron was taken over by Wing Commander C. M. Miller DFC* who had been well known to the Squadron when stationed at Hunsdon in 1942. Wing Commander Miller began ops in this war with No 9 Squadron of Bomber Command after which he served with No 148 Squadron, Malta. He subsequently occupied the post of Personal Assistant to AOC Mediterranean Command after which he returned to England to join No 24 Communications Squadron. He had command of No 29 Night Fighter Squadron in 1943 during which time he was awarded the second bar to his DFC. Wing Commander Miller comes to 85 Squadron now from 63 OTU, Honiley, where he has been in charge of training night fighter crews.'

By now though the Luftwaffe bomber forays over the British Isles had become so relatively insignificant that most 85 Squadron night fighter flights were assessed as 'Much Ado About Nothing'.

'30/3/44. Night flying done by "A" Flight. That night "B" Flight had their "Erks" party at the Royal Oak at Wrotham. Untold quantities of beer were drunk and Flight

*Charles Miller was a native of Kildare, Eire, proving once again that the wartime RAF was a family of nations.

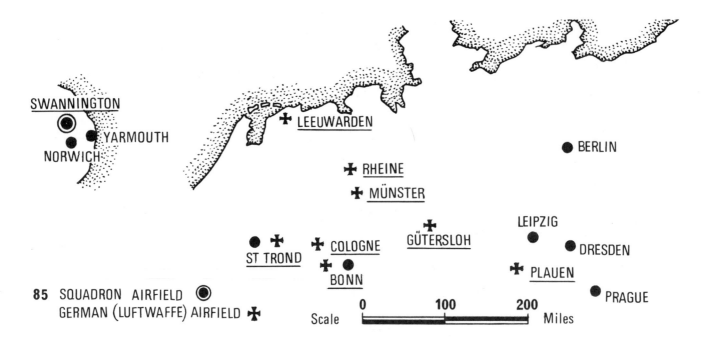

SWANNINGTON
● ●YARMOUTH
NORWICH ●

✠ LEEUWARDEN

● BERLIN

✠ RHEINE
✠ MÜNSTER

● ✠
ST TROND ✠ COLOGNE
✠ ●
BONN

✠
GÜTERSLOH

LEIPZIG
●
✠ PLAUEN

● DRESDEN

● PRAGUE

85 SQUADRON AIRFIELD ◉
GERMAN (LUFTWAFFE) AIRFIELD ✠

Scale
0   100   200   Miles

Above: 85 Squadron in the Bomber Support role — 1944-45.

Lieutenant Farrell gave his usual rendering of *She had to go and lose it at the Astor* into the inevitable microphone which didn't work. The "pièce de résistance" was the singing of *A long, strong black pudding* by the Station Master (station commander). As is customary this was voted the best party ever.

'Despite the revelry, night flying continued apace. Flight Lieutenant Phillips flew the dusk patrol while Flight Sergeant Gee did his first Ground Control Interception practice. Captain Weisteen was then scrambled but had no joy; Warrant Officer Alderton and Flight Lieutenant Ostaszewski then flew patrols. They were followed by Flying Officer Thomas who returned early with AI U/S. About 0300 hours several Huns appeared on the board and four were scrambled. The Squadron had no joy and Squadron Leader Thwaites was the last to land at 0540 hours. A rather long night.'

The last significant German manned bomber assault against Britain petered out in the spring of 1944, but the Luftwaffe was a far from spent force and nothing demonstrated this more forcibly than the fact that *their* night fighters were proving just as capable as the RAF in dealing with a bomber offensive. German night fighters accounted for most of the 40 bombers (or 8.7% of the force)* destroyed during the first of Bomber Command's attacks on Berlin in December 1943, and during the raid on Leipzig the following February, night fighters disposed of nearly all the 78 British heavy bombers that failed to return. Bomber Command losses were not always so high for bad weather, skilful routeing and subterfuge could thwart

*Anything over 5% was regarded as unacceptable in the long term.

the Luftwaffe fighter controllers, but when the skies were clear and the objective undisguised, German night fighters were directed into the bomber streams to wreak a fearful toll. The climax came on 30/31 March 1944 when the Luftwaffe accounted for the vast majority of the 95 Bomber Command aircraft that failed to return from Nuremburg. The problem promised to get worse as the nights got shorter, the weather improved, and Bomber Command chanced its arm deeper and deeper into Germany; something had to be done to protect the bomber streams or the RAF strategic offensive would be worn out of the sky.

Consequently, as on all previous occasions when 85 Squadron ran short of opposition, it was time for a move nearer to the action, and the action in the spring of 1944 was over continental Europe.

'26/4/44. For some considerable time, the air had been very thick with rumours of the Squadron moving from West Malling. Guesses were wild and inaccurate but it seemed probable that Hunsdon, the happy hunting ground of 85 Squadron, was to be the place. Today Wing Commander Miller went to see the AOC 11 Group and came back with news far different from anything ever imagined or suggested. No 85 Squadron was to move into 100 Group (Bomber Command) and on 1 May we were to go to Swannington near Norwich, once more to be an offensive Squadron both by nature and calling where recently only the former had applied. Bomber Command had been calling for increased close escort against night fighters and it had been decided to release Mk X AI for the job and, as the AOC put it, the best night fighter squadron to go with it. He even went so far as to say that Bomber Command had asked for us by name. Reaction to the news was mixed for while all felt it would be a blow to leave West Malling, it was generally realised that heavy bomber attacks on this country were on the decline and the new job would provide greater scope for destroying the Hun in the air. The rest of the day was spent in preparing for the party laid on for 27 April at the Manor House which would also serve as a "farewell party" now.'

Now poacher turned gamekeeper, No 85 moved out of Fighter Command for the first time in the war and was non-operational for four weeks while it adapted to its new role. It was an opportune break for some.

'1/5/44. A great honour was today conferred on the Squadron when six of its present members were invited to a private dance at Windsor Castle given in honour of HRH Princes Elizabeth's coming-of-age. Those who went were Wing Commander Miller, Squadron Leader Thwaites, Captain Weisteen, Flight Lieutenant Farrell, Flying Officer Hedgecoe and Flying Officer Thomas. The parties went by road and were met by Wing Commander Peter Townsend DSO DFC, Equerry to the King and former CO of the Squadron, who briefed them as to the desired etiquette. At Windsor the party was joined by Group Captain Cunningham, Flight Lieutenant Rawnsley and Flight Lieutenant Molony. The party was then introduced to the Guards Barracks where they were to spend the night. On arrival at the Castle, where they were the only members of the Royal Air Force present, they were received by His Majesty the King, Her Majesty the Queen, the Royal Princesses and Her Royal Highness the Duchess of Kent, before going into dinner. All were immediately affected by the great friendliness and warmth of their welcome and from then on felt quite at ease. After dinner, dancing with all members of the Royal Family continued until 0400 hours to the music of Ambrose and his orchestra, and everybody agreed that not only had the evening been a wonderful experience but also a most happy time.'

The drive back to the Guards Barracks was not without event. 'Most of those of the Squadron who were there seemed to be travelling in "Ginger" Farrell's car; a quaint vehicle which went — that was, when it could be induced to start — by the becoming name of "Lilly-Gal". Some of those who were with Ginger moved away from the lighted doorway into the merciful obscurity of the blackout. And to the remaining guests waiting for their cars there came from the darkness a vivid sound picture of what was happening.

' "Bet she won't start."
' "How's the battery?"
' "Flat as your hat. Where's the flamin' handle?"
' "Shush! We'll have to push."
'There came a scrabble of feet on the cobble-stones, a tinny clanking, and some hard breathing.
' "Now!" someone bellowed.
'There was a crack that shook the precincts, followed by muffled shouts of triumph as the engine started up. Then, with a roar somewhat like that of a flying-bomb, and with bodies clinging to the wildly swinging doors, "Lilly Gal"* was launched.'

The less fortunate humped crates and expended their energies in less regal surroundings.

'1/5/44. The day of the Squadron's move was fine but fairly hazy. This however did not prevent the "beating-up" of the aerodrome which is the custom on these occasions. "A" Flight flew up separately in the morning and caused more than one of the control officers to lie flat as they roared overhead. "B" Flight went up in the afternoon and did a formation run over the aerodrome at low level. At Swannington a further formation run was carried out and after a few individual beat-ups all landed successfully, the Squadron having brought 15 aircraft with it. All agreed that it was most enjoyable to land on runways again, particularly on such good ones. The aerodrome has three runways like billiard-tables, one of 2,000 yards and two others of 1,400 yards length, and full night lighting. However even the excellence of the aerodrome scarcely compensated for the chill emptiness and unadorned severity of a brand new station. But it was felt that it would be a good opportunity for the members of the Squadron to pull together to discover how good a place it could become. Flight Lieutenant Farrell was to look after the Mess and bar arrangements while Flight Lieutenant Burbridge kept an eye on the catering. The Officers' Mess is a very large country house, with good accommodation, but scarcely cosy as had been the Manor House. As the evening wore on, it was decided that with the best intentions of furnishing the mess, its emptiness could be borne no longer, so a party of fifteen resorted to a nearby pub where a Glee Club was started and good spirits restored with beer and song.'

'2/5/44. Most of the day spent in settling in and unpacking, organising dispersals and all the other paraphernalia attached to so extensive a movement. People had rather a tendency to go around looking lost. There was no flying by day or night.'

---

*Night Fighter; Rawnsley and Wright, Collins, 1957.

'3/5/44. Today began a series of talks outlining the functioning of Bomber Command and the role which the squadrons at Swannington might be expected to play.* Flight Officer Strang of the "Y" Service, whose job it had been to listen in to the R/T traffic of the Hun night fighters, told of the difficulty the German Controllers had in assessing the probable target, the main stream and the route of the bombers with a view to positioning the fighters to attack them. This was very interesting to us, knowing the snags we and our controllers had had in defending London. It seemed that in the general chase there was a chance for well-equipped AI fighters to move in with the Huns on their orbit beacons or over the target and destroy a considerable number with comparative safety to themselves. This, apart from the morale factor, would cause Hun pilots to imagine they were being followed all the time, contributing to a deterioration of efficiency. We were afterwards shown the bomber routes in conjunction with the plots of German night fighters, how they gathered at orbit beacons and, when properly led in, destroyed many bombers. If they were fed in late into the stream or over the target, they met with limited success. It seemed then that here was an opportunity for the two Swannington Squadrons to work out new methods of attack upon the German night fighters either on their beacons or as they flew into the stream. Certainly Bomber Command

*85 were to share Swannington with 157 Squadron.

expected good results from us. Flight Lieutenant Kelsey DFC, formerly of 141 Squadron* spoke to us in the afternoon of the High Escort aspect of the matter including the difficulties to be expected from inaccurate navigation, German flak and night fighters, and forms of radio interference. He said that if we navigated accurately, and got to the right place with our present equipment, there was practically no limit to the destruction of Huns. This we felt was a little optimistic but certainly as more was discovered about the job, so interest in it grew and all had high hopes for the future. There was again no flying.'

This pause for training and re-adjustment was most necessary, for on defensive night duties the radar navigators of 85 Squadron had had little navigating to do. Patrols close to England had always been under Ground Control Interception radar control while recovery to base had been achieved by homing onto a beacon, but the days of concentrating wholly on radar sets and blips were over — it was time to learn to navigate accurately into the heart of occupied Europe. Thus pilots began to read maps again and radar navigators got to grips with a new navigational aid called Gee on cross-country training flights. However, once they got themselves into enemy airspace, it was their new AI Mk X that was to make bomber support possible. Developed by the Americans, the Mk X had considerable advantages over the Mk VIII in that it could cope better with Duppel, and had a maximum range of 10 miles plus 180° forward coverage which made it an ideal search apparatus. This new radar was enclosed in the 'bull-nosed' Mosquito XIX, the first of which arrived at Swannington on 10 May, and it was hoped that this advanced version of the Mosquito night fighter with long endurance and the latest aids would take the Germans by surprise.

But before 85 could start to poach inside Germany, something else took priority:
'4/5 Jun 44. The weather was bad so night flying was cancelled. Unfortunately several people had a party. I say unfortunately because today was D-Day minus one and at eleven o'clock twelve crews were detailed to be at Colerne by one o'clock. Thanks to a splendid effort on the part of the ground crews, all aircraft were there on time.

AI Mk VIII

When the Mk VIII aerial reflected the beam dead ahead, it was in focus and therefore conferred a maximum range of 6½ miles. However, when it looked out to the side, the beam got out of focus and became degraded such that at an angle of 45° the maximum range was barely two miles.

AI Mk X

The Mk X was a great improvement over the VIII in that it enabled the radar operator to 'see' for 10 miles in all directions over a much wider radar scan.

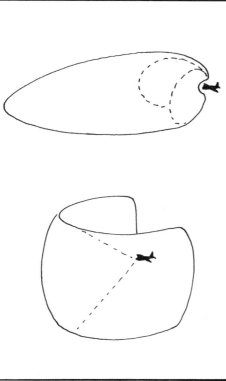

*In June 1943, 141 Squadron's Beaufighters had been fitted with 'Serrate', a device which gave a bearing on the transmissions from Luftwaffe AI radars. It was therefore hoped that 141 Squadron would go out and hunt down German night fighters but many potential interceptions were thwarted simply because the Beaufighter was outrun or outmanoeuvred.

'At 1500 hours, Group Captain Cunningham came down to brief us on the operation and generally to put us in the picture. Sea and airborne forces were to make landings on the beaches and as some 2,000 aircraft were to be engaged in the landings themselves and the bombing of ten coastal batteries which preceded them, considerable enemy night fighter reaction was anticipated. Thus six patrol lines were to be laid on about 50 miles West, South and East of the landing area. Of the six patrol lines, 85 Squadron was to do the four inside France from Vire to Argentan, Argentan to Bernay, Bernay to Pavilly, and Pavilly to a point 20 miles NW of Dieppe. It was thus hoped that at least some of the enemy fighters from known air fields in France would have to go through our patrols and we were to intercept all contacts that went in towards the landing areas. We were further strictly enjoined to be most careful about aircraft recognition, as nearly all the aircraft over France would be friendly with a proportion of perhaps one hostile in 50 aircraft. In fact with all the Dakotas around it was hinted that anyone claiming an He 111 would be most probably court martialled.

'It was certainly to be a most striking display of Allied Air Power for aircraft from every Command were taking part in it and practically every type of service aircraft. At night while waiting to take off, it was certainly amazing to see the glider trains going over the aerodrome, all with navigation lights on and appearing at first like an airborne flare path. These continued throughout the night, at times so low that people taking off had to fly under them. One could not but feel proud of being part of so inspiring and colossal an operation.'

'5/6 Jun 44. The night of D-1 was not as good as had been hoped, with considerable cloud at about 2-3,000 feet over England and the Landing Areas. The moon was full however and the visibility excellent below cloud. The first person off was Flying Officer Hedgecoe at 2235 hours who had the furthest distance to go to the Argentan-Bernay line where he was due to start patrolling at 2345 hours. He was relieved by Flight Lieutenant Cleaver while the last patrol on this line was by Flight Lieutenant Nowell. All had uneventful patrols over 10/10 cloud.

'Captain Ree was next off at 2240 hours to set course for the Vire-Argentan patrol, but he had to return early due to his AI breaking down. His place was taken by Flight Lieutenant Houghton who scrambled at 2330 hours and who was relieved by Flight Lieutenant Thomas. They also had uneventful patrols with nobody taking any interest in them at all. The first patrol on the line from Pavilly to Bernay was flown by Wing Commander Miller who was relieved by Captain Weisteen who was the only person to have any joy at all. He had six visuals but all were friendly and consisted of four Mitchells and two Dakotas. Flight Lieutenant Phillips did the last patrol here and had nothing to report.

'The final patrol line, that from Pavilly through Dieppe and to a point 20 miles NW thereof, was first flown by Flight Lieutenant Burbridge until 0100 hours when Squadron Leader Gonsalves arrived to take over. The

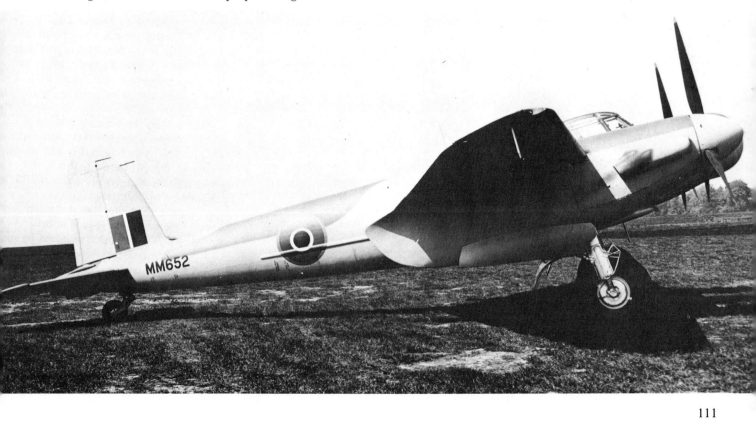

Below: A Mosquito NF XIX.

last patrol was flown by Flight Lieutenant House. All had nothing to report. Thus, although disappointed at having no combats, there was general satisfaction at having broken the ice and put all our training efforts to some use. We were no longer Freshmen.'

It was a measure of the importance of D-Day that it was the first occasion on which 85 Squadron had been given permission to risk their highly secret centimetric AI radar over enemy territory in case it fell into German hands. Having overcome that largely psychological hurdle, bomber support duties could begin in earnest on the return to Swannington. There were still a few hiccups to iron out first though.

'10/11 Jun 44. Night. Although the weather over the continent was not good, five intruder trips were sent off. Flight Lieutenant Nowell and Captain Ree went to Holland but both came back early in atrocious weather. While still about 40 miles from our coast, Captain Ree suddenly heard cannon fire and doing a very tight turn saw another Mosquito making an attack on him. It was still fairly light so there seemed little excuse for faulty recognition. Fortunately the aircraft sustained no damage and, on landing, subsequent inquiry showed that a member of 25 Squadron at Coltishall was the attacker. We were all glad that he was such a bad shot.'

The first 'kill' over enemy territory was not long in coming.

'11-12/6/44. Night. Tonight we had our first success in Bomber Command and as was fitting the enemy aircraft was destroyed by Wing Commander Miller. His report reads: 'While patrolling Melun airfield, height 3,000 feet, an aircraft was illuminated by searchlight and fired off enemy recognition signals. Turning towards this position, contact was obtained. A visual was obtained and the aircraft was recognised as an Me 110, the long range tanks being of great help in recognition. After a five second burst the 110 caught fire and exploded on the ground.' A note to the report added: 'It is suggested that enemy recognition signals and searchlights in the neighbourhood of airfields might prove profitable sources for contacts.' This was later proved.

Operations over enemy territory had many new implications for a Squadron that had previously stayed close to England.

'14/6/44. Today we had a rather long but interesting lecture on "Escaping from Germany" by a Flight Sergeant of Bomber Command who had made the trip after baling out of a Halifax. He had walked most of the way and then stolen a bicycle. The point which was most strongly felt by all was the real need to be pretty fit in case such an emergency arose, for very few of the audience

I feel sure could have walked through Germany on a full stomach let alone an empty one.'

But while the Germans still occupied France and the Low Countries, much of the action for 85 was nearer home.

'15/16 Jun 44. Night. Bomber Command sent out some 700 heavies tonight to bomb French targets once more so the aerodromes we patrolled were in Belgium and France. Warrant Officer Alderton did a Freshman to Brussels-Le Culot but was very severely shot at because he first flew over Brussels, then Antwerp, and finally over Ghent in his efforts to get away. He then came back, no longer a Freshman.

'The night's activity was not entirely profitless for Squadron Leader Gonsalves at long last broke his duck much to everyone's joy. While patrolling St Trond airfield* contact was obtained, and the aerodrome was then lit up. Contact was followed in a wide orbit of the circuit and at 2,000 feet from well below the aircraft was idetified as an Me 110 with long range tanks. Two bursts blew up the starboard engine and the aircraft crashed in the dispersal area of the field. A further contact was obtained a few minutes later, head on. A hard starboard turn brought the contact in again at 4,000 feet. It was recognised as a further Me 110. A long burst produced a concentration of strikes on the port wing but no fire. In view of the point of aim this struck the pilot as being rather odd so he pulled up to have another look at it, but the aircraft was diving and the contact was lost in the ground returns. Claims one Me 110 destroyed and one Me 110 damaged.

'We were naturally encouraged by this start and the defensive bogey was not only scotched but forgotten. What then was our dismay when a still small voice from North London whispered "Don't forget the Diver". At this critical moment we were snatched from our job of putting "round holes into square heads" and our status was shamefully, and I think unjustifiably, reduced to that of airborne ack-ack.'†

The cause of this outburst was the appearance over London of the V-1 flying bomb, and while the Squadron tried to keep a training programme going in readiness for

*St Trond then housed IV Gruppe of Nachtjagdgeschwader 1, commanded by Hauptmann Heinz Wolfgang Schnaufer. Known as 'The Spook of St Trond', Schnaufer was the ace of the Luftwaffe night fighter arm following the death of Oberstleutnant Helmut Lent, and as Schnaufer's men were a particular thorn in the side of Bomber Command, St Trond came in for its fair share of attention from 85.

† *A Short History of 85 Squadron in 100 Group*; author unkown; 8 May 1945.

Bomber Support,* most crews were temporarily re-assigned to try to shoot down V-1s in the air because the Mk X AI radar was accurate enough to detect flying bombs. 'The system of Anti-Diver patrols was to send one aircraft per hour to do a "joint" patrol with an aircraft from 157 Sqn. The aircraft made their own way to Manston and were then directed by Sandwich or Warring Ground Control radar to within AI or visual sighting distance of the flying bomb. The fighter was then left to continue its own interception.

'Captain Weisteen destroyed the first flying bomb for the Squadron. In view of the great speed of these missiles, around 360mph,† it was necessary to patrol at some 4,000 or 5,000 feet above the average height of the bomb, which was 2,000 feet. Thus cloud bases below 4,000 feet made chasing impossible. The most successful method of attack was found to be by the crossing flight technique, finally turning in on the flying bomb's course about a mile behind it with some two or three thousand feet in hand, giving an overtaking speed in the dive. Range was assessed by AI readings, about 200 yards being the most satisfactory range for firing.

'A further method of interception was to fly head-on to the target thereby assessing its course. This was followed by a hard turn on to reciprocal during which time the visual was lost. By turning on to the bomb's course and diving, it was then possible to obtain another visual and close on the dive. It was found though that if the fighter turned on to the target's course more than a mile behind it, it was practically impossible to close in to a suitable firing range. Thus by use of these various methods it was hoped to destroy a good percentage of flying bombs.'

The Squadron was moved back to West Malling for a time in response to a plea from HQ Air Defence of Great Britain (Fighter Command by another name) for greater control over the Anti-Diver patrols. The Squadron destroyed 33 'whizzers' by the end of August whereupon they returned to Swannington on 29 August. 'Not pleased to leave West Malling but pleased to be finished with "doodle-bugging".'

'On return we had once more to brush up on our navigation and AI, but after six days condensed training we accompanied the Main Force bombers to Karlsruhe on 6 September. Our first briefing in the new Operations Briefing Room was most impressive and became the standard method of briefing while we remained at Swannington. The entire night's operation by Bomber Command was depicted on the huge wall map. Coloured tapes were pinned to the map showing the route to be followed by Main Force bombers; while tape denoted the route to the target and black the return route; diversionary raids, that is, secondary and spoof raids, were also shown with tapes, usually of red and blue.

'Our patrol points were indicated by flat-headed pins with the numbers 85 or 157 on them. Group would allocate them to the squadrons en bloc and the Squadron and Flight Commanders would assemble before briefing to sort out each patrol separately for the individual crews. German fighter assembly beacons were shown by black-headed pins. All sorts of other relevant information was available — the disposition of searchlights and flak belts, for example — and all was presented in a manner easy to digest.*

'While we always aimed at complete flexibility in our tactics,' wrote the author of *Short History of 85 Squadron in 100 Group,* 'we concentrated on high flying. Flying high we had the added perk of witnessing night after night the most stupendous avalanche of fireworks that made the pre-war Crystal Palace and Blackpool Illuminations rolled into one look like a damp squib. From then on we never looked back.'

85 stood a better chance in high night flying once its aircraft were fitted with *Monica.* The Mk X AI was very good so far as it went but it could only scan forward, and if the Squadron hoped to achieve any great success as bomber protectors their crews had to be capable of detecting the Luftwaffe from all directions. Monica was designed to fill the gap and provided adequate warning of aircraft behind.

As individual Mosquitos were modified with Monica, the Squadron was quick to put it through its paces. 'The instrument is not designed to indicate the whereabouts of a pursuing aircraft, merely to indicate its presence. It was found that indications from 45° to port or starboard gave the best ranges (up to 12,000 feet), while from dead astern the range was seriously reduced, in some cases to as little as 2,500 feet. However, it was felt that as most people wouldn't be flying straight and level anyway, it was not too great a drawback.

* Between 1/2 and 19/20 July for example, No 85 found time to mount 28 Bomber Support missions.

† Squadron Mosquitos were given stub exhausts and engine boost pressure was adjusted to allow the use of 150-octane fuel so that they could reach 360mph too. Noses were strengthened to cope with the extra turn of speed and, with the exception of the exhaust shrouds, all these modifications were retained when the Mosquitos returned to Bomber Support.

Night Flyer, Lewis Brandon, Kimber (William) & Co Ltd, 1961.

'The best method for converting backward to forward contacts was found to be a steady weave, increasing in violence until the pursuer was at a range of 4,000 feet or so and well out to one side. At this point a steep turn in the right direction usually produced a good contact at about 9,000 feet range.'

Not that the conversion of Monica warnings to visual attacks was at all easy.

'Intruder Raid Report
15/16 Sept 1944
High Level

Mosq XIX
Pilot F/Lt Cleaver
Nav W/O Nairn

Arrived at enemy coast 0026 (4mins ahead of ETA) decided to go out again to lose time and to gain height. Made landfall again 00.30 when Monica warned 4,000ft range. Mosquito turned to port and hard turn starboard but unable to get a contact and Monica contact lost. Straightened out again and Monica warned again 6,000ft. Mosquito whipped round again but unable to get AI contact. Straightened out and the entire performace was repeated another couple of times. Cross coast once more approx 0045 when Monica warned minimum range. Mosquito did peel-off to port and then whipped round but unable to get contact. Another attempt made to cross coast but position this time uncertain and unable to pinpoint so returned to base.'

If all this smacks of groping in the dark, then that is the right impression. World War II was the first 'boffins' war with one side mounting a threat, the other countering it, the first responding with a counter counter-threat, and so on. Thus the RAF, being the foremost recipient of technological innovation, was constantly having to adapt and change its approach and techniques. However, although 'boffins' could produce black boxes and better aircraft, there were no 'experts' back home who knew best how to use them in battle. 85 were the experts and higher authority looked to them to determine how they should go about their business rather than the other way round. Consequently the early days of bomber support were a period of trial and error to determine how best to use the new aircraft and equipment to search out and destroy the enemy.

Right: Report of a bomber support mission flown by Squadron Leader Burbridge and Flight Lieutenant Skelton on the night of 27/28 June 1944.

S/Ldr. Burbridge
F/Lt Skelton
Biped 51:
Mosquito XIX (Mk X AI) VY-B

BOMBER SUPPORT *27/28th June, 1944*

We made rendezvous with the bombers at 02.30 hours at 5000 N - 0030 E.

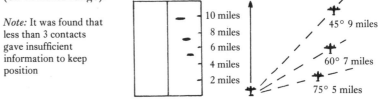

1. We found that we were on the right hand side of the bomber stream (all AI Contacts being to port): we thought it best to be on the left hand side, and therefore turned to port and crossed below.

2. We were able to keep position without difficulty, steering a DR Course at approximately 6 miles from the edge of the bomber stream. Here is a rough sketch of the B Scope and its interpretation: (on 10 miles range):-

Note: It was found that less than 3 contacts gave insufficient information to keep position

10 miles
8 miles
6 miles
4 miles
2 miles

45° 9 miles
60° 7 miles
75° 5 miles

3. The usual procedure of orbiting (in this case to port) to avoid overtaking, owing to our higher speed was adopted.

4. It is preferable, with AI Mk X, to keep about 1,000 feet below the stream. This eliminates ground returns and gives full 10 miles range. The estimated height of the stream was 15,000 feet: we therefore flew at 14,000 feet.

5. The expected direction of Hun fighter contacts is from side furthest from the stream. This may be a bit unreliable when near the target area, as some bombers may have arrived a little early and orbited: they then turn and run up from a direction out of the stream, thus giving a false impression (we chased one such, identifying same as a Lancaster over the target).

6. When chasing this Lancaster we were involved in a sea of Window. In this field it would be extremely difficult, if at all possible, to pick out an aircraft. However, this would presumably not arise to anything like the same extent if one were still positioned on the stream

7. If it is intended to patrol the target area after the bombers have passed, one should keep a patrol line clear of the steam and/or the Window, so that the remainder of the tube is kept more or less clear for picking out Hun fighter contacts. (Note: fighters patrolling on the up-wind side should conceivably have a better time.)

8. It will be appreciated that if the fighter hangs about at the target, the steam will get ahead on the return journey: this should not be done if protection from fighters being fed into stream is still required. (We, last night, got well behind the stream by reason of returning to investigate two separate areas where aircraft were seen to crash.) Window was still seen all the way out to the Enemy Coast.

Pilot (signed) B. A. Burbridge S/L
Navigator (signed) F. S. Skelton F/L

The conclusion drawn from missions such as this was that fighters could not stick like glue continually to the bomber streams at night. There were two reasons for this. 'One was the considerable difference in the speeds of bombers and night fighters and the consequent difficulty in maintaining station. The second and more important reason was that the main object for a Bomber Support fighter must be to destroy the enemy night fighters before they come near the bomber steam and lose themselves in it. Even with Mark X AI it would be impossible to pick out a German night fighter from a mass of British bombers who would probably be dropping Window. It was therefore necessary to throw a screen of fighters around the bombers' target and indeed, if possible, around the whole bomber route over enemy territory.

'The screen of fighters would operate at about the same height or slightly below the bombers' height, in order to intercept enemy night fighters climbing up on their way to attack the bombers. Patrol points for the Bomber Support fighters would be about 40 miles or eight minutes' flying time from our main bomber stream, so that once AI contact was obtained on an aircraft, the interception had to be brought to a swift conclusion. In other words, less than eight minutes must pass between the original contact, the chase, the visual, the identification and the destruction of the aircraft if it were hostile.'

No 85 was also to mount standing patrols over enemy territory, watching and waiting for the opposition around its beacons or airfields.

'We arrived at our patrol starting point,' wrote Flight Lieutenants Kendall and Hill in their Intruder Personal Combat Report for 12/13 September 1944, 'and turned on to our first patrol line. We got a head on contact in the vicinity of Limburg, range 9,000 feet. We turned in behind and followed the enemy aircraft round. It did two complete orbits well above us. We climbed with the aircraft on AI up to 17,000 feet. The enemy aircraft then levelled out on a course of 045°. We closed in and obtained a visual at 1,500 feet on a bright exhaust. Closing in to 50 yards and below we identified the aircraft as a single engine fighter with in-line exhausts, identified as an Me 109G. Dropped back to 75 yards and opened fire dead astern with one 3-4 second burst. Enemy aircraft blew up. Wreckage flew back past us. We peeled to port and saw enemy aircraft going down enveloped in flames. We took a cine camera shot of the aircraft as it went down. It burnt on the ground for a short while after impact.

'We continued towards Frankfurt where the bombing was seen to be going well. Large fires were noticed. Returned to base and landed at 0050 hours.'

Anything that moved was fair game on these patrols.

'Patrolled Gütersloh airfield from 0035. No lights, no activity. At 0055 a train was seen on the Hamm-Bielefeld railway just W of Rheda station going NE. Went down to 800 feet and attacked train, firing a medium length burst. Train stopped after this but resumed journey at about 0105. Mosquito was orbiting in area. Saw train leave Rheda and attacked again from 800 feet. Port quarter strikes were seen near centre of train. One train claimed as "damaged".'*

The Squadron prided itself on the fact that 'our crews always aimed at complete flexibility in our tactics.' Being roaming agents let loose on their own inside enemy airspace, with no ground control or massed formations for guidance and protection, it was important that Squadron crews were given a large measure of tactical freedom because they fell or prospered wholly by their own devices. But freedom necessitated something in return from crews if it was not to degenerate into wasteful lack of achievement, and the best night fighters were invariably those crews who worked together as a dedicated, intelligent and purposeful team. After the departure of Cunningham and Rawnsley, the most famous night fighter pair on 85 was 'Branse' Burbridge and 'Bill' Skelton.

Acting Squadron Leader Bransome Arthur Burbridge was born in 1921 at East Dulwich and, like Flight Lieutenant Frank Seymour Skelton, was commissioned from the ranks. Both men had first served on 85 Squadron back in October 1941 and January 1942 respectively, but they did not stay long on Havocs and they only 'crewed up' together when they returned for their second tour on the Squadron in July 1943. From the beginning, and for over 100 operational missions, they worked together with perfect understanding. Their first success was an Me410, which they shot down on 22/23 February 1944, and after that they never looked back. Five times they had to fly home on one engine and on one occassion their Mosquito was hit and caught fire over Hamburg, but Burbridge, by means of some expert flying skill and not a little luck, managed to put out the fire and limp home. Four times they destroyed two enemy aircraft during a single patrol, but their most famous achievement occurred on 4/5 November. That night eight Squadron crews patrolled at points around the Ruhr as Bomber Command aimed for Bochum, Hamburg and Wilhelmshaven: Burbridge and Skelton were one of the eight, and their

*2/3 October 1944 Intruder Raid Report by Flt Lt Phillips and Flt Lt Smith.

Intruder Raid Report signal not only laconically described their own success but also painted a pen picture of the melee over the target area.

'Airborne Swannington 1731hrs. Down 2223hrs.

Patrolled 1848/2100hrs.

1904 5040N 0750E (30 miles E of Bonn). 15,000ft contact 4mls range starboard/port same height. Closed to 1,500ft. Vis identified with night glasses as JU 88. Closed to 400ft. 2 short bursts. Port engine caught fire and E/A dived down and exploded at position approx 5040N 0740E.

1930 Set course for Bochum and patrolled to 6 miles N Koln. On turning on reciprocal greenish white flares seen over Koln and investigated. No contact. Resumed patrol leg.

1930 SE Koln 15,000ft. Aircraft seen to crash in target area.

1932 ESE Koln 15,000ft. Aircraft seen to crash in target area.

1940 ENE Koln 15,000ft. Aircraft seen to crash in target area.

1950 E Koln 15,000ft. Aircraft seen to crash WNW Koln.

1953 SE Koln 15,000ft. Contact 4 miles 30 degrees starboard slightly below. Chased for 10mins on SWly course with violent evasion jinking and diving. Closed to 1,200ft. Height 7,000ft. Identified at 800ft as JU 88. Short burst at 500ft range. Strikes and bright flash from port engine and visual lost. Contact regained and visual at 1,200ft. Height 3,000ft. Closed to 500ft. Height 2,000ft. Short burst with same results and visual lost below. Still on SWly course at 2002hrs. Position approx 5 miles SE Bonn airfield.

2005 Aircraft seen to explode on ground at position approx 5035N 0710E.

2007 Aircraft seen to explode on ground at position approx 5030N 0700E. Set course to rejoin bomber withdrawal route at Duren at 8,000ft. Flying on course of bomber route recognition signals seen fired 25 miles E. Set course to investigate diving and increasing speed. Red perimeter lights of an airfield sighted with aircraft landing. Snap contact and fleeting visual of aircraft above and head on.

2029 Hangelar 1,500ft. Contact 2 miles 60 degrees starboard same height. Turned in behind round south of airfield. Closed rapidly to 1,000ft. Vis identification of ME 110 from beneath. Dropped back and fired short burst from 500ft. Fuselage burst into flames and E/A crashed in river N of airfield at 2032hrs.

2037 Hangelar 1,500ft. Contact 2 miles 60 degrees starboard. Turned in behind and target made an orbit of perimeter as though to land E/W. Closed to 1,500ft and identified as JU 88 flying NNW from airfield. Short burst at 600ft. The whole fuselage exploded and E/A dived to starboard and crashed at position 1 mile N of airfield at 2040hrs. By this time intruder warnings were being fired from airfields in the vicinity. Set course base 2100hrs. Coasted out Blankenberg 2144hrs 2,000ft.'

And Squadron Leader Burbridge achieved all this with just 200 rounds of ammunition.

Christened 'The Night Hawk Partners' by the popular press, Burbridge and Skelton 'bagged' twenty enemy aircraft for which they received a DSO and bar and DFC apiece. Branse got one more Ju 88 after Bill Skelton was posted, bringing his final score to 21 confirmed kills, two probables and one damaged, thereby making him the RAF's most successful night fighter pilot. This achievement was even more remarkable in that 16 of Burbridge and Skelton's kills were achieved the hard way — deep in the heart of enemy territory.

'I asked,' wrote James Lansdale Hodson, a reporter who visited Swannington, 'the reasons for Burbridge and Skelton's great success. (It is advisable to speak of them as one.) The answer was: Intelligence. They know before they set out precisely where they will be at a certain time. They carry a picture in their head of the whole night's operation . . . the various bomber streams, times, targets. They try to read the enemy mind . . . they visualise at what time he will discover what is happening, how far he will be misled, what he will do, what airfields he will use, what times he will rise, whither he will fly, what his tactics will be. They act accordingly. If one expectation fails, they know which next to try. After they had shot down three on the night they shot down four, Burbridge said: "Time we were starting for home, Bill." To which Skelton replied: "Well, if you like, but I've got another Hun for you." They went round after him and destroyed him too. Then they had a further look round, "But", says Burbridge's combat report, "we found no joy and presumed we had outstayed our welcome."

'How far having "cat's eyes" is accountable for success is hard to say. Keenness, good shooting, eagerness to read "the gen" in the squadron Intelligence Library . . . all these are of high importance. But certainly good eyes are essential. Some pilots can see much further than others. The Wing Commander (and I think he was serious) said you can see an object better sometimes when you don't look straight at it but look ten degrees to right or left. Another trick is to get below it and see it against a lighter, different piece of sky or cloud. The Station Commander said: "I now use that dodge when finding my car on a dark night".'

How did an outsider like Hodson view the personnel at Swannington? 'The men struck me as lively . . . not quite so lively perhaps as men who fly single-engined fighters by day, not so given to coloured scarves and flying boots with maps stuck down the side, but livelier than the heavy bomber pilots (though there are a few of the latter among them, men who have done fifty trips in Halifaxes or Lancasters and now prefer this job to training men). It may sound (and be) absurd to suggest that these night fighter men are betwixt and between the other two sorts, but that's how it struck me. They've got humour. They fly Mosquitos armed with cannon which one successful but satirical pilot calls his "plywood pantechnicon". The pilot, who does the shooting, and the navigator who works the "magic boxes" and is the brains of the craft, sit side by side. There isn't half an inch to spare in the cockpit. They talk of being contortionists. "I've a permanent scar on my head from getting into my plane," a six-foot navigator told me. He added: "Your body learns to accommodate itself to all the projections." They say all these things with wry humour. The atmosphere was cheerful. I think you could say they enjoy the job. They are on top of it and on top of the enemy.

'Bailing out from a Mosquito isn't easy. The escape hatch is a small door on the right which you jettison. To get through it head first with your harness on requires determination and agility. A navigator who tried in November at first failed but was spurred on by a more incisive command from the pilot plus a lot of smoke and fumes in the cockpit. He says that the creditable impression of Dante's inferno behind him made that hatch now look positively cavernous. "The chance of being guillotined by the starboard propeller was dimmed by the flames." But they are not all as light hearted as this. Most combat reports are straightforward accounts of a workmanlike job portraying the steady determination of the men who write them.'

It was these workmanlike men who made a squadron, and for every 'ace' who was great or lucky enough to make the headlines there were dozens who lived and fought outside the spotlight of public acclaim.

'4/12/44. Five new crews arrived from 51 OTU (Cranfield) today. They are Squadron Leader H. A. G. Smith (Pilot) and Sergeant R. Hamilton (N/R), Flight Lieutenant F. D.

Win (Pilot) (New Zealand) and Flying Officer T. P. Ryan (N/R) (New Zealand), Flight Lieutenant B. Bonakis (Pilot) and Sergeant R. S. Garland (N/R), who go to "B" Flight: the remainder, Flight Lieutenant C. W. Turner (Pilot) and Flight Sergeant G. Honeyman (N/R), Flying Officer G. R. Night (Pilot) and Flight Sergeant J. J. A. McCormick (N/R) are to go to "A" Flight. Squadron Leader Smith has previously done a tour on Whitleys with 51 Squadron: Flight Lieutenant Win completed a tour with Coastal Command (614 Squadron) and his navigator, Flying Officer Ryan, a tour with 488 (NF) Squadron. Flight Lieutenant Turner did his first tour as an air gunner with 48 Squadron on Hampdens before training as a pilot and becoming a flying instructor. Flight Lieutenant Bonakis has been instructing in America and in Training Command. Flying Officer Night was in a Canadian Coastal Squadron and also instructed in Canada. All the NCOs are straight from training except Flight Sergeant McCormick who was on 157 Squadron for a short time. Warrant Officer Grimstone DFM, was also posted in today. He completed his first tour with 85 Squadron since when he has been instructing at 51 OTU (Cranfield).'

One such member of the Squadron was Jimmy Chipperfield from the circus family. The war had been a disaster for the Chipperfields commercially and Jimmy, because of his single kidney, could have avoided active service altogether but he wanted to make some contribution to the war effort. 'At first I had no luck. I tried to enrol in the Army, and was thrown out. I tried the Navy, fancying a career in submarines, but was thrown out of that too. Then I took a longer look at the RAF. The thought of becoming a pilot thrilled me, and I set my heart on getting into the air. Medical considerations apart, there was one major snag: the fact that I knew no mathematics, having

Above: An Me 110 bites the dust at the hands of Burbridge and Skelton at 17,000 feet near Wurzburg on the night of 21/22 November 1944. The enemy aircraft's fuselage is exploding after a second burst of cannon fire. Burbridge and Skelton then flew on to dispose of a Ju 88 over Bonn aerodrome after the German pilot, mistakenly under the impression that he was in friendly airspace, flashed his downward identification lights, fired a flare, and then switched on his navigation lights before coming in to land. The episode was regarded by the Squadron Intelligence Officer as 'a very good counter to enemy morale.' *Crown Copyright*

never learnt anything except the most basic arithmetic. At that stage, however, the Air Force was running a recruiting campaign with a poster which advertised "Three Months to Brush Up Your Maths", and I reckoned that if they gave me three months, I should be able to learn enough. I based my hopes on my father's philosophy which had been drummed into me all my life — that you can do anything if you really put your mind to it.'*

He was passed medically fit for service, largely because he had the forethought to send the RAF some photographs of himself, stripped to the waist and bulging with muscles — wrestling a bear, and he soon got to grips with the mathematics of navigation and triangular velocities. 'It was hard work, all right, but the concentration was exactly the same as I had needed when training wild animals or learning a new act in the circus (like walking the wire); and now, as soon as I saw the application of maths, the whole thing became both an exciting challenge and a joy.'

Then Chipperfield went through pilot training on Oxfords at Cranwell where he was awarded his wings and did an old-fashioned clown act at the party afterwards. He left Cranwell as a Pilot Officer to convert to twin-engined aircraft at Grantham, before going to the Charter Hall OTU outside Edinburgh to fly Beaufighters. From there he should have gone to Burma but the posting was changed at the last moment and he found himself on 85 as the new boy. There he crewed up with Jimmy Stockley and, having converted himself on the oldest, most clapped-out Mosquito they could spare, Chipperfield found nocturnal bomber support fascinating.

'The Squadron would take-off together, but once we were airborne we would separate and head for our allocated fields. Each pilot was allowed to choose his own route over the Channel, and I generally went across at some height between nine and fifteen thousand feet . . . As we approached the coast I would try to pick the blackest-looking spot, away from any lights that were showing; but no matter where we crossed the shore, guns would open up from all sides. Because of the engine-noise in the cockpit, I generally wore head-phones throughout the flight, and in them we would pick up the howl of the direction-finding radar. As the beams swept back and forth, hunting us, the sound would come and go, come and go, with a wow-wow-wow kind of undulation; but as soon as the operator got a fix on us the noise changed to a steady, penetrating yowl that went right through our heads. At the same moment, the searchlights would blaze on and the guns would start. I had a simple system for dealing with the lights; whenever one caught us I used to dive straight down the beam. Whether it made the aircraft any less conspicuous, I am not sure, but at least it enabled us to work up a tremendous speed — and that alone made us feel better . . .

'Our reception when we arrived over the fighter airfields was entirely different. Almost always, as soon as they became aware of us, the defenders would lie doggo, putting out every light in the place and evidently hoping that they could bluff us into thinking the airfield was a dummy, or that we had come to the wrong place. They hardly ever fired at us, and we were not allowed to fire at them, especially in Holland, because we knew that there were Dutch workers on the airfields. Our job was merely to sit there above them and do circuits at exactly the same height and speed for the alloted time, at the end of which — to the minute — another aircraft would arrive to replace us. But although the role was mainly passive, several members of our squadron caught German fighters coming in . . .

'Once, on one of my first intruder missions, our target airfield was Leeuwarden,* on the Dutch coast. Jimmy Stockley found it easily enough, but the place was absolutely dark and quiet, and after we had been going round for half an hour he said he reckoned the field was a dummy. I said to him: "Well — when we arrived here you seemed very sure it was the right place — and in any case, we can't leave now. But I tell you what I'll do. When one hour's up I'll get back a little and make a pass along the runway, and we can have a proper look."

'This we did. The runway lay at right angles to the sea, and I drew away inland a little to dive at it from the landward end, so that if anything happened we could shoot stright out over the water.

'The second we reached the end of the runway, every light on the airfield blazed on, and every gun opened up. Tracer came streaking over us from all sides like barrages of confetti. Jimmy, who had been so sure that there was nobody about, cried "Open the taps!" and I said "Don't worry — they're open!" The runway seemed a terrible length, even though we must have been doing the best part of 400mph, but luckily we were so low that the gunners could not hit us without also hitting each other, and we escaped unscathed into the friendly night — by which time Jimmy had no doubts that we were doing our job properly.'

The night of 4/5 December saw the

*My Wild Life, Macmillan Ltd, 1975.

*The home of two Gruppen of Luftwaffe night fighters.

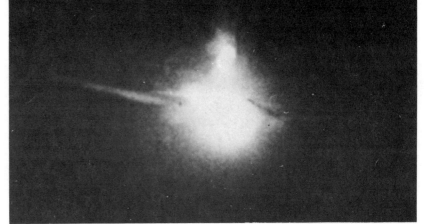

destruction of the Squadron's 100th Hun at night. Flying Officer A. J. Owen and his Nav, Flying Officer J. S. V. McAllister, got the Ju 88 concerned and this team ended the war with 15 kills to their name. There was even less Yuletide cheer for the Germans when both Burbridge and Owen went flying together.

'22/23 Dec 44. Six crews made high level patrols of the Ruhr. Flight Lieutenant Redfern returned early with oxygen trouble and Squadron Leader Burbridge destroyed another Me 110. Flying Officer Owen destroyed two Ju 88s and an Me 110. The first two were destroyed within seven minutes and in both cases the markings on the wings were clearly seen. The second chase resulted from a Monica contact. The third gave them a 15 minute chase with evasion but a short deflection burst hit the port wing and the aircraft went into a vertical dive.'

Such engagements must have had an adverse effect on Luftwaffe morale which was already taking a battering. 'The main idea behind all Bomber support operations was really to worry the German night fighters. Although a very large number of enemy fighters were shot down through these operations, the chief blow was at the morale of the German night-fighter crews. Any German night-fighter crew who managed to get airborne while his airfield was being patrolled, then made his way through the high-level patrol and found the bombers, faced up to their gunners, made his way back again through the high-level patrol, then landed at an airfield patrolled by one of our low-level fighters, could certainly be said to have earned his night-flying supper and ersatz coffee.

'A bomber shot down on or near its own base, either before or after a raid, is far more of a morale-destroyer than an aircraft "missing" after a raid.'

The Germans certainly agreed. 'Not only had we the enemy in front of us,' wrote Wilhelm Johnen,* a German night-fighter ace who finished the war in command of a night-fighting wing, 'but also in our backs. All this was a great strain on the German crews. The losses rose appallingly... The Mosquitos lived up to their name. They were the night fighters' greatest plague and wreaked havoc amongst the German crews... The Mosquitos not only pursued us in the bomber streams but, as a result of their enormous fuel capacity and endurance, waited for us as we took off from our airfields. They attacked us throughout the whole operation and interfered with our landing. It was almost a daily occurrence that shortly before divisional ops

*Duel Under the Stars, Kimber (William) & Co Ltd, 1957.

several Mosquitos would fly over the airfields and shoot down the Messerschmitts as they took off.'

The stories of bombers being shot out of the sky from nowhere must have lost nothing in the telling around the Luftwaffe and must have tightened already stretched nerves to breaking point.

'15/16 March 1945. Closed in below contact to 200 feet. Observer checked identification with night glasses and Ju 88 recognised. Dropped back to 600 feet astern, level, and fired a two second burst. Strikes seen between fuselage and port engine. Fired another long burst. There was an explosion and the port engine burst into flames. Observer, who was watching through night glasses while Mosquito closed in to fire a third burst, saw one member of the Ju 88's crew bale out from below the middle of the fuselage. A third burst was fired from 600 feet range and there was a bright explosion in the fuselage of the E/A. Observer saw two other crew members abandoning A/C in quick succession before pilot could fire the fourth burst which was intended to stop this happening. It is felt, however, that their morale will have been considerably impaired by the experience.'

Neither did spoof raids help matters for the Luftwaffe. On a night when a big Bomber Command raid was intended for a particular target, 100 Group would mount one or more decoy raids elsewhere. These would be co-ordinated in time with the main attack but the countermeasures aircraft would head on widely diverging courses and drop Window as hard as they could in order that all the raids would appear to be of equal strength. Thus the German controllers would have great difficulty in determining how best to deploy their fighters, and 85 accompanied the spoofers as well as the main force to deal with any German fighters seduced up the garden path.

'12/13 December 1944. A heavy bomber attack on Essen and a "spoof" raid on Osnabruck entailed 9 crews who carried out high-level patrols in the Ruhr. Squadron Leader Burbridge destroyed a Ju 88 and an Me 110. He saw one of the crew bale out of

Above: Flying Officer Owen captures the last moments of a Ju 88 on his cine gun camera. This was the Squadron's 100th kill at night. *Crown Copyright*

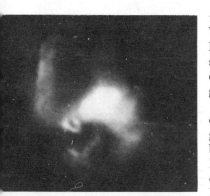

Top: The end of Flight Lieutenant Goucher's Ju 88. *Crown Copyright*

Above centre: Burbridge and Skelton dispose of a Ju 88 on 2 January 1945. *Crown Copyright*

Above: Win and Ryan's kill! *Crown Copyright*

Right: Menu for the dinner given to celebrate the Squadron's 250th kill of the war. The Party was held in the NAAFI on 14 February 1945 and many past and present members of the Squadron attended. 'It was unfortunate and unavoidable that many of the present aircrew and their associated ground crews could not attend because they were on operations, but for the remainder a good time was had by all.' However, by then the 250th kill was back in the past — to date the squadron had actually destroyed 270 aircraft of which 126 had been by night.

the Ju 88; the Me 110 crashed two miles West of the Essen fires. Flight Lieutenant Hedgecoe also destroyed two Me 110s and saw four V-2 rockets launched during his eventful patrol. Captain Fossum also did good work in destroying a Ju 88.'

The German night fighter's lot was not eased when 85 Squadron Mosquitos were given Perfectos, a device which gave a bearing from the enemy's IFF transmissions. In addition, by 1945, the Luftwaffe was crippled physically as well as mentally. Harried from all sides without respite by day and night, increasingly deprived of adequate warning and alert time as the Allied advance occupied more and more of its early warning radar stations, and throttled by shortages of aircraft, skilled men, spares and aviation fuel, those German aircraft that continued to fly were often lambs to the slaughter. 'Our job used to be a piece of cake,' said one Luftwaffe night fighter pilot, after he was shot down, 'but there's no future in it now.'

'1/2 Jan 45. Eight crews took part in a maximum effort in the Kiel and Ruhr areas. Flight Lieutenant R. T. Goucher at 1921 hours, after an eleven minute chase, obtained a visual on a Ju 188 which he shot down in flames after firing two bursts. The aircraft was seen to crash 10 miles north of Münster. Almost immediately after a second contact was obtained on an aircraft apparently dropping "Window". Closing in, a visual was obtained on a Ju 88G and a long burst was fired from dead astern as the aircraft made a diving turn to port. Large masses of flaming debris came back and struck the Mosquito which began to vibrate badly and lose height. The drop tanks were jettisoned and the port tank came over the top of the wing and damaged the tail plane, at the same time

shearing off the pitot head. A landing was finally made at Brussels Melsbroek after receiving instructions to bale out if height could not be maintained. Altogether a stout effort.

'3/1/45. Flight Lieutenants Goucher and Bullock returned from Brussels by Dakota and had triumphant journey across London in complete flying kit and parachutes. It has to be recorded that a London taxi driver refused an American Sergeant as a fare in their favour.'

'13/14 Feb 45. Patrols flown over widely dispersed parts of Germany, ranging from Berlin and Dresden westwards. Twelve crews flew. No hostiles but worthy of note is that not one of hundreds of bombers was brought down by enemy night fighters.'

'14/15 Feb 45. Ten crews were airborne in support of the bombers who were again attacking the Dresden and Chemnitz area. Patrols were scattered over a wide area deep inside Germany. At 2355 hours, while he was patrolling on a southerly vector at 14,000 feet alongside the bomber stream, Flight Lieutenant F. D. Win and Flying Officer T. P. Ryan (a New Zealand crew) in S for Sugar obtained a contact five miles away, below and almost head on. Turning on to the aircraft they followed it for a short time till it came to an airfield, thought to be Schwabioch/Halle, where it proceeded to orbit.

'Range was closed to 100 feet and for 10 minutes we held a "pow-wow" on the shape and position of the tailplane, fin and rudder, mainplane and the type of engine. The cupola was only faintly discernible, no exhaust flames were visible at any time, and the aircraft was without drop tanks. While closing in after the visual was first obtained

THE 250TH

menu.

Chicken Broth.

Cold Chicken & Ham - Chippolatas

Creamed Potatoes, Brussels Sprouts

Trifle & Cream

Cheese — Biscuits

SWANNINGTON — 1945

the navigator reduced the brillance of the AI, Gee and Monica. The U/V lighting was already turned well down and was not reflecting on the windscreen perspex, but as my face was glued to the windscreen for nine of the ten minutes spent at close range I should hardly have noticed it.

'When the identity of the aircraft was established as a Ju 88, I throttled back to a range of 150-200 yards, only to discover that the target became a blur again and that even with the gunsight turned well down the 88 could not be seen at all. I then further reduced the brillance of the gunsight until only the centre spot was faintly visible, aimed for the centre-section of the blur ahead, opened fire with a two-second burst and almost passed out with surprise on observing a wizard concentraion of strikes on the fuselage. Almost immediately fire broke out in the cockpit and as showers of sparks came flying back I deemed it advisable to position the Mossie to starboard to avoid the bits and pieces. Within seconds the 88 exploded and broke in half just aft of the mainplane, both sections burning fiercely. The fore section nosed sharply forward and then spun to starboard under our port wing and out of sight; the tail section fluttered down like a falling leaf. The sections finally crashed to earth two or three miles apart and still enveloped in flames.'

'This is a most satisfying victory in many ways,' declared the Squadron. 'Firstly it shows that the Hun is still to be found when he flies and that the lack of combats in the past month is not due to inefficiency. Secondly, despite the number of Gruppen alleged to be airborne it is likely that only a few (maybe only one) aircraft from each Gruppe operate. Thirdly, this is Flight Lieutenant Win's first combat since joining the Squadron, and finally, as on this night the Squadron was celebrating its 250th victory with an all ranks party, the stopping of the blank scoring days was most opportune.'

It is a measure of the efficiency of the bomber intruders, and their superiority over the Luftwaffe, that by the beginning of 1945 the two Swannington squadrons had accounted for 93 enemy aircraft for the loss of only six Mosquitos. But even at the end the Luftwaffe could still spring the odd surprise.

'I was the pilot detailed to fly with my navigator, Warrant Officer Grimstone DFM, on the night of the 14/15th March 1945,' wrote Flight Lieutenant Ian Dobie. 'We were airborne at 1912 hours from Swannington and set course. Made landfall North of the Hague at approx 1957 hours. Set course for Koblenz our height being 12,000 feet. At approx 2042 hours W/O Grimstone gave an alteration of course of 10° to port.

Immediately after making this turn the aircraft was hit by heavy flak. The starboard engine caught fire and I immediately feathered the prop. A second hit set the port engine alight. After the first hit I told W/O Grimstone to put on his parachute and after the second hit I told him to bale out. During this time I had been taking violent evasive action diving and turning to starboard. I told my navigator to bale out at about 7,000 feet. I saw W/O Grimstone get his head and shoulders out of the aircraft. The cockpit immediately filled with smoke and I could see nothing, not even my instruments. I became giddy and faint with the smoke and fumes. I then lost control, I immediately jettisoned the top hatch to try and clear the cockpit of smoke and fumes but nothing happened so I undid my straps, took off my helmet and tried to pull myself up for some air. I was half thrown out when the aircraft was on its back; I kicked myself clear, pulled the rip cord immediately, and touched the ground about two seconds later suffering no injury except being winded, deaf and finding my uniform smouldering on my right side. I did not know whether I was in enemy or friendly territory so I hid my parachute and crept around listening to see if I could hear any voices. The first voice I heard was German. I crept nearer to the centre of Kottenheim and heard two American sentries talking; I introduced myself to them and was escorted to the Officer i/c where I identified myself. I sent out a search party for W/O Grimstone but it was unsuccessful. It was not until next morning that I learnt that he had been found with this parachute open, but burnt, still attached to his body within fifty yards of the wreckage. I was told afterwards by watchers on the ground that the aircraft was seen to be out of control blazing furiously at about 500 feet. They saw it climb vertically and fall over on to its back in a sort of half loop. This must have been the moment when I managed to get clear of the aircraft.'

The Germans tried desperately to thwart the oncoming bomber streams — R/T interference in April was compared to 'heated arguments in Chinese' — and they even produced a purpose-built night fighter called the He 219 Uhu (Owl) which could meet the Mosquito on equal terms. Not that the Mosquito crew always knew what hit them when it did hit them.

'High Level Intruder Raid Report
6/7 Nov 1944   Pilot F/Lt Phillips
            Navigator F/Lt Smith
'Shortly after reaching patrol point, Monica warned and crew discovered it was almost completely U/S. Only warning at minimum ranges. This first pursuer was evaded and patrol continued. At 1920 hrs, 18,000 feet,

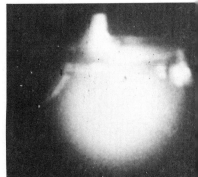

Top: Flt Lt Mellows' view of the Me 110 which he shot down on 1/2 February 1945. *Crown Copyright*

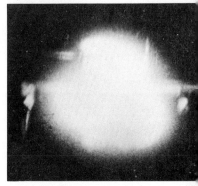

Above: Flight Lieutenant Win bags an Me 110 — 18/19 March 1945. *Crown Copyright*

Right: Flight Lieutenant H. B. Thomas DFC returning to the Squadron on 15 May 1945. Left to right: Unknown, Flight Lieutenant Patson (Senior Nav Officer), Flight Lieutenant Custance (Adjutant), Flying Officer Symons (CO's Nav), Flight Lieutenant Thomas, Major Weisteen (OC 'A' Flight), Signals Officer, Flight Lieutenant Duckett, Flying Officer Babington (Intelligence Officer).

Flight Lieutenant Thomas and his navigator, Flying Officer C. B. Hamilton, failed to return on 13 April 1945. Apparently a Lancaster, mistaking their Mosquito for an enemy aircraft, fired at them and set one engine on fire. While returning to base thus handicapped, Thomas and Hamilton were then attacked by an enemy night fighter and they were forced to abandon their aircraft. Thomas landed safely just inside the Dutch coast, from whence he was returned to Swannington, but there was no word of his navigator and it was feared that he landed in the sea and drowned.

Monica warned at minimum range. Pilot immediately commenced hard port turn and as he did so a burst of cannon shell struck Mosquito on starboard side setting fire to starboard engine and tanks. E/A did not make any further attack although Mosquito went down slowly on fire.

'The engine fire was extinguished but the propeller would not feather and the fire started again. The rudder and ailerons had been damaged by the attack or fire and the aircraft could not be turned starboard at all. Height was lost steadily and the aircraft became difficult to control.

'Crew endeavoured, but unsuccessfully, to put out the fire and prepared to abandon the aircraft. At 8,000 feet, pilot told navigator to jump. Pilot remained in A/C still trying to put out fires until cannon shells began to explode under his seat when he decided it was time to leave. Altimeter now read 4,000 feet. Pilot had no difficulty in leaving by exit door and made a successful descent into a wood.

'Both members of the crew were subsequently captured and after interrogation were imprisoned in Stalag Luft 1. At Barth until liberated by the Russians. They were finally returned to the UK on 13/5/45.'

Phillips and Smith fell foul of an He 219 but the Uhu and the jet fighters that followed it arrived too late to seriously trouble 85.

'20/21 Mar 45. Flight Lieutenant Chapman and Flight Sergeant Stockley were airborne from Swannington at 0145 hours on high level escort of bombers to Bohlen. Flight Lieutenant Chapman reports:

' "At 0255 hours just after passing Hamm on the way to escort the bomber stream, we got a Perfectos contact at 12 miles range, height 12,000 feet. Range was closed to one mile but no AI contact was obtained and the range started to increase again, so deciding that the contact must be below we did a hard turn to port down to 9,000 feet and finally homed on to the target's course at seven miles range. We closed in to six miles range and AI contact was obtained ahead and at 6 o'clock, 10° elevation. The target was climbing and we closed in rapidly and obtained a visual at 900 feet range — height was 13,000 feet. The target was still climbing straight ahead and was identified with the night glasses as an Me 110. I closed in to 600 feet and pulled up to dead astern when the Hun started to turn to port. I gave it half ring deflection and a three second burst, whereupon the E/A exploded in the port engine in a most satisfying manner, with debris flying back. It exploded on the ground at 0305 hours, 25/30 miles NW of Kassel. All this excitement was too much for the Perfectos which went U/S unfortunately, so we set course for the rendezvous with the bomber stream reaching there at 0322 hours.

' "The patrol with the bomber stream was uneventful until leaving the target when at 0400 hours at position 5045N 1215E (40 miles S of Leipzig) I noticed to port and 15 miles south a ball of yellowish flame take off and climb very rapidly (Plauen Airfield). I thought it was a flare or V-2 (a little out of position) until it started emitting a meteor tail several hundred feet long. We turned port towards it and lost height to 7,000 feet, that being the height of this phenomenon as far as I could judge, and continued watching. It travelled in a NW direction very fast and suddenly to our astonishment fired off some RPs (rocket projectiles) — four single and one pair — in the general direction of the departing bomber stream. We were pretty amazed at all this and, deciding that it must be an Me 163, I continued turning port and got behind it. It was heading 275° by this time and doing about 260mph, and using the AI to check range we closed in to 1,000 feet and visually identified a twin engined aircraft with rocket apparatus slung under the fuselage. Considerable quantities of flames and sparks were flying back preventing me from identifying the tail unit, so I decided to open fire at that range. I gave it several longish bursts as two of the cannon had stoppages and was gratified to see an explosion take place somewhere in the fuselage and debris fly back. The E/A nosed straight down through the patchy cloud and it exploded on the ground with a tremendous glare.

' "An interesting point about all this was that we could see plainly when the pilot opened up his rocket apparatus by the tremendous increase in size of the meteor tail. The E/A appeared to have a phenomenal rate of climb." ' '

Having won control of German airspace, the RAF could now make free with it.

'3/4/45. Attempts, with one or two successes have recently been made by Hun night fighters to interfere with Mosquitos on their nightly raids on Berlin. Germans believed to be using single-engined Fw 190s and Me 109s with "cat's eye" pilots. Trap laid for them this night. Only a few Pathfinder machines sent with strong escort of night fighters. Night fighters maintained radar silence almost up to Berlin to give the impression that it was usual bomber force. Plenty of searchlights but no E/A seen. The local inhabitants probably surprised to hear large number of aircraft overhead and to receive so few bombs but their disappointment (?) did not last long as usual Pathfinder force arrived shortly afterwards, when it was considered that any night fighters who had taken off would now be landing, and delivered the usual supplies.'

But 85 Squadron never underestimated the enemy, and up to the very end they were trying to learn lessons and perfect their techniques still further.

'17/18 April 1945. Wing Commander Davison* reports:

' "We were detailed to patrol Schleissmein and Fursten-Feldbrueck airfields in the Munich area in support of the raid on Cham by 5 Group ... We had not long been on patrol when we obtained a Perfectos contact at 30 miles. We overshot this target but the Perfectos remained and we soon again obtained AI contact at two and a half miles. He began to increase range and was well

above. I followed him using 2,850 revs and 18lbs boost and could just hold him though we lost ground when climbing. After about ten minutes we seemed to be closing very slightly but the temperatures were a little alarming. About ten miles before reaching the target the Hun switched off his IFF according to our Perfectos. He also reduced speed and levelled out. From then on it was like a practice AI, and we closed in and identified positively as a Ju 88.

' "I then pulled up and fired a two second burst, and immediately saw concentrated strikes inboard of the port engine. This was followed by a small white explosion and a hunk of the enemy aircraft, about the size of a Mosquito cockpit door, flew past. No fire or disintegration unfortunately resulted and the enemy aircraft went into a screeching port diving turn which I tried to follow but could not pursue without going out of control. We continued to turn as steeply as possible but obtained no further contact." ' '

The Wing Commander's comments on this engagement were very refreshing.

'1. It is quite unforgivable not to destroy a sitting target.

'2. This is a clear case where the Navigator Radar should be able to score a "confirmed visual" which only failed to be a confirmed destroyed by the inexperience of his pilot.

'3. It is remarkable that at this stage in the war, a Ju 88, re-engined of course but of prewar design, should outclimb and almost outpace "the fastest aircraft in the world".

'4. It might be of value to dissuade the Americans from discussing over the radio:

(a) Bottle Parties

(b) Interference on the Radar tube

(c) Approaching friendly bombers.'

But by May it was all over.

'7 May 1945. Day. In view of the lack of flying activity, permission was obtained to carry out "navigational exercises" over the Ruhr district in order that crews might obtain some idea of the damage that had been done there. In consequence, six crews set off in the morning on trips that lasted four and a half hours as a rule. All were amazed at the degree of devastation and were unanimous in their opinion that the photographs gave no indication of the complete destruction that did exist. It was while over the Ruhr and listening to the BBC over his VHF set that Wing Commander Davison heard a broadcast to the German people in Germany to the effect that Admiral Doenitz had agreed to the unconditional surrender to the Allied Armies of all German Armed Forces. The Wing Commander hurried back to base with the news that had been so eagerly awaited for days.

'The official broadcast of the news was not until 2000 hours. By this time the Squadron

*Wing Commander Miller became medically unfit for flying on 15 October 1944 and had to relinquish command of 85. It was a pity because he had hoped to make flying his future career, and his place was taken by the 'B' Flight Commander, Squadron Leader F. S. Gonsalves DSO, DFC. 'Gon' as he was known to everybody, had first joined 85 as a Flying Officer having learned to fly with de Havilland's at Hatfield before the war. Like many others he came back to 85 for a second tour and he was promoted to Wing Commander on 8 November. 'Gon' was posted in January 1945 and his place was taken by Wg Cdr K. Davison.

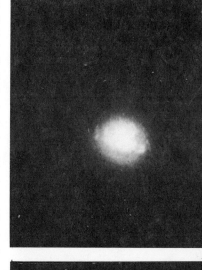

Top: 20 March 1945 — the end of a German jet fighter.
Crown Copyright

Above: Thomas and Hamilton record the demise of another Ju 88 — 8 April 1945.
Crown Copyright

Right: Cologne, as shattered by Bomber Command, photographed by Captain Fossum and Flying Officer Hider from their Mosquito as they did a Cook's Tour over Germany. *Crown Copyright*

Below: Remains of a V-1 flying bomb site in Holland, May 1945.

Bottom: Duren, between Cologne and Aachen, which once had the misfortune to house a German Army Brigade HQ.

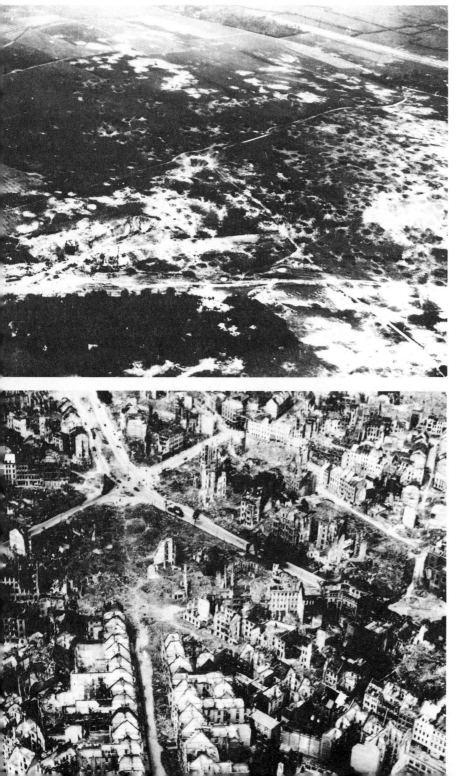

in variously decorated cars were already ranging through the countryside bent on suitable merry-making. It was generally agreed that our celebration of the peace was as successful as the part we played in winning it. Night. Night flying did not take place!'

'8 May. TODAY IS VE DAY. The first of two days' holiday granted at the conclusion of the war in Europe and the complete defeat of the Germans. All aircraft were grounded and the day was given over to individual celebration. Initiative in this direction was shown by everyone. In the evening the Sergeants came up to the Officers' Mess and brought the larger part of the neighbouring villagers with them, who finished off all the beer while the children revelled in "pop" and lemonade. Later all the parties gathered around a bonfire and watched with suitable decorum the burning of a very realistic and bemedalled effigy of Goering.'

'9 May. VE+ 1 DAY. The day opened with a Church Parade led by Wing Commander K. Davison DFC, followed by a Thanksgiving Service. A large contingent of the Squadron took part including most of the officers. This in turn was followed by a march past before the Station Commander.

'In the afternoon a full scale sports meeting took place in which everybody took part to some extent, even if all some could manage was to throw a cricket ball! Thanks to the ingenuity and resources of Flight Sergeant Dyas, BEM, of 85 Squadron Echelon, a very fine Fun Fair was set up in the Hangar complete with bar, dance floor and side stalls. By 1900 hours this was in full swing attended by all ranks and such local inhabitants as were still capable of continuing the celebrations. A satisfactory alcoholic time was had by all and a deal of money was handed over to the local War Charities.

'So ended the Victory in Europe celebrations and it is expected of all Squadron members that they will return tomorrow with renewed, if rather jaded, vigour to the

business of flying and whatever the future may hold.'

'10 May. Today we were all sorry to hear that our Norwegian aircrew were to be posted back to the RNAF Headquarters. The first to leave are Captain Sven Heglund DFC and bar, Captain Laff Lovestaad DFC and Captain Eric Fossum. Although of a different nationality, they quickly became most valuable and well-liked members of the Squadron, always keen to engage the enemy and efficient in their work. Captain Lovestaad was most outstanding in that he had flown operationally for about four years without a rest of any kind and had during that time assisted in the destruction of five enemy aircraft, the probable destruction of two more, and the damaging of yet another. Captain Heglund and Captain Fossum had both done 35 trips on Bomber Support, the former destroying three enemy aircraft and the latter two. It is with very real regret that we see them go and all our good wishes go with them.'

'17 May. There was a statement of policy for future flying by the CO today. It has been decided that night flying will take place on Monday, Tuesday, Thursday and Friday, with the proviso that pilots have a minimum of 10 hours per month by night and 15 hours by day. There will be no flying on Wednesday which will be given over to organised games, and apart from station duties and any Oxford flying, all crews will be free from midday on Saturday until duty begins again on Monday. Mornings will be devoted to lectures, link trainer, range shooting and other beneficial activities on the ground. This policy, on being put to the Flights, met with general approval and will in future be the basis of the week's activities.'

How did the Squadron assess its achievements at the close of World War 2? 'We would like as a Squadron to put it on record that we consider our time with 100 Group not only the most successful but also quite the most exciting and enjoyable chapter in our Squadron's life.

'While we were with 11 Group our job was difficult but we had the Sector, Radar and other aids. When we operated from Swannington we had no one but ourselves to rely upon to find the square headed needles in the European haystack. I must say it never ceased to surprise me that an aircraft should leave Norfolk and then, among a swarm of bombers, jammers, windowers and friendly fighters, search out, bring to combat and destroy a Hun perhaps near Leipzig even though he himself was armed with all the aids of a defensive fighter.

'For our success we relied implicitly on, and were never failed by, 100 Group. Our equipment was always the best, no idea however lowly was scorned, and never were we faced with anything but the widest and most generous co-operation from the Y-Service and Intelligence. It was their analysis of German prisoner of war reports and German fighter reaction to the counter double bluffs, super-duper spoofs and "modest feints", combined with the quite indescribably hard work and enthusiasm by our Station Intelligence, that took the place of the Section and Ground Control Interception and crowned our plans to search out the Hun with a tolerable measure of success.'*

The usual method of judging a fighter Squadron's record is to look at its scoreboard, and in the end 85 Squadron accounted for 278 enemy aircraft and 33 flying bombs confirmed destroyed and a further 120 aircraft probably destroyed or damaged between 1939 and 1945, thereby making it one of the highest scoring squadrons in the RAF. 'It may be of interest that we destroyed 67 Huns on night defensive work in the 'Battle for London" and again precisely 67 Huns on

*A Short History of 85 Squadron in 100 Group; 8 May 1945.

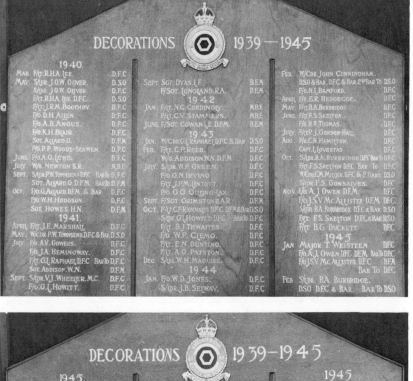

Above: Squadron Honours Board and Scoreboard.

The one thing that this history has tried to show is that the men who served on 85 Squadron were not supermen in the mould of epic films and pulp fiction to whom everything came easily. They were perhaps the cream of ordinary men but they were ordinary men nevertheless.

'12/13 April 1944. Lieutenant Fossum flew the last patrol and landed late at 0340 hours when the night's work was over. The only event of the night was that the Bofors guns were a little quicker on the trigger than is their wont and two aircraft were fired on in the circuit, fortunately without damage to either.'

'12/11/44. Day. Only one operational crew was asked for so Wing Commander F. S. Gonsalves DFC and Flight Lieutenant B. R. Keele DFC each tested the new Mosquito XXXs. Flight Lieutenant Keele had trouble with his port engine and returned to base on one engine, making a right hand circuit. Unfortunately he approached too high and found himself liable to overshoot. He attempted to make another circuit but had insufficient flying speed and the starboard engine twisted the aircraft round and they crashed near the perimeter track. Flight Lieutenant Keele was killed. His navigator, Flight Lieutenant R. C. Wright, was dragged clear* and apart from suffering from burns is expected to recover satisfactorily. Flight Lieutenant Keele had been with the Squadron for several months and was an experienced pilot with an extensive knowledge of AI. His loss is very much regretted.'

Even a relatively small fault such as a malfunctioning oxygen system could have potentially disastrous implications at height:

85 Squadron
RAF Station,
Swannington
30 November 1944

Report on abandoning operational flight in Mosquito XXX VY/X on the night of 21st/22nd November 1944

'Sir,

'I have the honour to report that on the night of 21st/22nd November I was Navigator to Flight Lieutenant P. A. Searle and we were detailed to carry out a patrol North of Strasbourg.

'We took off at 17.15 hours and set course for Furnes (Belgium) at 17.20 hours. At 17.50 hours I began to feel a little sleepy and as the oxygen was bubbling, I increased both of our

night offensive operations in the "Battle over Germany". This figure beats our "Battle of Britain" score of 54 but falls short of our score of 90 during the "Battle of France".

For this, the Squadron received 8 DSOs (plus 3 bars), 51 DFCs (plus 8 bars), 6 DFMs (plus 1 bar), 2 St Olaf Medals, 3 MBEs and 4 BEMs.

On the other side of the coin, the Squadron lost 28 men killed or missing on active service. Given that each of the 278 German aircraft shot down carried a crew of two on average, and that most of the Squadron 'kills' took place over Britain or completely destroyed the opposition, it can be argued that 85 Squadron took some 500 German aircrew out of the war for the loss of only 28 of their own number. Statistics can prove anything however, and it would be a rash man who could imply from this that the RAF was some 20 times superior to the Luftwaffe.

*Corporal Tom Woodhead, one of the Squadron groundcrews, dashed right into the fire and pulled Bob Wright, unconscious and badly burned, out through a hole in the blazing fuselage. For this most courageous act, Corporal Woodhead was awarded the BEM.

regulators by 5,000ft. After this I felt quite normal and proceeded to take Gee fixes. On arriving at Furnes at 17.55 hours, Flight Lieutenant Searle turned starboard instead of port, but he noticed the error before I had time to tell him and queried the course he should have been steering; I told him the heading and this time he turned on to the correct course.

'Three minutes later, I was checking our position with Gee, when I felt the aircraft behaving in rather a strange manner and I turned to ask Flight Lieutenant Searle if everything was OK. To my horror he was slumped forward over the control column as far as his harness would allow. Immediately I turned his oxygen on to emergency, pulled him off the control column and after a struggle managed to induce the aircraft to fly something like straight and level. Before pulling out the aircraft had seemed to be diving and at the same time, side slipping; Indicated Air Speed was 325mph and the tail was vibrating.

'When levelled out we had lost about 8,000ft. I turned off the cabin heater and, being afraid of further trouble, decided it would be better to climb a little. On pulling back the stick, the aircraft nearly stalled. Luckily I sensed what was wrong and eased the aircraft into a shallow dive to regain a little speed. I then knelt on the floor of the aircraft and by keeping the stick more or less central with my right hand, I opened the throttles with my left. When 220 to 230mph appeared on the Air Speed Indicator I tightened up the locking nuts as tight as possible from this position and climbed very gently to 12,500ft. Flight Lieutenant Searle very probably pulled the throttles back when he collapsed.

'I jammed one leg under Flight Lieutenant Searle's thighs so that he could not move his legs easily if he came round and accidentally moved the rudder bar. I then gently eased the aircraft to starboard on to an average heading of 300 degrees estimated to take us towards Manston; following this I opened pilot's fresh air vent.

'Holding the stick with my right hand (with left knee on the floor and right leg under Flight Lieutenant Searle's thighs) I hit him in the chest, slapped his face, and shouted over the intercom, until at last he showed signs of regaining consciousness. When he came to he seemed to think I had gone mad and said, "What the hell are you doing on the controls?" I tried to explain the situation but he would not believe me and said, "I am quite OK, we will press on." He tried to grab the stick and although I was grasping the stick succeeded to a small degree in turning the aircraft to port. My efforts to keep the aircraft on course seemed to work him into a frenzy and he commenced to fight me, tearing my battle-dress blouse, clawing my hands, beating my head and finally grabbing my throat. I decided things had gone far enough, especially, as the aircraft was getting out of control, so I hit him in the solarplexus with my left elbow and he passed out.

'About 30 seconds later he came round again although he could not see and for the first time realised something was wrong with him. I suggested that I should read his instruments for him if he would try and fly the aircraft; this proved fairly satisfactory and enabled me to change my position which was cramping me by this time. I then asked him to call up Manston, and, after telling him which button to use and rehearsing his message he called up in a rather drunken fashion. After talking to Manston he became much more sensible although still acted as though he were very drunk. He asked me if I wanted to bale out I replied that I did not wish to, but put my parachute pack in position as a safety precaution.

'As we approached Manston, some 20 to 25 miles away, his sight began to clear and by the time we arrived over the airfield, at a height of 11,000ft he was just able to read his instruments; for safety we decided I should watch them as well. We then lost height to 1,500ft and Flight Lieutenant Searle obtained permission to pancake; and he asked me to check everything that he did as he still felt pretty hazy. This I did and had to remind him of radiator flaps and 10 degrees of wing flaps. When we came to the funnel lights, he put on full flap, and instead of turning on to the runway commenced to lose height as if he intended landing on circuit lights. I shouted at him and pointed to the runway; he immediately levelled out but did not pull up his wheels until I told him to. I asked him what he was troubling him, and he replied that the outer circuit lights has fascinated him, but that he realised something was wrong just as I shouted.

'On going round again everything went quite well; he asked me when to put his wheels down and instead of putting on 10 degrees of flap first he put on full flap. He made a fair, wheel landing at rather a high speed (160mph) and did not pull his tail down until I had told him to three times. When we came to a standstill we found we were 300 yards from the far end of the runway. Flight Lieutenant Searle managed, with difficulty, to taxy to the end and turn off clear of the runway, but could go no further.

'I helped him out of the aircraft with the assistance of the waiting ambulance driver. He was unable to support himself and was still talking indistinctly. I helped him into the ambulance and he was taken to hospital.

'After this, I returned to the aircraft, switched off, made arrangements to have it towed to a safer position and then reported to Flying Control, notifying Swannington soon after.

I have the honour to be,
Sir,
Your obedient Servant,
B. J. P. SIMPKINS, Flying Officer
"B" Flight 85 Squadron'

Thus the strains of operating on a squadron in war were ever present and could make the bravest men crack.

'7/10/44. Flight Lieutenant X DFC and Flight Lieutenant Y DFC were grounded today prior to going on a rest for medical reasons. This is a great blow to the Squadron for they constituted a keen and experienced crew who have done well during their three months with us, having destroyed two enemy aircraft and one flying bomb.'

It is therefore not surprising that men lived the social life to the full, for none knew what tomorrow would bring when Lady Luck was so fickle. However it would be wrong to over-emphasise this point. The Squadron was 'glad to boast that we never asked for, or obtained, a stand-down on any occasion for any Squadron celebrations or Mess parties', and morale on 85 was always very high. Many crews worked hard to return to the Squadron from their 'rest' tours in order to get back to the action, and Rawnsley records that there was a constant stream of visitors to Hunsdon who tried to wangle a posting to 85 Squadron. A notice was even put up by one of the Flying Control Officers; 'Aircrew applying for jobs in 85 Squadron please sign here.' It was only put up in fun but seven signatures appeared on it in one day.

Jimmy Chipperfield probably summed up life on 85 for the majority. 'No one could pretend that my war career had been very dramatic or distinguished. I never killed a German, because the chance of doing so never came my way — although had the need arisen, I have no doubt that I should have met it without any qualms. And yet, even though I achieved nothing spectacular, I was pleased to have played a modest part in the national struggle for survival; if I had taken advantage of my physical disability, I should never have felt easy afterwards, for people would surely have assumed that I had fiddled things. As it was, whenever someone asked "What were you in the war?" I could cheerfully answer "Petrified", because it was true. I had been as frightened as anyone else, and I didn't mind admitting it. But at least I had been *there*.'

For many people therefore their time on 85 Squadron was the highlight of their lives, in that it gave them a measure of excitement, commitment and ésprit de corps that they were never to experience again once the war was over.

The Short History of 85 Squadron in 100 Group, written the day after Germany surrendered, even referred to 'that dreadful day in May 1945 when the war collapsed'. Nevertheless there were also some who, despite the effort they put into winning the conflict with their fellow man, became affected by the violence of it all. Suffice to say that the top scoring night fighter pair in the RAF, Burbridge and Skelton, took up totally different lives on leaving the Service. They both went back to the studies that had been interrupted by the war, Branse eventually becoming a lay preacher with a particular interest in the formation of religious groups in schools, and Bill being ordained a clergyman in the Church of England.

On 19 May 1945, Squadron Leader 'Ginger' Farrell DFC* and Squadron Leader Bill Skelton DSO, DFC set off on a navigational exercise over France to view some of the results of Allied bombing. Somewhat inconsiderately, their Mosquito developed engine trouble and Farrell had to land at Buc, whereupon who should walk out to greet them but Tim Molony, the longest serving member of 85 Squadron 'who entertained them royally'. This reacquaintance was something of a coincidence, given that the RAF at its height in July 1944 numbered 1,011,427 men and 174,406 women, but it only went to show that the RAF was really one large family. Bases, equipment and roles could alter, but the same familiar faces clung to the Squadron they knew and loved for as long as possible, and stayed with it in spirit once they had left. 'It's a sad world when you need a war to achieve that wonderful spirit of unity and glad comradeship,' wrote Jimmy Rawnsley in February 1946, but it was this feeling of 'belonging' that was to enable men to eventually overcome all odds and which was to embody all that was great in a Fighter Squadron at War.

*Ginger Farrell joined the RAF at the age of eighteen soon after the war started, and after completing pilot training he was posted to 85 at Hunsdon from September 1941 until August 1942. After a spell on Defiants he returned to 85 in December 1942 and continued with the Squadron until September 1944. He then moved on to another Mosquito unit, was posted to a headquarters staff on a convalescent rest after being on the sick list (during which time he flew the odd trip with 85 as on 19 May to keep his hand in), and finally returned to the Squadron officially in September 1945 as CO. Even at that stage he was only 23 years of age, and on leaving the RAF after six years of intensive operational flying, he went straight to work and qualified as a doctor. Unfortunately, once he started up in practice it was time to settle the account and Ginger suffered an almost complete breakdown in his health.

BOOK TWO

BOMBER SQUADRON
AT WAR

Bibliography

'For my son
Charles'

The following books were those chiefly consulted during the preparation of this book:

Notes on the History of RAF Training, 1939-44; Air Ministry
Special Operations; Raymond Alexander; 1979.
The Thousand Plan; Ralph Barker; Chatto & Windus, 1965.
Fair Stood the Wind for France; H. E. Bates; Michael Joseph.
The World in Ripeness; H. E. Bates; Michael Joseph, 1972.
Winged Squadrons; Cecil Beaton; Hutchinson & Co, 1942
Guns in the Sky; Chaz Bowyer; J. M. Dent & Sons, 1979.
History of the RAF, 1912-77; Chaz Bowyer; Hamlyn, 1977.
2 Group, RAF; Michael J. F. Bowyer; Faber, 1974.
Action Stations, East Anglia; Michael J. F. Bowyer; Patrick Stephens, 1980.
The Second World War; Winston Churchill; Cassell & Co, 1950.
Lancaster at War, Vols 1 & 2; M. Garbett & B. Goulding; Ian Allan Ltd, 1971 and 1979.
Action Stations, Lincolnshire; Bruce Barrymore Halpenny; Patrick Stephens, 1981.
'Lincolnshire Life' article; Bruce Barrymore Halpenny.
British Air Policy Between the Wars 1918-1939; H. Mongomery Hyde; Heinemann, 1976.
I Hold my Aim; C. H. Keith; Allen & Unwin, 1946.
The Mint; T. E Lawrence; Penguin, 1978.
The British Bomber Since 1914; Peter Lewis; Putnam, 1967.
Practical Flying; W. G. McMinnies; Temple Press, 1918.
The Nuremberg Raid; Martin Middlebrook; Allen Lane, 1980.
The Battle of Hamburg; Martin Middlebrook; Allen Lane, 1980.
Normandy to the Baltic; Montgomery of Alamein; Hutchinson & Co, 1947.
The Strategic Air Offensive against Germany; Webster and Frankland; HMSO, 1961.
101 Nights; R. Ollis; Cassell & Co, 1957.
Instruments of Darkness; Alfred Price; Macdonald & Jane's, 1977.
The War in the Air; Raleigh & Jones; Oxford UP, 1922.
White Rose Base; Brian J. Rapier; Aero Litho Co, 1972.
The Royal Air Force; E. Sargeant; Sampson Low, Maston & Co, 1942.
'Faygate Report'; via Andy Saunders.
The Great Raids — Essen and Peenemünde; J. Searby; Nutshell Press, 1978.
The Air Force of Today, 1939; E. C. Shepherd; Blackie & Sons.
Slipstream — An Autobiography; Eyre & Spottiswood, 1946.
The Royal Air Force; T. Stanhope Sprigg; Pitman, 1935.
Confound and Destroy; Martin Streetly, Macdonald & Jane's, 1978.

Contents

Preface

It is an interesting observation on modern society that as the years of peace increase from 1945, so popular interest in the happenings of World War 2 grows rather than diminishes. Perhaps this is due to the increasing number of young people who know nothing of war and want to learn, or perhaps it is an indictment of future prospects that people need to seek inspiration in the great deeds of the past, but there is no denying that histories of war grow ever more numerous and popular with each passing year. This is particularly true of the history of wartime aircraft, and the Ian Allan series on 'Aircraft at War' is foremost in this field, but we all know that the finest technology can be as nothing if the right men and women are not available to put it to good use. The heart of an aeroplane is undoubtedly its engine, but the people who maintain and fly it are its soul.

This book therefore is not so much a history of machinery as an attempt to round off the Ian Allan 'at War' series by underlining the human dimension of World War 2. 'I had meant to go on to a Squadron', wrote T. E. Lawrence in *The Mint*, 'and write about the real Air Force', and in similar vein, I have tried to show what it was like to serve on an RAF bomber squadron up to 1945, having performed a similar task in *Fighter Squadron at War* (Ian Allan Ltd, 1980).

The unit I have chosen had a varied and exciting combat history, but I have made no attempt to put together a complete 'official' history of one particular unit — rather this is more of a kaleidoscope of life in wartime as seen through the medium of the official reports, letters, diaries and mementoes that the members of one squadron left behind. This is how they saw themselves, and how others saw them; the words are theirs, the pictures are theirs, the emphasis is theirs, and if this book reinforces some points and neglects others it is only a measure of what the Squadron personnel regarded as important and, by implication, what they deemed of less consequence.

In selecting my bomber squadron at war, I have deliberately not chosen one of the more glamorous squadrons such as 'The Dambusters' because, for all their bravery and achievement, they were not typical of Bomber Command. This is the story of a very good squadron, but one whose personnel were at pains to impress upon me that they were only one of the best and that they were never the be all and end all of Bomber Command. In their opinion, the bomber war was a combined Command effort, and to do justice to that effort I have chosen a squadron that served within Bomber Command throughout World War 2 and which was to typify the rest if for no other reason than that it lost more men on operations than any other squadron in the Command.

Bomber Squadron at War should therefore be regarded as a scrapbook of an age, for it attempts to portray how men and women in RAF uniform worked and played, fought and died. This is the story of a perfectly ordinary generation which was plucked from its studies and civilian jobs to take part in a conflict which was not of its making, which was often beyond its understanding, and which promised not ripe old age but rather death on the morrow. This story therefore is dedicated to everyone everywhere who served in the RAF, and in particular to those who fought for a peace they did not live to see.

Acknowledgements
Most of the material in this book comes from members of the 101 Squadron Association and their families, and I must say how grateful I am for all their generous and unstinting help. I also wish to record my gratitude to the many authors from whose works I have taken quotations and inspiration, and a full bibliography appears at the front of this book. The H. E. Bates quote on p116 is produced by permission of Lawrence Pollinger Ltd and the author's estate. Finally I must pay tribute to the help and assistance I have received from the staff of the Imperial War Museum and the Public Record Office, Kew, and I gratefully acknowledge permission to reproduce Crown Copyright material.

In the Beginning

The Royal Flying Corps came into existence as a form of airborne cavalry which sent out aeroplanes to reconnoitre on behalf of the army below, but by 1916 each side had become so tired of being spied on by the other that fighting in the air had become a regular adjunct to reconnaisance work. Yet once fighting machines arrived, it became obvious that their use would not be restricted to attacks on enemy aircraft — bombing raids on enemy positions also became a regular duty of the Flying Corps.

However, a machine laden with bombs in 1917 was clumsy and slow to manoeuvre — it stood little chance of outflying the attacks mounted upon it by light enemy scouts, and as such became, in the words of the time, 'cold meat in the air'. Hence it was decided that heavy bombing raids could only stand a chance of success if they were carried out at night.

No 101 Squadron was therefore formed at South Farnborough on 12 July 1917 as the Royal Flying Corps' second specialised night bomber unit. Lt C. H. Wallis was one of the first to report to the Squadron headquarters which were temporarily housed in a bell tent, but as 101 at the time comprised little more than the Adjutant, Capt Errington, there was not much for the new arrivals initially. The Squadron remained at Farnborough for all of a fortnight, whereupon its presence was demanded in France so 101 moved across the Channel to the RFC headquarters at St André-aux-Bois.

The first Squadron Commanding Officer was Maj the Hon L. J. E. Twistleton-Wykeham-Fiennes, and his first priority on arriving in France was to find his 18 crews something to fly. Their pleas were answered in the shape of the Fighting Experimental (FE) 2b, a somewhat elderly aircraft by 1917 and one which the Squadron was probably given because its low ceiling made it unsuitable for Zeppelin interception work back home. No 101 Squadron's FE 2bs, with their top speeds of 81mph at 6,500ft, came from No 22 Squadron and were fitted with 'luminous instruments comprising compasses, rev counters, aneroids, air speed

1
FE 2b night bomber floodlit on the Western Front. The cost of an FE 2b 'pusher' fresh from the factory but minus engine, instruments, and guns was £1,521 13s 4d — the 160hp Beardmore engine fitted to each 101 aircraft cost an extra £1,045. *IWM*

2
Crew positions in the FE 2b. The pilot sat in the rear cockpit by the main fuel tank while the observer/gunner sat in an exposed and unprotected plywood-skinned semi-circular nacelle at the front.

3
Mechanics attach a 230lb bomb in preparation for a night raid.
IWM

Squadron, 'and a weird-looking contraption it was. The whole thing had an appearance of insecurity. Painted black, those old night bombers certainly presented a terrifying sight. It made me shudder every time I looked at mine.'

Perhaps his fear was compounded by the fact that night flying was then a somewhat novel and imprecise art. As W. G. McMinnies said in *Practical Flying by a Flight Commander* (Temple Press, 1918): 'A prospective night pilot is seldom given any dual control for night flying. His instructor can tell by his daylight flying if he is likely to make a successful night pilot, although it does not follow that because a pupil is only a fair daylight pilot he will be no use for night flying. He is generally considered fit for night flying, under moderate conditions, if he can make six or ten successful landings and attain a height of 6,000 feet in the dark. He must familiarise himself by daylight with the aerodromes equipped for night flying where he may have to land. He must possess a good knowledge of the country and be familiar with those parts of it which are open, and those which are wooded or otherwise dangerous. He can acquire this knowledge by moonlight nights as well as by day.' Not that the Squadron had much time to practice because it was soon moved closer to the front line and the action. 101 was assigned to the Ninth Wing of the RFC at a time when the August rains had halted the Battle of Ypres, but as the ground began to dry preparations went ahead to resume the offensive. So 101 was moved north to Clairmarais to take part in the Battle of the Menin Road Ridge which was planned to start on 20 September. Such was the stalemate on the Western Front that the average depth of objectives at that time was 1,000yd, and 101's first contribution to this war of attrition was to attack Hooglede, Rumbeke, Ledegham and Menin before dawn on 20th as these were rest billets which housed German reserve troops behind the immediate battle area.

The Squadron bombed Menin and other detraining centres on the night of 20/21 September, but the following evening air reconnaissances reported that German reinforcements were 'still pouring into Menin by rail, whereupon they were transported by motor-buses to the front'. The Germans were trying to sneak reinforcements through under cover of darkness so 101 was ordered to attack the town as well as the roads along which the troop transports were reportedly moving. By the light of parachute flares dropped from time to time, it was possible to see that the Menin-Ypres road was crowded with troops and vehicles: 101 Squadron crews began their attacks as soon as it was dark, and that night they dropped two 230lb

indicators and watches' plus navigation lights.

Bombing raids in those days were of the short distance variety, aimed at the aerodromes, munition stores and communications of the German forces on the Western Front. Racks were therefore fitted to the Squadron FE 2bs to allow them to carry one 112lb bomb or eight 25lb bombs on either side of the fuselage, and another rack underneath just behind the axle to carry one huge (for the day and for the aircraft) 230lb bomb. Finally, the aircraft top planes were painted brown with standard red, white and blue roundels, but to prevent detection from the ground the rest of the machine was finished in dull black with dark grey nacelles and the usual underwing roundels were replaced by white circles.

'I was now allotted an FE 2b,' wrote a brand new pilot when he arrived on the

bombs on Menin, and five 230lb and 12 112lb bombs on Rouliers station to the north. Such bomb loads seem relatively inconsequential by later standards, but it took a long time for an FE 2b to get anywhere and return to re-arm. Notwithstanding, on the night of 26 September, 101 and its sister night bombing squadron, No 100 Squadron, dropped a total of nearly five tons of bombs on enemy billeting and railway centres, interspersed with salvos of pom-pom shells. RFC Operation Orders instructed 101 Squadron to pay 'special attention to the attack of troops' and such night forays, which supplemented concentrated attacks by day, must have had an effect on tired enemy nerves if not property. Then the fog came down.

The Battle of Ypres dragged on throughout the autumn of 1917 and on the typical night of 20/21 October, 101 dropped three 230lb, eight 112lb, and four 25lb bombs on Ingelmunster station and aerodrome. The following night, a bomb dropped on Ingelmunster was seen to explode among aeroplanes lined up to leave the ground, so it was a contented crew that returned to base. The Squadron was now running up to speed and on the night of 27/28 October they dropped the following loads:

'Aerodromes: Gontrode (one 230lb), Rumbeke (six 112lb, four 25lb), Moorseele (four 112lb), Abeele (two 112lb), and Bissengham (two 112lb). Also Ingelmunster station (12 112lb, two 230lb), Isegham station (four 25lb) and various trains (one 230lb and 12 112lb).'

The method of attacking trains at night was to glide down with the engine cut and then open up for a slow run along the track. Bombs were then dropped in sticks along the

Life during the day on 101 Squadron at Clairmarais.

4–5
'Swinging' the compass of an FE 2b.

6
Lieutenant Basker indulging in a little gun firing practice.

7
Captain Vickers' aircraft comes to grief after colliding with a plough. The airfield at Clairmarais was an expanse of grass approximately ¾ml long and 300 yards wide alongside a forest. Being so narrow, it forced aircraft to take off either due East or due West, which eventually produced ruts in the soft earth. The wheels of an FE 2b were only held on by a collar and split pin, and under the strains imposed by a cross wind take off these wheels sometimes fell off, causing two crashes and the death of one pilot.

8
Captain Vickers after his contretemps with the plough; he was eventually to be awarded the Military Cross for later gallantry.

9

such features as railway junctions, woods of various shapes, bends in rivers and so on which would be sure to stand out at night. As new crews came to us, they were flown in daylight to the southern outskirts of Ypres town and had all the landmarks pointed out to them.'

The aircraft were housed in Bessoneaux hangars — huge, wooden-framed buildings covered with camouflaged canvas — and during the day the riggers, fitters and armourers cleaned the guns, loaded the ammunition drums and generally prepared the FE 2bs so that they were ready for operations. Another officer wrote in his diary:

'Just before dark the machines would be got out of their hangars and loaded up with bombs in accordance with the armament laid down in the daily operation orders. Then they would be got into line of flights, and ready to be taxied out to the flare path. Flares were out and ready for lighting at the appointed time. Pilots and observers would arrive, climb into their machines, and await the order to start. Presently an orderly is seen doubling down to the flight ordered to start first. Directly afterwards the roar of an engine was heard, and machine number one was on its way to the flare path. A hurried shout to the Flares Officer, conveying to him the names of the pilot and observer, together with the number of the machine and time away, and in less than a minute machine number one was on the flare path, engine all out, and fast disappearing in the failing light, until its navigation lights fast dwindling into twin stars were all that could be seen. Hardly had this machine left the ground, when the second was after it, soaring into the night, its twin lights following the first, and so on until all the machines were in the air, which seemed full of the drone of engines, getting fainter and fainter until the silence of a summer's evening once more reigned supreme. The mechanics who had been engaged in the dispatch of the machines are seen strolling back to pass the time in what manner they cared until the return of the machines. The average time taken on a raid was about two hours, according to the distance away of the targets. Quickly the time slips by, and all are beginning to cast their eyes around the sky to try and pick up the lights of a returning machine. Soon the drone of an engine could be heard, the pilot could be seen blinking his lights, intimating that he was going to land, and required the flares on to give him his position. These were put on and sometimes a searchlight beam was displayed on the ground. One last turn to get into the wind, and the machine is gliding towards the flare path, the roar of the engine gradually lessens and dies away, and in a few moments the slight shock of the machine landing is heard.

9
The sort of target Squadron crews had to find and bomb at night — a railway station by a field in France in 1918.

10
Officers of 101 Squadron at Catigny in March 1918. Notice the differing uniforms — officers were only attached to the RFC from their respective regiments. The Bessoneaux hangar in the background housed the Squadron aircraft. It was protected by an armed guard but the rest of the aerodrome was left unguarded — sabotage was unknown in those days.

trucks or carriages and a flare released afterwards to observe the results.

By the time of the Battle of Cambrai at the end of November, when the main targets were again the railway stations that supplied the battle area, the Squadron had settled into a distinctive pattern of operations. 'Being nocturnal,' said Lt Wallis, 'pilots and observers were not required to put in an appearance until lunch time. Having acquainted themselves with the orders of the day, they went at the specified time to the Operations Room to get their orders for the target of the night. On receipt of these, each pilot and observer studied maps to acquaint themselves with the best way of reaching their objectives — they had to memorise

Immediately the engine roars out again and the pilot taxies the machine towards the hangars. He shouts his name to the Flare Officer who notes the time of arrival of the machine, and then hands his machine over to the mechanics, who either overhaul it and load it up for another raid, or put it away in its hangar. The pilot then makes his way to the CO's office to hand in his report, and then retires to the mess for a little well-earned refreshment.'

On 16 February 1918 the Squadron moved south to Catigny in the Fifth Army area primarily in order to attack those airfields such as Etreux which housed German night bomber squadrons that were active against the Third and Fifth Armies as well as Paris. However, the Squadron was actually given a wide choice of objectives depending on weather conditions, and it was also briefed that attacks were to be 'concentrated, ie attacks on a particular target, once begun, were to be continued for several nights'. Thus 101 hit the aerodrome at Vivaise on the night they arrived at Catigny, but although they were ordered to bomb Etreux between 20 February and 4 March, such was the effect of bad weather on flying in those days that a raid on Etreux was only possible on 21 February. At 17.20hr, 15 FE 2bs set out, not in formation but individually, and all crews found the German airfield without difficulty, reporting that it was well protected by anti-aircraft guns. Thirteen hits were claimed on aerodrome buildings, mostly with 25lb bombs, and the same crews returned to attack again at 22.35hr. By this time the visibility had worsened considerably but direct hits were reported again and a total of two 112lb and 300 25lb bombs were dropped. Some 4,400 rounds of machine gun ammunition were also expended against hangars and searchlights.

The weather having lowered its protective shield over Etreux, the Squadron attacked alternative short-distance targets at Mont-brehain on 24 February and rest barracks in the woods east of Fontaine-Merte the following night. This latter raid involved all pilots making two or more trips, and the men of the German 352nd Regiment at Fontaine-Merte had their rest disturbed that night by a total of 378 25lb bombs and 12 40lb devices.

One man who flew on that occasion was Lt Edgar Hall. Born in Batley, Yorkshire, on 3 April 1889, he was apprenticed as an electrical engineer before joining the Northumberland Fusiliers in February 1915. He transferred to the RFC in October 1916 and completed flying training with No 76 Home Defence Squadron, Ripon, on 12 May 1917. By this time the flying training syllabus for pilots had been standardised by the Central Flying School, a good description of which

11
An FE 2b night bomber pilot examines a 25lb bomb before it is attached to his aircraft. *IWM*

was given in The War in the Air (Raleigh and Jones; Oxford UP, 1922): '... lectures on engines, aeroplanes, wireless telegraphy, meteorology, tactics, and organisation. Flying was taught in four flights of service machines, two of them being made up of various types of BE machines, while the other two consisted of Henri Farmans and Avros. The pupil was first taken up as a passenger, and the method of using the controls was demonstrated to him. He was then allowed to attempt flight for himself, either on a machine fitted with dual controls, or with a watchful instructor on the pounce to save him from dangerous mistakes. If he prospered well, the great day soon came, which, however carefully it may have been prepared for, is always a thrilling experience and a searching test of self-reliance, the day of the first solo flight ... The training was almost wholly directed to producing airworthiness in the pupil. The various activities which had developed at the front, such as ... bombing, had no counterpart as yet in the training establishment.'

By the time he graduated in May 1917, Lt Hall had amassed 80hr solo flying on Maurice Farmans, Avros, BE 2cs and 2es, RE 7s and FE 2bs. However his 'Report on Posting to Expeditionary Force' records that his 'Total Hours on most advanced type of machine flown' was '25 minutes on FE 2bs'; moreover, his 'Total Time Night Flying' was '4hr 50min'.

Lt Hall had gained more flying experience by the time he joined 101 Squadron in October 1917, and such was to be his proficiency in night bombing that the French eventually awarded him the Croix de Guerre.

'CITATION
BY ORDER OF THE ARMY

'Lieutenant Edgar Dean Hall, 5th Battalion Northumberland Fusiliers (Territorials) and 101 Squadron Royal Flying Corps.

'For his part in 34 squadron night bombing raids, notably on 21 February 1918 on Etreux airfield, and on 25 February at Fontaine-Merte barracks, displaying the greatest courage in spite of extremely adverse weather.

'A most fine example to all.

Grand General HQ
6 January 1919
Commander-in-Chief
Pétain'

Night navigation was always something of a hit and miss affair. 'But for the excellent system of lighthouses used on our side of the line, it was quite an easy matter to get lost. These lighthouses were placed at intervals of roughly 15 miles apart, some running toward the line and others parallel. They each flashed a letter in morse, so that any pilot, once he picked up a lighthouse, knew his position. Unfortunately, the enemy was not so considerate towards us. He put nothing out to guide us, and once over the line it was a matter of "by guess" plus a very erratic compass, which often acted in such a way as to make us doubt its accuracy.'

Thus on 22/23 March 1918, when 101 made many raids against German positions that were being strengthened opposite the Fifth Army front between St Gobain Wood and Bellicort, crews had roving commissions and 'were to judge their targets by lights displayed by the enemy'. In all, 484 25lb and six 40lb (phosphorous) bombs were dropped that night, and dumps near Travecy and Castres were set on fire. For part of the time operations had to be stopped when German aircraft bombed 101 Squadron's airfield in retaliation, but in spite of poor visibility, Squadron pilots and observers brought back a fair amount of useful information, notably that there was a great deal of westward troop and transport movement on the Mont d'Origny — St Quentin road. The last great Battle of the Somme was under way.

Such was the pace of the initial German onslaught that 101 could do no bombing on the night of 23/24 March because the Squadron had to pull out of Catigny before it was overrun and withdrew to No 2 Aeroplane Supply Depot at Fienvillers. From here the FE 2bs struck out the following night and dropped 284 25lb bombs on the Somme bridges and roads to the east, claiming four hits on the bridge at Béthencourt.

The next day saw the Squadron move again to Haute Visee where it was ordered by RFC HQ to attack Ham as heavily and con-

12
Sunday at Fienvillers being celebrated from the best available 'pulpit'.

tinuously as possible, paying particular attention to the roads through the town and bridges over the Somme. But after the attacks on Ham had begun, the Squadron received new instructions to direct all further efforts against Cambrai instead. Between 25 and 27 March, nine new divisions reinforced the German Second Army on the Cambrai front: 'It is hoped,' declared an RFC HQ message, 'that a record number of bombs will be dropped. It is of the utmost importance to delay enemy reinforcements coming up at this crisis, and to inflict casualties on him.'

Bombing by the Squadron was continuous for seven hours and 502 25lb bombs were dropped on Cambrai 'where great activity was seen'. Cambrai station was hit twice, a bomb fell on a canal bridge in the town, five hits were recorded on a transport column, two bombs struck a train, and another blew up an ammunition dump. In addition, 4,270 rounds of machine gun ammunition were fired at moving lights, into streets at Ham and Cambrai, and at trains. Ironically, 101's operations were hindered to some extent by the frequent passage over Haute Visse of enemy bombers on their way to inflict the same sort of damage on British lines of communication as the FE 2bs were handing out to the Germans. 'One machine, with Lieutenant Dunkerley and Lieutenant James (observer) met an enemy aircraft east of Arras with its lights on — one red and one white. They immediately proceeded to engage it. On observing that he was being attacked, the enemy LVG at once endeavoured to get well across the line, but after some manoeuvring Lieutenant Dunkerley succeeded in getting within 25yd, whereupon Lieutenant James opened fire. This lasted some minutes, Lieutenant James firing 100 rounds in all. The enemy aircraft was seen to make a vertical nose dive and appeared to crash finally apparently out of control.'

The orders for 101 Squadron on 27/28 March were as follows: 'The enemy have been attacking all day between the river Somme and Rosières, and will without doubt send up reinforcements in personnel and material during the night through Péronne and along the main Péronne-Amiens road. As it is most important to hamper this as much as possible, you will bomb Péronne and the bridge over the river Somme at Brie throughout the night.' Subsequently 101 crews found great activity at Péronne and claimed many direct hits on transport columns. A large tent encampment near the town, foolishly showing lights, was hit and partly set on fire, and a dump east of Brie also received a direct hit and blazed throughout the night.

The independent Royal Air Force came into being on 1 April 1918 but 101 Squadron personnel probably slept through most of that momentous day because there had been considerable bombing of enemy communications the night before. The Squadron had been given objectives on the Amiens-Roye road where German troop concentrations, estimated at two divisions, had been reported from the air. The FE 2bs operated for 10hr and their crews claimed many direct hits on billeting villages with 78 112lb and 150 25lb bombs. At 0530hr on 1 April, just as the last aeroplane was landing, German bombers hit 101's airfield after apparently following the final FE 2b back from the lines. The Germans obtained their revenge by killing one officer and two men, wounding two others, and wrecking four aeroplanes. It was not an auspicious beginning for the new RAF so far as 101 was concerned, but it did not prevent the Squadron from launching 14 aircraft the following night to bomb enemy billets and roads south of the Somme.

This was a very hectic period in 101's history as the fledgling RAF tried to stem the German advance without being overrun. On their way to attack the railway station at Chaulnes on 19/20 April, Lt S. A. Hustwitt and his observer, Lt N. A. Smith, saw a train near Rosières and attacked it with three 112lb bombs which hit the train and started a series of explosions that continued for most of the night. On the same night, 2-Lt Day crossed the line and bombed his objective in spite of a failing engine. 'On the return journey his engine stopped twice, but by skilful piloting he succeeded in reaching the aerodrome despite the fact that he was losing height all the way.'

Four nights later, 2-Lts Brooke and Chantrill obtained three direct hits with 112lb bombs on the railway junction at Chaulnes, while at 2250hr, 2-Lts Preston and McConville made a direct hit on an ammunition dump on the south side of the railway near Rosières. 'A great explosion took place immediately, followed by a tremendous blaze and further explosions. The fire and explosion were seen by several other pilots, who reported the matter on their return. When the second raid took place the fire was again observed by all pilots, who reported that it had increased enormously and was rapidly spreading; at one place it had crossed the railway line and was burning on the north side as well as on the south, and explosions were still taking place.' The fire served as a useful landmark as it could be easily distinguished from Amiens, and it guided crews as they went on their way to and from Chaulnes throughout the night.

FE 2b observers such as Smith, Chantrill

and McConville were worth their weight in gold; to quote again from *War in the Air*: 'The observer's duties were usually undertaken by officers or non-commissioned officers who volunteered for the business ... It has always been the tendency of our air forces to make more of the pilot than of the observer. When battles in the air became frequent, this tendency was strengthened. The pilot is the captain of the craft. If he is killed, the craft cannot keep the air. But if more depends on the pilot, it is equally true to say that a higher degree of cold-drawn courage is demanded from the observer. He suffers with the pilot for all the pilot's mistakes. For hours together he has nothing to do but sit still and keep his eyes open. He has not the relief that activity and the sense of control give to strained nerves. He is often an older man than the pilot, and better able to recognise danger. There is no more splendid record of service in the war than the record of the best observers.'

Eventually Ludendorff's last throw ground to a halt and it was time for the Allies to regroup and prepare for their final telling blow. For instance, a minor operation which began in the early hours of 4 July was preceded by the Squadron's FE 2bs flying up and down the front line to mask the noise of tanks while they were assembling. But this was small fry, and on 8 August 1918 the 17 aircraft and crews of 101 Squadron were thrown in to the Amiens Offensive which marked the beginning of the end.

The Squadron was then at Famechon where its role was to make life as difficult as possible for the troops, transport, and billeting villages facing the British Fourth Army which was detailed to lead the assault. Field Marshal Haig had selected 101 for 'independent action' and they acted under the direct orders of the Army Commander, Gen Sir Henry Rawlinson, with a brief to bomb selected targets at night. By the afternoon of 8 August, the enemy was retreating in no little confusion and reports indicated that German troops were converging on various bridges spanning the Somme. If these could be cut, the enemy would be trapped, so the FE 2bs carried on where the day bombers left off and attacked the bridges throughout the night. Although this intense activity was probably the first example of 'round the clock' bombing, it had to be acknowledged as a failure because of the lack of concentrated accuracy and the limited bomb loads involved. Nevertheless, there was no denying the commitment of the 101 Squadron crews to the offensive. They attacked stations at Péronne and Velu when the targets were invisible and the bombing was therefore of little practical value, but 'these attempts may be looked upon as an expression of the will of

the pilots and observers to take an outside chance to help the attacking infantry'.

September saw 101 attacking defended villages opposite the Fourth Army in preparation for the assault on the Hindenburg Line, and it was here that Captain Stockdale earned the DFC. Stockdale had joined the Squadron at the end of July after lengthy military service which included command of a company during the Boer War, and he took part in 24 raids and reconnaissances during his first two months on 101. However his most famous exploit came on the night of 17/18 September, his CO's description of which could have come straight out of the *'Boy's Own Paper'*:

'CONFIDENTIAL 2/Lt (Hon Capt) HENRY WALTER STOCKDALE
'Sir,

'I have the honour to lay before you the name of the above-mentioned Officer for immediate award of a decoration for gallantry and devotion to duty.

'While bombing Bohain from a height of about 2,000ft, he was caught by at least 10 searchlights. His efforts to evade them by clever manoeuvring of his machine were useless and accordingly he dived steeply, but in doing so received a direct hit by an anti-aircraft shell in his engine. As there was considerable moonlight at the time he succeeded in landing without using his parachute or flares thereby escaping notice. He was at this time about 15 miles behind enemy lines and as his machine could be of no further use to the enemy, he took a rough direction West and commenced to walk home. He succeeded fairly well in avoiding enemy traffic and movement along the roads by laying in a

13
Lt S. Golding with his gas-operated Lewis gun on its tube mounting. The Lewis gun was fed from an ammunition drum which revolved as the gun fired and the canvas bag hanging down caught ejected cartidges before they went back through the propeller. A 101 Squadron observer also carried a second Lewis gun placed on a pillar mounting to fire backwards over the top plane. It was a hazardous business for the observer had to undo his solitary lap strap, climb on to the ammunition lockers situated between him and the pilot, and stand precariously with his legs astride so that the pilot could see where he was going. The observer's only means of security while his pilot was manoeuvring violently was to cling to the pillar mounting with one hand and fire his gun with the other, and the RFC did not issue parachutes to its crews in those days!

ditch and then, when it had passed, running still further west.

'He and his observer, Second Lieutenant Shergold, were almost overcome with thirst and they attempted to drink water from ditches and shell holes but found it unfit for drinking and had, therefore, to carry on without it. At this point the observer was overcome by fatigue and Captain Stockdale had to half drag and half carry him further. By this time they had reached the St Quentin Canal about Bantouzelle and it was necessary to ford this. The observer was the first to get in and the immersion in cold water caused him almost to faint. Thereupon, Captain Stockdale jumped in and succeeded by his own sheer physical strength, which was by this time practically exhausted, in reaching the opposite bank with the observer. They then walked along a road towards Gouzeaucourt and while walking down the main street of this village, had the greatest difficulty in avoiding German soldiers.

'After passing through the village they came to a sunken road. At this point they were challenged by a German but they attempted to walk straight past without heeding him. He kept shouting and to avoid attracting attention, Captain Stockdale and his observer went back. The German, seeing that they were British officers, shouted something in German and struck Captain Stockdale in the mouth. Immediately they attacked the German and succeeded in knocking him down, rolling him in the mud, thereby dazing him for a few moments. They then took to their heels and bolted for the British trenches which they found by the Very Lights which were being sent up. They had considerable difficulty in crossing the barbed wire but after searching for a short while, they found a gap and reached the lines in safety.

'The time taken by them to reach their own lines was about eight hours during which they were running or walking the whole time. The fatigue must have been very great. I cannot speak too highly of the brave way in which Captain Stockdale succeeded in escaping and getting his observer back with him.

E. L. M. L. Gower
Major
In the Field   Officer Commanding
21.9.18   No 101 Squadron, RAF'

As the Allied advance grew in momentum, other Squadron personnel were congratulated by the General Officer Commanding, RAF France, for their sterling work on night bombing raids. Capt Halford for example, who completed 90 bombing missions in all and who three months earlier had made three trips to Bray in one night and dropped 52 bombs in the process, took off from Famechon to bomb Busigny junction. When he got there, he found the searchlights and anti-aircraft guns to be very active so he flew in as low as possible to escape the hail of fire. Unfortunately the bomb release gear was faulty so, rather than take the weapons back, the observer, Lt Anderson, crawled along the bottom mainplane to drop his bombs by hand. He scored direct hits.

A few nights later the weather was so bad along the British front that only 101 Squadron got airborne. Capt Beeston took off in heavy rain to carry out a low patrol over an area where tanks were assembling; after this 'most demanding and arduous patrol' he set course to bomb Levergies, finally landing back at Famechon after having been up in the drenched and cold night air for three hours.

Not that the bad weather was unwelcome to some. The Squadron also possessed a Special Duty Flight of BE 2cs, though no one talked about them much because they were set apart from the FE 2bs and were out of bounds to most personnel. The role of the Special Duty Flight was to drop spies by parachute behind enemy lines, a task that was accomplished by fixing a special type of sidecar to the fuselage side behind the mainplane trailing edge. The sidecar had a trap-door bottom which was operated by the pilot and the parachute was enclosed in a tubular container which was fixed to the side of the sidecar. The parachute cords came out through stout paper and led through a hole in the trap door to a harness worn by the spy. As the pilot sent him on his way, the falling agent dragged the parachute from the container and hopefully landed in one piece, to be picked up later at a prearranged time and place by a pilot who landed secretly behind enemy lines.

The Squadron was at Hancourt when the Armistice was signed, whereupon it moved into Belgium to unwind. In 16 months of active service the Squadron had earned four MCs, eight DFCs and four DSMs among its awards for gallantry; on the debit side, 101 recorded the loss of seven men killed in action or died of wounds, 13 killed and seven injured in accidents, and 23 taken prisoner of war. These figures are small beer by World War 2 standards but the mental and physical demands made on men who had to fly exposed to the elements as well as to the enemy night after night must have been as great. For example, on the night of 1 October only one of the Squadron's aircraft managed to get through the bad weather and bomb the target. The pilot, exhausted with the strain of it all, fainted when the aircraft was 10 miles behind enemy lines. His observer, Capt

Harold Smith, could not fly but he leant over his pilot, took hold of the controls, and after turning the FE 2b round in a series of flat turns, headed towards base. He 'landed safely on our side of the lines' even though the engine started to give trouble.

Not only pilots succumbed to cold and exhaustion. On 7 September Lts Stockman and Cock claimed a direct hit on a train at Vermand which caused a fire, but shortly afterwards Lt Cock fainted. Nothing daunted, Lt Stockman pushed him to the bottom of the nacelle and went on to complete the reconnaissance, staying in the air for over three hours. Thus, although 'our number of casualties was extremely light', World War 1 was just as much a battle of nerves as World War 2 because 'most of our losses were caused by forced landings, the pilot's worst enemy at night'.

Not that the old FE 2b let many people down. 'It can truthfully be stated,' wrote an officer in August 1918, 'that there was no machine that served its country so well as did the FE 2b. It was undoubtedly a most excellent machine for night bombing, all Squadron personnel made the best of the machine and it did them more than credit.'

Maj W. J. Tempest DSO MC took over the Squadron on 28 January 1919, but he soon found himself in command of a unit that was disappearing into thin air. In March the Squadron returned to an England where the prewar £1 was worth 9s 6d, where wartime service expenditure of £1 million per day had dropped to £1 million per week, and where there was little demand for night bomber squadrons.* Consequently, 101 was initially reduced to cadre status at Filton, Bristol, and eventually, on 31 December 1919, it was disbanded, its faithful FE 2bs sold for scrap, and its pilots and observers mostly demobilised. So it came about that Capt Edgar Hall received another letter to add to his Croix de Guerre citation:

'Telephone No.   AIR MINISTRY
Regent 8000   KINGSWAY
                    LONDON WC2
                    9th January 1920
'Sir,

'I am commanded by the Air Council to inform you that you have been placed on the Unemployed List of the Royal Air Force with effect from 8-5-1920 and you will cease to draw pay from the Air Force funds from that date.

*The RAF had to cut its personnel from 22,000 officers on 31 March 1919 to 3,280 during 1920, and suffer a reduction in other ranks from 160,000 to 25,000.

'I am to say that, on demobilisation, you will retain the rank of Captain but this does not confer the right to wear uniform, except when employed in a military capacity or on special occasions when attending ceremonials and entertainments of a military nature.

I am,
Sir,
Your obedient Servant,
H. McAnally.'

14
101 Squadron bases and principal bombing objectives during the First World War.

15
Squadron aircrew wrapped up against the night elements and noise of open cockpits. Standard flying kit at the time was a lined, leather jacket and thigh-length, sheepskin-lined boots plus thick gloves. The pilots here are wearing goggles.

14

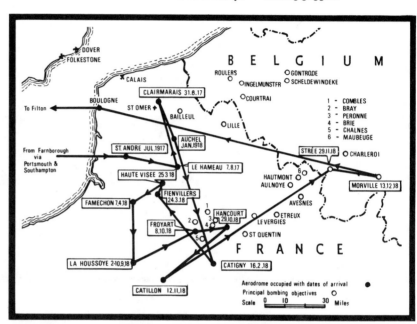

15

The Lean Years

In the years immediately following 1919, neither the Navy nor the Army looked with much favour on the fledgling RAF. At a time when funds were scarce, the two elder Services fought to regain control of aerial forces operating within their own spheres of influence; consequently Sir Hugh Trenchard, now Chief of Air Staff and chief sustainer of the RAF, laid special emphasis on aerial bombing over and beyond the armies and battlefleets as the prime raison d'etre of his independent air arm.

It was not until the Interim Report of the Salisbury Committee was published in June 1923 that the issue was finally settled and the RAF could look forward to a secure future. By that time the Government had realised that the postwar run-down of the RAF had gone too far and the Salisbury Committee enunciated a new principle in its Report — 'British air power must include a Home Defence Force of sufficient strength adequately to protect us against air attacks by the strongest Air Force within striking distance of this country.' But in Trenchard's view this did not mean mere reliance on a defence force of fighters — it meant being in a position to go on the offensive and strike at the very aircraft factories and airfields that sustained the enemy's bombing might. Here lay the foundations of total war and the main justification for a separate air arm — as Trenchard told his staff in 1923, 'The Army policy was to defeat the enemy Army — ours to defeat the enemy nation'.

Thus Trenchard insisted that the ratio of bombers to fighters should be increased in the force to be raised, which was christened the Air Defence of Great Britain Command (ADGB) in 1925, and the intention was to have 52 squadrons (ie 35 bomber and 17 fighter squadrons) operational by 1928. Yet the only possible enemy at this time was France, and as it soon became apparent that she posed little threat the RAF's ambitious expansion programme was slowed down to save money. Consequently, although 25 of the 52 planned home squadrons were in being by the autumn of 1925, the growth rate was reduced to two regular squadrons a year

16
A Boulton Paul Sidestrand with the Squadron number boldly emblazoned on its side. The Sidestrand's bomb racks are just visible underneath — they did not impose a drag penalty as they were hidden within the contour of the fuselage.

17
101 Squadrons Sidestrands in formation. Although the Squadron practised formation flying, the standard day bomber operating procedure in the early Thirties was that 'a single Sidestrand should go out by itself on a bombing raid'. *Aeroplane*

by 1927. Another four units were added the following year, one of which was 101 Squadron which re-formed on the authority of H.D./730 dated 21 March 1928 just in time to greet the RAF's 10th birthday.

Not that there were many Squadron members to celebrate anything in the beginning. 101 came back into being at Bircham Newton, Norfolk, as an ADGB unit within the Wessex Bombing Area, but when Sqn Ldr J. C. P. Wood was posted in from RAF Uxbridge on 28 March 'to command on formation' he found that the Squadron had only 23 airmen to its name. On 2 April, 'Flying Officer J. W. Duggan and Flying Officer J. G. Elton were posted in from No 100(B) Squadron and No 11(B) Squadron respectively. Both officers then proceeded to Martlesham Heath [the home of the Aeroplane and Armament Experimental Establishment] for a short course of instruction on the Sidestrand'.*

This Sidestrand aircraft at Martlesham was the first to be constructed and it ushered in a new era. Sir Hugh Trenchard was insistent that his precious aerial resources should not be frittered away on long-range fighters to protect his bombers: in his view, fighter squadrons should only consist of short-range interceptors for home defence to placate civilian susceptibilities. As it was generally agreed that the RAF could only strike to maximum effect if it bombed by day

*This, and many subsequent quotations, are taken from the *Squadron Operations Record Book* (RAF Form 540). 'The Object of the Operations Record Book,' declared *King's Regulations for the RAF*, 'is to furnish a complete historical record of the unit from the time of its formation . . . During major operations, or when a unit is placed on a war footing, the Operations Record Book is to be compiled from day to day'.

18
A magnificent view from the pilot's cockpit of the Sidestrand looking over the front gunner into sun.

and night, the day bomber squadrons would lack the protective cover of darkness and would therefore have to fight their way through to their targets unescorted.

No 101(B) Squadron was to be a day bomber squadron, and as this role demanded more speed and manoeuvrability as well as armament if it was to be credible, the Squadron was to receive the Boulton and Paul Sidestrand. Named after a village near Cromer in Norfolk, for Boulton Paul's factory was then located at Norwich, the Sidestrand was to mark the return of the twin-engined, high performance bomber to the RAF inventory after a gap since the retirement of the DH10.

The first year of 101's new life was taken up with ironing out such snags on the new aeroplane as the replacement of balanced ailerons with Frise ailerons and the fitment of a servo rudder for better control. By 25 January 1929 the Squadron complement had grown to 13 officers and 117 airmen, but it still had only one Sidestrand so continuation training had to be carried out on a couple of elderley Avro 504s and some DH9As donated by 39 Squadron when they left Bircham for India at the end of 1928.

The first production Sidestrand appeared on 101 in March 1929 and the Squadron establishment of an HQ and two Flights only materialised as more aircraft rolled out from Boulton Paul.

Having gained considerable twin-engined bomber experience through the Bourges and Bugle, Boulton Paul's Chief Designer, John North, was in a good position to produce a Sidestrand bomber that was very shapely and efficient aerodynamically for its time. It displayed remarkable manoeuvrability for a twin-engined aircraft and not only could it fly on one engine but it could also be looped, spun and rolled without difficulty. Once in Squadron service it soon became known as a superb pilots' aeroplane and, although the controls demanded considerable muscle, the Sidestrand was a pleasure to fly.

Unfortunately, some became too exhilarated for their own good:

'17 September 1929. Flying Officer X tried by General Court Martial for low flying at Hunstanton, Norfolk on 17 July 1929. Sentenced to be severely reprimanded and to have his seniority to date from 17 September 1929.'

The Sidestrand carried a crew of four — pilot, observer and two gunners — and its offensive load consisted of two 230lb or 250lb bombs plus a single 520lb or 550lb bomb, two more 230lb or 250lb bombs, or four 112lb bombs. 'Recently the position of the man who releases the bombs has been changed. He used to lie prone on his chest in

19
The whole of No 101 (B)
Squadron at No 1 Armament
Training School, Catfoss (near
Hornsea, Yorks) in 1931. At
Catfoss a year later, 'secret
experiments have been carried
out by this Squadron. The object
is to climb to an altitude of
10,000ft, glide down at a speed
of 135mph for 2,000ft, and
whilst gliding down drop bombs.
Then we flattened out and flew
straight for a certain period,
before repeating bombing by
gliding down another 2,000ft.
The effect of this is more
accurate bombing and it defeats
the ground defences.
Experiments are being
continued.'

a very uncomfortable position but now he sits in a very comfortable seat in the nose of the machine in front of the pilot. Panels of glass have been inserted in the nose in front of him, through which he can see his target as the machine approaches the position from which the bombs are to be released. This is a great improvement and leads to much greater accuracy of aim.' Thus endowed, and being a very stable aiming platform, the Sidestrands of 101 and their crews soon set new records for accurate delivery:

'1 September-27 September 1930. RAF Practice Camp, Catfoss. Combined results of A and B Flights are as follows:

'Bombing 84 yards, Gunnery 33%.

These results place the unit on top of all the other day bomber squadrons.'

'29 September 1930. Flt Lt Collins (pilot) and Cpl Thrussell (bomb-aimer), bombing from 6,000 ft, broke the record for Catfoss. Their error from 6,000ft was 21 yards.'

By now the Squadron was at Andover, Hants, where, as the only day bomber unit in the Wessex Bombing Area, it could be closer to any continental conflict. Andover was then commanded by Wg Cdr W. B. Hargrave, a 101 Squadron CO back in 1917, and from here his old unit settled down to formalising such serious business as the design of the Squadron tie — 'diagonal lines coloured dark blue, light blue, red and black.' More importantly, 101 also set about demonstrating the Sidestrand's ability to strike and survive far and wide.

'28 July-4 August 1930. Affiliation with No 111(F) Squadron. Results of Affiliation Exercises carried out with fighter squadron proved that the Sidestrand was a difficult proposition to tackle and that fighters at present had no attack to meet them.'

'12 August-14 August 1930. Air Exercises. These took the form of Redland against Blueland. This unit was allocated to Blueland and operated from Andover. Long distance bombing raids were carried out chiefly against Cranwell and Hucknall. The raid against Cranwell was most successful. On one raid to Catfoss the aircraft reached their objective and returned in a 60mph gale to land after a flight lasting $5\frac{3}{4}$ hours.'

Informed observers were very impressed by all this. Maj F. A. de V. Robertson in *Flight* of 24 April 1931 wrote: 'During the Air Exercises of last summer a formation of Sidestrands made an effective raid on the HQ of Air Vice-Marshal Dowding at Cranwell. But generally speaking the idea is that a single Sidestrand should go out by itself on a bombing raid. There is more than one reason for this. Naturally a single machine is not such a conspicuous object in the sky as a formation, and therefore it has a better chance of winning through to its objective than a Flight or a complete Squadron would have. A Sidestrand can carry a bomb load of 1,000lb and so even one is a formidable weapon of offence. Finally, the fighting powers of the Sidestrand are such that it is considered very well able to take care of

20
A good view of the Sidestrand's defensive weaponry of one forward gun, one rear upper gun amidships, and a third in a ventral turret pointing downwards towards the tail. All three Lewis guns were moveable and their very extensive field of fire left few blindspots.
Because of its manoeuvrability, excellent rate of climb and top speed of 140mph, the Sidestrand was the best light bomber of the decade. The Sidestrand's crew of four could talk to each other through a revolutionary new 'electrical inter-communication system'.
Aeroplane

21
Squadron dispersal at Andover.
Aeroplane

22
On Air Defence of Great Britain air exercises during May 1931. The Squadron was part of 'Blueland' forces and here its ranks are supported by Hawker Harts. Not that such fighter protection was necessary — 'Blue' forces were attacked en route by Siskins of 29 and 111 (F) Squadrons from the 'Redland' Air Defence Brigade and 'afterwards the fighter pilots admitted they had no definite form of attack which they could bring off safely against Sidestrands'.

23
A Sidestrand on a visit to Waddington, Lincs, in 1931. The Sidestrand was equipped with W/T radio, and when the trailing aerial was wound out crews could listen to broadcast morse messages 'as well as the ordinary wireless programmes which makes for brighter flying'.

itself. It has three machine guns, all of them moveable ... This gives a very extensive field of fire and leaves very few blind spots on the machine. The gun mountings, too, are made simpler and therefore easier to work. Important details such as these often make all the difference between a hit and a miss, and a single-seater fighter runs a particular risk when he attacks a Sidestrand ... It is reported that two fighter squadrons have been very puzzled to arrive at a plan of attack on Sidestrands which would not involve risk of heavy casualties to themselves. The guns of a fighter are fixed, and the whole machine must be aimed at the target. The fighter is only dangerous when flying towards his target. When turning off after an attack, usually in a zoom with speed diminishing, he presents a more or less helpless target to the gunners on board the bomber.'

By the end of the year, therefore, the Squadron had cause to be pleased with itself, and no one more so than the latest CO, Sqn Ldr F. H. Coleman, DSO, who was something of a perfectionist:

'20 November 1930. The Air Officer Commanding's Inspection by Air Vice-Marshal Sir John Steel KBE CB CMG was held in No 12(B) Squadron's hangar owing to bad weather. The AOC congratulated No 101(B) Squadron on its excellent results at the Practice Camp, and also the Squadron spirit and teamwork. He further congratulated the Squadron on being the best turned out and efficient Squadron on parade. During the inspection of aircraft, the AOC had a level half-crown bet with Squadron Leader Coleman that he (the Squadron Leader) had not read and understood properly an Engineering Servicing Instruction on a mechanical tail trolley. It is sufficient to say that the AOC lost and paid the half-crown.'

1931 was the first year in which no wooden aircraft were ordered for RAF squadrons, and this gradual modernisation of the Service had its impact on the front line.

'8 April 1931. The Squadron was selected to carry out Bombing Trials against HMS *Centurion* in September 1931, and in this connection was supplied with Gyro-rectors, Tail drift-sights, Mk VIIA Vector bombsights, electrical inter-communication sets and an electrical bomb release. In addition, new Jupiter VIII engines with 4-bladed propellers were supplied along with Mk II starters. All this modification work was completed at the unit in three weeks with the help of Messrs Boulton and Paul Ltd. The Squadron is now the most up-to-date equipped Unit in the Royal Air Force.'

This growing prowess was justified to the British public in the following manner in *Flight* of 24 April 1931.

'Bombing is becoming more and more of an accurate art — one might almost say, an exact science. The civilian who dreads outbreaks of "frightfulness" in the next war takes comfort in the thought that a pin-point target can still only be hit by good luck rather than skill. But the most useful targets, namely aerodromes, railway junctions, factories and such like can be seriously damaged and thrown out of gear even though the bomber and the bomb sights do not possess quite the accuracy of a King's Prize-man at Bisley. Moreover, the British citizen, who perhaps has lost more than any other national through the coming of air power, should find his chief comfort in the thought that the aim of British bombers is more accurate than the aim of any possible enemies. In that lies his best hope of security.'

No 101 (B) Squadron continued to impress throughout the early 1930s, be it among the hierarchy at ADGB Headquarters or in front of the crowds at the annual Hendon Display who delighted to watch the Sidestrand looping in mock combat with Bulldog fighters:

'25 June 1932. To OC No 101(B) Squadron. On behalf of the Flying Com-

24

24
The officers and men of 'A' Flight in 1932.

25
The Prince of Wales approaches the officers and men of 101 Squadron during a visit to Mousehold Heath aerodrome at Norwich. Notice the Boulton Paul hangar in the background. Sqn Ldr Coleman and his two flight commanders are in the front row. Notice the other ranks' uniforms in 1933. Lord Swinton, the Secretary of State for Air from 1935 to 1938, hated the tight cloth collar which he considered both uncomfortable and unhygienic. To improve comfort and efficiency, and thereby recruiting during the RAF's expansion programme in the late 1930s, Lord Swinton and the Air Council decided to make some radical changes — 'We substituted the open collar on the tunic and a shirt, collar and tie. We also got rid of the useless puttees.'

26
Sidestrands, together with their crews and groundcrews, prepare for flight.

mittee of the Royal Air Force Display, I shall be obliged if you will convey our thanks to Sergeant Pilot Methven who flew the bomber in this event. Whether the event was a success or failure depended more upon him than any other individual.

Hendon Display
Air Vice-Marshal F. W. Bowhill CMG, DSO'

Nevertheless, officialdom never felt the need to equip any other squadrons with the Sidestrand though it did allow development of the big biplane to continue. One particular problem associated with the relatively high speed of the Sidestrand was that its front gunner had difficulty aiming his Lewis gun satisfactorily in the increased pressure of the slipstream. John North concluded that the only solution was to enclose the gunner in a protective, power operated turret. This was a revolutionary feature for the time, and together with an enclosed pilot's cockpit, warm-air cabin heating, and an autopilot, altered the Sidestrand to such an extent that the modified airframe was rechristened Overstrand after another Norfolk village. The RAF ordered 24 Overstrands in all, but once again only 101 Squadron took operational possession of the type, its first aircraft arriving on 24 January 1935. (In fact this was a converted Sidestrand; the first production Overstrand 1 did not arrive until early 1936).

By now 101 was at Bicester in Oxfordshire to whence it had moved in December 1934 to replace 33 Squadron within the Central Region of ADGB. Having achieved the distinction of being the first RAF squadron to operate an aircraft with a power-operated gun turret, 101 then set about commemorating the fact in its Squadron crest.

Back in 1929, the unofficial crest had centred on the figures '101' with an eagle emerging from the 'O' carrying a bomb in its talons. Underneath were the words *Mens Agitat Molem* (Mind Over Matter); this was taken from the motto of Rossall School and it was doubtless adopted (with the Headmaster's approval) because the CO of the time was an old boy who wished to instil a few good old fashioned virtues into his men.

This motto stuck, if not the bomb-toting eagle, for in February 1938 King George VI gave approval for the new Squadron crest which was officially described as 'Issuant from the battlements of a tower, a demi-lion rampant guardant'. Symbolism was everywhere — the lower battlements signified the power-operated turret and the lion, being a fierce fighter, represented the Squadron's fighting spirit. *Mens Agitat Molem* remained, interpreted by the irreverent as 'They don't mind and I don't matter': on a more serious note, some argued that the words should have been transposed because there was very little that the mind could do against the small 'matter' of a high explosive bomb.

The Overstrand was an advance over the Sidestrand in that it was regarded as the prototype modern medium bomber, and so 101 found itself reclassified as a medium bomber squadron with a brief to pave the operational way for the introduction of the Blenheim by investigating new techniques such as intensive night flying. In fact the Squadron had started night flying in a cursory fashion back in March 1932, but most of the old tactics of the Sidestrand age were hardly adequate for a modern European war in the late 1930s.

'21 May-23 May 1935. The Squadron took part in a demonstration given at Porton

150

27

28

27
Sqn Ldr E. B. C. Betts DSC, DFC, Officer Commanding No 101 (B) Squadron from 21 December 1933 to 12 January 1936, in full dress uniform. Sqn Ldr Betts was a crack shot who represented Ireland at Bisley, but he did not have to suffer the discomfort of the full dress uniform for much longer — it soon went the way of puttees.

28
The official 101 Squadron crest which was approved by King George VI in February 1938. The badge is described as 'Issuant from the battlements of a tower, a demi-lion rampant guardant.' Officially these Squadron crests 'stand for tradition and foster an *esprit de corps* and this promotes the very necessary efforts of the individual.'

29
The unofficial 101 Squadron badge in the early 1930s.

No. 101 SQDN

29

30
An Overstrand (foreground)
stands next to one of the
Sidestrands it was to replace on
the Squadron flight line at
Bicester. Note the enclosed
pilot's cockpit and front turret on
the newcomer — on the
Overstand service trials, gunners
enjoying the protection of the
powered front turret achieved an
average success rate as high as
85%, whereas the average on the
Sidestrand had only been 15%

31
In 1933 the Under Secretary of
State for Air, Sir Philip Sassoon,
presented a trophy for
competition between the night
bomber squadrons of the Wessex
Bombing Area of ADGB. This
trophy was subsequently
awarded for prowess in aerial
photography, for all bomber
squadrons carried plate or film
cameras for reconnaissance work
when required. In between
bombing and gunnery therefore,
Pilot Officer Williams (pilot), AC 1
Goad (observer) and LAC Gregory
(camera) won the Sassoon
Trophy in 1935 for 101
Squadron with a score of 89.5%,
which was the best result in the
competition to date.
   This photograph, taken after
the Trophy presentation, shows
(L–R): Sqn Ldr Betts, Sir Philip
Sassoon MP, Air Cdre H. R.
Nicholl (AOC Central Region,
ADGB), and Wg Cdr M. L. Taylor
(School of Photography). Another
reform later initiated by Lord
Swinton was the abolition of field
boots for officers. 'They were the
last things that anyone would
rush to fly in, and we had no
horses.'

32
The first Squadron Overstrand on
parade for a royal inspection by
King George V, the Prince of
Wales and the Duke of York at
the Mildenhall Jubilee Review on
6 July 1935. 'The King inspected
the turret of the Overstrand and
Sgt J. L. Thrussell was presented
to His Majesty as the best bomb-
aimer of the year on day bomber
squadrons.'

31

32

and Andover to students of the Imperial Defence College. The task was distributed salvo bombing against a target representing a bridge 200yd long by 30yd wide over which three salvos were dropped, all hitting the target.'

It was great stuff for the uninitiated, but hitting undefended, immobile, short-range targets in friendly airspace and in fair weather proved little. Certainly the Squadron tried to fly more realistically with its Overstrands, as during the ADGB Air Exercises of 1936 when the aircraft raided in flight formation at dawn and dusk, but at least one leg and the bombing had to be undertaken during daylight because Squadron crews had no means of finding a target at night. 101 won the Armament Officers' Trophy for the second year running because they completed the Long Distance Bombing Exercises with an average bombing error of 53.7yd, but the Overstrand could not get to Germany and back even from the south coast and such bombing scores were unlikely to be repeated in the blitzkrieg war around the corner.

The Squadron soon had two flights of Overstrands with four aircraft held in reserve, and each flight normally had around six aeroplanes for use at any one time. The Overstrand could carry 1,500lb of bombs and had a top speed of 153mph, but its normal operating altitude was only around 7,000ft and this restriction, like many others, only highlighted the deficiencies of the RAF in the mid-1930s. The daily flying programme was displayed on a blackboard in

the flight office showing aircraft number, type of exercise, crew, time of take off and approximate duration, but there was not much more organisation. For a start there was no real air traffic control as such. The duty pilot sent off a signal to the destination airfield informing them that an aircraft was on its way; if he felt that the Overstrand might arrive before the telegram he might try to telephone, but as likely as not he kept silent on the matter.

Neither was there a station meteorological office, so the Squadron crews had to rely on weather forecasts which were transmitted several times a day in morse code from the Air Ministry in London. Not that there was a specialist navigator on board to use up-to-date 'met' if it had been available. The Overstrand crew numbered five — pilot, bombardier, nose and two rear gunners, who also operated the wireless — and not only was there no professional navigator but also four of the crew were only part-timers. Such navigational duties as there were on the relatively short-range and slow Overstrand were left to the pilot, the only full-time aircrew member on board, who map-read from ground feature to ground feature backed up by wind speed and drift calculations derived from an elementary computer disc strapped to his knee.

Aircrew members of the RAF in the 1920s fell into just two categories — pilots and observers — and the bulk of the 'back seat' jobs were left to volunteer ground tradesmen who were eager to fly. T. Stanhope Sprigg wrote in *The Royal Air Force* (Pitman,

33
Squadron Overstrands over Oxfordshire in June 1936. Apart from the powered turret, the chief differences between the Overstand and its predecessor were an increase in top speed of 153mph, an enclosed pilot's cockpit, warm air heating for the pilot's and rear gunner's cockpits, a wind shield for the rear gunner's cockpit, a tail wheel, larger main wheels with wheel brakes and servo operated elevators. 'Essentially though,' recorded the Squadron, 'the aircraft were identical.'
Charles E. Brown

34
The Overstrand's famous powered turret, the front of which was closed by a zip fastener when not in use. The 'power' came from a compressed air bottle though the cylindrical cupola turret could only be fully rotated when its Lewis gun was elevated by 70°. One RAF staff officer, who expressed a wish to try it for himself on the ground, commenced rotation only to become so overwhelmed by the turret's speed that he remained transfixed, whirling like a top, until both he and the air system were exhausted.

34

33

35
An Overstrand in its natural
element.
Chaz Bowyer Collection

1935): 'It is the Air Ministry's intention to draw from airmen entered as boys the bulk of observers required by the Service. Ex-boy entrants recommended for these posts will usually be selected during their seventh year of service, provided they are willing to re-engage to complete 24 years total service. They will be given a short course of training, promoted to Corporal, and thereafter employed on such observer duties as aerial gunnery, signalling, navigation, photography and look-out, until they have completed 18 years' service or have been promoted to Flight Sergeant. Whilst serving as observers they draw additional pay at the rate of 1s 6d a day.'

It all sounded good in theory, but in practice, gunners and bomb aimers were just as often chosen from amongst the keenest Squadron groundcrew who were then taught the rudiments of the job. These men did not even receive automatic advancement to the giddy heights of Corporal, but despite the 'second-class' nature of rear-crew duties there was never any lack of volunteers from among the other ranks. They might attain AC1 (Aircraftman First Class) or LAC (Leading Aircraftman), and they might have to service the machine they had just flown as soon as they landed, but merely to fly was sufficient reward in itself and therein lay the chance of advancement to 'real' aircrew status as a pilot.

Once a year, 101 Squadron crews were given a chance to drop real bombs and fire live ammunition at Armament Training ranges such as Catfoss or North Coates Fitties. Small smoke bombs were deposited with enthusiasm from high or low level, in steep or shallow dives, while the air gunners blazed away at ground targets or banners towed behind apprehensive aircraft. Back at Bicester, the crews could only refine their bombing skills by using a rudimentary 'camera obscura' device in a small room. Thus, in spite of new drift sights and electronic release mechanisms, precision in bombing only came by dint of experience, and the Squadron crews had no means of finding and accurately identifying targets which were masked by bad weather or night.

That the RAF was still largely geared to bomber techniques that were not far removed from those of World War 1 was due almost entirely to the many intervening years of retrenchment and neglect. The deteriorating international situation after 1933 put a stop to this and provided sufficient impetus for the RAF to embark on its first expansion scheme in July 1934, but the fact that Scheme A was to be superseded by no fewer than 10 other such schemes during the next four years gave some indication of the uncertainty of the time. Parity with the emerging Luftwaffe was to be the aim of the game as the Government strove to deter possible German aggression by sheer weight of numbers. Consequently, as aircraft rolled off the production lines the metropolitan air force became too large and unwieldy to be effectively controlled from a single ADGB Headquarters. Moreover, the work of its various branches was becoming increasingly specialised, so in July 1936 ADGB was separated into four independent Commands. One of these was Bomber Command, and its first Group was to be No 2 (Bomber Group) commanded by 101's first CO, Laurence Twistleton-Wykeham-Fiennes, who was now a Group Captain.

Having been forced in the name of 'parity' to go for quantity in the short term rather than quality, the RAF had to accept a pre-

An Overstand in its unnatural element, having come to grief outside a Bicester hangar at the hands of an embarrassed flight commander!

ponderance of light and medium bombers which were cheaper and easier to build, needed fewer crew members, and demanded smaller airfields and support facilities to keep airborne. Not that this was necessarily a bad thing because the Service needed time to absorb the implications of the rapid advances in airframe and engine technology that were then taking place. For example, when the Bristol Aeroplane Company designed a high-speed, twin-engined, personal transport monoplane for Lord Rothermere, its sleek, low-winged design together with retractable undercarriage, variable pitch propellers, and advanced engines gave it a top speed some 50mph in excess of the RAF's latest production fighter. Lord Rothermere generously presented his aircraft to the nation for further tests, and Bristol redesigned it as a medium bomber to be known as the Blenheim.

No 101's Overstrands graced the Hendon Display for the last time in 1937 because events had rapidly overtaken this stalwart of the biplane age. The Squadron began to re-equip with the Blenheim I on 27 August 1938, though conversion on to type was pretty rudimentary. 'One or two pilots did a quick circuit at Bristol's airfield, Filton, in the company of the firm's test pilot, but not in a dual control aircraft. Then we took off in the Blenheims allocated to the Squadron and we flew in formation back to base. That was the conversion course in its entirety.'

No 101 was 're-allocated from a training to a mobilisation Squadron' on 16 September, just in time for the Munich crisis which the Squadron Adjutant discreetly referred to in the following manner:

'26 September 1938. As a result of events in Central Europe, an International Situation occurred which necessitated the Squadron immediately preparing for a major war. Intensive training was done in an attempt to make as many crews as possible fit to perform long distance bombing raids by day and night. These preparations were somewhat hampered by the shortage of air observers and wireless operator air gunners, and the non-availability of certain essential items of equipment.'

Although the Squadron continued training after Munich was over 'so as to achieve complete operational fitness as soon as possible', there was no immediate solution to the manpower problem. RAF personnel, who numbered 31,000 officers and men in 1934, totalled approximately 118,000 by 1 September 1939; thus in these few years the aggregate intake amounted to some 4,500 pilots and 40,000 airmen and boys compared with the annual pre-expansion entry of 300 pilots and 1,600 airmen. The implications of this rapid expansion rate were considerable. Blenheims for instance were readily forthcoming — the Squadron was up to its established strength of 16 IE (Initial Equipment) plus 5 IR (Immediate Reserve) by 5 October 1938 — but skilled groundcrews to service them and proficient aircrews to fly them took longer to arrive.

Back in 1919 Trenchard had laid the foundations of his officer corps by pushing through the unprecedented proposal that permanent commissions should only be offered to one-third of his future officers, and that the remainder should be recruited on a short-term basis 'in order to give a good curve of promotion to those officers who were permanent'. The principal method of obtaining a permanent commission was either through a university or via the RAF College, Cranwell. Entry through either of these doors was theoretically open to all, but although there were scholarships available to those of limited means there were no university grants in those days and the fees for the two years' training course at Cranwell were £300 in 1934. To enter Cranwell a boy had to be between 17½ and 19½ years of age, of proven academic ability, and impress a board of officers as to his 'Interview and Record' which gave information as to 'mentality, character and athletic prowess'. Yet the fact that a member of the 'officer class' in the prewar RAF had to maintain a social standard alongside brother officers who might keep a private horse in the Mess stables or even a private aeroplane in the hangar makes it clear that the ranks of the permanently commissioned were more likely to be filled by boys who went to public schools such as Rossall rather than to grammar schools. This is not to say that the average prewar RAF officer on a permanent commission was a chinless blockhead — in fact much of the Service's success in World War 2 was undoubtedly due to the standard of leadership and example set by men taken into Cranwell during the 1930s. Rather, it was more a question of glamour and challenge. Neither the Army nor Navy had come out of World War 1 with overmuch glory, and to sons of men who had suffered at the hands of uninspiring admirals and generals, the RAF in the thirties often promised a brighter and less conservative prospect than the other two services. As a result the RAF was able to select the elite of the

elite because it could afford to pick and choose from the best youth in the land.

The Cranwell men were the 'career' stream who would eventually fill such prime executive posts on the squadron as CO and flight commanders. 101 Squadron was divided into two operational Flights: OC 'A' Flight and OC 'B' Flight were then flight lieutenants each responsible for eight crews, their aircraft and their groundcrews. Only pilots on the Squadron held the King's Commission before the war and, excluding the executives, these were either young Cranwell men or officers who could not gain, or did not aspire to, a permanent commission. The latter served on short-service commissions which were available to 'those between 18 and 22, unmarried, and of pure European descent' and which allowed a man to serve for four years followed by six in the Reserve. A £100 gratuity was paid for each year served, though those of proven worth were allowed to transfer to a permanent commission if they so desired.*

Yet there were only 10 officers on 101 at this time, and as each Squadron Blenheim carried a crew of three — pilot, navigator/observer, and gunner — some of the pilot posts and all the rear-crew positions were

*The rank of flight lieutenant could be reached by a Cranwell graduate in 3½ years, but could not be reached by other officers for 4½ years, by which time a short service officer would have transferred to the Reserve.

37
Line-up of Squadron Blenheim Is. As the threat of war increased, bomber squadrons painted out all their unit markings and replaced them with code letters. Thus 'LU' identified 101, though after August 1939 this was changed to 'SR' for the remainder of the war. Eventually a third letter was added after the unit code to identify individual aircraft.

37

filled by lesser mortals. The non-commissioned pilots were drawn from men who had worked their way up from direct entry into the ranks or from apprenticeships. A newly commissioned (and unmarried) pilot officer fresh out of Cranwell earned £381 14s 7d a year in 1938, which was more than an experienced sergeant pilot, but few SNCOs complained because they were flying as well as earning 3s a day more than when they had been on the ground.

The status of an SNCO pilot was certainly much higher than that of the remainder of his crew. Now that the modern Blenheim had arrived, the old unsatisfactory state of navigation affairs was improved somewhat by the decision to put selected rear-crew men through a 16 weeks' course in navigation and bombing, on successful completion of which they would receive the acting rank of sergeant. After six months duty as 'Acting Observer' they would be confirmed in rank and crew category, and allowed to wear the winged 'O' flying badge of an air observer above their left tunic pockets.

This advance placed non-commissioned observers on a par with non-commissioned pilots, but even so there was always a shortage of trained navigators during the expansion period. At a time when the Air Ministry was producing no fewer than 13 grandiose Western Air Plans for use in a forthcoming war, all of which presupposed pinpoint accuracy to strike at German military, industrial and transportation targets, the facilities available to RAF bomber navigators were totally inadequate. Too much flying was done in the local vicinity of aerodromes, and anything farther afield relied on a hit-and-miss method known in the Service as 'by guess and by God'. On 17 May 1939 a report to Bomber Command declared that dead reckoning navigation by day when above cloud could be expected to bring an aircraft only to within about 50 miles of a long-range target. Thus it was only gradually being realised that accurate navigation was a full-time job and one moreover that, if it was to prove successful over reasonable distances and unfamiliar terrain, not to mention in bad weather and at night, required special training and facilities. This in turn would necessitate such an education as would often make commissioned rank as desirable for the navigator as for the pilot.

The third man in the Blenheim was the gunner who sat in a power-operated semi-retractable dorsal turret containing a single Vickers K or Lewis gun. Although the advent of the 'new' generation of RAF bombers had seen the first regular inclusion of straight air gunners into each Blenheim crew, the role of 'Air Gunner' as a specific aircrew 'trade' was not formally recognised by the Service until 19 January 1939. Air Ministry Order A.17/1939 finally gave full-time employment to air gunners, but then only in the category of wireless operators. Existing air gunners were expected to take the wireless operators' course but henceforward all new recruits had to train first as W/Ops at RAF Yatesbury before undertaking a course of gunnery instruction at Jurby on the Isle of Man. The men who succeeded at all this became WOp/AGs but they could still remain aircraftmen first class or leading aircraftmen until well into the war at a maximum pay of 5s 6d a day plus 1s 6d a day flying pay. Prospects of further advancement in status were restricted by the Air Ministry Order to the possible selection, after some three years' crew service, for training as an air observer.

Yet it was impossible to train hordes of new RAF aircrew overnight. As Viscount Swinton, the then Secretary of State for Air, wrote in *British Air Policy Between the Wars 1918-1939* (H. Montgomery Hyde; Heinemann, 1976). 'We had to mobilise and improvise by every means in our power. For the training of pilots we proceeded on the basis of separate initial training and advanced training. For the initial training we used and expanded all the existing Civil Training Schools, and the men who had pioneered and persisted without much encouragement in these schools played a notable part in the expansion; most, if not all of them, old Air Force officers. The advanced training schools were entirely run by the RAF. For the intructional staff in both initial and the advanced schools we drew largely upon the Reserve of Officers. Then we had to expand the specialist schools, and build new ones for navigation, gunnery and the like.'

So manning levels on 101 remained a headache and cockpit seats had to be left empty, 'resulting in monthly flying hours being often well below the required number'. The situation was not helped when the Squadron lost a considerable proportion of its skilled manpower in the first three months of 1937 to form the nuclei of 90 and 144 Bomber Squadrons. Thus, although 101 was 'mobilised' in response to Munich, this was largely a cosmetic exercise because, in the words of the Air Ministry, 'Less than 50% of the crews in the mobilisation squadrons were fit for operations as judged by Bomber Command's peacetime standards.' But the quest for the right sort of manpower went on:

'The new bombers require not only extra pilots but crews, wireless operators, observers and gunners,' wrote Viscount Swinton to the Prime Minister. 'These we cannot improvise . . . These men are vital to sustain a war effort.'

The remainder of the 114 non-commissioned members of 101 Squadron who were the maintainers and sustainers were equally vital. In *The Mint*, T. E. Lawrence praised the aircraft mechanics as more important in their way than the pilots themselves since, but for their conscientious work, the pilots could not carry out their tasks. This was a very sound attitude and one that was certainly reflected in the aircrews' approach to the groundcrews of 101.

Direct entrants to the ranks swelled in number with the RAF Expansion Scheme and they were initially paid between 2s and 3s 6d a day depending on their trade group. At the end of the training course, say for a flight rigger at No 2 School of Technical Training, Henlow, there came the great day of the Control Test Board. 'A senior NCO took each trainee on the oral part of the subject. There were practical jobs to be done, a built-up riveting and a splicing exercise. There was also a written paper to complete. The results were collated from each part and the average of all was the final result. Below 40% was a fail, 40-60% made one an air-craftman 2nd class, with 60-80% one became 1st class, and 80% and over elevated one to the dizzy heights of leading aircraftman. It was a good man indeed who passed out LAC with the high standard demanded.'

The longest serving engagements in those trades most directly associated with aircraft maintenance was reserved for those who undertook an RAF apprenticeship. Introduced by Lord Trenchard, the apprentice scheme was designed to provide the service with a nucleus of highly skilled technicians at the end of an intensive three-year course, and from this cadre were to come the engineering officers and NCOs of the future. Boys between the ages of 15 and $17\frac{1}{4}$ could sign on for 12 years from their 18th birthday if they were accepted for apprenticeships, but like the permanent commission, an apprenticeship was a coveted prize only awarded to the elite.

Having said that, there was still much that was anachronistic about the attitude of the RAF before the war. E. C. Shepherd could write in *The Air Force of Today, 1939* (Blackie and Sons Ltd): 'The maintenance of aircraft, like the care of horses, is a specialist job... The apprenticeship ideas was one of Trenchard's best, for it combined an engineering training with an education in the ways and traditions of the Service. In effect it permeated the units with a mechanical aristocracy who... were familiar with the way the Service tackles its work and with the reasons why certain things are important... The boys arrive at the squadrons *full of the spirit of the game...*'

Unfortunately, if airborne warfare was ever a game, the Germans were then in the process of unilaterally re-writing the rules.

A skilled LAC on 101 Squadron in 1938 earned 35s a week less 7s for food and accommodation. Good conduct badges were worth an extra 3d a day, these being awarded after 5, 8 and 13 years. 'There was a tremendous esprit de corps, and comradeship was the operative word.' Life revolved around the barrack block for 'very few personnel lived, or had their homes within, easy reach of the camp and weekends were invariable spent at Bicester. Fewer still could afford the luxury of a car or even a motorcycle although I remember a few "souped-up" bangers usually with two or three or even four bods in part ownership, and their antics were not altogether in favour with the station warrant officer. ... Booking IN and OUT was compulsory at the Main Guardroom where each individual would come under the scrutiny of the duty service policeman and, unless you were dressed to the required standard, you would be refused permission to leave camp.

'There were no exceptions when administrative duties were promulgated in daily routine orders — duty crew, fire picket and station guards come quickly to mind. The duty crew consisted of a corporal and six airmen (mixed flying and ground personnel) and the duty lasted for one week. The duty crew were responsible for opening and closing the hangar doors daily. They remained at the flight line until all the aircraft had returned, manually moving each aircraft into its allotted position; if outside the hangar, they ensured that each aircraft was pegged down into wind, chocks positioned, and aircraft searched for 'left overs' etc. Working parades were held daily when both flights would assemble outside their respective barrack blocks and, after inspection, would be marched to the hangars and be dismissed. The reverse would take place at the cessation of work.'*

Nevertheless, despite numerical deficiencies, the quality of the manpower from the top to the bottom of 101 Squadron was excellent. The man largely responsible for this, Lord Trenchard, certainly found cause for satisfaction in September 1940: 'I have also been round nearly every squadron. The spirit they are all imbued with is wonderful... They are what I had not thought possible, — better than in the last war. On the RAF I feel will fall the heavy burden of fighting all through the winter in very hard conditions, but I know their spirit will pull through whatever happens.'

*Aircraftmen First Class V. Noble, 1936 — via *Special Operations*; R. Alexander, 1979.

158

Trial and Error

Although 101 was always short of aircrew right up to the war, the RAF was right not to lower its standards in order to make up numbers. This policy was to create a pool of superb manpower which was to stand the Service in very good stead in the long term, but in 1939 it only added to the problems facing Bomber Command. New Blenheim air gunners might be better motivated, but they had such little opportunity to perfect their skills on the armament practice ranges 'that their results were not very satisfactory'. In addition, although the gunners were now encased in power turrets, the weapons they fired were little different from those their fathers had used in World War 1. Consequently the C-in-C Bomber Command, Air Chief Marshal Sir Edgar Ludlow-Hewitt, felt moved to write in the following manner to the Air Ministry on 17 July 1939:

'As things are at present, the gunners have no real confidence in their ability to use this equipment efficiently in war, and captains and crews have, I fear, little confidence in the ability of the gunners to defend them against destruction by enemy aircraft. Under these conditions it is unreasonable to expect these crews to press forward to their objectives in the face of heavy attack by enemy fighters.'

Even more crucial were the failings of the aircraft themselves. Back in 1935 the Blenheim had been a fleet-footed beast, but by the end of the decade, the Blenheim I was some 70mph slower than the Me109. In April 1939 the post of Officer Commanding No 101 Squadron was elevated to wing commander status, reflecting the growing number of personnel on 101; and just as Wg Cdr J. H. Hargroves was settling into the post his Squadron started to equip with the Blenheim IV. This aircraft sported a longer nose to improve the navigator's position, but it was no faster than its predecessor, and as soon as the RAF's eight-gun fighters became the mock adversary it became clear that the Blenheim had neither the speed, manoeuvrability nor armament to take on the Luftwaffe in daylight.

Operations under cover of darkness were the only alternative, but the problems of training bomber crews in night operations were never really faced in the prewar period. It was impossible for instance to simulate blackout conditions with no lights visible from the ground, and blind flying aids were in short supply. 'Consequently group commanders hardly dared to send up their crews on flights of any length at night or if the weather was not set fair. While all squadrons were required to do some night flying, only a small proportion of it was done in the dark, though it was generally recognised that in war time it would probably often have to be done.'*

Observations such as these only added weight to the view put forward by an air marshal at the time of Munich that, 'We have during the past few years been building up a front line Air Force which is nothing but a facade'. In an even more damning indictment of his 'shop window' force, Air Chief Marshal Ludlow-Hewitt reported that if a determined attack was made on Germany his

*From *The Strategic Air Offensive Against Germany* (Webster and Frankland; HMSO, 1961).

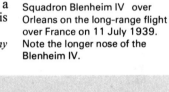

38
Squadron Blenheim IV over Orleans on the long-range flight over France on 11 July 1939. Note the longer nose of the Blenheim IV.

38

medium bomber force would be eliminated in only $3\frac{1}{2}$ weeks. In the end, the only Western Air Plan which was endorsed with any degree of enthusiasm involved the dropping of propaganda leaflets by night; it might have bored the Germans into surrender but would have achieved little else.

Not that nothing was done to try to improve matters in the last months of peace. Some 50 new air stations were authorised during the expansion period, many of which were built in eastern England to get as close as possible to northern Germany. Thus between 6 and 9 May 1939, '101 moved from Bicester to West Raynham, Norfolk, and transferred from No 1 Group to No 2 Group'.

As befitted part of a 'shop window' force, 101 also set about displaying its wares for the benefit of all potential customers. 'Massed formation practices' with 90 Squadron were in vogue in February, and then on 21 March the Squadron took part in a 'flypast' over Dover during the state visit of the French President, M. Lebrun. This Anglo-French entente progressed into a series of sorties over France to prove that Bomber Command was capable of operating into Europe.

'11 July 1939. On this occasion, No 101 Squadron led a formation of 18 aircraft (9 from 101 Squadron and 9 from 110 Squadron). The route followed was: Tangmere-Le Treport-Orleans-Le Mans-Barfleur-St Catherine's Point-Tangmere. The flight was without incident. The formation of 18 aircraft covered 615 miles in 3hr 20min.'

Finally in August 'the Squadron took part in major air exercises as part of the "enemy force". High and low level attacks were carried out on distant targets. The weather was consistently bad with rain and low cloud. All attacks were successful'.

On 12 August the Squadron detached to No 5 Armament Training School, Penrhos with nine aircraft and crews for their last peacetime live bombing and gunnery practice. Training proceeded satisfactorily but the international situation deteriorated to such an extent that at 0915hrs on 24 August, Readiness State C came into force. This involved the delivery of official green envelopes bearing the word 'MOBILISA-TION' — hastily overstamped as a security afterthought — to the main body of the RAF Reserve and Volunteer Reserve. The signing of the Anglo-Polish Treaty of mutual assistance the following day eased the situation slightly but, although 'Mobilisation' was cancelled, 'the Squadron was recalled to West Raynham in view of the National Emergency'. Flying training was to continue but personnel were briefed to hold themselves ready for recall from leave at six hours' notice.

Readiness State D came into force on 26 August whereby aircraft were to be dispersed around the perimeter of the airfield to minimise the destructive effects of possible air attack. Only essential air test flying was now permitted, and although bombs were not yet to be fused all personnel were recalled from leave and all aircraft made serviceable. Mobilisation began in earnest on 1 September as 'E' class Reservists (the reserve of all airmen in all trades with and without previous service in the RAF) started to arrive, and on 2 September 'the peacetime Squadron

records were closed in concurrence with Mobilisation Instructions'. The following day the Squadron heard that they were at war with Germany.

'3/9/39. No 101 Squadron on the declaration of war was stationed at West Raynham as part of No 81 Wing within No 2 Group. The Squadron Commander was Wing Commander J. H. Hargroves. Establishment — 22 officers and 207 airmen. Equipment — 21 Bristol Blenheim Mk IVs. Squadron Adjutant — Flying Officer D. S. Dawson. OC "A" Flight — Squadron Leader W. R. Hartwright; OC "B" Flight — Squadron Leader T. E. Morton, Today is the third day of mobilisation which is proceeding satisfactorily.'

As Blenheims from Wyton had attacked the German fleet in the morning, retaliation was feared likely and, in order to give potential Luftwaffe bombers less to aim at, at 1415hr eight of the Squadron aircraft and crews were hastily ordered to deploy to West Raynham's scatter aerodrome at Brize Norton.

Mobilisation was completed on 5 September 'except for certain items of equipment such as oxygen bottles, rubber dinghies, anti-gas clothing, field dressings etc'. Like all 2 Group squadrons, 101 had been ordered to stand by for 'ops' against German naval units off Wilhelmshaven and electricity and oil plants in the Ruhr, but after a few days a feeling of anticlimax set in. On 9 September after six days of sitting around the Squadron record still had 'nothing of importance to report'; two days later, the eight dispersed aircraft and crews were recalled from an uneventful sojourn at Brize Norton on the amusing grounds that 'the enemy might discover the Scatter Plan'. Whatever hopes there were of action always came to nought.

'12/9/39. Squadron standing by from 0700hr at 45min notice to operate against fleeting targets on North Sea. Squadron stood down at 2000hr without operating owing to bad weather conditions over North Sea.'

Higher authority soon saw the need to reduce this feverish pitch of inactivity:

'HQ 2 Groups 17/9/39. 1714 hr. The following message was received from Bomber Command: "In order to allow Groups to proceed with training with the minimum amount of interruptions, the Air Officer Commanding-in-Chief is willing for one squadron only to be regarded as at four hours' readiness for operations. Remaining squadrons may be regarded as free for training at 24 to 36 hours notice for operations."

'2008hr. Wings informed of the preceding message. The Squadron standing by at four hours' notice is to be known as the Duty Squadron. Thanks to this arrangement,

satisfactory training programmes can be made.'

101 took their turn as 2 Group's Duty Squadron, not that it got them any nearer to the action.

'HQ 2 Group, 21/9/39, 2020hr. Orders issued to West Raynham to the effect that NINE aircraft from 101 Squadron are to attack German surface warships during daylight hours on 22 September. Aircraft to standby at 60 minutes' readiness from 0930hr.

'22/9/39. Nine aircraft of 101 Squadron stood by at 60 minutes' notice from 0930hr to attack fleeting targets at sea, but at 0940hr the Squadron was instructed to stand down and revert to four hours' readiness.'

Bomber Command's greatest problem at this time was that it lacked the strength to undertake any far-reaching bomber offensive. Of the 33 front-line squadrons available on the outbreak of war, 10 had gone to France with the British Expeditionary Force and the remainder were wholly equipped with aircraft that could do no more than pin-prick the outer fringes of German territory. Thus it was of paramount importance to conserve Bomber Command's limited manpower resources and not to fritter them away on all-out bombing of the enemy until the Command was fully equipped with four-engined 'heavy' bombers backed by adequate reserves. For this reason Bomber Command was initially authorised to do little beyond reconnoitring, dropping a few token bombs on enemy ships at sea, and depositing propaganda leaflets.

In the first year of the war, Bomber Command dropped some 74 million leaflets.

40
Blenheim IV merging with the fields below where hay making is in progress.

Known as 'bumphleteering', it was not a very popular pastime on 101 because crews felt that they were being exposed to a great deal of danger for not much purpose. So one day, while they dropped leaflets proclaiming in German that 'This might have been a bomb', one Squadron wag took along a huge brick, wrote on it in German, 'This might have been a leaflet', and heaved that out.

Unfortunately 101 Squadron's chances of glory were now to be reduced even further. One of the main problems with the Blenheim I had been its range — it could manage no more than 900 miles when bombed-up* and so it was decided that the Blenheim IV should have additional fuel tankage in the outer wings. However, this modification was only incorporated on the Bristol production line with the 81st Blenheim IV, and so the previous 80 had to be modified at station level. By 27 September, 101 was one of only two squadrons left with unmodified aircraft, bringing them down to what was known as Range State 1; it was a bad time to be so underendowed.

World War 2 transformed the whole social fabric of the Royal Air Force. Before 1939 it had consisted of a small, regular élite of officers and men, but now the gates were open to a growing influx of volunteers to swell the aircrew ranks. 'By the end of 1937,' wrote a young Scotsman by the name of Scrymageour Wedderburn, 'it was obvious to me that war was coming as sure as fate, so I decided that I would rather fight *my* war in the RAF, if they would have me, rather than in either of the other Services. I therefore applied for a Short Service Commission, was accepted for training, and set off in my £100 car (a Ford 8) for the Civil Flying School at Ansty.'

The Air Ministry decreed in *Air Ministry Pamphlet 101*, 5th edition of July 1940, that 'direct appointment commissions for flying duties are only made in exceptional circumstances. Entry into the General Duties (Flying) Branch is normally through the ranks . . . As vacancies occur for commissions, they are filled by promotion from the ranks, either on completion of flying training or subsequently.'

Having learned the basics of flying at Ansty and Little Rissington, Scrym Wedderburn was then sent down to the RAF depot, Uxbridge, 'where we were taught how to become officers and gentlemen in the space of two weeks. I always remember one senior

officer summing it all up when he said, "Gentlemen, officers do not frequent pubs, they visit hotels!" '.

A newly commissioned officer received an outfit allowance of £40 in 1940 and if he was suitable for immediate posting to a service unit he was paid 14s 6d a day as a pilot officer. He was provided with free accommodation and rations and if he was separated from his family 'by the exigencies of the service', he received an extra 4s 6d per day to put a roof over their head. He also knew that if he was 'invalided in consequence of wound, injury or disease directly attributable to the conditions of service, he may be granted disability retired pay or other award calculated according to his rank and the degree of disablement. Disability retired pay will not be granted or continued if the degree of disablement is assessed at less than 20%.'

Having completed advanced flying training, Pilot Officer Wedderburn found himself posted to 101 at the beginning of 1940 to join other prospective bomber pilot, observers and WOp/AGs. Whereas Training Command had taught them the basic skills, it was left to Bomber Command to weld individuals into fighting crews and to familiarise them with the type of aircraft in which they would have to operate. Before the war such conversion training had been left to the front-line squadrons, but now they were unable to cope with both training and wartime operations so in September 1939 13 squadrons were 'rolled up' and made into advanced training centres. These Group Pool Squadrons (rechristened Operational Training Units (OTUs) in April 1940) did sterling work but the operational squadrons could only absorb a limited number of replacement crews at any one time; something had to be done with the remainder, and on 21 September 1939 Air Chief Marshal Ludlow-Hewitt made the following poposals to the Under Secretary of State for Air:

'There is a further requirement which has become apparent, namely the provision of reserve operational squadrons to absorb the output of Group Pool Stations in excess of requirements. It is most necessary to avoid cluttering up the training units with surplus crews. The syllabus of a Group Pool Station is the very minimum necessary to put crews into an elementary state of operational efficiency. It is most desirable that they should get more operational practice and experience if time is available, before going to operational squadrons.

'Hence it is necessary to provide a unit into which crews from Group Training Stations can go pending absorption by operational units. These intermediate units will be called Reserve Squadrons, and . . . in each Reserve Squadron, a minimum of three

*From East Anglia, the approximate distance to Berlin and back was 1,100 miles; to Hamburg and back 900 miles; to Hamm and back 800 miles, and to the Ruhr and Cologne and back 700 miles. More distant targets such as Turin, Danzig, and Prague were way beyond the range of the 'medium' Blenheim.

of the most efficient and experienced crews in each flight will be retrained for training purposes...

'I propose to use the balance of the non-mobilising squadrons for this purpose. In the case of the Blenheims, I have had to put one squadron down from the operational first line for use as a second line reserve. This will bring the Blenheim organisation into line with the other Groups, namely six operational squadrons, one reserve squadron and three group pool squadrons.

'Any reduction in the strength of our Striking Force is, of course, undesirable, but it must be accepted if it is the only means of conserving our strength. Under existing circumstances it is necessary to take the long view.'

Thus, although all 2 Group's Blenheims would receive their long-range fuel tankage by October, someone had to be Reserve Squadron and it might as well be one of the Range State 1 units. 'HQ 2 Group, 25/9/39, 1255 hours. Duty Squadron is 101 Squadron which, with effect from today, is the Reserve Squadron for this Group and was ordered to stand down.'

101 eventually became a very large unit with 27 aircraft compared to the usual Blenheim squadron complement of 16 aircraft plus five reserves. Its size reflected the scale of the task foreseen in supporting the other six Blenheim squadrons in 2 Group, and for the next six months the Squadron spent its time converting new crews to operational flying and ferrying them around for all the other Blenheim units. 'On 101 pilots converted from the Blenheim I to the Blenheim IV and learned what it was really like to work operationally with navigators and WOp/AGs.' Not that life for the fledgling aircrew was without incident:

'2/11/39. A Blenheim IV piloted by Plt Off C. H. Keedwell crashed on landing after carrying out air firing exercises. The aircraft was written off.'

'14/11/39. The port engine of a Blenheim piloted by Plt Off T. R. Goodbody, with Sgt Eden and AC Jeffries as crew, failed in cloud on descending from a height test up to 20,000ft. Pilot ordered crew to abandon aircraft when at 2,000ft. Sgt Eden made a successful landing in a field at Sohan near Mildenhall with a torn parachute. The canopy was probably torn on the light series bomb carriers beneath the fuselage through pulling the rip cord too soon. The aircraft broke cloud and pilot ordered AC Jeffries not to jump. The pilot then landed successfully at Mildenhall aerodrome. Engine failure was probably due to hot air intake shutters being buckled due to backfire.'

Then at last something came along to really make the adrenalin flow. Back in August Germany had signed a non-aggression pact with the USSR which left Hitler free to make war in the west while the Soviet Union could absorb its Baltic neighbours. Once 'pacts' were imposed on Estonia, Latvia, and Lithuania, it was Finland's turn, but the Finns, with great courage, refused to accept Soviet demands on their sovereignty and at the end of November war broke out. Given the respective might of the two nations, the Soviets should have wrought a swift and crushing defeat, but initially the Finns not only held out but also inflicted humiliating losses on their aggressors. This David and Goliath struggle aroused considerable British sympathy for the gallant Finns, and though they were both at war with Germany, Britain and France were prepared to send an expeditionary force if Finland asked for it. In the event this joint initiative floundered over transit arrangements, but in February 1940 the Finnish defences finally cracked and the French government unilaterally decided to send 50,000 volunteers and 100 bombers to Finland. 'We could certainly not act on this scale...,' wrote Winston Churchill in *The Second World War* (Cassell & Co, 1950); 'however, it was agreed to send 50 British bombers.'

As the Finns had acquired 18 Blenheim bombers after 1937, it made sense to supplement their air arm with similar aircraft. Unfortunately the Bristol Aeroplane Company did not have any aircraft immediately available for dispatch, so it was decided to use aircraft from the RAF's second line reserve.

On 16 February 1940, Bomber Command signalled HQ 2 Group that '12 short-nosed Blenheims are to be flown to Finland. Aircraft are to be flown by volunteer crews'. As 101 was non-operational, five Squadron crews — captained by Sqn Ldr J. F. Stephens, Sqn Ldr P. E. Meagher, Flt Lt E. J. Little and Sgt Hill (with Flg Off E. J. Palmer's crew in reserve) — had no hesitation in volunteering for some action. 'It was all cloak and dagger stuff,' recalled one Squadron member. 'The Blenheim did not have the range to fly direct, so the route was to be Bicester-Dyce-Stavanger-Basteras — finishing up at a Finnish aerodrome to be named later.' But Norway was then neutral, 'so we were all to go as civilians'. They were told to wear 'plain clothes' and they were to be 'relegated to the reserve without loss of pay'. The crews had to be given passports describing them as 'Bristol Engineers', but 'at the outbreak of war, our civilian clothes had been sent home, so all our passport photographs were taken with everyone wearing the only civilian jacket that anyone could find on the station'.

Subsequently it was announced publicly that '36 British volunteers have been engaged by the Finnish Government to ferry aircraft to Finland'. 'In time our civilian outfits were assembled, and our forged passports stowed in the Intelligence Officer's safe. We were due to take off in two days, taking our bomb loads with us, when a signal came direct from the Air Ministry telling us to hold everything. The whole exercise was called off a few days later when Finland capitulated.'

So it was back to the old routine of bombing practice and formation training, for it was felt that the unescorted Blenheims could only survive if they massed together for mutual protection.

However, once France fell and the Germans started massing across the Straits of Dover, the RAF could no longer afford the luxury of reserve squadrons. Too many good men had been lost over France and so, on 4 July 1940, 101 went to war at last when three aircraft and crews were sent to attack oil targets in northern Germany.

'First crew Flg Off Messervy, Sgt Forgeard and Sgt Whiteman carried out first run over target but bombs failed to release, so in spite of heavy fire pilot made second run up at 1725hrs to drop 4 × 250lb bombs in salvo from 2,000ft. Bombs burst large pipeline at Ostermoor between fuel tanks and Kiel Canal, and obliterated scene.

'Second crew returned owing to lack of cloud cover. Third crew, captained by CO, Wg Cdr Hargroves, failed to return.'

Official recognition of the Squadron's new status came through the following day.

AIR MINISTRY
'SECRET   LONDON SW1
S.5457/DCAS   5 July 1940
To: Air Officer Commanding-in-Chief
    Bomber Command.
'Sir,
'I am directed to say that, in view of the present critical state of the war, you are requested to convert all Reserve squadrons in your Command to first line operational squadrons.
2. The functions heretofore carried out by the Reserve squadrons will have to be shared between the operational training units and the first-line squadrons.

I am, Sir,
Your obedient Servant
Douglas
Air Vice-Marshal
Deputy Chief of Air Staff'

However, the Squadron's experiences the day before served to illustrate the problems facing Blenheim units in the summer of 1940. For a start, the loss of an experienced crew such as the Wing Commander's underlined the question of Blenheim vulnerability in daylight. Lacking either speed, manoeuvrability, or ceiling, the Blenheim's only hope of avoiding destruction lay in its armament, yet initially the turret was only endowed with a single machine gun which stood little chance against modern wing cannons. Not that the workman could always blame his tools:

'19/9/40. One aircraft took off at 0600hrs to attack Dunkirk. This aircraft returned

owing to lack of cloud cover. Two aircraft took off at 0640 hours and 0730 hours respectively to shoot down drifting balloons in Norfolk area. Balloons were located but shooting was not successful.'

Where possible Blenheims still sought sanctuary in darkness, but as the situation in Western Europe became desperate, the AOC 2 Group deemed it 'essential that the destructive efforts of our night bombing operations over Germany should be continued throughout daylight by sporadic attacks on the same objectives. *The intention is to make attacks only when cloud cover gives adequate security.*'

As a result the second 101 crew to visit Kiel on 4 July was probably wise to return when their main means of defence failed to materialise, whereas Wing Commander Hargroves probably pressed on for too long and paid the penalty.

As German preparations for the Battle of Britain got under way, Bomber Command's attentions moved nearer home, to quote from Operational Instruction No 38 dated 3 July 1940: 'The enemy are using airfields and landing grounds in France, Belgium and Holland... The intention is to destroy as many aircraft as possible on the ground thus forcing the enemy to withdraw. Airfields are to be attacked by sections escorted by fighters, or sections of individual aircraft using cloud cover when definite information is received from fighter reconnaissance.' The latter was something of a let-out clause because Fighter Command has its own duties to perform in 1940 — thus there were no fighter

42
'Bomb train' of 250lb GP bombs and incendiaries on its way out to the Blenheim dispersal for loading. *IWM*

43
Observer at his position in the Blenheim nose. *IWM*

43

escorts available when 101 flew off to attack airfields in northern France and Belgium, and Squadron Blenheims had to run the gauntlet of the German air defences alone by day when their crews were sent to bomb the long-range guns on the Pas de Calais or invasion barges in the Channel ports. It was the price that had to be paid in a crisis. 'You must bear in mind,' signalled the AOC, 'that your forces may have to play a most important part in repelling an invasion of this country, and you should be prepared at short notice to divert your squadrons to the attack of the invading enemy force at ports of departure and subsequently at sea, and points of landing in this country. To meet the threat of invasion, twelve aircraft (at each station) are to stand by every morning at 20 minutes notice from twilight to sunrise.' These daily stand bys in Squadron rotation did nothing to ease the Blenheim crews off the horns of their dilemma. If the skies were clear enough to see the target properly, they were probably clear enough for the enemy to detect the intrusion. On the other hand, if the skies were cloudy enough to prevent detection or destruction, they probably restricted visibility sufficiently to thwart accurate navigation and bomb delivery. After all the recommended minimum safe weapon delivery height to avoid bomb blast was 1,000ft for 250lb bombs and 700ft for 40lb weapons, and as attacks from great heights reduced accuracy, this kept the Blenheim crews right in the optimum firing bracket for the anti-aircraft guns which ringed the invasion ports. Despite the gravity of the national situation therefore, Blenheim vulnerability was such that on 14 August 1940 'the Squadron ceased to operate by day and commenced night operations'.

Yet even with inadequate aircraft, 101 Squadron crews still gave of their all. 'On the night of 9 September 1940, Plt Off Bicknell and crew were ordered to carry out an attack on Antwerp aerodrome. Whilst flying across the North Sea, their port engine gave trouble and finally stopped completely just before reaching the Dutch coast.

'The Captain decided to abandon the original target and bomb Haamstad aerodrome instead — this was located by his observer and bombed from 5,000ft.

'On return journey, the aircraft commenced to lose height and continued to do so despite every precaution taken by crew. Before reaching English coast and flying just above the water, the aircraft started to lose speed and captain decided that a landing on the sea was necessary. He warned crew and landed in every rough sea near a trawler. Pilot and observer forced a way through broken perspex and then went to assistance of air gunner. He was unconscious and trapped in cockpit but in spite of heavy sea, pilot and observer struggled to try and release him until aircraft sank five minutes later.

'Pilot and observer picked up by trawler some 30 minutes later. Pilot was cut about head and observer unconscious. The crew had already carried out a number of successful raids over enemy country and have always shown greatest determination, skill and coolness in reaching and attaining their objectives.'

On 29 September, 'Plt Off N. Bicknell and Sgt W. B. Gingell were awarded the DFC and DFM respectively for their courage and devotion to duty in operations against the enemy on the night of 9 September'.

There was no let-up in the tempo of night operations against the invasion ports and the lines of communication that supported them; 101 launched six aircraft on the night of 31 August/1 September alone, but such con-centrated effort only resurrected the old problem of finding precise targets in darkness after a lengthy flight with very limited navigational aids.

'4/9/40. Operations — Night. Four aircraft took off to attack Hamm marshalling yards and one to attack Berck-sur-Mer aerodrome. Owing to searchlight activity and poor visibility, no aircraft succeeded in locating Hamm.* Alternative targets attacked were — a ship by one aircraft, an unidentified aerodrome by one aircraft, a cluster of lights by another aircraft, and Berck-sur-Mer by two aircraft.'

'8/9/40. Operations — Night. Ten aircraft took off to attack Boulogne Harbour and shipping in harbour. Five aircraft did not reach target area owing to bad weather conditions and returned to base. Three aircraft succeeded in reaching target, bombs released but results unobserved. Two aircraft and crews did not return; one was captained by Flt Lt Palmer who had been with this Squadron since May 1937.'

Nevertheless, there were successes to sustain morale:

'18/9/40'. Twelve aircraft were ordered to attack Dunkirk barge concentrations and to complete two raids during the hours of darkness. The first series of raids commenced at 1930hr and were completed at 2300hr. The aircraft proceeded in the second series of raids commencing at 2359hr and ending at 0340hr on 19 September. All aircraft attacked target under ideal weather conditions with satisfactory results.

'19/9/40. Following telegram of congratulations received:

'To OC West Raynham. From AOC-in-C Bomber Command. I have noticed with much pleasure the extreme keenness and efficiency behind your recent night operations which reflect great credit on all concerned with flying, arming and maintenance.' The AOC 2 Group also sent his congratulations to 'the CO and crews of 101 Squadron for their efforts last night and to the ground personnel who effected the rapid turn round'.

As winter approached though, the crews had to face another foe besides the Luftwaffe, and that was the weather.

---

*Hamm was a natural target in that it possessed the largest and best equipped railway marshalling yards in Europe. It was of crucial importance to the German war effort because it not only maintained and reinforced the invasion forces in France and the Low Countries but it was also the focal point for the supply of raw materials to and armaments from Germany's great industrial centre, the Ruhr. The main consideration here though was its sheer size - Clapham Junction would have been swallowed several times over in the Hamm yards and its connections which covered an area four miles long by about ¼ mile wide — yet the Blenheim crews could not even find it.

'2/3 October 1940. One crew (Plt Off Brown, Sgt Collis and Sgt Loughlin) took off at 2331hr. They did not succeed in locating target owing to 10/10 cloud extending from 1,000ft to 15,000ft. Severe icing conditions encountered with this aircraft causing pilot to abandon task and return to base with bombs.'

'20/10/40. Five aircraft dispatched to one target and four aircraft to another target with 4 × 250lb bombs. Three crews managed to bomb first target at heights between 7,000 and 11,000ft. One aircraft returned to base owing to illness of pilot and one aircraft unable to locate target after search lasting 20min, so crew released bombs "safe" in sea and returned to base. A ground mist covered aerodrome during this night's ops, causing some considerable difficulty to pilots locating aerodrome. All flares were finally illuminated ie Money flares, gooseneck flares, hooded gooseneck flares and glim lamps.* All aircraft finally landed safely on aerodrome. Some anxiety was felt for last two aircraft until they both arrived over aerodrome boundary on their approach to flare path in line astern with an interval of approximately 50 yards. They did land successfully in formation however.'

But the most insidious enemy of all was the cold. Time and time again aircraft returned because a crew member was ill, and usually it was because he was sick with cold. 'It is cold of a different kind to that experienced on the ground. It seems to bite into you and attacks your will-power making you physically and mentally incapable of doing anything except going to sleep. The half-open turret in which the gunner sat was the coldest place in the aircraft and after a time I found it difficult just to reel out the trailing aerial to pass the relevant code to the ground station to prevent us being shot down.'

Later, electrically heated suits would be provided, but in the winter of 1940 crews had to make do as best they could. 'Having put on as much clothing as possible and still able to walk, I now added inner and outer flying suits and three pairs of gloves — silk, woollen and leather. I collected my gas-operated Vickers machine gun, plodded out to the waiting lorry and was driven to our faithful Blenheim.'

At the dispersal the crews were met by groundcrew who were often frozen

*Although 101 had been operating at night as far back as 1917, such was the unpreparedness of the RAF for night wartime operations that, apart from these flares, almost every other airfield lighting aid had to be improvised. Thus, on many occasions, two motor cars were positioned 100 yards either side of the up-wind end of the runway to act as touch-down markers whilst an early attempt at providing an approach funnel consisted of four goosenecks taken out by a lorry.

FORTUNA II (RIGHT) AN

44
Although this photograph was taken from an aircraft belonging to 18 Squadron, 101's one-time stablemate at West Raynham, it gives an interesting view from the gunner's position of a Blenheim. The blur in the foreground is the single gun barrel of a Vickers gas-operated machine gun with drum feed. Squadron aircraft sported yellow stripes on their trail planes for a time to catch the gunner's eye because, despite the fitment of an interrupter gear, it was still possible to shoot off the Blenheim's tail.

themselves after hours spent preparing the aircraft on the open airfield. Everyone stood patiently by as the swaddled air gunner struggled to fix his machine gun on to its mounting, and then the crew taxied out to await a 'green' for take-off. 'We were away. A watery haze spread over the countryside... Like a great strip of silver paper the North Sea hove into view. It looked cold, unfriendly, and I always had the feeling that once you started to fly over it you cut your last link with everything that meant safety and warmth.' (Quoted from *2 Group RAF* by M. J. F. Bowyer (Faber, 1974).

Now that they were airborne, the freezing conditions became even more intense.

'The clouds congeal with ice and snow as the aircraft passes through them; this collects, often to a thickness of six inches, on the surfaces of the planes and windscreens, cutting off the crew still further from the outside world. In the form of fine rime it penetrates through the interstices of the aircraft, covering the crew with white powder and freezing on clothes and equipment.' Sometimes thick ice formed inside the cockpit — instruments froze, oxygen bottles were known to freeze to crew fingers, and on occasions the oxygen system failed too. 'Worst of all, ice accumulates on the controls, jamming them and rendering the aircraft temporarily uncontrollable. Despite the fact that the majority of these aircraft are equipped with de-icing gear it has proved often ineffective in conditions of this kind. Neither will heating equipment stand up against temperatures of −20° to −30° Centigrade.' (Quoted from *The RAF in Action*, Adam & Charles Black, 1940).

Given all this, it is remarkable that there was never any lack of men to fly the Blenheim on 101. 'When I finished my WOps course at Yatesbury,' recalled Jim Marshall, 'you stayed on the ground if you remained just a WOp. Men who wanted to fly had to do the air gunners' course, and I remember an air commodore who visited Yatesbury saying that the operational life of Blenheim aircrew was five hours. But there was never any shortage of volunteers — men cried if they weren't accepted as aircrew.'

On 25/26 October the Squadron hit German targets in the Cap Gris Nez area. 'All aircraft located the gun positions and dropped their bombs. This attack was carried out for its nuisance value and Squadron aircraft were over the target area for 30 minutes and released their bombs singly, to be followed over the target by another squadron.' If the object was to arouse the enemy, it succeeded admirably:

'27/10/40. West Raynham. 1815hr. Six enemy aircraft made two attacks dropping 50 bombs (50 kilos and 250 kilos). Aircraft believed to be Ju88s; six Blenheims, one Battle and one Tutor damaged, all aircraft capable of repair by unit. One hangar hit, one bay blown in, offices and crew room destroyed. Ground defences opened fire immediately at low flying enemy aircraft but were themselves machine-gunned by raiders. Aerodrome rendered U/S (unserviceable) by bomb craters.'

The Luftwaffe also sought revenge on West Raynham's satellite airfield at Massingham just up the road.

'27/10/40. Massingham Satellite, 1800hr. Three enemy aircraft, (believed Ju88s) made three attacks. Ten bombs dropped. One Blenheim destroyed and 11 Blenheims damaged — capable of repair by unit. One hut destroyed and one hut damaged. Landing ground rendered U/S by craters. Casualties — four killed, three seriously injured, four minor injuries. All aircraft attacked below 300ft — one aircraft known to have been brought down by ground defences. Operational ability of Squadron not affected.'

These raids immediately led to a decision to disperse the aircrews away from the airfield for their own safety, and on 9 November, 'Weasenham Hall was taken over by this Squadron to accommodate flying personnel. A provisional "house warming" was held during the evening'.

But such light relief could not disguise the fact that the winter of 1940/41 was no picnic for Blenheim bomber crews.

'24/11/40. Target — Wanne Eickel oil refinery in the Ruhr. Owing to 8/10 to 10/10 cloud cover over target, it was only with considerable difficulty that five crews were able to bomb target area. Results could not be observed although bomb flashes were seen under cloud. One aircraft crashed near West Raynham village. The lock nut on the spider

in the reduction gear of starboard engine of this aircraft became loose, causing reduction gear casing to be churned away. Airscrew shaft and airscrew left engine on return over North Sea and pilot (Sgt Redmond) returned on one engine. He located aerodrome but crashed during circuit of airfield, pilot and gunner (Sgt Woodruff) received minor head injuries but air observer (Sgt Green) received fractured skull and is dangerously ill.

'Two other aircraft abandoned task — bombs brought back — one owing to ice accretion and one because fixed aerial broke away from mast and wrapped around tail plane. One aircraft overdue and presumed lost. The crew took off at 1703hr, were heard on R/T at 1905hr, and then no further communication was received.'

'26/11/40. Sgt Observer Green died today as a result of injuries received.'

'16/12/40. Target — Mannheim. Seven aircraft detailed and three aircraft attacked primary target, bombs seen to burst in target area. One aircraft unable to locate target and bombed small town with railway at 2310hr from 12,000ft. Bomb bursts observed in town but railway missed by 100yd. One aircraft abandoned task owing to sickness of WOp/AG.

'Two crews were lost — Sgt Plt Clarke's aircraft was heard sending SOS from St Quentin, France. W/T fix passed to aircraft but no further communication received.

'Sgt Plt Skipworth had broadcast SOS, and a W/T fix and courses to steer were given to crew. Aircraft crashed at Fairlight Place Farm, just east of Hastings, at 0235hr on 17/12/40, and burnt out. All crew were killed.

'Three more aircraft got lost on return flight. Plt Off Brown and crew landed wheels-up in a field at Cornwood near Plymton, Devon. Plt Off Hill and crew ran out of petrol off Plympton and abandoned aircraft — all crew landed safely. Flt Lt Graham and crew landed at Christchurch aerodrome without a flare path. Aircraft landed without sustaining any damage. Wing Commander Singer was only pilot to land at base after proceeding to target.'

In fact, Wg Cdr N. C. Singer continued to command 101 right through to the end of his tour on 31 March 1941 when he was posted to HQ 2 Group. Perhaps survivors like him survived because they lived long enough to learn when to press on and when not to push their luck too far. Fortune certainly smiled on the favoured at times:

'13/12/40. Primary target not attacked as cloud cover proved insufficient, so crew (captained by Sqn Ldr Cree, OC B Flight) turned for Flushing. When flying at 500ft, pilot saw ship of between 800 and 1,000 tons in entrance to Flushing in vicinity of Jouteland. Beam attack made from about 400ft with two 250lb bombs and 13 40lb bombs. A steep turn was made and it was seen that the stick had straddled the ship. The ship was down at the stern and listing to port with steam escaping. Ship did not open fire as it appears they were taken by surprise as aircraft came out of broken cloud at 500ft.'

But Lady Luck could also be a fickle mistress, and she was at her cruellest when crews, mentally and physically exhausted as well as frozen stiff, had to land back at base in cloud and darkness after a five-hour raid into Germany.

'24/9/40. Aircraft crashed one mile south of Swaffham at 0530hr. This aircraft exploded and caught fire on impact with the ground. Sgts Lorimer, Booth and Simms killed.'

'27/9/40. One aircraft (Sgt Turner — pilot) crashed on landing, 350yd to right of landing lights. Two aircraft on ground damaged.'

'30/31 October 1940. One aircraft crashed at Coleby, Lincs, and all crew were killed.' Squadron morale was not helped by the fact that the Blenheim had a reputation as a bad aircraft to evacuate in the event of a crash.

By the end of 1940, 101 Squadron had lost 27 officers and NCOs killed in action, but for those who came back there was a welcome breakfast of eggs and bacon and a thorough intelligence debriefing before drifting off into the fitful sleep of exhaustion. For the fortunate few though, there were also the honours and awards.

'23/10/40. Plt Off C. R. Brown awarded DFC. Sgt (now Plt Off) Collis awarded DFM. Sgt Loughlin awarded DFM. This crew has shown great skill and determination in locating their targets and pressing home their attacks in spite of encountering heavy AA fire on nearly every occasion. A telegram of congratulations received from AOC 2 Group.'

But for the unlucky ones, like Sgt Skipworth's crew who died on 16 December, it was left to the Recovery Inspector to pick up the pieces.

'No 49 Maintenance Unit, Faygate.
AIRCRAFT COLLECTION ORDER.
Date 18/12/40
To. Messrs NICHOLLS & CO (BRIGHTON) LTD
100 NORTH ROAD, BRIGHTON.
Please arrange to collect immediately and dispose of aircraft as follows:-
TYPE & DESCRIPTION. BLENHEIM.
P.6953   M.U's SERIAL NO. B/10
LOCATION.   FAIRLIGHT.
HASTINGS.   CATEGORY. E.
DISPOSAL INSTRUCTIONS: To Faygate Confirmation of phone message.
Ref CSO/FAY/10125.

(Driver's copy of this order to be delivered to the Receiving Depot with aircraft).
Superintendent, CSO
No 49 Maintenance Unit, RAF
at Faygate, Horsham, Sussex'

But even bravery was not enough in the long run — '31/3/41. Plt Off Brown DFC, Plt Off Collis DFM and Sgt Loughlin DFM reported missing after raid on Wilhelmshaven.'

Nor did the experience that usually went with senior rank necessarily mean much in the lottery of Blenheim operations, as Wg Cdr Singer's successor found out within four days of taking over command of 101.

'3/4/41. Eleven aircraft detailed to attack Brest, taking off at 1915hr from West Raynham and landing back at Boscombe Down. Three aircraft reached target and landed without difficulty at Boscombe. Four aircraft returned to West Raynham on considering weather conditions hazardous. One aircraft landed South Cerney owing to weather and poor visibility. One aircraft landed at Shrewton owing to adverse weather. One aircraft crashed at Warmwell on return from target — all crew killed. The remaining aircraft was missing and the crew — Wg Cdr Addenbrooke, air observer Plt Off Fenton and WOp Sgt Blomely — presumed lost. No results of bombing were observed by the three aircraft which attacked target owing to cloud cover and ground haze.'

If the Blenheim crews were chancing their arm in September 1939, they were certainly pushing their luck over occupied Europe in the spring of 1941. Protection was the answer, and now that the threat of invasion had receded it was decided to send fighter-escorted bombers on daylight raids against 'fringe' targets in France. Any bombing results they achieved would be a bonus — the main aim was to entice German fighters to battle in the hope that this would prevent the Luftwaffe from either renewing daylight attacks on Britain or deploying aircraft to the impending assault on Greece. These forays were known as 'Circuses' and 101 led one on 17 April.

'17/4/41. Weather — light haze, cloud 4/10 at 3,000ft. Visibility — 3-4 miles. Two boxes of six 101 aircraft, together with six aircraft from 18 Squadron, carried out formation attack on Cherbourg with fighter cover. Course was set at 1600hr from Tangmere — formation in three boxes of six aircraft led by OC 101 Sqn, Wg Cdr McDougall.* First six aircraft attacked

*Wg Cdr J. McDougall took command of 101 following the death of Wg Cdr Addenbrooke. He remained on the Squadron until 5 May 1941 when he was posted to 90 Squadron.

45

46

45
101 Squadron Blenheim dives for
the sea. *IWM*

46
Blenheim runs in at 50ft to attack
enemy shipping. *IWM*

target at 1633hr, followed by other two formations at two-minute intervals. Good view
of target obtained by all bombing leaders,
and majority of bombs were seen to burst in
target area. All aircraft returned safely to
base.' As was customary the bombs were
released on their leader's signal and, although
this was the first time that as many as three
boxes were employed on a Circus, the enemy
fighters still did not react to the increased
bait.

With the conclusion of the Battle of Britain
and the dispersal of the invasion barges, at
the beginning of March 1941 Prime Minister
Churchill directed that the Battle of the
Atlantic was now to have full priority with
Bomber Command concentrating on naval
targets. Coupled with this was the tightening
of the sea blockade around Germany, and
orders were given to halt the movement of all
coastal shipping between the Brittany
peninsula and Germany. Any Axis vessel
that was sighted in these waters was to be
sunk, and the AOC 2 Group, Air Vice-
Marshal Stevenson, was ordered to see that
this was done irrespective of cost.

On 24 April Sqn Ldr R. O. M. Graham
led a detachment of nine Squadron aircraft
down to Manston in Fighter Command's
No 11 Group. Now assured of immediate
escort, the Flight set about implementing
'Channel Stop', an exercise designed to close
the Straits of Dover to enemy shipping by
daylight while MTBs continued the task by
night.

The trouble with the enemy ships which
plied these coastal waters was that they were
generally small, so the maximum number of
available aircraft had to be launched to make
a concentrated attack. Moreover, the enemy
protected his merchantmen with flak ships,
each of which had tremendous fire power, so
surprise was essential and this could only be

achieved by flying very low over the sea. This
was no picnic for the Blenheim crews
because the visibility at low level could be
very poor and a momentary lapse of concentration could lead to a watery grave, but
as wise Axis merchantmen clung to the
European coast, low flying was the only way
to avoid radar detection and the adjacent
fighter and anti-aircraft battery protection
that the early warning stations could
summon up. To lessen the odds against them
therefore, Squadron crews were briefed to
remain in their allocated areas for only a few
minutes, even though fighter escorts were
supposed to keep the enemy off the backs of
the Blenheim crews while they concentrated
on their destructive errand. The laid down
instructions were for the Blenheim formation
to fly extremely low in line abreast — 50ft
was the maximum suggested altitude though
many flew lower — at the start of the 'beat'.
On arrival at the allotted start line, usually
some 30 miles from the coast, the Blenheims
would fly towards the coast until the leader
was approximately three miles from the
shoreline, whereupon he led the formation
parallel to the coast for three minutes before
turning home. Any ship that saw them
would surely report them, so the order was to
sink the first vessel sighted, and indeed any
ship in the beat area, with the minimum
delay. With these tactics in mind, the
Manston detachment set about its business.

'27/4/41. Weather fine and clear with
good visibility. Three aircraft from 101
Squadron detachment at Manston carried
out attack on enemy shipping off Calais at
1100hr. These aircraft encountered nine
trawlers and attacked them in trail from 50ft
with 12 250lb bombs fused for 11sec delay.
Much opposition from shore batteries and
machine-gun fire from ships encountered, as
a result of which one of Blenheims shot down
— crew posted as missing. Other two aircraft claimed to have sunk one trawler and
damaged another. One of these aircraft was
engaged by Me109 but not hit. Fighter escort
of six Spitfires from 74 Squadron, Manston,
was provided.'

'29/4/41. Weather cloudy with bright
periods. Visibility moderate. Squadron
detachment at Manston sent out three aircraft to attack four merchant vessels — one
large and three small — reported in
Zuydcoote Pass steaming towards Dunkirk.
An interception made three miles off
Nieuport at 0908hr and large merchant
vessel and one small ship (of 2,000 tons and
500 tons respectively) were attacked from
50ft with four 250lb bombs. No results
observed by bombers owing to low level of
attack and violent evasive action which had
to be taken to avoid flak, but it is believed
that the large ship was hit and damaged. A

gun crew on one ship put out of action by rear gunner. High fighter cover provided by 12 Hurricanes of 609 Squadron, Biggin Hill, and close fighter escort by six Spitfires of 74 Squadron, Manston, who beat off three Me109s. However, one Blenheim (Captain — Sgt Pilot Deane) was badly damaged on both wings, fuselage and rudder, and port engine also damaged. Observer (Sgt Jordan) was wounded in the elbow but in spite of all this, aircraft made a safe landing at base.'

There was nothing easy about shipping strikes even with fighter protection.

'3/5/41. Weather fine and clear, visibility good. Six aircraft from Squadron detachment at Manston, with close support of 12 Spitfires from 74 Squadron, took off at 1330 hours to intercept steamer of 2,000 tons heavily escorted by four trawler-type vessels and five E-boats. Leader of first section of three aircraft returned to base at 1340hr owing to U/S rear guns*; his No 2 and 3 aircraft turned off track near ETA (estimated time of arrival) to attack what they thought to be target but proved to be two wrecks off La Panne. These two aircraft returned to base with their bombs.

'Second section sighted and intercepted target, a motor vessel (MV) of 2,500 tons, heavily escorted and positioned two miles west of Ostend. The Section leader (Pilot Officer Brown) scored three hits on large vessel and claimed it sunk whilst other two aircraft hit two escort vessels and claimed them as sunk. All ships heavily machine-gunned. Height of attack was 50ft, dropping four 250 pounders with 11-second delay.

'Again at 1930hr, six aircraft in two sections of three made rendezvous with 12 Spitfires of 74 Squadron at Dungeness and set course to intercept convoy estimated to be eight miles SSW of Boulogne. Convoy, consisting of large motor vessel (5-6,000 tons), smaller MV of 2,000 tons and two flak ships found 1½ miles south of DR (dead reckoning) position and formation, led by Sqn Ldr Graham, went in to attack each ship by sections at 1956hr. Attack pressed home in face of concentrated and accurate fire from ships, their escort vessels, and from French coast. Larger ship hit just above the beam with four 250lb bombs and was observed later to emit a violent explosion and catch fire. This vessel claimed as sunk by formation leader, No 2 and No 3 of whose section also scored near misses.

'The second section attacked smaller MV and although thought she was probably hit,

*By now, Squadron Blenheims carried twin Browning guns with higher rates of fire and continuous belt feed, but survival aids such as these together with armour plating and self-sealing tanks also increased aircraft all-up-weight which in turn reduced performance still further.

this was not confirmed. The Section leader (Plt Off Brown) was hit by fire from ship and last seen heading for French coast on fire. No 2 of this section (Sgt Deane) also hit and was observed by one of fighter escort to go down in sea bearing 110° Dungeness at 10 miles. Pilot and navigator seen to get out of aircraft but although Air Sea Rescue service carried out search very soon afterwards, no trace of them was found. No 3 of this section also hit in fuselage and port engine, but made safe return to base.'

The Manston detachment returned to West Raynham on 9 May. For their outstanding efforts in making 'Channel Stop' as good as its name, Sqn Ldr Graham, Flt Lt McLaren and Plt Off Redmond, were awarded the DFC, and Flt Sgt Cooke received the DFM. Life in their absence had not been dull. 'I did three daylight low level shipping strikes,' recalled Sgt H. L. Mackay, a Wop/AG, 'and although we flew in formation on all of them for protection, they were still very grim. My first mission was not only terrifying but also we were the only aircraft out of three to return. In my fearfully paralysed state, I sent a request back to base in *very* shaky morse for an ambulance and doctor to meet us. On landing, I was met by an angry and abusive Squadron signals officer who asked what the hell I was doing sending it all in "long" and thereby wasting signal time. The fact that five of us were sent direct to West Raynham from gunnery school without an OTU so that I didn't know many of the operational procedures didn't bother him at all. I did notice that in his outburst he had a very chronic "twitch" — a bad case of ops fatigue.

'Incidentally, of the five of us who joined 101 together, four were lost on ops within three weeks. Perhaps I was destined for a charmed life!'

To lighten the load Squadron crews periodically participated in high level 'Circus' operations which all agreed were 'a piece of cake compared with those low level strikes'. One particularly appealing idea to emanate from the planning staffs was the blocking of the Kiel Canal, and on 8/9 May five 101 Squadron crews were ordered to attack Holtenau at the Baltic end of the Canal. 'Four of these aircraft, although carrying out correct identification procedures when returning to base, were fired on by a large convoy on crossing the English coast near Cromer. All managed to return to base. The remaining aircraft did not attack primary target owing to intense searchlight activity.' Like many that had gone before, it was not a particularly war-winning raid, and so there were few tears shed when it was announced that this was to be the last mission that 101 would ever mount with the Blenheim.

The Wellington Era

In the middle of April 1941, while one flight commander was leading 'Channel Stop' from Manston, the other, Sqn Ldr Cree, was somewhat more comfortably employed on detachment at No 14 OTU Benson, gleaning 'information on conversion to Wellington aircraft'. By the end of the month, Wellington flying was taking place at West Raynham and on 11 June 1941, Sqn Ldr Jones and Sgt Caunt captained the first two 101 Squadron Wellingtons to be sent on an operational mission. Both crews successfully attacked the docks at Rotterdam, dropping a total of 6,000lb of high explosive (HE) bombs, before returning safely. 'It is worthy of mention,' recorded the Adjutant proudly, 'that 101 Squadron carried out their last operational sortie on Blenheim aircraft on 9 May 1941 and their first operation on Wellington aircraft on 11 June 1941 after only one month in conversion, during which period only one aircraft was very slightly damaged while night flying'.

Squadron Wellingtons hit Germany, or Cologne to be more precise, for the first time on 21 June 1941, and thereafter 101 settled down to employing their new aircraft operationally.

'27/6/41. NFTS carried out during day. (Night Flying Tests — during the day before each night raid, all aircraft designated for duty would be flown around the aerodrome for about half an hour to test all the systems.) Operations — of the nine aircraft that took off tonight, four crews successfully attacked Bremen. (Captains — Plt Off Todd, Sgt Caunt, Plt Off Redmond and Plt Off Rickinson.) Of the rest, Sqn Ldr Jones located primary target but bombs failed to release — he subsequently successfully attacked Den Helder. Sgt Fooks abandoned primary target owing to adverse weather conditions and attacked Oldenburg. Sqn Ldr Colenso and Sgt Taylor abandoned primary task owing to adverse weather conditions and each attacked Den Helder instead. One crew set out to attack Dunkirk (Captain — Plt Off Hardie) but they abandoned task owing to technical failure. They returned to base, changed aircraft and took off again within 45min of landing but were recalled by Group. Sgt Plts Taylor, Hart, Cook, Caunt and Allen granted commissions in the rank of pilot officer on probation.'

The Squadron mounted seven operations (or 55 sorties) with its new aircraft from

47
Wg Cdr D. R. Biggs — OC 101 Squadron from 16 May 1941 to 14 January 1942 — with his officers outside Weasenham Hall in the early summer of 1941. The lady seated in the middle was the owner of the Hall, and she was known somewhat cryptically to the Squadron as 'The Pheasant'.

47

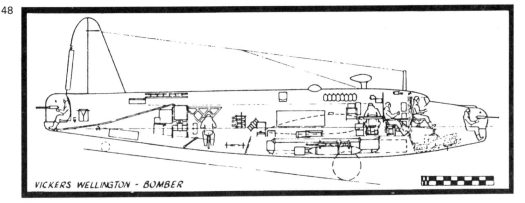

West Raynham, but it made little sense to keep a solitary Wellington unit in 2 Group, so on 6 July 101 moved to Oakington near Cambridge and transferred to 3 Group the following day. Two nights later 101 was back in business when it detailed 11 aircraft for operations.

The Wellington I was certainly a welcome improvement over the Blenheim in that it could carry twice the bomb load over nearly twice the range, ie 2,000lb to Danzig or northern Italy. The Wellington was also superior in terms of defensive armament — 101 Squadron was equipped with Wellington ICs and these carried a pair of .303in Browning machine guns in the hydraulically-powered nose and tail turrets, plus beam guns in the midship position. Barnes Wallis' famous geodetic construction also endowed the Wellington with a considerable reserve of strength, enabling some aircraft to return home with appalling battle damage.

Nevertheless, despite its strengths in comparison with what had gone before, the Wimpy (in view of its rotund, 'well fed' appearance, the Wellington was soon likened by its air and groundcrews to Popeye's stout, Hamburger-eating friend, 'J. Wellington Wimpy') was still too lumbering and under-powered for comfort, and its drawbacks were underlined when it came to attacking those targets that were either so precise or so important that they could only be profitably

bombed in daylight. Two of these were the battlecruisers *Scharnhorst* and *Gneisenau* which had wrought havoc in the North Atlantic between January and March 1941, and in order to curtail their future activities it was decided to bomb them in a surprise daylight raid on 24 July. Even so, in order to stand a reasonable chance of hitting such relatively small and well-defended targets, it was considered necessary to dispatch between 140 and 150 heavy and medium bombers against them (the Wellington was classed as a medium bomber).

The plan was to open the attack with unescorted Fortresses operating at high altitude, followed 15 minutes later by 18 Hampdens closely escorted by long-range Spitfires. It was hoped that these would draw off the German fighter cover, leaving the main force of Wellingtons and heavy bombers free to attack, without escort, in the shortest possible time. But the best laid plans often seem to go astray — at the last minute the *Scharnhorst* moved to La Pallice and so the heavy bombers were redirected there.

The Fortresses and escorted Hampdens went in as arranged, but unfortunately they did not exhaust the defences by the time the main force arrived. 'Sqn Ldr Colenso led the 101 Wellington element, supported by crews captained by Sgt Fisher, Flt Lt Craig and Plt Off Rickinson.' This section had to keep station to enjoy the protection of mutual fire-

```
No. 101 Squadron.                    BATTLE ORDER.              24th July, 1941.
SECRET.

A/C Letter.

   B. O      S/Ldr. Colenso . P/O. Ashton, P/O. Street, P/O. Osbon, Sgt. Rainbock, Sgt. Cormack, Sgt. Hatton.

   F.        F/Lt. Craig. Sgts. Sainsbury, Love, Hesmondhalgh, Price, Smith,

   V.        P/O Rickinson. Sgts. Watson, Bridgett, Jinkinson, Litton, Thompson.

   D. )      R E S E R V E   A I R C R A F T.


BOMB LOAD  -  5 x 500 lbs. S.A.P.,  fused .12 seconds delay.

FUEL   +  692 galls.                          BRIEFING -  0845 hours.

DISTRIBUTION:
Officer Commanding.       Met. Officer,        Armoury.          O.C. "B" Flight, 101 Sqdn.
Operations.               Officer's Mess.      Signals.          Regional Control.
W/Cdr. Biggs.             Sergeants' Mess.     O.C."A" Flt, 101 Sqdn.   Instrument Section.
```

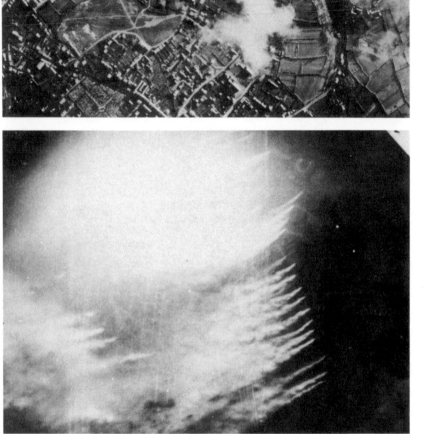

50

Wellington, 'which lacks armament, speed and handiness, and especially rate of climb, is a most unsuitable type of aircraft for daylight operations . . .'. This view was endorsed by a signal from Bomber Command declaring that henceforward, 'No 101 Squadron will be used for night bombing only, undertaking tasks similar to those of the heavy bomber Groups'. Not that concentrating on raids under cover of darkness was necessarily easier, and the Squadron lost 19 aircrew killed in action during August alone.

What of those aircrews on 101? The Squadron manning establishment increased as more Wellingtons arrived because not only did the larger aircraft, with their new hydraulic and electrical systems, need more groundcrew support to keep them in the air, but also they required more aircrew to operate them once they got up there. Squadron Wellingtons carried a crew of six — pilot, co-pilot, navigator (after April 1942, the title of 'observer' was officially changed to 'navigator'), WOp/AG and nose and tail gunners. Gone therefore were the days when most of the responsibility fell on the pilot; bigger teams demanded closer crew co-operation and operational training revolved around the motto, 'United we fly, divided we fall'.

A typical description of a bomber crew at this time was provided by an Air Ministry publication entitled *Bomber Command*, which was issued by the Ministry of Aviation in 1941. 'The men of Bomber Command are appointed to fulfil a special mission. Their life is not that of other men — not that even of those in the other branches of the service. Its very physical conditions are different. For them nowadays much of the night is the day, much of the day a time for sleep and repose. Discipline is constant yet flexible . . . Triumph and disaster are met and vanquished together.

'The captain and his second pilot do the actual flying, the observer navigates and drops the bombs; the wireless operator helps the navigator and with the air gunners does the fighting. The same spirit and practice of co-ordination is required of a bomber crew as of a crew of a racing eight or the members of a football eleven . . .

'The bomber pilot differs in training and environment from his colleague flying a Spitfire or Hurricane. A pilot of the Royal Air Force is subjected at an early stage to a process of selection by which it is determined whether he is better fitted to fly a fighter or a bomber. Both will have to fly aircraft; both will wear pilot's wings; but here their ways diverge. The fighter pilot is in action for an hour and a half to two hours at most, often far less. He is usually led into the fight by his squadron leader.

50
The *Scharnhorst* and *Gneisenau* berthed in Brest (upper left). On such a clear day they looked an easy target.

51
Spot the battlecruisers — Brest obscured by a German smoke-screen.

power, 'but they lost the main formation south of Point de St Mathieu while waiting for Flt Lt Craig to catch up. His aircraft was seen to be attacked twice by enemy aircraft and was eventually shot down by an M109, crashing into the sea. Two more enemy aircraft were seen over the mainland so Sqn Ldr Colenso decided that his three aircraft would not attack alone. They turned and brought their bombs back.' It was a wise move because, of the 99 bombers that attacked Brest that day, 11 were shot down by fighters and flak. 'Subsequently reported that Sergeants Smith and Hesmondhalgh (Craig's air gunners) are prisoners of war.'

Thus the AOC 3 Group, Air Vice-Marshal J. E. A. Baldwin, echoed the opinion of his subordinates when he declared that the

'Very different, but equally important, qualities are required of a bomber pilot. He must be capable of considerable physical and mental endurance, for it may be necessary for him to remain nine, ten, eleven, or even twelve hours in the air, and to fly for the most part of that time over hostile territory or across the unfriendly sea. During much of the flight he may find his aircraft the object of an attack by enemy fighters far faster and more heavily armed. By reason of their greater speed his assailants can break off and renew their assault at any moment. Surprise, that weapon which more than any other wins a fight, is theirs to wield at will. The bomber pilot must fly doggedly on, defending himself with the aid of darkness and cloud outside and with the skill of his crew and their machine guns inside. The bomber pilot must not forget that he is one of a team and that that team is not flying separated from him in another Hurricane or Spitfire, but in the same aircraft, crouched over the navigator's table or hunched up in the gun turrets. He must be imaginative, yet not dismayed by his own imagination, brave yet cautious, cool yet daring.'

Nevertheless, in spite of these stirring words, the author of the propaganda pamphlet was in no doubt that 'the key man in the bomber aircraft is the navigator. His task is threefold. He must give his pilot the directions necessary to enable the bomber to reach the target at the right time; he must aim and release the bombs, and he must bring the aircraft and its crew safely back to base. Under ideal conditons his task is not difficult, but conditions are rarely ideal. Darkness, clouds, air currents, all singly or together, are his foes. His main pre-occupation is with air currents for he finds himself, unless the wind is directly ahead or astern, in much the same predicament as a man trying to swim straight across a river disregarding the force of the current. It cannot be done. The speed and direction of the wind have to be calculated and taken into constant consideration throughout the flight.

'The navigator has certain aids to help him in his calculations and enable him to check his position. These are: radio position finding, usually known as "radio fix", map reading and astro navigation. The first is limited by distance; the second is useless unless landmarks can be seen; the third can be used only when the stars are visible. The skilful navigator makes judicious use of all three. He is usually working in conditions opposed to accurate calculations, for he carries out his duties in a cramped space, wearing bulky clothes and an oxygen mask. Yet the proportion of bombers that reach their objectives, always very high, is growing higher. "The wind and waves are always on the side of the ablest navigator," runs a quotation from Gibbon upon the wall of the briefing-room of one bomber squadron. In the past many of the greatest sea navigators were British. Today our air navigators are showing themselves to be worthy of their for-bears.'

Somewhat surprisingly, there was no eulogy in similar vein on behalf of the air gunners. The poor old gunners always regarded themselves as 'tail-end Charlies' in every sense, probably because most were still only of airman rank at the start of the war. Then on 12 December 1939, the familiar air gunners' brevet was introduced and on 27 May 1940 all air gunners were suddenly promoted to the rank of sergeant and their pay increased accordingly to 7s 9d a day — shortly afterwards, commissioned air gunners started to appear. It was not before time. Gerry Hingley was waiting to undergo pilot training at the beginning of 1940, and it 'made a deep impression on me that the wireless operator/air gunners were still not sergeants. It seemed tough on these men that they should join the long food queues still wearing their flying boots and straight back from gruelling ops'.

Aircrew candidates — those destined to be trained as pilots, navigators, WOp/AGs or just air gunners — were carefully selected by a board of specialist officers. These selection boards sat regularly at many different centres throughout the Empire, and civilian candidates were considered according to their mental, educational and physical suitability. One aircrew selection board president, Grp Capt C. H. Keith, recalled in *I Hold My Aim* (Allen & Unwin, 1946) that 'there was never a shortage of volunteers, as nearly every youngster who comes into the RAF is consumed by a desire to fly . . . They came from every walk of life, from every trade and profession, and represented some of the finest manhood in the country — and a few who were "not so good". Most of them wanted to become pilots, although the educational standard necessary for the training of an observer had to be higher. They could volunteer for any one or two or more of the various crew categories. The type we welcomed was the lad who said: "I'd like to be a pilot, but if you can't take me for that, I'll go for observer or air gunner or anything you like, so long as I can become a member of an aircrew and have a crack at the Hun." '

'Gallantry and keenness are not sufficient alone to make a successful air-gunner; he must have a certain minimum of education or he could never stay the course during train-ing. It was heart-breaking to have to explain this to some of those we had to turn down . . .

'Cold, bitter vengeance by those who had been bombed was the motive that brought

52

Battle order for the first Squadron attack on Berlin.

53

250lb bombs being loaded on to a 101 Squadron Wellington at Oakington. Like the defensive guns, the bombs carried by British bombers in the early years of World War 2 were little different from their World War 1 counterparts, and as such were largely unsuited to the demands made on them. The standard 250lb and 500lb GP (General Purpose) bombs were an unsatisfactory compromise between strength of casing and weight of explosive, and their charge/weight ratio was only about 27% compared with 50% for their German equivalents. To add insult to injury, British explosive fillings were also less efficient and all too frequently they failed to detonate. No serious attempt was made to remedy the situation before the end of 1940 (by which time 1,000lb GP bombs were in use), and although bigger and better high explosive (HE) bombs were developed, notably in two main types — the medium capacity (MC) and high capacity (HC) — their arrival into service was slow.

No. 101 Squadron.					BATTLE ORDER. 7th September 1941. Serial No. 52.	
SHORT.						
Flight.	Aircraft.	Letter.	Captain of A/C.	2nd Pilot.	Crew.	
B.	Z.8842	T.	P/O. Robertson.	Sgt. Dil	Sgts. Mason, Treeby, Dennis, Little.	
B.	T.2846	S.	P/O. Polmore.	Sgt. Claneder.	Sgts. Pearson, Johnson, Williams, Edmond.	
B.	R.1219	R.	P/O. Imeson.	Sgt. Denning	Sgts. Fowler, Parkington, Lowden, Highfield.	
A.	R.1781	B.	F/L. Todd.	Sgt. MacKenzie.	P/O. Carroll, Sgts. Pidgeon, Dorr, Weston.	
A.	R.1399	D.	P/O. Allen.	Sgt. Christenson.	Sgts. Saxton, Campbell, Spooner, Highton.	
A.	R.1790	D.	P/O. Willson.	Sgt. Page.	Sgts. Morrison, Redford, Appleby, MacFay.	
A.	R.1778	G.	Sgt. Fooks.	Sgt. Dowling.	Sgts Ryan, Davies, Polloc, Holmes.	
A.	X.9822	K.	P/O. Hardie.	Sgt. Moran.	P/O. Miller, Sgts. Mawhennetson, Perry.	
A.	X.9920	F.	Sgt. Muin.	Sgt. Wilson.	Sgts. Fenwick, Drors, Clderphese, Perry.	

* FITTED WITH CAMERAS.

BOMB LOAD. Aircraft B.D.C. 1 x 1000lbs, 2 x 500lbs, 1 x 250lbs G.P. Fused .025.
" K.G.T.S. 6 S.B.C of 501bs Incendiaries; 2 x 500lbs, 1 x 250lbs G.P. Fused N.D.T.
" R. 1 x 1000lbs, 4 x 500lbs G.P. Fused .025.
" F. 6 S.B.C of 501b Incendiards, 3 x 500lbs, 1 x 250lbs G.P. Fused N.D.T.
All aircraft fitted with Lex. Flares.

BRIEFING 1820   BRIEFING FOR CREWS NAMED F 1800 HOURS.

TRAINING.

B.	L.7889	P.	Sgt. House.	Sgt. Newton.	P/O. Pilkington, Sgts. Sullivan, Williams, Sykes.	F Landing first then X go Northampton-Marwell, Halesworth-Thrupston-Lane.
B.	X.9819	V.	Sgt. Raybould.	Sgt. Watts.	Sgt. Spencer, Lott, N/S. Woodgate, Treacy.	
A.	X.9807	A.	Sgt. Williams.	Sgt. Diemer.	Sgt. Kennea, Hooper, Maxwell, Crichton.	X Cross Country as above, no practice landings.

TAKE OFF. 1955
APPROX TIME OF RETURN. 2030   BRIEFING 1830 HOURS.

Offr. I/c Night Flying W/C. E.L. BIGGS.   (Signed) E.L. BIGGS, W/C.

many before us. Tragedy came into my office the day one volunteer answered my query by throwing down in front of me a pair of tiny baby's shoes. He swallowed and did not say anything for a moment. Then he pointed to the shoes and exclaimed: "That's why. They got my wife and they got my baby, and now by God I'll get them." He passed, and I do not envy the Hun who met him in the air!'

Each squadron in Bomber Command lost an average of one crew a week on operations and one crew a week from operational fatigue, not counting other factors such as moves on promotion. Replacement crews came from the Operational Training Units and each Wellington OTU pushed out 20 crews plus five spare pilots every fortnight. Some of these came to 101 in proportion to its loss rate, and having gone through the OTU training mill together, crews were kept together on their arrival at Oakington if at all possible.

Pilots arrived on the Squadron with 30-hour OTU flying to their name and they were then required to complete five trips on ops as second pilot with an experienced crew to learn the ropes. They then flew two or three sea-mining sorties and one or two missions to 'easier' targets in occupied Europe with their own crews. After this, a new crew was deemed ready to be let loose on its own for a raid into Germany. This Squadron conversion schedule was regarded as the best compromise in the circumstances, but going into the deep-end against the hot spots of the Reich, like a first solo flight, was a plunge that had to be taken sooner or later.

Once ensconced in their Wellingtons, the Squadron crews could certainly range farther afield than their predecessors on Blenheims.

'7/9/41. Six aircraft successfully attacked Berlin by night.'

'10/9/41. Four aircraft are known to have successfully attacked Turin by night.'

A fifth aircraft, captained by Plt Off Allen, also reached the target but engine trouble on the return leg forced the crew to crash-land in France. The Allen crew (who were 'posted as missing') had been one of the most experienced on the Squadron, but some of them managed to return to Britain with the help of French sympathisers. Afterwards they were fully debriefed on their experiences, and one man who listened in on the grapevine was the author H. E. Bates, then visiting Oakington as a public relations officer from the Air Ministry. He was so impressed and moved by their story that he used it as the basis for one of his most successful novels, *Fair Stood the Wind for France*.

To chronicle every bombing mission that 101 subsequently carried out against the enemy would be to produce a list that would often make dull and repetitive reading, not that the Squadron crews would have minded for the most successful raids from their point of view were those on which no incident occurred. Ironically, the best crews were not necessarily those who won awards and accolades for bravery but were those who took their aircraft 'unseen and deadly to the target, bombed it and flew home again through the silence of the night' (*Bomber Command*, HMSO, 1941). Yet no matter who went where and did what, the essentials of 'ops' on 101 remained the same — 'to bomb the primary target or, failing that, the secondary. In every case the bombs are carried by aircraft manned by crews who act on orders issued in accordance with a prescribed pattern, who follow the same technique learnt after long months of training, who encounter the same obstacles of wind, weather and darkness, whose success or failure is measured by the same standard.'

The main priorities for the air offensive were drawn up by the War Cabinet who passed them down through Air Ministry directives to the AOC-in-C Bomber Command. At 0900hrs in the morning, the C-in-C would hold a conference with his operations, intelligence and meteorological staffs to determine which targets could most profitably be attacked that night and by what proportion of his force. The instructions finally transcribed into the 'C-in-C's Daily Allotment of Targets' were then passed down to the Group Headquarters by teleprinter, where the Group Commander would decide how many of his squadrons he would use and from what stations. At the Oakington Station Headquarters the station commander, a group captain, would then send for the squadron commanders of 7 and 101 Squadrons, plus his operations officer, and they would divide the station commitment between them on the basis of serviceable aircraft and crews available.

'The size of the bomb loads is laid down in the Group Operation Orders, but the load may be reduced by the Station Commander if he thinks it is necessary to do so for local reasons. It must be emphasised that, once the target has been chosen and the aircraft "bombed up", to change it at short notice, although not impossible, is difficult. It means changes in the fuel and bomb load. These cannot be made in a few minutes, and if the decision is left too late, it may mean that an unsuitable bomb load will be delivered at the target.'

'As soon as the preliminary orders for the raid have been received, the work of fuelling and bombing-up is put in hand. To do this in a hurry with bombs weighing a thousand pounds or more is not easy and requires skill,

54
Flight mechanics service one of the 1000hp, Pegasus engines on a Squadron Wellington IC. The more powerful Wellington III, which first arrived on 101 in February 1942, was fitted with the 1,500hp Hercules engine.

53

54

55
Crew boarding their Wellington
for a night 'op'. *IWM*

56
Interior view of a Squadron
Wellington rear gun turret as
seen through the entrance doors.
The reflector sight midway up the
centre window provided an
illuminated circle through optical
lenses directly in line with the
gunner's eye. Adjustment of the
circle's diameter by means of a
range knob gave the gunner
automatic deflection angle in
proportion to the target's known
wing span.

56

practice and team work. An expert **55**
"bombing-up" squad of 28 men can load
fifteen aircraft in two hours' (from *Bomber
Command*).

Back in station headquarters the Squadron
crews, who had had a preliminary warning
that they would be required that night, have
assembled in the briefing room. Facing them
were the target and route maps and from the
dais the Intelligence Officer would open the
proceedings by delivering his brief:

'The target tonight is the synthetic oil plant
at Gelsenkirchen. It produces petrol from
coal and the output capacity is 325,000
metric tons per annum. The most vital
section of this plant, and also the most vulnerable, is the hydrogenation plant itself. It
lies in the top half of the target and a direct
hit with a large bomb on the compressor
house will put the whole plant out of action.
The plant lies on the northern bank of the
Emscher Kanal, which at this point runs
parallel and very close to the Rhein-Herne
Kanal.'

Particulars would then be given of the 'opposition' with crews being shown maps of where night fighters operated and where the flak, searchlight belts and barrage balloons were situated. A description of the landmarks by which the target could be found and the suggested lines of approach were then given, but these were only guidelines. Crews were given a great deal of latitude in the choice of routes to the target once the area in which it was located had been entered; after the briefing, captains and navigators would spend some time together working out the course that suited them best. 'This is natural, for it is impossible to foresee the exact circumstances in which they will be called upon to make the attack.'

Back in the briefing room the navigators, who were also the bomb-aimers, would then be issued with target maps. These maps were kept as simple as possible and were printed in various colours to represent woods, built-up areas, water and other easily distinguishable features. Photographs of the target were also shown to the crews and it was a wise bomb-aimer who studied these carefully because his memory and the simple map would be all he had to go on on the bombing run.

The crews were then addressed by the signals officer who informed the wireless operators of the frequencies to be used for identification, 'fixes', and in emergency. The homing and distress procedures were also explained, together with the position of friendly defences and searchlights. The met and armaments officers would then take up the tale and the briefing would be concluded by questions from the crews.

This mass briefing may have lasted as long as 45min but 'the atmosphere in which it is conducted resembles nothing so much as a lecture at a university, though the attention paid by the audience would certainly flatter most lecturing dons. Everything is very matter of fact. There is no straining after effect. The information is imparted clearly, briefly and without embellishment. Questions are answered in the same way. The object, aimed at and achieved, is to leave no member of a crew with the excuse that he did not know that a certain procedure was to be employed or a certain course to be avoided.'

The crews then had a meal, after which they donned their flying clothing over their uniform. The pre-flight meal was somewhat irreverently termed 'the last supper'. Crews had to wear uniform on operations so that if they baled out over enemy territory, they could claim POW status under the Geneva Convention rather than be shot as spies. Crews were then conveyed to their individual aircraft, which were dispersed around the station, in a lorry. The navigator took on board with him a green canvas satchel con-taining all his gear. In amongst the protractors, dividers, coloured pencils, Very pistol cartridges, forms and astro navigation tables were the 'flimsies' on which were typed the procedures to be adopted if the aircraft got lost and needed emergency wireless assistance. These 'flimsies' were made of rice paper so that they could be destroyed by eating in emergency. It was said that the taste of the ink left much to be desired.

'The aircraft are sent off at short intervals of between two and five minutes by means of a green signal from the air traffic Watch Office. On reaching 1,000ft, course is set for the objective. If the wind is favourable, the captain turns for the coast straight after take-off; if not, he circles the aerodrome to gain height or to make sure that they are right on course from the start. Generally, there would be little chat on the "inter-com" on the way out because the crew members would be too much occupied and they wished to conserve oxygen; the silence would only be broken by staccato changes of heading from the navigator. Lights were kept down as much as possible while the gunners tested their turrets and loaded and cocked their guns. Over the seas the bombs would be made "live".'

'The striking thing about a tail turret,' wrote one rear-gunner, 'is the sense of detachment it gives you. You're out beyond the tail of the plane and you can see nothing at all of the aircraft unless you turn sideways. It has all the effects of being suspended in space. It sounds perhaps a little terrifying but actually it is fascinating. The effect it has on me is to make me feel that I am in a different machine from the others. I hear their voices; I know that they are there at the other end of the aircraft, but I feel remote and alone.'

Time passed and the aircraft would approach the Dutch coast. If the night was clear, the coastline, rivers or bursts of flak would act as signposts; if ground features were obscured by cloud, the navigator would have to shoot the stars to find his position. 'Few bomber men will forget the magnificent spectacles to which we were treated night after night. Arcturus, Vega, Deneb, Polaris were familiar as the fingers of one's hand. Old stuff, some might think, but to the bomber crew they remained sure and certain signposts' (from *The Great Raid — Essen*, J. Searby, Nutshell Press, 1978).

As the crew neared their target zone, the navigator would go forward to lie prone in the bomb-aiming position, and on his command the captain would turn in. By this time the captain would have decided whether to attack direct or make a gliding attack. Either way he would be 'jinking' and flying with engines desynchronised to confuse the anti-aircraft predictors and listening devices on the ground, but on the final bomb-run

57
Examples of propaganda leaflets
dropped by 101 over occupied
Europe and Germany.

57

where a steady platform was desirable, he might glide down to confuse the sound locators still further. As the bomb doors opened, the navigator would pass last minute refinements to his pilot. 'If he wishes him to turn to the left he will say, "Left, left". If, however, he wishes him to turn right he will say, "Right", once only. The reason for this is that there is often a considerable amount of crackling on the "inter-com" which makes it difficult to distinguish the exact words spoken. If he hears two words, the pilot knows that they must be Left, left; if only one word, it must be Right.'

A bomb-run lasted from four to five minutes and these were probably the longest minutes of most crews' lives because they felt themselves at their most vulnerable. A straight and level course was essential for bombing accuracy as well as for the night camera nestling in the aircraft's belly which could tell the whole Command where the crew had (and had not) been. As the navigator gazed through his bomb-sight, he would shout 'Steady, steady, steady' in ascending pitch until the emphatic 'Bomb gone'. At the moment of release a magnesium flash illuminated for the benefit of the night camera, and then it was time to close the bomb-doors and beat a retreat back home through the flak and searchlight batteries once more.

Wireless silence would be maintained as far as possible throughout the sortie, but approaching Britain the wireless operator would switch on the IFF (Identification Friend or Foe) and transmit the code-letters of the aircraft in morse for a 'fix' if necessary. The IFF allowed friendly aircraft to superimpose a distinctive mark over the radar blip it made in the air defence radar screen to enable Fighter Command controllers to differentiate between the RAF and the Luftwaffe. 'It was always good to hear the welcome station call-sign greeting you on your return,' recalled one pilot, and as soon as a Wellington arrived back over base, the watch office would pass landing instructions depending on such factors as the number of aircraft simultaneously recovering, which were lowest on fuel, and which were in emergency. Each bomber would circle the aerodrome at its designated height before dropping down for the final approach. A brightly illuminated 'T' would mark the beginning of the flare path and on the ground would also shine the Chance light — so-called after its inventor, not as some crews believed because it was only switched on haphazardly.

On landing, the crews would once again be picked up by lorries from their dispersal points and brought back for individual interrogation on route weather, defences and targets by the intelligence officers. Then, as the dawn broke, they would go to breakfast and then to bed — it took 9hr 40min to make the round trip to Berlin, and 10hr 20min to get to Turin and back.

However, at the end of the day, travelling long distances deep inside enemy airspace and surviving to tell the tale counted for little if the bombs were not dropped in the right place. Clear and bright nights were a boon to navigators, for even the blackout could not mask the illuminating effects of the 'bomber's moon'. But there are not many cloudfree days and nights a year in Western Europe, and the winter weather of 1941/42 only served to highlight the problems of navigating and bombing accurately without adequate aids.

Vic Redfern, an instrument repairer in the Squadron photo section at Bourn in April 1942, with some of the night cameras that now accompanied all 101 aircraft on their raids. 'Once the Squadron had learned to accept the night camera,' said one pilot, 'we became very keen to use it properly such that when Bomber Command started what might be termed a photographic competition by publishing the monthly photo results, 101 always came in the top four.

59
Having loaded and tested his photographic charges, Vic Redfern poses for the ground camera from the pilot's window. The attractive WAAF driver was Eileen 'Bobbie' Clarke who served on 101 for four years.

59

'12/2/42. Four aircraft did a daylight op against battlecruisers *Scharnhorst*, *Gneisenau* and *Prinz Eugen*. Targets not sighted owing to bad visibility.'

'16/2/42. Sgt Cowley's crew went on a Nickel raid (propaganda leaflet dropping) to Lisle. Eight packages of leaflets dropped on ETA above 10/10ths cloud.'

Cowley's men were reduced to dropping on time because they had no better means of accurately determining where they were. It was an old problem. Before 1939, numbers of aircraft were everything in Bomber Command. Little thought was then given to what was operationally possible, what targets could be reached, how accurately they could be bombed, and the effects of the bombs if they did fall accurately — to have a large number of aircraft that could carry bombs seemed to be sufficient in itself.

The weight of bombs dropped by bomber Command during May 1941 was more than twice that dropped in May 1940, and the weight of bombs dropped in June 1941 was half as much again as the total for the previous month. But like the 'shop window' force of 1939, these figures meant little in themselves because they took no account of whether the bombs were being deposited to good effect or not. After being driven out of the sky by day to all intents and purposes during the first year of the war, Bomber Command continued to think that it could cripple the German war effort by hitting crucial pinpoint targets such as oil refineries by night. Yet this again was far too ambitious — in November 1940 the evidence revealed that no fewer than 65% of the bombers dispatched had failed to find their targets.

After the Luftwaffe attack on Coventry,

60
Sergeant 'Mac' Mackay standing by B-Beer, or Beer the Bitch as she was known affectionately to her crew. B-Beer was a Wellington IC which had the unique distinction of being the only aircraft of her genre to live through service on 101 to be retired back to Vickers.

Bomber Command was allowed to aim for larger targets in the hope that the crews could at least find these. But it was not to be. There were cases in the Command of navigation errors up to 100 miles, yet on these occasions 'the pilots, relying blindly on a met wind forecast and flying above 10/10ths cloud, have been convinced that the area bombed through the gap in the clouds was their target'.

Thus the brave claims that considerable destruction was being heaped upon Germany, and eloquent propaganda such as *Bomber Command* which declared authoritatively that the proportion of bombers reaching their objectives was 'always very high' and was 'growing higher', were simply not borne out by reality. No blame could be attached to the crews for this — at the end of a long and arduous outbound leg, lasting up to 700 miles in darkness and with virtually no navigational aids or accurate meteorological data to help them, Wellington navigators were expected to place their bombs to within 1,000 yards of a target they could not see. It was asking too much of crews, even though they never failed to operate to the best of their ability with the limited equipment they had to hand, and the aerial photographs now being taken during and after raids drove the point home. The Butt Report of August 1941 made a careful study of a large number of these photos, and concluded that only one in ten aircraft was getting through to bomb within an area of even 75 square miles around assigned targets in the Ruhr, and a radius of five miles around any German target other than Berlin consisted very largely of open countryside. 'The

air photographs showed how little damage was being done,' wrote Winston Churchill. 'It also appeared that the crews knew this, and were discouraged by the poor results of such hazard. Unless we could improve on this there did not seem much use in continuing night bombing.'

Added to this was the problem of vulnerability. Throughout 1941, Bomber Command dropped a total of 31,704tons of bombs but at the cost of 333 aircraft crashed and 701 'missing', or nearly 20 aircraft and crews a week. In all, close to 4,000 individual crew members had been taken out of the front line in a single year of not very effective offensive effort; it was only thanks to the superb courage and determination of individual crews that squadrons such as 101 achieved as much as they did with so little. The first two years of the war were basically ones of trial and error as Bomber Command adapted its philosophy from what was theoretically desirable to that which was operationally possible, but the fact that morale in the Command remained as high as it did throughout, and formed the springboard without which future expansion would have been unthinkable, says wonders for the dedication and preserverance of the squadron personnel who bore the brunt of it all.

Fortunately for them, there were bright lights on the horizon. The first was the appointment of Air Marshal Arthur Harris to the post of Air Officer Commanding-in-Chief, Bomber Command, on 20 February 1942. 'What did we think of Harris?' mused Sgt 'Mac' Mackay, a 101 rear-gunner. 'He was *always* known to us as "Butch" or "The Butcher", nothing else, and our opinion of him varied in accordance with our losses. If they were heavy, then his "popularity" — if that is the right word — suffered. You must remember that most aircrew never saw him. I can see him now on the only occasion he visited Oakington — stone faced, severe and even cynical over our efforts — but I disagree with those who dubbed him arrogant. He certainly was not.'

Nevertheless, if his crews did not see enough of Harris to love him, they certainly appreciated what he was doing for them. For a start, he gave his Command a much needed sense of purpose. Up to the end of 1941, many people both inside and outside the RAF tended to regard strategic bombing as little more than a wasteful sideshow. It was Harris who proclaimed loud and long that Bomber Command was vital to the war effort and that his crews should be given the best of everything because their efforts would be decisive in the final outcome. After a particularly successful raid the C-in-C would send a signal to the Squadron saying, 'Good show, keep it up, you are winning the war', and this meant a great deal to men who knew that they stood a less than an even chance of surviving a tour of operations.

Harris was also a great innovator. Before his appointment, poor bombing results were often excused on the grounds that crews were not putting in enough effort. Harris saw differently and he not only campaigned for better bombing and navigation aids but he also tried to solve the problems of bad weather and night flying. To this end he demanded a better instrument panel for blind flying and had car headlights mounted as landing lights which could swivel so that the beam angle could be altered during the approach. He also called for an electrically-lit flare-path to replace the crude paraffin flares of the time. All this reinforced the view at Squadron level that here at last was somebody in high places who *cared* about them.

The nickname 'Butcher' hurt and surprised Harris when he first heard of it, but he soon came to regard it as a term of endearment from his crews. 'One point,' recalled a Squadron pilot, 'which I think shows the respect in which our C-in-C was held, was that the bomber offensive was such an entirely new method of warfare that very senior officers could obviously not have taken part in it. Nonetheless, I never heard anyone suggest that Harris himself would not have gone into battle with us if he could have done so and that he would not have made a first-class operational pilot.'

The second problem to be faced was that of vulnerability, which previously the crews on 101 had only been able to overcome by raw courage. Sgt A. C. Spencer for instance was navigating on the Raybould crew when their aircraft was shot up on the way to Germany. Although the captain avoided further trouble and carried on, Sgt Spencer was badly wounded in the thigh by shrapnel: notwithstanding, he continued his navigational duties until the pain became so intense that he collapsed. On recovering, he noticed that not all the bombs had been dropped so he dragged himself forward to the release gear to jettison them. Then he crawled back to his seat where he succeeded in fighting off unconciousness until he had navigated his crew back to safety. For the exceptional courage and dedication displayed on this sortie, Sgt Spencer was awarded the DFM.

Sgt Ward was also rewarded with an immediate DFM on 9 March 1942 when he brought back his aircraft after it had been riddled with flak: he had to crash-land at Oakington and, although the crew were injured when the Wellington caught fire, they all survived. But such bravery and dedication by itself was not enough. The answer was to replace twin-engined 'medium' Wellingtons with more powerful, longer ranging, four-engined 'heavy' aircraft such as the Lancaster which would be far more capable of taking care of themselves. But this would take time, and in the short term the momentum of the strategic offensive could only be sustained by concentrating the bombers closer together in time and space. A loose gaggle of aircraft stumbling about all over Germany on a raid that could encompass seven hours was not only inefficient but it also meant that individual aircraft could be picked off at will. A concentrated force on the other hand, routeing in with far greater accuracy, dropping their bombs in quick succession, and beating a retreat 'en masse', would provide protective cover for each other and stood a better chance of getting in and out before the enemy had time to do much about it. But this goal could only be achieved if every navigator knew precisely where he was all the time, and this in turn demanded better equipment and techniques.

The first of these devices was 'Gee', which enabled a navigator to plot his position relative to a ground station and the introduction of which, in the words of one navigator, 'turned navigation from an art into a science'. Fortunately Gee came into service just after Air Marshal Harris' arrival at High Wycombe (HQ Bomber Command had moved to High Wycombe, Bucks, in March 1940); at the same time, the Commander-in-Chief received a directive ordering his Command to commence a prolonged and specific offensive against Germany with particular emphasis on '. . . the morale of the enemy civil population and in particular the industrial workers'. In blunt terms, this meant 'area bombing' against German industrial towns and cities because, in all honesty, these were the only targets that Bomber Command stood any chance of hitting at night at the beginning of 1942.

61
B-Beer showing the battering she had taken during her operational life. But why the change to U-Uncle? The original U-Uncle had suffered somewhat on her last raid and was to be out of action for some time, leaving her crew with only five trips to complete to the end of their tour and no aircraft of their own in which to fly them. As the Millson crew were in the process of converting to Wellington IIIs, it was decided to give B-Beer to Uncle's crew. But 'we were all understandably a superstitious lot', and since Uncle's crew refused to fly under any other code letter than 'U', B-Beer became U-Uncle.

61

Selection of many targets was restricted by the range of Gee — up to 400 miles — but this encompassed the urban and industrial complexes of W and NW Germany. It was appreciated that there would be a period when only a proportion of Bomber Command aircraft would be equipped with Gee, so some means had to be found whereby the Gee crews could guide their less fortunate brethren to the target. Consequently, the 'Shaker' technique was devised whereby the attacking force would be divided into three sections — the illuminators, the target markers and the followers. The first of these were the illuminators, consisting of 20 Wellingtons fitted with Gee, which were expected to drop bundles of flares to illuminate the target. The target markers were then briefed to drop incendiary bombs into these flares to produce a concentrated area of fire into which the followers, not yet endowed with Gee, could drop their high explosive bombs.

Throughout the latter half of 1941, 101 Squadron operated Wellington ICs from Oakington in company with the Stirlings of 7 Squadron. Occasionally the Squadron operated from Oakington's satellite landing ground at Bourn, a few miles to the South-West, but as the tempo of Stirling operations increased at Oakington, it was decided to relieve the pressure on the parent station by moving 101 and its newly received and more powerful Wellington IIIs permanently into Bourn on 11 February 1942. Gee was not yet available for operations, but on 3 March Bomber Command decided to test the flare aspect of its 'Shaker' plan by sending 235 aircraft to attack the Renault motor and armaments factory at Billancourt near Paris. Three 101 crews, captained by Wg Cdr Nicholls, Flt Sgt Raybould, and Sgt Attwood, 'successfully attacked' the factory, and aerial photographs taken the following day revealed that 'very great devastation of the target' had been achieved. It seemed that the force concentration had been excellent and it was estimated that 40% of the Renault machine tools had been destroyed. The Squadron recorded that 'a message of congratulation was received from the AOC on the effect'.

Yet Paris in good weather conditions was a far cry from the Ruhr, which was the primary target given to Air Marshal Harris in the 'area bombing' directive and which was protected by a formidable defence system supported by almost perpetual smoke haze and searchlight dazzle. On the other hand, Bomber Command soon had 150 aircraft equipped with Gee, and one of the first units to be so endowed was 101. Thus within a week of the Renault raid, Bomber Command, with 101 Squadron in the van, was ready to test the 'Shaker' technique against the supreme target — the giant Krupps Konzern at Essen.

'8/3/42. Eight squadron aircraft attacked Essen. Plt Off Luin and crew failed to return.'

'9/3/42. Six aircraft successfully attacked Essen.'

These were the first of eight major attacks which employed the Shaker technique or a variation of it against Essen during March

62
Oakington Ops Board for the raid on the Renault factory at Billancourt on the night of 3 March 1942.

and April. Yet on none was any substantial success achieved. 'I had joined 101 as a navigator on 1 January 1942,' recalled Plt Off A. A. Castle, 'and I did four sorties during that month. My log book shows that I did no operational flying at all during February, but I did 13 cross-country flights and this fits my recollections that we were withdrawn from ops whilst training to use Gee. The last of these training flights was on 26 February and my next flight was the Paris raid'.

The first time Plt Off Castle used Gee operationally was against Essen on 8 March. 'I flew with Sgt Don Attwood as pilot and we were briefed to drop flares over the target not by visual means but simply when the two Gee blips coincided. It was rudimentary pathfinding but we were not really good enough at it. I still have my navigation log and I am not proud of it, but I was only 19 and it was only my sixth operational trip.' In all fairness to Plt Off Castle and his contemporaries, although Gee was an admirable aid to dead-reckoning navigation it was not accurate enough for precise blind-bombing.

Back in the autumn of 1941, the Air Staff had concluded that saturation incendiary attacks were likely to prove far more destructive than attacks with conventional high explosive. This theory was still to be proved so, on the night of 28 March, 234 Bomber Command aircraft were dispatched to Lübeck, an old Hanseatic port on the Baltic beyond Gee range but which, being largely of medieval wooden construction, was built to burn. The moon was nearing full and the weather was excellent as the first wave of Wellingtons dropped their flares. Sgt Attwood's crew, who took-off at 1945hr and landed six and a half hours later, were the first 101 Squadron aircraft to reach the target, and they were to record: 'Incendiaries dropped in centre of town, many fires already started.' The next three Squadron crews (Captains — Sgts Llewelyn, Cowley and Earley) all dropped their incendiaries in the centre of Lübeck too, then Flt Sgt Raybould's crew dropped a stick of bombs — one 1,000lb and six 500lb General Purpose — into the fires. To help the conflagration, the Millson and Callender crews dropped 12 bundles of flares across the town, while the 101 Squadron contribution was completed by Flt Lt Watts' men who dropped another stick of bombs across a factory. This practice of combining a general area attack against a city with a specific assault on a particular target, such as an aircraft factory, within or near that urban centre, was becoming the standard Bomber Command procedure.

Post-strike photo-reconnaissance carried out in daylight on 12 April revealed that 'large areas of total destruction amount to probably 45-50% of the whole city'. It was estimated that some 200 acres of Lübeck had been devastated, mainly by fire, and that additional heavy damage had been caused in the suburbs. Two thousand houses, the central power station, and four factories appeared to have been destroyed or damaged beyond repair. The main railway station and workshops were damaged, as were a number

63
An eventful landing.

64
A Squadron Wellington III which came to grief on 20 April 1942 as a result of 'finger trouble'. Thankfully no-one was hurt in the accident.

of warehouses, and the cathedral, Reichsbank, and Market Hall were destroyed. Despite the fact that the town was particularly vulnerable to fire, the raid on Lübeck was an outstanding success and far exceeded anything previously attained by Bomber Command. By way of comparison, Coventry had 100 acres destroyed by enemy aircraft between 1939 and 1945.

On 5 April, nine Squadron crews were detailed to form part of a raid on Cologne. Flt Sgt Machin's and Sgt Chuandy's aircraft failed to take off because both had become bogged down on the soggy grass airfield* while taxying. The other seven aircraft got through without incident but cloud over the target prevented accurate identification of the point where the incendiaries and high explosives fell. Three nights later, nine crews flew to Hamburg but 10/10th cover ensured that 'no damage was seen by some aircraft or glow of fires seen under clouds'.

However, life was not always so hectic on 101. '23/9/41. Weather — fog and drizzle in morning. Overcast until the afternoon. Vis poor. Squadron stood-down — organised sport in afternoon.'

'24/12/41. The Squadron stood-by at two hours notice for a daylight op throughout the

*Although the RAF laid its first concrete runway in 1937, only three operational bomber stations had concrete runways by March 1941. These soon became essential however, following the introduction of heavy, four-engined aircraft.

day. No aircrew were allowed off camp in the evening.'

Nor was every operational flying hour devoted to bomb-dropping deep inside enemy airspace. '2/4/42. Three aircraft went "gardening" at St Nazaire. Each crew dropped two 1,500lb mines from 650ft.' Minelaying was known as 'gardening' and periodically crews spent a relatively relaxing night planting 'vegetables' in evocatively named enemy waters such as 'forget-me-not' and 'wallflower' areas. A very nice crop was to be harvested from these 'vegetable' missions over the next three years.

But it was back to the hard stuff all too quickly. 'On Friday 8 May 1942,' recalled Plt Off Castle, 'we joined some 300 other aircraft detailed to attack an aircraft factory at Warnemünde. Of these, about 18 of us were briefed to go in at low level (50ft) while the main force attacked from high level as usual. I was flying with Sgt Don Attwood in G for George and we were told that there were almost no defensive guns around the target but this was far from the fact — there was quite heavy fire from the ground, starting on the jetty into the sea which we were to use as an aiming point before turning west on to the target. My only vivid memory as we neared the target was just missing hitting a church spire with the port engine and then immediately after dropping our bombs, the whole aircraft started to vibrate. It quickly became apparent that there was something wrong with the port engine; Don Attwood

tried to feather it but he was unable to do so and we had no alternative but to put up with the vibration. I remember very clearly that I could not write properly. I had to write very slowly to stop my pencil skidding about the paper and all that I did write was composed of wavy letters and figures — it looked quite amusing really! The vibrations continued as we made our way home and as we did not know the cause, we were quite apprehensive that we would finish in the drink. However, we landed back at Bourn and then found that we had lost all three tips off the port propeller and that the propeller boss was crushed. The only explanation was that we had hit a barrage balloon cable and that it had wrapped around the propeller boss before breaking. This explanation was borne out by a photo of the target taken before the raid which showed a single barrage balloon, whereas one taken immediately after showed no balloon.

'I recall that the BBC reported on the raid the following day and stated that "one of our Stirling aircraft had hit a barrage balloon cable but had got back to base". We were quite annoyed that the Wimpy was denied the credit it deserved. The raid itself was quite costly in aircraft, and did little damage to the factory — this was perhaps why we attempted no more low level attacks at night.'

Thus in 1942 long range targets did not succumb easily to Bomber Command, and notwithstanding the introduction of Gee, difficult objectives nearer home such as the Ruhr were no less difficult to bomb. Billancourt and Lübeck had been unrepresentative in that their defences were light and the skies above clear enough to allow crews to come down low and identify their target visually. Over the Ruhr, where the defences forced the crews up high and gave them a nerve-wracking run-in, and where the industrial haze made visual identification of whole towns impossible, the results were nothing like as good — of the 212 aerial photographs showing ground detail taken by bombers during the attacks on Essen, only 22 of them proved to have been within five miles of the target.

The staffs at High Wycombe believed that they would solve some of their problems if they could concentrate even greater numbers of bombers in the target area to swamp the enemy defences thereby giving crews a better chance of an uninterrupted run-up to the aiming point. This proposal also had political advantages. At the very time when he was arguing for even more aircraft and better equipment, Air Marshal Harris was under pressure from many in high places who saw strategic bombing as an expensive waste of valuable manpower and resources while more immediately pressing matters such as the Battle of the Atlantic had still to be resolved. As April passed into May, the Admiralty and War Office presented an urgent demand to the War Cabinet for the immediate transfer of 50% of the bomber force to be divided between the Atlantic, the

65

Wg Cdr Nicholls and his officers at Bourn in May 1942. (L-R) Back row: Plt Off Waterkyn (just off photo), Plt Off Castle, Plt Off Beer (Bombing Leader), Plt Off Tregea, Plt Off Beechey, Plt Off Spencer, Plt Off Osbon, Plt Off Davidson, Plt Off Stratton, Flg Off 'Tubby' Whitbread (Eng Off), Flg Off Ross (Medical Off). Front row: Plt Off Gardner, Flg Off Doig, Flt Lt Pilkington, Flt Lt Harper, Sqn Ldr Watts, Wg Cdr Nicholls, Flg Off Eagleton (Adjutant), Flt Lt Edwards, Plt Off Callander, Plt Off Pidgeon, Plt Off Muggleton.

Squadron NCOs at Bourn. The aircraft in the background, F-Freddie, was lost over Cologne on 30 May.

Middle East, and India. It was Harris' moment of truth. 'If only we could put on something really big,' he mused. 'One spectacular raid, big enough to wipe out a really important target. Something that would capture the imagination of the public.' (From *The Thousand Plan* by Ralph Barker; Chatto & Windus, 1965.) So he decided to gamble everything on a massive 1,000-bomber raid. If it succeeded, or more accurately, if his crews proved his point for him, the war-winning potential of the strategic offensive would be plain to all; if the grandoise scheme failed, and his force suffered unacceptable losses or inflicted insignificant damage, there would be no worthwhile expansion of Bomber Command.

By committing not only the whole of his front-line strength, but also by mobilising as many aircraft as possible from his second-line and Operational Training Units, Harris amassed over 1,000 bombers in preparation for a night attack against either Hamburg or Cologne as soon as possible on or after 27 May. This was a moon period, for Harris insisted that the raid take place in bright moonlight or not at all, but for three frustrating days the operation was postponed until the weather was right. Then at 0920hr on 30 May, the weather forecast became acceptable; there were to be no more delays and that night over 2,000 tons of bombs in 1,046 bombers set course for the fourth largest city in the Reich, Cologne.

'Towards the end of May 1942, I was in the final stages of Bomber Command training with my crew at 23 OTU, Pershore,' wrote Plt Off L. R. Sidwell. 'Suddenly a flap blew up which called for scratch crews to be hurriedly formed from instructors and a few pupils for an unknown purpose. So I (an Air Gunner) came to be in a detachment of five crews to take our old training Wellington ICs

to Bourn. All we knew was the official line — a "practice Liaison Scheme for an indefinite period".

'Hopes of enlightenment when we arrived at Bourn were dashed; the blokes of 101 Squadron were equally in the dark but rumours were plentiful. We found that Bourn was one of the wartime aerodromes that had hurriedly come into being — it had the unfinished air of newness about it and lacked many comforts but our welcome helped to make up. The officers' mess was only a small Nissen hut — a bit rough and ready but the friendliness was typical of many such temporary wartime aerodromes.

'Our venerable Pegasus-engined ICs looked down-at-heel and ancient compared with the Squadron's latest Wellington IIIs with higher powered Hercules engines. A bad hold-up for weather meant we were cooped up at Bourn with 101 in great secrecy with rumours running wild. We checked and rechecked our old IC bangers and we filled in many sessions in friendly rivalry with the Squadron blokes on the popular shove-halfpenny board in the little ante-room. The eventual briefing came amidst mounting excitement. Group Captain Adams, Station Commander at Oakington (Bourn's parent station), came over for the briefing — then we knew it was to be the first Thousand Bomber Raid.'

As in every other bomber briefing room, a special signal from the Commander-in-Chief was read out to the 101 Squadron crews:

'The force of which you form part tonight is at least twice the size and has more than four times the carrying capacity of the largest Air Force ever before concentrated on one objective. You have an opportunity therefore to strike a blow at the enemy which will resound, not only throughout Germany, but throughout the world.

'In your hands lie the means of destroying a major part of the resources by which the enemy's war effort is maintained. It depends, however, upon each individual crew whether full concentration is achieved.

'Press home your attack to your precise objective with the utmost determination and resolution in the foreknowledge that if you individually succeed, the most shattering and devastating blow will have been delivered against the very vitals of the enemy. You are a thousand strong. Let him have it — right on the chin.'

Twelve 101 Squadron aircraft took-off for Cologne that night. Their bomb load, as for most of the force, was incendiaries and the whole raid was to be concentrated into the space of 90min. The force ran into dirty weather as it crossed the North Sea, but conditions improved markedly beyond the Dutch coast and there were only small amounts of high level cirrus over Cologne. The moon was above the horizon and 90% full, and the visibility was reported as good both by attackers and defenders.

Most of the first aircraft to bomb came from 3 Group, with selected crews from 101 Squadron in the van. These crews in the leading Gee aircraft had no difficulty identifying the target on arrival, and by the time the main force arrived there were 'considerable' fires to help them identify the aiming point.

'30/5/42. Cologne.

Captain	Time Off	Time Down	Bomb Load	TOT*	Comments
S/L Watts	22.55	03.40	9 SBCs†	01.05	Height 12,000ft. Weather good. Many fires seen.
F/L Harper	23.00	04.10	9 SBCs	00.55	Height 15,500ft. Weather good. Many large fires seen. Started two more fires.
F/L Edwards	23.15	00.00			Returned safely — mag drop.
Sgt Attwood	23.00	03.10	9 SBCs	01.02	Height 18,000ft. Weather good. Many large fires seen.
P/O Callender	23.05	02.55	9 SBCs	00.55	Height 19,000ft.
Sgt Llewelyn	23.05	03.35	9 SBCs	01.03	Height 14,000ft.
P/O Gardner	23.15	MISSING			All killed.
Sgt Earley	23.05	03.15	9 SBCs	00.55	Height 16,000ft. Weather good. Many large fires seen.
Sgt Deimer	23.05	03.00	9 SBCs	00.59	Height 18,000ft.
P/O Read		MISSING			All POWs.
P/O Kennedy	23.10	02.15			Returned early — rear turret U/S.
F/S Williams	23.10	03.05	9 SBCs	00.50	Height 18,000ft.'

*Time on Target.

†Small Bomb Containers, which were long aluminium boxes holding 90 incendiaries each. Thus, each aircraft carried 810 4lb incendiaries.

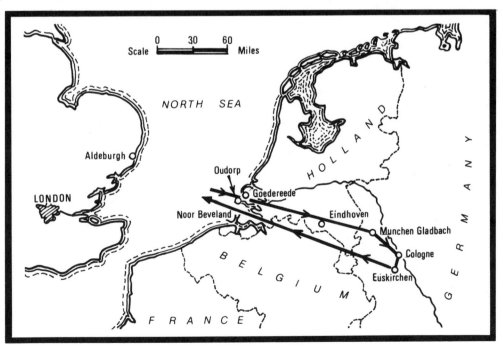

67
Route to and from Cologne on 30 May 1942.

When at last the smoke had cleared, the daylight damage assessment photographs showed that the damage inflicted on the unfortunate Cologne was 'heavy and widespread' and that it was 'on a much larger scale than any previously inflicted on a German city'. Six hundred acres of Cologne, including some 300 acres in the city centre, appeared to have been completely destroyed, and there was no 'considerable' part of the city which appeared to have escaped damage. No less than 45,132 people were rendered homeless and while some of these were only displaced temporarily, there was no denying that the 1,046 bombers dispatched that night inflicted far more damage than the 1,364 aircraft sent against the city over the previous nine months. Harris' crews had unmistakably proved his point for him, and the vindication came in the shape of the following message to the C-in-C from the Prime Minister:

'I congratulate you and the whole of the Bomber Command upon the remarkable feat of organisation which enabled you to dispatch over 1,000 bombers to the Cologne area in a single night, and without confusion to concentrate their action over the target into so short a time as one hour and a half. This proof of the growing power of the British bomber force is also the herald of what Germany will receive, city by city, from now on.'

Moreover, the victory over Cologne had been achieved without unacceptable losses. Two 101 Squadron crews had failed to return but they went down in circumstances that said much about Bomber Command in 1942. The first crew to fall was captained by Pilot Officer Reece Read. Read had always wanted to be a doctor but there was no money in the family during the Depression to send him through university so he eventually went to West Africa to work as a mining engineer. He was still there eight years later when war broke out.

When he joined the RAF, Reece Read was 'short and unremarkable in appearance', but his dogged perseverance and sympathetic handling of people marked him out as a big crew leader rather than a dashing, solitary fighter man. He was posted to bombers and early in 1942, after five trips as a second pilot, he was made a captain on 101 and given a crew. Since then he had been on three missions to French ports and had never operated as a captain over Germany. At the relatively elderly age of 28, Read was to receive his baptism of fire against Cologne.

Soon after take-off Read's engines began to run roughly and he was unable to get full climb power. One by one his crew called him up to pass comment on the matter and it was at this stage that Read learned about the loneliness of captaincy. He knew that it would be a popular decision to turn back but he also knew that if every captain with a small mechanical fault opted out, the mass impact of the Thousand Bomber Raid would be negated. So, although he was unhappy, Read did as most others would have done and 'pressed on'. At first his engines seemed to settle down, but as he neared the Dutch coast the trouble returned. The starboard engine suddenly lost power and the Wellington began to lose height rapidly. Then the port engine went the same way — Read called his gunners out of their turrets and, as the aircraft dived ever more steeply, he gave the order to bale out. Everyone got out safely and the next thing Read knew was that he was on his knees in a muddy field. Like the rest of his crew, he eventually finished up as a prisoner of war where he occupied his mind with what he had always wanted to do — the study of medicine. Perhaps there was a moral there somewhere.

Plt Off Gardner's crew from 101 Squadron was not so lucky. They were in the bulk of the force, rocking in the slipstream of other aircraft, altering course to avoid collision and weaving continually to upset the flak predictors and to give the gunners a view of the blind spots underneath. All this had been foreseen, but what the planners had not been taking into account were the bomber crews' long-standing habits of independence. The anti-collision element of the Thousand Plan hinged on the assumption that all the crews would fly in approximately the same direction, but some crews who found themselves south of the target simply looked for a pinpoint on the Rhine and then flew northwards to drop their bombs, against the stream. Other attacked across the stream, while some crews added to the confusion by orbiting over the target like a moth round a candle, fascinated by the sight of the burning city below.

The illuminated night sky probably lulled some crews into thinking that they could get away with shortcuts if they kept a good lookout, but there were always blind spots. A pilot in a 408 Squadron Hampden was trying to avoid the mêlée when he noticed two aircraft not more than 400yd ahead of him and slightly to starboard settling down into the most dangerous configuration of all — one on top of the other. The top aircraft was a Stirling and the one underneath was a Wellington, and unless someone in the lower was looking straight up from the astrodome, neither crew would spot the other. It was obvious that no one in a Wellington over Cologne would have the time to gaze at the heavens, and in the space of 10 seconds the inevitable occurred. As it weaved, the Wellington rose slightly, while the Stirling sagged and then levelled out. Then the Wellington came up again and, as the two aircraft touched, the Wellington's propellers cut the Stirling's tail completely off. Both aircraft rose together for a moment and then fell to earth — Plt Off Gardner's Wellington blew up and no parachutes were seen to come out. It was the Squadron's second casualty.

After Cologne, Harris was not content to rest on his laurels and while the moon was still up, and his force still in being, he launched it against the Ruhr. This time 101 exacted a measure of revenge for the loss of their comrades over Cologne.

'1/6/42. Wg Cdr Eaton assumed command of 101 Squadron in place of Wg Cdr Nicholls who was posted. Once again over 1,000 aircraft operated, their target being Essen. Ten out of ten Squadron aircraft took-off and bombed Essen successfully. All aircraft returned safely. Sgt Earley's aircraft received superficial damage to its port wing but his rear gunner, Sgt Ferguson, shot down an Me 110 and damaged a Ju88.'

But, as usual, industrial haze was on duty over the Ruhr and the force leaders had to drop their flares on ETA and blind Gee fixes rather than visually. In consequence, although no less than 767 crews claimed to have dropped their bombs on or near Essen, post-strike photographs showed little damage in Essen and none to the Krupps works. Some 30 or 40 houses in the suburbs were hit

but it was clear that most of the bombs had fallen elsewhere.

Immediately after the Essen attack and with the waning of the moon, the Thousand force was disbanded and 101 returned to normal 3 Group attacks on Germany. They returned to Essen twice again in the next seven days and, on 26 July, Wg Cdr Eaton led 14 Squadron aircraft on a raid to Hamburg. 'Thirteen crews attacked the primary target between 0110 and 0155 hours and all of them attempted photography from between 15,000 and 19,000ft. Bombs dropped — 4,050 4lb incendiaries, 30 500lb, five 1,000lb and two 4,000lb GP bombs. Whole town a sea of flames, especially old town. Smoke pall up to 17,000ft. Sgt Raymond's crew failed to return.'

Two nights later, 13 Squadron crews were detailed to attack Hamburg again, but it was an unlucky number for some. 'Three attacked the primary target, three attacked the secondary target (Cuxhaven) and six returned early after experiencing severe icing (three brought bombs back and three jettisoned them over the sea). Sgt Teall collided with a Stirling after take-off and all his crew were killed. Results of raid seen — nil.'

The Squadron lost 35 officer and NCO aircrew in July, and airborne collisions such as befell the Teall crew seemed to be an unavoidable consequence of trying to cram a large number of aircraft into the crowded skies over Britain without a radar system to

68
101 Squadron's partner at Oakington, 7 Squadron, had flown Stirlings since 1940, and on 5 May 1942 a Bomber Command letter announced the intention to convert 101 Squadron to Stirlings also. At that time, each heavy squadron was obliged to set up a conversion flight, and 101 went so far as to establish 101 Stirling Conversion Flight on 1 June 1942 under the command of Squadron Leader Crompton. This photo shows a Stirling of the 101 Conversion Flight at Oakington before they had time to paint 'SR' on it, but a shortage of aircraft prevented the rest of the Squadron, then at Bourn with Wellingtons, from following suit. 101 eventually converted to Lancasters and 101 Stirling Conversion Flight combined with three others to form 1657 Heavy Conversion Unit on 7 October 1942.

69

The King and Queen at Oakington railway station on 12 June 1942 when they came to inspect 7 and 101 Squadrons. They are talking to AVM Baldwin, AOC 3 Group, while on the far left is Grp Capt Adams who was known to all as 'Daddy'.

70

The Duke of Kent and Wg Cdr Eaton leaving the Control Tower at Bourne on 30 July 1942. Wg Cdr Eaton was a great personality and a fearless man who was killed on ops two years later. He was buried in Durnbach War Cemetary in S. Germany alongside several other members of 101. The Duke of Kent was also to die in an air crash in Scotland less than a month after this photograph was taken.

70

exercise effective control over them. These wasteful accidents due to haste, tiredness or misjudgement were just as frustrating to the Squadron as the failure to bomb effectively.

'6/8/42. Accident, in which two aircraft collided on runway, prevented circuits and landings being carried out. War ops over Duisburg. Eight crews carried out attack — all attacked primary target and returned safely. 8/10ths cloud over enemy territory plus ground haze made identification of target difficult. Haze also rendered flares useless.'

At least there was hope around the corner. After a period of musical chairs, when 101 moved to Stradishall on 13 August to make way for 15 Squadron's Stirlings, which had themselves been manoeuvred out of Wyton by the Pathfinder Force, the Squadron received orders on 27 September to prepare to move to Holme-on-Spalding Moor. Holme was north of the Humber between Selby and Hull, and the Squadron was being transferred from 3 Group to 1 Group 'in order to rearm with the Avro Lancaster'.

71

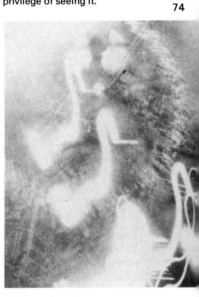

The remains of a Ju88 intruder which tried to sneak into the circuit to shoot down returning bombers. The German aircraft itself however was dispatched by an outer perimeter defence point and crashed in a nearby cornfield. All the airfield lights were then switched off in case there were other intruders in the vicinity and returning Squadron aircraft had to land without visual aids — fortunately there was a full moon that night.

72

The Rhine at night near Dusseldorf. 'The extraordinary beauty of the Rhine,' wrote one pilot eloquently, 'will never be forgotten by anyone who had the privilege of seeing it.'

72
▼

73

74

73

The moment of release — incendiaries starting to fall over Nuremburg at the end of August 1942. Pictures like this proved that crews were dropping their bombs in the right place at last.

74

Hamburg from four miles up on 26 July 1942. The wavy lines are flak. 'There was an army officer who studied German flak and who visited 101 on a number of occasions,' wrote a W/Op. 'We called him 'Major Flak' and each time he flew with us he asked to be taken close to the flak wherever it might be so that he could study it a little more closely. I can assure you that we were not too happy whenever we saw him around.'

75

Battle order for the attack on Hamburg on 26 July 1942.

75

No: 101 Squadron
SECRET
Officer i/c Night Flying :- S/Ldr: Watts

BATTLE ORDER
Serial No: 194

SUNDAY, 26th: JULY, 1942

Duty Plotter :- P/O: Lincoln

Flt	Aircraft	Let	Pilot	Observer	W/T: OP:	Front Gunner	Rear Gunner	E.T.D.	Time Off	Time Down	Capt: u/t
A	X:3654	K	F/S:Brown	Sgt:Baker	Sgt:Justice	Sgt:Oakley	P/S:King-Scott	22:10			Sgt:Waterhouse
A	X:3391	A	P/L:Harper	P/O:Weterboyn	Sgt:Mullin	Sgt:Skinner	P/S:Mullineaux	22:15			Sgt:Spinney
B	BW:699	T	Sgt:Mahoney	Sgt:Calhoun	Sgt:Sauve	Sgt:Springer	Sgt:Martin	22:20			
D	X:3657	Q	S/L:Paterson	P/S:Cafferty	Sgt:Sibbald	Sgt:Sundborg	P/O:Doooly	22:25			
B	BJ:698	U	W/O:Ollier	Sgt:Caldwell	Sgt:Lewis	Sgt:Shore	Sgt:Musgrove	22:30			
D	X:3547	P	W/C:Baton	W/L:Pilkington	P/O:Pinucane	Sgt:Otter	Sgt:Jade	22:35			Sgt:Brown
A	X:3650	B	F/O:Vauteur	Sgt:Daniel	Sgt:Ward	Sgt:Sine	Sgt:Skipsey	22:36			
A	Z:1661	F	P/O:Fahnestock	Sgt:McBride	Sgt:Cleadleigh	Sgt:Carter	Sgt:Hill	22:37			
A	BJ:590	H	Sgt:Raymond	Sgt:Miller	Sgt:Lyle	Sgt:McGregor	Sgt:Jarvis	22:38	Missing		
D	BJ:689	O	P/O:Delartok	Sgt:Drury	Sgt:Haskins	Sgt:Dyehouse	Sgt:Bailey	22:39			
A	BJ:844	C	Sgt:Foderingham	P/S:Gordon	Sgt:Stewart:A	Sgt:Cobbett	Sgt:McFadyen	22:40			
A	X:3541	E	Sgt:Foxcraft	Sgt:Clarke	P/S:Cook	Sgt:Coleman	Sgt:Angelo	22:41			
A	Z:1662	D	Sgt:Bannee	P/O:Jefferson	Sgt:Buckland	Sgt:McLennan	P/O:Selover	22:42			
A	X:3668	G	Sgt:Teall	Sgt:Webster	P/O:Stubbings	Sgt:Bridge	Sgt:Corber	22:43			
B	X:3455	V	Sgt:Beale	Sgt:Rowles	Sgt:Rundell	Sgt:Roberts	P/O:Butcher	22:44			
B	X:3366	N	Sgt:Yellott	Sgt:Bennett	Sgt:Swann	Sgt:Kearns	Sgt:Armstrong	22:45			

OPERATIONAL LOAD:-

Aircraft K:A:T:Q:U:P: to carry Incendiaries (810 x 4lbs)
Aircraft B:F:H:O:D:G:V:N: to carry 1 x 1000lbs: + 6 x 500lbs:
Aircraft C:E: to carry 1 x 4000lbs:
All aircraft to carry GAILLES
All aircraft to carry 750 gallons of fuel

Time of Origin:- 16:00 hours:

Briefing   :- 17:00 hrs
Supper   :- 19:30 "
Transport leaves Sgts: Mess   :- 20:15 "
1st: Briefing   :- 20:25 "

(signed) E: C: BATCH,
Wing Commander, Commanding,
No: 101 Squadron, R:A:F;

193

Holme Sweet Holme

On 28 September 1942, 'the Advance Party under WO Beesley, consisting of 18 NCOs and 57 aircraftmen, left for Holme. Wg Cdr Eaton and Flt Lt Ross travelled by road'. They were joined the following day by the main party which 'proceeded to Holme by rail and by Squadron vehicles in convoy. Fifteen officers and 86 airmen aircrew proceeded by air, while two officers and 23 airmen aircrew travelled with the main party under the charge of the Adjutant, Flt Lt E. W. Eagleton'.

These figures give some idea of the size of 101 at the end of the Wellington era, and the Squadron was going to increase once the new bombers arrived. On 30 September, '10 complete aircrews proceeded to No 1654 Heavy Conversion Unit, Wigsley, Notts, for conversion training on to the Lancaster. Some were ferried by air, the others by rail'. The remaining crews continued to fly the Wellington because Bomber Command could not afford to take a complete squadron out of the front-line, and in between carrying on the fight against Germany they helped the ground staffs unpack and settle into Holme. There they were welcomed personally into 1 Group by their new AOC on 1 September. 'He explained the damage being done to Germany both materially and morally, and he enjoined the Squadron to "keep it up".'

The No 1 Group Summary for September 1942 was equally pleased to record that 'No 101 Squadron has arrived at RAF Station, Holme, from No 3 Group. This is an excellent piece of news and we are very pleased to welcome this Squadron with its fine record. We wish it the best of luck in its new surroundings.'

Holme-on-Spalding Moor was a typical purpose-built Bomber Command station with the sleeping accommodation dispersed away from the Messes, which in turn were removed from the work areas and aircraft to minimise the effect of any enemy bombing. Such were the distances involved that '125 bicycles were issued to Squadron personnel, the control of which was a continual headache for the Adjutant'.

The huts in which both officers and men lived were 'poorly heated by a small coke stove with one bag of coke being supplied per week, if the residents were lucky. Water for washing was more often than not cold, but life was lived to as full an extent as possible'.

No 101, 103 and 460 Squadrons were the first units in 1 Group to re-equip with the Lancaster, and there followed a hectic race between them to see who would be quickest to get the new type into operational service. The first two 101 Lancasters arrived at Holme on 11 October 1942, and eight days

76
On 23 October 1942, Wg Cdr Bruce Bintley of 102 Sqn, Pocklington, landed his Halifax at Holme after a raid on Genoa. The airfield was shrouded in fog and before the Wing Commander could leave the runway, a Lancaster also returning from Italy landed on top of the Halifax, killing Bintley and his wireless operator. It was just one of many tragic accidents to result from the strain of ops.

76

WO Oliver AFM and his crew after they finished their tour of ops on the last night that 101 flew Wellingtons in anger. (L-R) Back row: Sgt Franchuk (Rear gunner), Sgt Moore (Bombardier), Sgt Lewis (W/Op). Front row: Sgt Caldwell (Observer), WO Oliver, Grp Capt Blucke (Station Commander, and member of the station hockey team when he could find the time).

77

later 'the first party of aircrews to complete their conversion training returned from Wigsley: they are full of enthusiasm for the Lancasters and are itching to get operational with them to show the world, and Hitler, what 101 can do with them'. By the end of the month, no more Wellington sorties were being flown and 101 was the proud possessor of 14 Lancasters. 'The entire Squadron is keen to get on ops with our new machines,' but there were unavoidable delays while the new aircraft were checked on their receipt from the manufacturers and modifications such as the fitment of flare-chutes were carried out. 'The supply of spares and necessary parts is very difficult,' lamented the engineers, 'but aircraft are being initially checked at the rate of three every $2\frac{1}{2}$ days.'

They need not have worried — 101 dispatched eight Lancasters to attack Turin on 20 November 1942, just winning the race with 103 and 460 Squadrons.

The Avro Lancaster was regarded by many as the ideal bomber. 'There can be no doubt at all that until 1942, the success of Bomber Command was extremely limited,' declared an experienced Squadron navigator. 'The Wellington was not really suited to the type of work being asked of it, and even newer four-engined bombers like the Stirling had their limitations. I rather liked the Stirling but without going into rich mixture, when the enemy could see the cowlings many miles away and the fuel consumption soared to around 300 gallons an hour, the Stirling was incapable of getting anywhere above

78
The photographic beauty of impending destruction over Duisberg. All the lines are tracer shells converging upwards towards a point represented by the light mass at the bottom right. The curved nature of the tracer lines is caused by the bomber taking evasive action. 'Personally, I disliked flak more than fighters,' said Flt Lt Misselbrook. 'Needless to say, flak was most heavily concentrated in the target area. I know this to my cost as I got a direct hit over Munich in December 1942, and it took the side of the aircraft away just where I was sitting plus some of the controls. We had a rough old trip back home.'

20,000ft.' Unlike the Wellington III, which could only carry 4,500lb of bombs over 1,500 miles, the Lancaster I could transport 14,000lb of bombs over 1,660 miles. Moreover, on 101 Squadron trials during January 1943, Lancasters reached heights of between 26,800ft and 28,100ft with full fuel loads and they could cruise at 185mph fully laden. For a large aircraft the Lancaster was also extremely manoeuvrable, and the combined all-round view from front cabin, mid-upper and rear turrets was good. Consequently Sir Arthur Harris spoke for all on 101 when he declared that the Lancaster soon proved immensely superior to all other types in the Command and that, measured in no matter what terms, the Lancaster was incomparably the most efficient and far surpassed all its rivals in range, bombload, ease of handling, freedom from accident and casualty rate.

Until the spring of 1942, 101 Squadron Wellingtons had always carried a first and second pilot, but Bomber Command lost 107 aircraft in the first 18 nights of August 1941 alone and the continual replacement of two pilots for every bomber lost eventually imposed an unacceptable strain on the training organisation and diverted too many men away from other roles. Experienced operational personnel had to be conserved until the Command received more potent aircraft and up-to-date equipment, and so at a meeting held on 29 March 1942 it was decided to dispense with the second pilot altogether. From now on, a 20-aircraft Squadron such as 101 would have its quota of pilots reduced from 40 to between 23 and 26. As a result, from 4 May 101 Squadron

'discontinued second pilots and came down to five man crews'. In fact, if all the aircraft concerned had required two pilots, the 1,000-bomber raids of 1942 could not have been launched.

The meeting on 29 March was also innovatory in other ways. For a start, none disagreed with the Chief of Air Staff when he 'considered that the title of 'observer' should be changed to 'navigator', but more importantly the staff officers were not happy with the practice of the navigator leaving his post some 50 miles from the target in order to concentrate on bomb-aiming — in the age of new devices such as Gee, it was felt that he should remain with his black boxes and charts throughout the raid. Consequently it was decided to add a specialised bomb-aimer to the heavy bomber crew, to be known as the 'air bomber', together with a flight engineer to assist the solitary pilot.

A 101 Squadron Lancaster crew henceforward numbered seven highly specialised individuals. Up front were the pilot, who was always captain, and the flight engineer. The navigator was now solely responsible for the navigation, leaving the air bomber to drop the bombs or occupy the front turret whenever he was not dropping bombs. The wireless operator was also released from gunnery duties and mid-upper and rear gunners were no longer required to undergo wireless training. These changes had a considerable effect. Up to now, there had been no clear idea of what a bomber crew did beyond the general rule that the pilot flew the aircraft. The rest of the crew had titles and seats, but the precise nature of their duties on the Wellington, and the extent to which they required pre-operational training, was obscure. Once Bomber Command got its crew specialisations right on the 'heavies', it opened the way for each crew member to specialise to a much greater extent and thereby receive a much more thorough training than had hitherto been possible. It was all part of the growing efficiency and sophistication that was enveloping Bomber Command, and nothing demonstrated this more forceably than the fact that in 1940 an embryo 101 Squadron Blenheim crew could be rushed through training in a matter of months whereas it took around two years to train 101 Squadron Lancaster aircrew in 1944. However, one less satisfactory by product of this extension of the training period was the increase in training casualties: one in seven (8,000 men) of all the Command's casualties occurred during training.

The RAF took no pressed men for its aircrew but relied wholly on volunteers. 'During the war the normal method of providing flying personnel for the RAF is by

HOPE BROTHERS LTD.

Military & R.A.F. Tailors & Outfitters

Established 1874:   Head Office :- 44 & 46, Ludgate Hill, London, E.C.4.

Local Address: 78, BRIGGATE, LEEDS. 1.

Telephone No: LEEDS 26191

R. A. F. Price-list

UNIFORM Ready for Wear					Shirt	R.A.F. Regulation		12	6
Tunic & Slacks from	...	£9	5	3	Collar	,, ,,		1	10
Slacks	... ...	3	1	9	Gloves	Unlined from		8	6
Greatcoat ···	... ...	12	15	11	,,	Lined from		10	3
Raincoat		4	19	0	Socks	from		2	2
					Ties	from		2	9
UNIFORM Tailored to Order									
Tunic and Slacks from		£10	9	0	R.A A.F. Uniform To Order Only				
Slacks	... · ...	2	12	0	Tunic & Slacks ...		£12	14	0
Greatcoat	... ...	13	13	0	Greatcoat	...	15	0	0
Peaked Cap with Badge		2	6	5	Raincoat [In stock]		4	19	0
Folder ,, ,, ,,		1	7	11	Cap with Badge	...	2	6	5
R.A.F Regulation Shoes		1	17	6	Folder Cap With Badge		1	7	11

All Wings, Shoulder-tabs etc. in stock.

We are well known for Ready - to - Wear Uniforms of which we hold
large stocks in a wide range of fittings. You are invited to inspect
our store — You can be fitted out in a few hours

establishment in the ranks of the RAF Volunteer Reserve for training as a member of an aircraft crew.' The RAFVR age limits were 18-31 for pilots and 18-33 for navigators, wireless operators and air gunners. Whereas a School Certificate was demanded from prospective regular aircrew, by 1942 no prescribed educational standards were laid down for RAFVR men 'except for elementary mathematics. A short and simple test is given in this, but should the candidate fail and otherwise be suitable he is permitted to remain in his civilian occupation while receiving instruction locally.'

Trainee aircrew received their basic flying training in safety overseas under the auspices of the Empire Air Training Scheme, but the Dominions themselves also contributed large numbers of first-rate aircrews to Bomber Command. Such a large proportion of young volunteers travelled from all corners of the globe — including neutral Americans before 1942 thinly disguised as Canadians — that by 1 June 1943 some 37% of the pilots in Bomber Command were Canadians, Australians, or New Zealanders. Thus, like the majority of Bomber Command squadrons, 101 eventually became a very cosmopolitan unit. 'We had a couple of Yanks and when the USA entered the war, they merely changed uniforms and stayed with us. It was the same with the Canadians — they did not join the separate Canadian Bomber Group when it was established. We were very Commonwealth orientated by 1945.'

With the ending of second pilot posts, bomber pilots entering Squadron service had to be up to full captain standard from the start. Additionally, new types such as the Lancaster were far more sophisticated and demanding than Blenheims or Wellingtons so, at a time when it cost £1,000 to train a pilot, it become economically as well as militarily essential 'that those selected for pilot training should have the highest degree of inherent piloting ability and would consist of those most likely to get the greatest value from their training' (from *Notes on the History of RAF Training 1939-44*; Air Ministry, 1945).

As a result, it was decided to introduce what was to be known as the Pilot, Navigator, Air Bomber, or PNB Scheme. Basically this marked a change of training emphasis from the system of 'survival selection' to 'quality selection'. Under the old scheme, volunteers were arbitrarily classified as pilots or observers merely on the basis of a short interview at the Aircrew Selection Board — many designated pilots then went on to struggle at Elementary Flying Training School because they lacked the required aptitude, but just as importantly many who might have had the necessary pilot aptitude never had a chance to show it because they did not impress at an interview.

This wasteful system was altered by the new scheme in that volunteers accepted by the Selection Boards entered training as an unidentified bunch of aircrew known as PNB. Some 10% volunteered for non-pilot categories, but the remaining 90% who hoped to become pilots were sent to grading schools where they were given 12 hours flying instruction. Their performance in the air was then marked and the prospective pilots were listed in order of merit: depending on the number of training vacancies available at the time, the RAF started at the top of the list and went down as far as necessary. In this way, those who demonstrated the most aptitude went on for full pilot training while the rest were classified as navigators or air bombers.

A typical volunteer was Sgt C. North, information on whose career was gathered from 'RAF Operational Training' in *Aviation Week* by Ray Sturtivant. He was accepted for PNB training in late 1942, but owing to a reduction in pilot and navigator requirements at the time he was re-mustered for air gunner training. After a course at 3 Air Gunnery School, Castle Kennedy, he was posted to 29 OTU, Bruntingthorpe, where 'we gunners were the first to arrive and had to await the remainder of the aircrew. Following this there was a period of about a fortnight when we received ground training mainly according to category. During this period we were expected to sort ourselves into crews.' Sufficient men for the 16 crews who usually comprised a course would be assembled in a hangar or large hall and left to sort themselves into crews of kindred spirits. In this apparently casual manner crews had to band together for the supreme test of their lives, but it was a good system — there would be no place for square pegs in round holes when it came to working as a single entity over the hectic skies of the Ruhr.

Having learned the basics of operational techniques, and how to operate as a crew instead of as individuals on Wellingtons at the OTU, a prospective 101 Squadron crew then had to convert to a four-engined heavy bomber. And as the Wellington for instance did not have a mid-upper turret or carry a flight engineer, these crew members only joined a crew at the end of the OTU course. By October 1942 four-engined conversions were performed by the Heavy Conversion Units within each Group but, because precious Lancasters could not be spared from the front-line, the HCUs had to make do with Stirlings and Halifaxes. Consequently, at the end of the HCU course, crews destined for Lancasters then had to pass through a Lancaster Finishing School (one per heavy bomber Group) before joining the Squadron. It all took time, and because a crew could cost well over £5,000 to train, and because the Lancaster they would fly would be worth around £40,000, Bomber Command had to look after its men for more than humanitarian reasons. Thus when Sqn Ldr St John, a New Zealander on a short service commission, joined 101 in April 1943, he did a 2nd pilot trip with the Squadron Commander to Spezia on 18 April, followed by a cross-country trip over the UK with his own crew the following

night, before finally being let loose to bomb Duisberg on 26 April.

More aircrew were lost on their first six operational trips than at any other stage of their career. Until then, they lacked the experience that training could not teach, and it was war itself that acted as the final trade test. These first operational missions were known as 'Freshman' flights, and a keen crew who put them to good use became alert to most of the enemy's tricks. It was reported on the Squadron that 'Butch' Harris had said that a bomber crew had justified their training and the cost of their aircraft if they flew two successful missions and were lost on the third *after* they had bombed.

Similarly, no matter how steel-hearted or hardy he was, no man was officially allowed on operations once he had reached the age of 40 because the RAF Medical Branch had thought long and hard about such matters. 'A man subjected to prolonged or repeated fear due to battle stress,' wrote the experts, 'will usually persist in fighting that fear as long as his supply of courage lasts. When his courage is exhausted he may either refuse to continue the struggle or develop a psychiatric illness if he has not already suffered death or injury at the hands of the enemy.' It was this kind of dilemma that led the wartime bomber crews to jest that the only alternatives open to them were 'coffins or crackers'.

By mid-1943 it had been decided that 30 operational sorties in Bomber Command were as much as the bravest man could tolerate without a significant risk of developing psychiatric illness. This number could be completed in anything from four months to a year, and survival rates varied throughout the war. Only three crews in 10 could expect to survive their first tour in the most dangerous year of 1942, but later on an average man had a 50% chance of living to see the end of 30 operational missions. Very occasionally, all members of a crew who came through this feat of endurance were rewarded with a 'survival gong' — a DFC or DFM depending upon whether they were commissioned or not — but if a crew had not done particularly well they got nothing at all. Generally, if a crew had had a good tour, they got one or two awards — 'It all depended on the Commanding Officer,' recalled one air gunner, 'and some wing commanders only "gonged" the skipper and nobody else.'

A tour-expired crew would then split up to be posted away as individuals for a minimum 'rest' of six months, to recharge the batteries of courage, usually at a training unit within Bomber Command where they could pass on their expertise. After this, aircrew could volunteer or be called back at any time for a second tour of 20 operations on heavies:

given that only one man in four completed two front-line tours in Bomber Command, it says a great deal for the dedication of the personnel involved that many Squadron aircrew volunteered to stay on 'ops' immediately after their first tour rather than move on to safer but less exciting instructional duties. Either way, those who survived their second operational tour could not be ordered to fly on bomber operations again.

It is probably true to say that 101 Squadron was not in particularly good spirits by the middle of 1942. Life on the Wellington had not been very happy and casualties had been heavy, so the arrival of the Lancaster was good for Squadron morale. But it took leaders as well to motivate men. 'Successful leaders,' observed one Squadron navigator, 'were those who got the best out of their men. "Butch" Harris, despite his critics, was a great commander. Below him came the Group commanders, and they were just as important. I would say that 5 Group would never have achieved the success it did achieve without Air Vice-Marshal Cochrane, and I also believe that Air Vice-Marshal Bennett *personally* had a tremendous amount to do with the success of the Pathfinder Group. In similar fashion, I believe that within 1 Group we had a wonderful combination in the Air Officer Commanding, AVM E. A. B. Rice and his senior Air Staff Officer, Air Cdre Constantine. I only appreciated all this after I came from another Group where, although the Air Officer Commanding was a very nice man, his Group was a bit of a giggle.'

The Station Commander at Holme was Grp Capt R. S. 'Bobby' Blucke, 'and I think one would have had to go a very long way before one found a greater gentleman.' Blucke was a World War 1 pilot and an expert in blind flying techniques, but despite his experience and seniority he was known as an extremely easy person to get on with and one who 'always stopped to talk to everyone, regardless of rank. He was a man of tremendous humanity and understanding, who could also be tough when the need arose.' Grp Capt Blucke was very much part of 101 and, although he was 46 years old in 1943, he periodically exercised his 'droit de seigneur' to take a Squadron crew on operations.

Below the Station Commander came OC 101 Squadron who, after 26 January 1943, was Wg Cdr D. A. 'Tony' Reddick. Before the war, if a squadron commander was posted away he was usually replaced by a man from another unit — to promote a man from within a squadron and to ask him to stand apart from comrades who the day before would have been equals and might have been confidential drinking partners

often led to difficulties. It did not matter if the man was not conversant with the aircraft on his new unit — so long as his personality and powers of command were adequate there was time in peace for him to learn the ropes.

Although this arrangement continued in war as career officers returned to the front-line from staff appointments, more and more squadron commanders and flight commanders came to be promoted from within. 'The crux of the matter,' wrote the AOC 2 Group in Novmber 1939, 'would appear to be that a squadron commander requires sound knowledge in current tactics and a capacity for leadership established on operational experience to get the best from his command, and that under war conditions administrative ability in a squadron commander, although desirable, is nevertheless of secondary importance.'

This view was endorsed by Air Marshal Portal on 18 June 1940 when he was C-in-C Bomber Command. 'Squadron Commanders *must* be active and experienced pilots. They should be regular pre-war officers nearing the end of their flying careers and aged about 30 to 35 years, or else they should be the cream of the short service and war entry, aged somewhere between 26 and 30. The pilot aged about 40, who does a minimum number of hours flying yearly, is in most cases utterly useless and ought never to be sent to an operational squadron. The flight commanders should be the best of our young officer pilots aged about 23 to 26.

'The above suggestions are idealistic and may present some difficulties in personnel and posting arrangements. Nevertheless, it is felt that if the introduction of such arrangements can be gradually effected we shall be maintaining and increasing the high standard of efficiency which is vital in all operational units.'

Air Marshal Portal was correct when he foresaw difficulties in implementing his suggestions. As the war dragged on, the hard core of career officers and men on short service commissions became too depleted to fill all the vacancies brought about by casualties and wartime expansion. Consequently, 'two tour' men began to fill flight commander posts in growing numbers, and by the end of the war there were 21-year old squadron commanders. It did not matter if a man came from Cranwell or the RAFVR — if he was good enough, he did the job. The only difference came in substantive rank — an officer on a permanent commission would probably be a substantive squadron leader or wing commander, whereas a VR man could be a substantive flying officer with acting wing commander rank.

Wg Cdr Tony Reddick was an old hand though. He had joined the RAF in the 1920s

199

as an apprentice armourer at Halton, and he appeared on 101 for the first time as a sergeant pilot back in 1932. He was such a good pilot that he was chosen to fly an Overstrand in mock combat with a Hawker Fury at the Hendon Display of 1936, and those who witnessed the event said that Reddick was quite brilliant and outflew the opposition.

Whilst none doubted his flying ability, Tony Reddick was not an outgoing person and so he, like many others, may well have remained an NCO pilot had not the demands of war swept aside the old shibboleths about 'background' and allowed many good non-commissioned men to become officers. He rejoined 101 as a squadron leader in charge of a Flight in 1942, and when 'Ginger' Eaton was posted in January 1943, Reddick was promoted to command 101.

In those days a squadron commander remained in post for only six months, during which time he was supposed to fly two operational missions per month. He had no aircraft or crew of his own, so he usually slotted in when a captain was not available or sick. Scrym Wedderburn converted to Wellingtons at 25 OTU, Finningly, in 1942, and afterwards he was given the choice of a posting to any squadron in 1 Group. For him there was no question but that he would rejoin 101 at Holme. 'It always gave me great pleasure,' he recounted, 'to contemplate the enthusiasm with which Tony Reddick managed to wangle an aircraft to go on ops — he would use a new one, not yet

allocated to a crew, or something like that. By these means Tony managed to get more than twice his appropriate number of operations in his six months as OC 101 Squadron.'

At the beginning of 1943 there were two flight commanders under Tony Reddick, each of whom was responsible for 10 aircraft and their crews. The Squadron complement however was growing all the time and it eventually reached 30 aircraft (plus three initial reserves). These were divided into 10 aircraft per flight, which meant that a 'C' Flight had to be added to 'A' and 'B'. But who was to command it? The selection criteria had certainly been laid down:

'BC/C.23068/P dated 20 Oct 42

Squadron Commander and Flight Commander posts in operational Squadrons are normally to be filled by pilots, but recommendations for the appointment of outstanding Observer officers to these posts may be forwarded as special cases for consideration by the Commander-in-Chief. All submissions are to be passed through Group HQ.'

Wg Cdr Reddick had no pilot in mind to take over 'C' Flight, but he certainly had a navigator readily available. Flt Lt A. B. 'Sandy' Greig had arrived on 101 on 1 October 1942 after serving on Wellingtons and Stirlings, and he soon made a name for himself at Holme as Squadron Navigation Officer. As an experienced hand, Greig appreciated the improvements that were taking place within Bomber Command. 'With Harris and Reddick in command, we

Flt Lt A. B. 'Sandy' Greig on the left of the front row. Behind him are Sgt Howells (flt eng), Sgt Teasdale (mid-upper), Sgt Webb (bomb-aimer), and Sgt Fryer (W/Op). Seated next to Sandy Greig are Grp Capt Blucke and Flt Lt Beechey, the Gunnery Leader who had 94 ops under his belt by the time he eventually left 101. This photo was taken on 13 February 1943, just after Grp Capt Blucke had flown his first mission on a Lancaster to drop five 1,000lb bombs and 600 incendiaries on Lorient from 12,000ft. 'A most successful and enjoyable trip.'

started doing things we had not done before. In the old days we flew a mission and the air test beforehand, and that was that. Now we did formation flying practice and bombing and gunnery exercises (known as "Bulls Eyes") over the UK. Our ground training programme also increased considerably — as Squadron Navigation Officer I tried to improve the standard of navigation by discussing errors made with the crews. By doing other things like dinghy drills, the whole crew discipline on the Squadron improved. It was noticeable that those crews whose discipline on the ground and in the air was good were the ones most inclined to survive.* In fact I would go so far as to say that for those of us who had done a bit of operational flying, it wasn't difficult to pick out the crews who wouldn't survive. Of course, good crews didn't come back if luck was against them, but the most efficient crews were usually the lucky ones, and we used to say that the more crews practised, the luckier they got.'

The enthusiasm and professionalism that Sandy Greig put into improving standards on 101 soon earned its reward.

*The price of sloppy crew discipline could be severe. On 28 August 1943 the air bomber, W/Op, and two air gunners on one crew abandoned their aircraft without orders when they saw that two engines were on fire over Nuremburg. By the time their captain had sorted out the emergency, he found that he had only two crew members left to take him home. The four unfortunates who abandoned their aircraft too quickly spent the rest of the war as POWs.

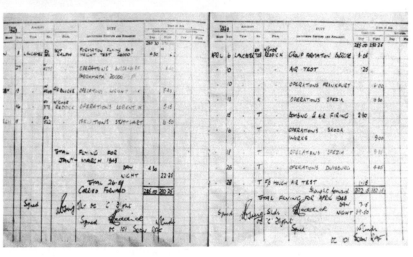

'25 March 1943
Flying Officer (Acting Flight Lieutenant) A. B. Greig DFC — 68753
Navigator — No 101 Squadron — Holme
1. Under the provisions of your letter BC/C. 23068/P dated 20 Oct 42, authority is requested for the above named Navigation Officer to be re-posted to No 101 Squadron to fill the post of a Flight Commander consequent on the formation of a third Flight.
2. This officer has completed one operational tour and six sorties of his present tour. He is an exceptionally able officer and moreover, has an outstanding enthusiasm for flying, particularly operational flying, in which he has shown great ability not only as a navigator but also as an officer. He possesses pronounced organising abilities and has powers of leadership and personality which

82
A page from Sandy Greig's log book.

mark him as fully qualified for the post of Flight Commander.

3. I strongly recommend this appointment as a special case.

E. A. B. Rice
Air Vice Marshal
AOC 1 Group'

This request was approved on 2 April and a few weeks after his 21st birthday Sandy Greig found himself an acting squadron leader in command of 'C' Flight with its preponderence of Australians. Sandy was only the second navigator in the Command to be so favoured, though it was to be a mixed blessing. 'My Australians were absolutely magnificient in the air but on the ground they were just about uncontrollable. They were a law unto themselves — they overstayed their leave, they did as they pleased — and a severe reprimand meant nothing to them while the loss of a day's pay was like water off a duck's back. The Aussies were the most courageous bunch on the Squadron and I was very happy to see them board an aeroplane but on the ground they put years on my life.'

Sandy received an immediate award of a DSO on 20 August 1943 — a far from common occurrence — 'but I did not regard it as an award to me personally, rather I saw it as an award to my crew and as an appreciation of the work of the Squadron.' At the end of his tour on 101 he was posted to instruct at an Empire Training School in South Africa where he married a local girl and settled down to become the father of the future England cricket captain, Tony Greig.

In concert with the flight commanders were the specialist leaders — bombing leader, navigation leader, gunnery leader, etc. They were all experts in their jobs, as befitted veterans of many missions, 'and they formed a sort of permanent Brains Trust to guide and advise the aircrews for which they were responsible as well as the Squadron executive officers'. The leaders also gave directions to their particular charges at the mass briefings, and typical of the breed was Flg Off 'Dagwood' Durringer who was the W/Op on Sqn Ldr St John's crew.

'On the occasion of a visit by Butch Harris to the station, we pulled "Dag's" leg and instructed him to take no nonsense from the C-in-C and to tell him that he favoured 5 Group too much as far as specialised targets were concerned. Of course, it was meant as a joke, but nonetheless "Dag" stood up and said "Would it be possible, Sir, if any specialised targets come up, for 1 Group to have a go instead of 5 Group?"

'The result of this was that 1 Group got the Breda works in Milan while the Main Force was bombing the town itself.'

But the 200 or so aircrew on 101 Squadron would have been the first to admit that they could not have done half the things they did without their magnificent ground-crew. 'As far as I am concerned,' said Sandy Greig, 'the non-flying personnel of 101 were quite outstanding, and that applied to everyone on the station.'

A potential recruit for an RAF technical trade spent 4-5 days at a reception centre where he went through a selection procedure similar to that for aircrew. This consisted of what were known as the GVK tests — General, Verbal and Practical — and they were so successful in fitting the right person to the right job and cutting down subsequent remustering that Sir William Beveridge gave the RAF credit for making the best effort of all the services to avoid misdeployment.

From the reception centre a recruit passed to a training centre where the basics of service discipline were instilled. In the middle of 1943 this course lasted eight weeks for men and three weeks for women, a discrepancy accounted for by the fact that the latter were excused combat training. Then it was off to specialist training in a host of occupations.

'Trade Groups in the Royal Air Force

The RAF trades and the groups in which they are placed for purposes of pay are as follows:

GROUP I

Blacksmith and welder	Fitter MT
Coppersmith and sheet metal worker	Fitter (torpedo)
Draughtsman	Instrument maker
Electrician, grade I	Instrument repairer, grade I
Engine driver (fitter)	Link trainer instructor
Fitter, grade I	Machine tool setter and operator
Fitter, grade II (airframe)	Metal worker
Fitter, grade II (engine)	Radio mechanic
Fitter (armourer)	Wireless mechanic
Fitter (armourer) (bombs)	Wireless operator mechanic
Fitter (armourer) (guns)	
Fitter (marine)	

GROUP II

Acetylene welder	Armourer (bombs)
Armoured car crew	Armourer (guns)
Armourer	Balloon operator
Blacksmith	Miller

Bricklayer
Carpenter
Coppersmith
Electrician, grade II
Electrician (wireman)
Flight mechanic (engine)
Grinder
Instrument repairer, grade II

M.T. mechanic
Photographer
Plumber
Radio operator
Sheet metal worker
Steel erector

Turner
Wireless operator

GROUP III

Balloon rigger
Balloon fabric worker
Concreter
Cook and butcher
Drainlayer
Driver (winch) (Balloon)

Fabric worker
Hydrogen worker
Motor boat crew
PAC operator
Shoemaker
Tailor

GROUP IV

Clerk (accounting)
Clerk, equipment accounting
Clerk, pay accounting
Clerk (general duties)

Clerk (special duties)
Equipment assistant

Teleprinter operator

Radio telephony operator

GROUP V

Aircrafthand
Aircrafthand (under trade training)
Batman
Driver (MT)
Ground gunner
Ground observer
Groundsman
Machine-gun instructor
Maintenance assistant
Messing duties

Armament assistant
Barber

Musician
Motor cyclist
Parachute packer
Pigeon keeper
PT instructor
Service police

Telephone operator

Torpedoman

GROUP M

Dispenser
Laboratory assistant
Masseur
Medical orderly under training
Mental nursing orderly
Nursing orderly
Operating-room assistant

Radiographer
Sanitary assistant
Special treatment orderly
Trained nurse

Dental clerk orderly

Dental mechanic
Dental orderly under training

'The minimum daily rates of pay, ie for Aircraftsmen, 2nd class, to the maximum, ie Warrant Officer, are as follows:

Group I, 3s 9d to 16s 6d
Group II, 3s 6d to 15s
Group III, 3s to 13s 6d
Group IV, 3s to 14s
Group V, 2s to 13s 6d
Group M, 2s to 13s 6d

'War pay of 6d per day is issued to all, in addition to the above. Additional payments are made when good conduct badges, etc are awarded. These badges are awarded for very good conduct after three, eight and 13 years' qualifying service rendered after the age of 18 has been reached. Good conduct pay of 3d per day is awarded for each badge. Airmen are eligible for an allowance of 2s a day while under instruction as pilots. Airmen while under instruction as air observers are eligible for an allowance of 1s 6d a day.

'Age limits may vary from time to time, but, roughly, the minimum age for all Groups or trades is 18 and the maximum for any one is 50.'

It is obvious from this pecking order that, not only were a vast number of specialists needed to keep the RAF airborne in wartime, but also that the highest paid personnel, and thereby those with the most status, were those most closely associated with the aircraft themselves. A flight sergeant was in charge of the groundcrew on each 101 Flight, and each bomber was entrusted to a sergeant 'usually possessing trade qualifications of a Fitter, grade I, the highest grade of any trade in the RAF'. Under his direction came an NCO engine fitter plus a flight mechanic for each engine, and an NCO rigger with three or four riggers. They were assisted by varying numbers of electricians, wireless mechanics, instrument 'bashers', and armourers depending on the daily work load, and although the number of tradesmen grew as more sophisticated aircraft systems arrived, the general technical routine remained the same.

'Aircraft must be constantly examined, for upon these expert examinations depend their success and reliability in the air. Fitters examine the engine and all its details. They run over the cooling system, check magnetos, look for leaks, examine the airscrews, and so on. Riggers examine the airframe. Controls are tested. Fabric and metal are carefully searched. Tyre pressures are made exact etc. The wireless mechanic will examine and test the receiving and transmitting set, re-charge the accumulators, and replace any damaged coils. He will also run over all the wiring and see if there is anything wrong. Electrical installations are also tested. These are many and include the intercommunication system between all the members of the crew, the bomb circuits, signal lamps, batteries and circuit fuses etc.

'The instrument repairer tests all the aircraft's many delicate instruments. The armourer looks over the guns and cleans them; he tests the gun-turrets and the bomb releases.

'To sum up, the ground crew maintain the aeroplane. They are as important as the crew who fly. They must be constantly ready to do an urgent job and they cannot afford to make mistakes, for upon their diligence and skill depend the lives of those who fly'. (From *The Royal Air Force*; E. Sargeant; Sampson Low, Marston & Co, 1942.)

With an establishment of 30 Lancasters, 101 not only needed highly trained tradesmen to cope with the sophisticated aircraft — it took nine months to train a fitter grade II — but the Squadron also needed many more of them. In May 1943 the total complement of airmen and airwomen on 101 numbered 757 and, even allowing for the NCO aircrew element within this number, it still left a Squadron groundcrew of considerable size. In addition, this figure did not include all the other station personnel at Holme who were there purely to keep the bombers operating.

Reg Humphries was an electrician, grade I at Holme, and his routine was typical. 'I was

with a set of lads who had come from a strange collection of pre-war jobs — a cardboard box maker, a cigarette packet maker, a grave digger, a shoe salesman, an insurance man, and a lad who professed to have "put the nuts in milk chocolate".

'A normal day started with carrying out routine inspections and repairs in the hangars. These inspections were carried out at 40hr flying time intervals whilst repairs mounted up after operations had taken place. There was always a rush to ensure that the squadron had its full quota of serviceable aircraft. This was often achieved by taking parts off grounded planes to put others into service. Once it was announced that operations were on for that night there would be a rush to do the Daily Inspections on all those aircraft scheduled for the raid. As the kites were spread around the 'drome on dispersal sites it meant a long walk if you did not own or could not borrow a bike. Usually these inspections were done in pairs, one inside the kite while the other did the outside. You can imagine the crush as all the trades were trying to do their own inspection on time and all trying to get in and out of the same small hatch in the front of the aircraft.'

There were two engineering officers, a medical officer, and an administrative officer in charge of the various 101 'erks' in 1943,

83
Tea break on the Squadron line with sustenance provided by the NAAFI van: (L-R), Jock (electrician); Vic and Freddie (photo section): Mary (driver).

83 ▶

but the lynch pin of the whole Squadron engineering organisation was the squadron warrant officer. This post was filled by WO Joe Beesley, an ex-Halton man who, in the opinion of one navigator, 'was quite the most magnificent Warrant Officer I have ever come across in the RAF. He was a big man in all respects who commanded respect wherever he went. I remember that two other warrant officers were posted back from the Middle East and they both actually applied to the Air Ministry to be allowed to come back to 101 with the reduced rank of flight sergeant to serve under Beesley. Thus we ended up with a warrant officer and three flight sergeants who I maintain were second to none on any squadron I have been on before or since. As a result, maintenance was magnificent — there was nothing one could ask of the ground staff that they would not try to do. This I believe was where success on 101 started, the spirit and basis was there, and Reddick, as an ex-ranker who had a happy knack of dealing with people, got the very best out of them.'

Despite its size, 101 still had the cohesion of one large family and as such the successes and failures were shared by all. 'Just about the saddest job,' wrote 'Mac' Mackay, 'was to be on the "Committee of Adjustment" which usually fell to an officer who had been on ops the previous night plus two ground NCOs. This entailed collecting all the personal effects of those who did not return. One night we lost several crews and I had the heartbreaking job of going to each bunk of nearly 50 chaps, collecting their photos of wife, kids, parents, etc, and other personal belongings. Of course there was always the usual letter to loved ones that crews left on their beds for posting, and at the end of it all I went to the Mess and stood there until friends dragged me off to bed paralysed with drink.'

Nevertheless, according to most, 'We were a happy Squadron. The vacant chairs around the breakfast table spread gloom for a while, but then new crews came to take their place and we got on with it.' Perhaps this sense of resignation accounted for the black humour that periodically surfaced in official reports: '17/1/43. Five aircraft took off in evening to attack Berlin, one returning early owing to nav, Flt Sgt J. C. Brown, collapsing. Reports that this was due to his bomb-aimer having told him that he was dead on track were untrue.'

Although there was not much to laugh about in Bomber Command at the beginning of 1943, one story had a happy ending. The strategic offensive certainly ranged far afield and, on 14 February 1943, 'Wg Cdr Reddick led five crews from A Flight and seven crews from B Flight to attack Milan. A very

successful attack was made in good visibility at target and photos were obtained. Sgt Miller's and Plt Off Bennee's crews returned early, and Sgt Hazard's Lancaster was attacked by a CR 42 biplane fighter coming back over the Alps. Contrary to popular belief, the Italian was pretty persistent in his attacks, wounding the rear gunner, Sgt L. Airey, and setting fire to the rear fuselage of the Lancaster when "hung-up" incendiary bombs started to explode.' Sgt Airey collapsed over his guns but the mid-upper gunner, Flt Sgt G. Dove, waited for what seemed like 'ages' for the fighter to return whereupon he shot it down. Though burnt about the hands and face he then went back through the flames to drag his friend, Sgt Airey, out of the rear turret. While this was going on, the W/Op, Plt Off F. Gates, together with Sgt W. Williams (navigator) and Sgt J. F. Bain (flight engineer) extinguished the fire. In the meantime, Sgt Hazard had found that his port outer engine was on fire and he was forced to dive to 800ft before he regained full control. Having given the order to 'Prepare to Abandon', he was informed of Sgt Airey's condition and so the captain elected to stay with the aircraft. Unfortunately the bomb-aimer, Plt Off Moffatt, misunderstood the instruction and baled out. With one engine out, Hazard

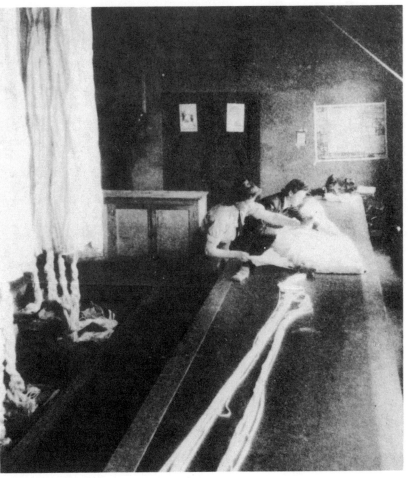

84
One of the many tasks behind the scenes at Holme — parachute packing.

84

205

85
Sgt Williams on a 4,000lb bomb. Known throughout the Command as a 'Cookie', the 4,000lb bomb was no more than a thin-cased can with over 80% of its weight being explosive. It was primarily intended as a blast bomb for use among compact building complexes such as factories, and it was complemented in the bomber armoury by a variety of incendiary bombs. The most common and effective of these was the hexagonal-shaped 4lb incendiary, a simple stick of highly inflammable magnesium which burned fiercely on contact and was difficult to extinguish. Incendiary bombs, unlike high explosives, did not destroy their targets but set fire to them so that they could destroy themselves. Consequently incendiaries did not grow greatly in size during the war as the overall aim was to produce a great number of small fires, with all their cumulative effects, rather than a small number of large ones.

86
One of the cartoons drawn to illustrate the 1 Group Monthly Summaries, which recorded the achievements of Group squadrons and disseminated specialist advice on operating procedures.

managed to coax his bomber across the Alps, 'and ably assisted by his crew, with Plt Off Gates hovering between his post and the badly injured rear gunner, he made the long haul back to England, landing at Tangmere'.

'How Hazard got that bomber back, I'll never know,' said Sandy Greig in wonder, and for this feat of courage and determination Plt Off Gates was awarded the DSO and Sgt Ivan Henry Hazard, together with all other SNCO aircrew, received Conspicuous Gallantry Medals. Plt Off Moffatt's feelings

as he floated down alone over Italy remain unrecorded.

Some five months earlier, Hazard's mid-upper gunner, Flt Sgt George Dove, had met a Leading Aircraftswoman called Christine who worked in the battery-charging room at Holme. They were married a week before Flt Sgt Dove received the CGM at Buckingham Palace to add to the DFM he had earned two years earlier. 'Nice work. Congratulations,' said the King, and the subsequent photograph of George and Christine Dove gained a prominent place in the *Evening Standard*. This was one of the good occasions on 101 that helped to compensate for the bad.

Nevertheless, Italian targets remained a sideshow as the Casablanca Conference, held between Mr Churchill and President Roosevelt in January 1943, issued the following directive to both British and US bomber forces: 'Your primary object will be the progressive destruction and dislocation of the German military, industrial and economic system, and the undermining of the morale of the German people to a point where their capacity for armed resistance is fatally weakened.' Yet as these words were being formulated, the daily average of aircraft with crews available to Sir Arthur Harris for operations was still only just over 500, of which approximately 200 were either obsolescent or of little long-range value. Thus the success or otherwise of the Casablanca directive would continue to rest heavily on the shoulders of Lancaster squadrons such as 101.

There were some strategists who believed that 'it is better to cause a high degree of destruction in a few really essential industries

than to cause a small degree of destruction in many industries', but 'Butch' Harris was not one of them. He poured scorn on the 'Panacea mongers' and their fixation with selective attacks on oil refineries or ball-bearing factories — to Harris there were no key points in the Axis war economy where destruction could not be countered by dispersal, the use of stockpiles, or the provision of substitute materials. Consequently the Commander-in-Chief became the main proponent of the general area attack — in his opinion, the only effective policy was to hit all the major industrial centres so hard and so often that organised German industrial activity would cease under the weight of material and moral devastation.

Yet even larger targets had to be found before they could be destroyed. Navigational standards in Bomber Command had certainly been much improved by the introduction of Gee, but it had already been proved that this device was not sufficiently accurate to bomb blindly through the murk and overcast which perennially shrouded the Ruhr. Nor did it have the range to support operations much further east, and, as expected, the Germans took to jamming Gee from August 1942. To complicate matters still further, intense anti-aircraft defences were forcing the bombers higher and higher while the growing Luftwaffe night fighter force was driving Bomber Command to operate on darker and darker nights so, if crews were to strike as repeatedly and effectively as their Commander-in-Chief wanted, more blind bombing and target marking aids would have to be provided. They were not long in coming and by early 1943 Bomber Command found itself the proud possessor of two new radar blind bombing aids known as Oboe and H2S, target indicator markers to illuminate the aiming point, and a Pathfinder Force to put them all to good use. With these new devices, Sir Arthur Harris felt confident enough to announce that 'a new era in the technique of night bombing was initiated . . . At long last we were ready and equipped.'

Oboe relied on transmissions from two ground stations and its accuracy could be measured, not in miles like Gee, but in hundreds of yards. However Oboe was limited in range and could only guide one aircraft at a time, so H2S was also needed. This airborne radar was precise enough to differentiate between ground features such as waterways and large buildings, and it was a potent bombing aid in that it relied on no signals from ground stations, was unjammable, and was capable of simultaneous use by an unlimited number of aircraft. However, unlike Oboe, it did not always produce clearcut answers, for the amount of data gleanable from a radar screen of varying shades of obscurity depended heavily on the skill of the operator.

In view of the limited availability of such new aids initially, and as they needed good men to get the best out of them, it made sense to give priority in both to the Pathfinder Force — henceforward the main force followed on behind, relieved of the responsibility at last for finding the aiming point.

The strategic air offensive was therefore resumed in earnest in March 1943 against the ultimate target, the Ruhr. To the crews on the bomber squadrons, 'the Ruhr' was a grim phrase that always sent a shudder down the spine: it was known familiarly as 'Happy Valley' but there must have been some on 101 who groaned inwardly when they filed into the briefing room at Holme on 5 March to be told that they were to form part of a force of 442 aircraft to be dispatched that night against Essen. This was to be the first occasion on which the Oboe marking technique would be used to guide the main force in a major attack on a German target, and it would not be an easy test. Essen, with the Krupps Works lying at its very centre, was not only one of the most heavily defended targets in Europe but it was also protected by the close proximity of many other heavily built-up areas which easily confused the inevitably harassed and frequently blinded bomber crews. Moreover the Germans had even gone to the trouble of cleverly camouflaging the only significant geographical feature in the area — a stretch of water known as the Baldeney See. For three years therefore Essen had remained immune from any serious damage — it remained to be seen if Bomber Command could do any better in 1943.

The massed attack on 5 March was to be condensed into a mere 40min during which time over 400 bombers were expected to go over the target. Oboe worked best at height, so the high-flying Pathfinder Mosquitos would go in first. Zero hour, or 'H-hour', was to be 2100hr, and at this time the first of eight Oboe-equipped Mosquitos was to drop a salvo of red target indicator bombs over the aiming point, which belonged to Herr Krupp. The second Mosquito would follow three minutes later, the third seven minutes after that, and so on until H+33, when the last Mosquito would drop its indicators. All these 'reds' were to be aimed blindly on Oboe and, to make sure there were no gaps in the marking, 22 Pathfinder Lancasters were detailed as backers-up. They were spread over the 40min of the attack and their crews were briefed to drop green target indicators on to the red markers. By this means it was hoped that either red or green target indicators would be visible to the main force throughout the whole bombing attack.

The main force consisted of three overlapping waves with the Halifaxes first, then the Stirlings and Wellingtons, and finally 143 Lancasters bringing up the rear from H+20 to H+40. Eleven of these Lancasters came from 101 and all Squadron bomb-loads were to be in the proportion of two-thirds incendiaries to one-third high explosive of which one-third of the latter were to carry long-delay fuses. Crews were briefed to bomb the 'reds' if they saw them, otherwise the 'greens' — the 'reds' were deemed the most accurate and bomb-aimers were told to get a red in their bomb-sight on release if at all possible. 'The method of placing target indicators for this target is a new and very accurate one,' recounted the Intelligence Officer at Holme as he read out the Bomber Command Operations Order. 'It is to be impressed on all crews that they should make every effort to concentrate their bombing on the target indicators. If this is done this most important target will be destroyed. Crews are to be warned of the necessity for carrying on after dropping their bombs before turning off.' These injunctions were repeated to captains before take-off — it was feared that Oboe's life would be short because the enemy would soon jam it, so it had to be employed to maximum effect while the going was good and therefore no bomb should be wasted. The order to carry on across the target after release reflected the high density of the attack and was intended to minimise the risk of collision.

Such was the plan, and it was revolutionary in that at no stage did it depend on visual identification of the target. 'Up to this time,' wrote Flt Lt T. D. Misselbrook, then on his first bomber tour, 'each bomber crew used to fly to the target with little or no aids (certainly not over enemy territory) and had to identify the target by visual map reading. The Germans were pretty clever at setting decoys and we often stooged around for five to ten minutes trying to identify the aiming point.' Much had changed therefore from the old days when there was no such thing as an H-hour — navigators for instance now got together to prepare and compare their charts to lessen the chances of stupid collisions or misunderstandings — and this all convinced the crews that strategic bombing operations were now much better organised and this boosted their confidence accordingly.

Flt Lt Misselbrook's log book records that the raid on Essen was 'quite straightforward' and the Squadron diary reinforces this impression. '5/3/43. Aircraft took-off in evening to attack Essen. Sqn Ldr Fisher's crew had to abandon mission over base (Squadron aircraft and crews would join up together overhead base before setting course to meet up with the rest of the bomber stream) owing to port inner engine running a big end, and Sgt Smitheringale had to return owing to rear turret U/S. A very concentrated and successful attack was made on this raid and Krupps received heaviest battering that Bomber Command has been able to hand to it.'

The aerial photographs bore out this assessment. When the Intelligence Officers examined the pictures taken at the time of release, they estimated that one-third of the crews had dropped their bombs within three miles of the aiming point. Moreover post-strike daylight photo reconnaissance indicated that the heaviest concentration of damage was right in the centre of the town which was 'virtually devastated'. An area of 160 acres had been 'laid waste' and at least three-quarters of the buildings in as many as 450 acres had been demolished or damaged by high explosive or fire. The Krupps works also suffered heavily, losing 13 of its main buildings and suffering damage to at least 53 of its separate workshops. Nearly 1,000 tons of high explosives and incendiaries fell on Essen that night, and for the first time Bomber Command squadrons had been able to concentrate massive destruction in an area crucial to the German war effort. Only a year previously the first Gee raid on Essen had come to nought — 5 March 1943 heralded the long awaited 'breakthrough' and it inaugurated the start of the Battle of the Ruhr.

To many, the results at Essen that night gave rise to optimistic expectations of a crushing and immediate 'knock-out blow' to Germany, but wiser heads knew otherwise. Bomber Command lacked the means to fell the Reich at a single stroke, and Harris realised that his strategic offensive would be a war of attrition. Unfortunately, as the trench warfare of World War 1 so amply demonstrated, a war of attrition had the one great drawback that the attrition handed out by the enemy might ultimately exceed that inflicted upon him.

101 Squadron certainly appreciated this point for it had lost 35 aircraft in 1942, but in some ways the Squadron could live with these losses because they appeared remediable. The Wellington for instance had only two engines, so if it lost one it was in a far worse position than a four-engined Lancaster. Similarly, when the Lancaster arrived it could operate at levels above the attention of the flak batteries and its new navigation kit allowed crews to eschew the bombers' moon which also doubled as the anti-aircraft gunners' moon.

Even the stupid accidents that were an unavoidable consequence of war could be borne:

'17/12/42. Sgt Fussell and crew — a new but promising crew — were shot down in N-Nan to the regret of the whole Squadron after completing a "Freshman" trip sowing "Vegetables". Their IFF beacon was out of order, and as they returned in very difficult weather conditions they were shot down by our AA fire over the Yorkshire coast at Redcar — all crew were killed.'

Three days later the crew of Q-Queenie made a 'heavy' landing at Holme in bad weather, and on 23 December another Lancaster swung on landing and was written off. A Squadron crew crashed on the beach at Hornsea on 20 March 1943 whilst the second Q-Queenie went the way of the first and hit a tree at Southcliffe nine days later. Yet in such cases there was hope it was possible to improve procedures and skills to prevent repetition — what was less remediable was the impact of the enemy.

Just as Bomber Command was employing the latest radar technology to strike with increasing accuracy over Germany, so too the Luftwaffe was not slow in adapting these same laws of physics to their defensive advantage. In the early years of the war when individual bombers had meandered around Germany under cover of darkness, they could only be found by an enemy fighter force that stumbled around to the same extent trying to pick the attackers off by night vision alone. Now that the serried bomber ranks had arrived, they became much more conspicuous to a German system that was increasingly served by excellent ground and airborne radars. The Luftwaffe was attracted to the bomber stream like moths to a flame.

Some 101 crews were lucky. '21/12/42. On return from raid on Munich, Sgt Wiltshire's crew encountered an Me110 and port tailplane trailing edge was shot away. The rear and mid-upper turrets were also badly damaged, all the electrical circuits except W/T and Gee were destroyed, and the port tyre riddled. In spite of this, good landing made at base in bad weather conditions and captain reported good attack. 180 bullet holes were later counted in this machine and it is fortunate that crew escaped with only slight injury to mid-upper gunner.'

Nor was it always possible to sneak through gaps in the German defences. On 20 April 1943, 16 101 Sqn crews took-off to take part in a raid on the Baltic port of Stettin with the intention of flying low over the North Sea and Denmark to keep under the German radar screen. Sgt Yates was the mid-upper gunner on Flt Sgt Gray's crew and he remembers that 'the sense of speed over the undulating swell of the North Sea in moonlight was exhilarating. We crossed the coastline in a flash — I wondered how people felt with scores of Lancasters whistling overhead at 50ft, seemingly from nowhere. A muttered exclamation from the pilot notified "off track" and then it happened. Dull thuds, a smell of burning, smoke below my turret which stopped rotating. I felt for my legs, remembering you don't feel anything at first; still there thank God. We climbed frantically to gain height; the barrage ceased and everything seemed strangely quiet and unreal. It was then that I realised we had flown over a defended area and were extremely lucky to be alive. By some miracle we were still airborne and, it appeared, not too badly damaged although my turret had been knocked out. We had been lucky and I thought nothing worse could happen on this trip. Tempting fate? We were now over the Baltic and an urgent voice interrupted my musing — "Ships below!" Even as he spoke, red, orange and white lights came up towards us, slowly at first then gathering speed. A jagged hole appeared in the starboard mainplane, a port engine burst into flames, the aircraft shuddered in protest as we savagely banked and dived back towards the coast. "Jettison bombs" was the next sharp command — this was one target we couldn't reach.

'Out of the bomber stream, an alien place to be, the countryside below was bathed in moonlight as the crippled Lancaster limped painfully back the way it had come. The knots in my stomach tightened: I was painfully aware of our vulnerability and isolation. The aileron controls were damaged and the Lancaster complained at every change in course and height. Thankfully clouds began to obscure the moon but we were approaching a German night fighter station. I wondered how I would react when the inevitable happened. At first it was just a shadow on the port quarter, then a blur registered as an Me110. He came in fast, seemingly impervious to the rear gunner's bursts. Instinctively I reached for the turret controls, then realised I was immobilised. I could only watch helplessly as the tracer gathered speed towards us and blasted cannon shells into the starboard mainplane — our evasive action was too laboured to be effective. He came in again dead astern — it was the moment of truth. This time our evasion was more desperate and he missed, breaking away above us and flying on a parallel course at the same speed. He waggled his wings, banked to starboard and disappeared. To this day, I do not know why — was it my imagination or did he really slide back the canopy and wave. Later, as we approached the English coast, I felt completely detached from reality; had it all happened. It was 0430hrs when Lancaster EO422 made a rather bumpy landing at Holme-on-Spalding Moore.'

It would be wrong to give the impression that the Luftwaffe had it all their own way. On 17 January 1943, Flt Lt Misselbrook's crew were detailed to take part in a raid on Berlin. They had visited the German capital the night before when the moon had been near enough full and the target easily identified, and the overall picture at the briefing on 17 January appeared the same. This time, however, 'We were told that a diversionary raid was being carried out on Kiel in the hope of hoodwinking the enemy into thinking it was the main target. As on the previous night it was clear and moonlit until we got near to Berlin. All over the target area there was a thick layer of cloud and it was impossible to see the ground. After stooging about for a bit hoping to find a gap, and the flak getting more intense, I said to my crew that rather than waste our bombs we could divert to Kiel on our way back, which would be easy to find, so the navigator gave me a course. Needless to say this tended to take us away from the main force and it was not long before someone (the mid-upper, rear gunner or the wireless operator used to take turns to look out of the astro dome) said he thought there was a fighter on the starboard side. Everyone was on the alert, including me, and instinct must have prompted me to look to the right just as he opened fire because I remember seeing the flame from his guns as though I were waiting for it. I gave a slight twitch back and rolled towards him. Both upper and rear turrets opened fire and hit him. I didn't know this at first, and thinking he would make another attack I told the bomb aimer to jettison our bombs, which he did. But almost at once there were excited shouts that he was hit and on fire. However, we had managed to get a few stray bullets into us as the starboard outer engine appeared to be on fire, but I feathered it and the fire went out. The flight engineer said one of the fuel tanks was losing fuel so he ran all three engines off it, but after a short time (we had self-sealing tanks) this eased off. Unfortunately by this time we were picked out by searchlights and a lot of desperate weaving and loss of height got us clear. There was no flak so no doubt there was another fighter trying to find us. This was the end of the excitement until we got back to base which was fogged out and we were diverted up to Middleton St George. The aircraft received some bullet holes in the starboard wing and engines and also perspex in the upper turret was broken slightly but no one was hurt. Needless to say, I couldn't see much of the action except tracer flying in all directions and it was the opinion of mid-upper and wireless operator who considered Pat Harrison (rear gunner) actually dealt the mortal blow. Anyway he received an immediate award of the DFM for his efforts'. Unfortunately Sgt Harrison DFM was shot down on the third or fourth trip on his second tour.

But generally the Lancasters did not possess the armament to seriously challenge the German night fighter force. Browning .303in rifle-calibre machine guns were adopted as standard bomber armament in 1937, mainly because of their rapid rate of fire, but although the Lancaster sported machine guns in the three turrets they were almost invariably outranged and outweighed in fire power by cannon-equipped fighters. The only answer was to try to avoid trouble in the first place. 'If we saw a German fighter before he saw us,' recounted Sandy Greig, 'the chances were that we could get away from him. We didn't want to enter into combat and the only way to avoid it was to keep a good look-out. If we saw a fighter, we would turn inside him and "corkscrew" — you had to keep inside him all the time. Unless you were caught unawares by a German fighter sneaking up underneath — and a good crew constantly rocked the wings up and down to check the blind spots below — and you kept your wits about you, the chances of getting away from a fighter and going on to bomb the target were very good indeed.

'Against flak, you had to get out of the searchlight cone as quickly as possible because that controlled the predictors. There were often flak barrages over the target and other hot spots, and the only way past was to fly straight through the barrage as quickly as possible. The chances against you were lessened if you did that. Of course an unlucky shell could get a good crew, but once again, those crews who had practised their procedures and whose discipline in the air was good — they didn't chatter and only spoke when they had to — these were the crews who survived. You could see that some crews were basically survivors while others were basically losers.'

The Corkscrew Manoeuvre

The 'Corkscrew' Manoeuvre enabled a bomber crew to make good their course while at the same time presenting a difficult target to an attacking fighter and hopefully shaking it off in the process. It must be remembered that this manoeuvre was designed for use at night.

'This form of evasion,' described the RAF Trial Report, 'consists of a steep diving turn of about 30° and 500ft, followed by a steep climbing turn of 30° and 500ft in the opposite direction. The manoeuvre must be as violent as possible, particularly at the top and bottom of the corkscrew, to avoid giving an easy deflection shot. It should begin when the fighter attacking is at 600yds and should be continued throughout the engagement unless the fighter attacking can be clearly seen to be out of position, when normal flight can be resumed. This evasion is tiring for the pilot and must be stopped immediately it is clear that no immediate attacks are developing... This evasion does not affect the air gunners' shooting as much as a tight turn.'

Nevertheless, despite the growing offensive might of Bomber Command during the Battle of the Ruhr up to July 1943, the bomber casualties grew heavier and heavier.

88
Flt Sgt Bowyer and his crew. They were one of the first on 101 to complete an operational Lancaster tour on 30 April 1943 against Spezia, but it had taken them 30 trips and 13 abortives to do it. The Squadron now loses the services of another good experienced crew but we are glad to see them safely through a tour.'

88

89
The Ops Board at Holme for the night of a raid against Essen on 27 May 1943.

'21/1/43. Five air tests flown by A Flight in the morning and in evening, five aircraft took-off to attack Essen. Misselbrook and Hazard crews forced to return early owing to severe icing.' Flt Sgt R. E. MacFarlane's crew in C-Charlie had a more eventful flight, as the national press vividly described:

' "UNFLYABLE" BOMBER GOT HOME

A Lancaster which was attacked and shot up by three night fighters while returning from a raid on the Ruhr, dropped 10,000ft to escape from searchlights and flak, and finally dived to 80ft above the sea when it sighted five more fighters.

'The captain, a young Canadian, managed to get back to Britain although the plane was almost unflyable.

'Three Ju88s suddenly attacked. The Lancaster was raked with bullets. The rear-gunner was wounded and the mid-upper gunner killed.

'Throughout the pilot was weaving about, trying to shake off the fighters, and at length his evasive action was successful. By then the hydraulic and electrical equipment had been damaged and the gun-turrets were out of action.

'The rudder controls had been hit so badly that the pilot could only turn the aircraft very slowly. One starboard engine caught fire, and although the flames were extinguished, it was out of action for the rest of the trip.

'A few miles over the Channel he sighted five single-engined fighters. One turned to attack.

Defenceless because his gun turrets were out of action, the captain put the Lancaster into a steep dive and did not level out until he was 80ft from the water.

' "He lost the fighters and set course for home," nonchalently comments the Air Ministry News Service.'

Nevertheless, the RAF was grateful, and this engagement, which saw Sgt Singleton killed and Sgt O'Brien wounded, was rewarded by an immediate award of the DFM to Flt Sgt MacFarlane.

There were other losses on that mission to Essen. 'Sgt Wiltshire's crew failed to return and no news heard of them, to the regret of the whole Squadron who lost another first class pilot and crew. The losses of good crews this month has been heavier than the Squadron can afford with intakes from the Conversion Units being so slow.'

'4/5/43. A black day for the Squadron. Operations were ordered against Dortmund and we put up 18 aircraft. Sgt Nicholson and crew, and Flg Off Stanford and crew failed to return. It was Sgt Nicholson's first operational trip as captain but he had been spoken well of by his Flight Commander. Flg Off Stanford and crew had been well tried in previous raids and had achieved a very good reputation indeed — with them, doing his second tour, was Plt Off Lewis (WOp) who had come back to the Squadron to fly again.

'All other aircraft returned to base but some had to be diverted because of weather.

Four of these aircraft crash-landed, killing seven men and injuring seven more.'

At a time when it was calculated that an overall loss rate of 7% would prove lethal to the fighting efficiency of Bomber Command and that a loss rate of over 5% would produce an 'unacceptably low' standard of effectiveness, slightly over 16% of the bombers dispatched on the 43 major attacks during the Battle of the Ruhr became casualties of one sort or another. Although Squadron morale remained good throughout, there was no denying that the tactical and technical developments of the period tended to favour the defenders rather than the attackers. Night fighting techniques were steadily reducing the value of the cover of darkness which had succoured Bomber Command for so long, and it seemed to be only a matter of time before the night fighter mastered the night bomber just as effectively as the day fighter thwarted the day bomber during the Battle of Britain. Consequently it became even more imperative to throw everything into the bomber offensive in an effort to crush the German will to continue before the German defences wore Bomber Command out of the sky.

90

90
Hamburg at night showing the vast docks and waterways which stood out well on H2S radar.

91
The bombers' route to and from Hamburg.

91

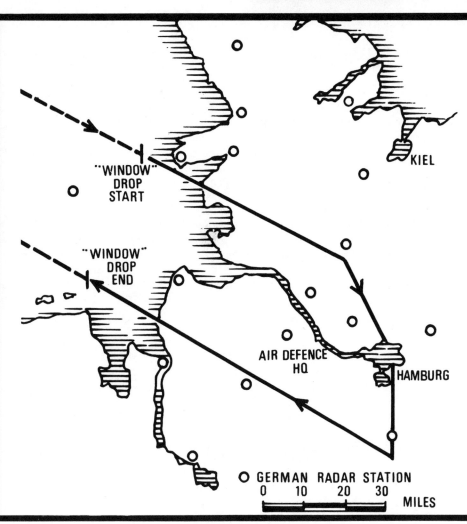

The result was that, in the course of five major operations spread over nine nights between 24 July and 2 August 1943, Bomber Command inflicted catastrophic devastation on Hamburg and struck the heaviest blow yet against Essen. The force of 791 bombers dispatched to Hamburg on the night of 24 July included 24 aircraft and crews from 101, and the whole exercise revolved around the second new bombing and navigation aid, H2S. The massed ranks of Lancaster, Halifaxes, Stirlings, and Wellingtons were routed well to the north so that they could turn on the target from a NW direction and coast-in over the north bank of the Elbe estuary. Water stood out well in H2S radar, and this coast-in point was to be signposted by yellow route markers dropped by six H2S-equipped aircraft and 30 backers-up. Also at this point, the marker aircraft would transmit wind information back to the main force, enabling the latter to cross the enemy coast with far more accurate meteorological information than they were used to. It was all to lead to far greater force concentration and accuracy than before.

The Hamburg raid was also to be the first on which Bomber Command crews were allowed to drop 'Window', those bundles of tinfoil strips which produced echoes equal in magnitude to those of aircraft and which thereby confused the air defence radars. 'Tonight you are going to use a new and simple counter-measure to protect yourselves against the German defence system,' declared the Bomber Command instruction which was read to all crews at briefing. 'The German defences will, therefore, become confused and you should stand a good chance of getting through unscathed while their attention is wasted on the packets of "Window".'

Two points were underlined for the crews. Firstly, the benefit of 'Window' was communal in that the protection afforded to a bomber was not so much from its own foil as from that dropped by aircraft ahead of and above it. Concentration and adherence to the bomber stream was therefore vital both to and from the target area. Secondly, the task of discharging 'Window' would be physically demanding, but it was essential that the correct number of bundles be released at the appropriate times.

As it approached the enemy coast therefore, the whole force prepared to drop 'Window' at the rate of one bundle per minute. The bomb-aimers crawled back to the rear fuselage where the 'Window' bundles were stacked around the flare chute. At the Lancasters' altitude the temperature was −20°C, so it was no fun to stand in the cold darkness, encumbered with parachute, oxygen lead, torch and stopwatch, and heave out aluminium foil with precise regularity. As the leading aircraft crossed the enemy coast, the flight engineers crawled back to the flare-chute to relieve the bomb-aimers, who would shortly have more pressing duties to perform. Ten minutes later the bombers turned right on to their attack heading, and the large radar echo that was Hamburg, the second city of the Reich and the largest port in Europe, gradually moved into the centre of the H2S screen.

The appointed H-hour was 0100 on 25 July, but the attack opened three minutes before this when 20 H2S-equipped aircraft dropped yellow target markers and flares blindly on Hamburg. These pointed the way for a further eight crews, also with H2S, to try and visually identify the aiming point in the centre of the city which they were to mark with red target indicators. Fifty-three backers-up were then to put down green markers from H+2 to H+48 minutes, during which time the whole main force was ordered to bomb into any reds they could see. If no 'reds' were visible then the bomb-aimers were to aim at the centre of the green concentration, but either way they were to ignore the 'yellows' because these had not been aimed visually. This acceptance of the fact that H2S could not work miracles, and that its role was to guide the Mark 1 eyeball which could not be surpassed when the weather was good, paid ample dividends in that night photography showed that some 306 crews had placed their bombs within three miles of the aiming point.

The unfortunate Hamburg was hit again on the nights of 27 and 29 July, and 2 August, with a total of 66 No 101 Squadron crews playing their part, and the cumulative weight of destruction inflicted on the four nights of Operation 'Gomorrah' was catastrophic. The city was tinder dry, and under the torrent of incendiary bombs the conflagration grew into a fire storm. 'People who thought they had escaped fell down, overcome by the devouring force of the heat, and died in an instant,' reported the distraught local civil defence chief, Major-General Kehrl. Refugees had to make their way over the dead and the dying. The sick and the infirm had to be left behind by the rescuers as they themselves were in danger of burning. Nearly a million people streamed out of the city between dawn and dusk, leaving behind a total of dead alone estimated at 50,000. 'Gentlemen,' observed Goering's deputy, Erhard Milch, to his colleagues, 'we are no longer on the offensive... I am beginning to think that we are sitting out on a limb and the British are sawing that limb off...'

To drive the point home, in between the raids on Hamburg 101 contributed 23 crews to the force which hit Essen on 25 July, and nothing demonstrated Bomber Command's new-found potential more than the Squadron observation that Essen should now be known as 'the Dead City'. Moreover, the Command had achieved all these victories at extremely low cost. 'On our return from Essen on 25 July,' recorded Scrym Wedderburn, 'I went to make my report when I was grabbed by Grp Capt Blucke who was obviously very moved. He said to me, "Come and look at my operations board. It is the first time that you have all come back from Essen".'

Flt Lt Wedderburn was also pleased to note that the defenses around Hamburg, when faced with 'Window' for the first time, 'were feeble in the extreme'. They were still 'disorganised' on the following attacks such that only 86 bombers (or 2.8%) of the 3,095 dispatched to Hamburg on the four nights failed to return, and Flt Sgt D. P. P. Hurst's crew were the only casualties from 101. 'Window' had enabled Harris to concentrate his forces against a single target for long enough to encompass its complete destruction without suffering the usual penalty for such concentration. In vain the German night fighter crews waited impatiently over their radio beacons for instructions from their ground controllers, but in the words of the drinking song that Squadron crews often sang in the Mess, they called for help and no help came. The ether was thick with confusion — as Alfred Price in *Instruments of Darkness* quoted: 'The enemy are reproducing themselves.' 'It is impossible — too many hostiles.' 'Wait a while. There are many more hostiles.' 'I cannot control you.' 'Try without your ground control...'

Never again would 'Window' have such an effect because the Germans would not be slow to counter it, but the destruction it helped to inflict on Hamburg staggered the imagination. As his tour as CO of 101 drew to a close, Wg Cdr Reddick could take comfort from the fact that things seemed at last to be going right for his Squadron. When he first arrived at Holme, Bomber Command had finally learned from bitter experience that the bombing results were far from what they were made out to be, and in the depressing winter of 1942 there did not seem to be much point in going on. Then in the spring of 1943 the sun started to shine, the new Lancasters were settled into service, training was seen to be greatly improved, and the revolutionary bombing and navigation equipment was entering service. 'I wouldn't like to say whether a happy squadron becomes an efficient squadron or vice-versa,' said Sandy Greig, 'but the fact remains that 101 then became superbly efficient and tremendously happy and I think these two factors complemented each other. As efficiency grew, so did the happiness, and as the happiness grew, so did the efficiency'. Hamburg put the icing on the cake, and one Squadron member spoke for them all when he proclaimed that 'at last we seem to be winning'.

PLEESE! I CHANGE-A DA COAT IF YOU STOP-A DA BOMB!!

92
Further evidence that the men of 1 Group did not hold the Italians in overmuch esteem.

THE RUHR

- Huls
- Hamm
- Kamen
- Castrop Rauxel
- Soest
- Bottrop
- Gelsenkırchen
- Dortmund
- Oberhausen
- Essen
- Schwerte
- Mulheim
- Wûppertal
- Dusseldörf
- Remscheid
- efeld

Ruhr

0   10   20   30   40
MILES

INTERNATIONAL BOUNDARIES AS AT
THE OUTBREAK OF WAR ━ ·━ ·━

DISTANCE CIRCLES MEASURED FROM
LINCOLN (IN MILES)

- Danzig
- Marienburg

Vistula

WARSAW

- Posen

POLAND

Oder

700   Upper   Silesia

RAGUE

CZECHOSLOVAKIA

VIENNA

BUDAPEST

HUNGARY

As Easy as ABC

Wg Cdr Reddick was posted to Lindholme on 27 July 1943 and his successor, Wg Cdr G. A. Carey-Foster, took over 101 just after it had moved home yet again. The expansion of 6 Group to the north of York had forced 1 Group to hand over all its stations north of the Humber to 4 Group; personnel from Linton therefore moved into Holme with the result that 101 was ordered south to the Lincolnshire Wolds and its final wartime base, Ludford Magna.

'15/6/43. We moved to Ludford Magna with A Flight sending nine aircraft, B Flight 10 aircraft, and C Flight 12 aircraft. The movement of the whole Squadron as well as the Station Headquarters was accomplished without a hitch, and it was noticed that all sections buckled down in a whole-hearted attempt to make the best of what will no doubt prove a long job.

'The incorrigible Squadron members of course operated on the first night. A very low level attack was staged on Louth, the "Mason's Arms" being the target.'

Situated between Louth and Market Rasen, Ludford airfield had been built by the firm of George Wimpey in the space of only 90 days, and in the beginning it was as bleak as the countryside on which it lay. Every bit of equipment that could be carried from Holme was loaded into the aircraft — 'We must have been hopelessly overweight,' observed Sergeant Schofield, 'because we flew like a Mark I Wellington. The new station was, if anything, worse than the last. There were no perimeter or runway lights, so we had to taxy with the aid of our landing lights and an Aldis out of the bomb-aimer's window which was not a good idea'. At first the aircrews and groundcrews had to set up the Squadron among the shovels and cement mixers, but 'if you couldn't take a joke you shouldn't have joined' and 101 was soon back in business against Mulheim on 22 June.

After the Battle of Hamburg the whole of Bomber Command was not to be concentrated against another single target until November 1943. However there was one famous raid in between against the rocket

93
101 Squadron bases and principal enemy targets during World War 2.

weapon research establishment at Peenemünde. This attack, on 17 August, demanded precision because the usual heavy-handed area bombing tactics were inappropriate against a number of specific buildings, so this was to be the first major raid to employ the 'Master Bomber' technique. In addition, it also illustrated some of the advances that Bomber Command had made in the science of bombing over the previous year.

Peenemünde was beyond the range of Oboe but, being a coastal target, it promised to stand out well on H2S. The bombing force, to which 101 contributed 20 aircraft, was ordered to attack in three waves against three different targets; all three aiming points were in line with a tiny island three miles north of Peenemünde, and it was felt that timed runs from this island would be accurate enough for the Pathfinders to lay down target markers with a considerable degree of accuracy. Radar-placed yellow parachute flares were to illuminate the area around the target, whereupon Visual Marker crews would drop red target indicators supported by Pathfinder 'backers-up' who would drop green markers and bombs. The main force following on behind would consolidate the attack until the time allotted for the first target had expired, when a new marker — known as the 'aiming point shifter' — would appear on the scene and switch the weight of the onslaught on to the next objective. It would be precise and concentrated mass bombing as never before, and the whole force of 597 aircraft was to be through in 45 minutes.

The crews assembled in the Ludford briefing room were hushed by the news that the night's target was a mystery 'research station' which was engaged upon the production of a 'new form of radiolocation equipment' which promised to work wonders for the German night fighter organisation. Such information was doubtless calculated to inspire the bomber crews to maximum efforts and the station Intelligence Officer drove the point home by saying that, 'in order to retard the production of this equipment and thereby help maintain the effectiveness of Bomber Command's offensive, it is necessary to destroy both the Experimental Station and to kill or incapacitate the scientific and technical experts working there.'

There were other signs that this raid was out of the ordinary. Up to now, 'security had not been rigidly adhered to on pre-flight briefings, but prior to this attack police were on duty at the briefing room door recording the names of those who entered and locking the doors after they all went in. Such strict security became the norm at Ludford thereafter and, once a raid was announced, not only were crews not allowed to leave the camp but also they were denied all telephone links with the outside world'.

Such was the plan, but unfortunately as the first Pathfinder crews ran in towards Pennemünde, they found that the H2S picture was not as clear as had been predicted: some of the first flares went down two miles to the south, which cost the lives of several hundred foreign workers trapped in the Karlshagen labour camp. But the correct aiming point — the scientists' housing estate — had been

Award promulgated in the London Gazette dated 20.8.43
DISTINGUISHED
SERVICE ORDER
Acting Squadron Leader Alexander Broom GREIG DFC (68753)
Royal Air Force Volunteer Reserve, No 101 Squadron

This officer, who has completed many sorties since being awarded the Distinguished Flying Cross, is a fearless and courageous captain. His great navigational ability and fine fighting qualities have inspired all with whom he has flown and have played a large part in the many successes obtained. His record of achievement is worthy of the highest praise.

94
Sandy Greig's citation for his DSO (see p76).

95
Praise from the highest quarters followed the award.

R.A.F. Form 1924   **POSTAGRAM.**   Originator's Reference Number :—
BC/C.23191/P.

To: F/O(A/S/L) A.B. Greig, D.F.C. (68753)   Date:— 4th August 1943.
No.101 Squadron,
R.A.F. Station, Ludford Magna.

From: The Commander-in-Chief, Bomber Command.

My warmest congratulations on the award of your Distinguished Service Order.

A.T. Harris
Air Chief Marshal.

Originator's Signature   Time of Origin

accurately marked by a single yellow flare dropped by Wg Cdr John White of 156 Pathfinder Squadron, and four or five of the following Marker crews placed other yellows close by to reinforce the glow. Grp Capt John Searby, the master bomber, or 'master of ceremonies' as he was known to the main force crews, was content with this marking, and when he saw three backers-up correctly reinforce the aiming point yellows with greens he ordered the main force to 'Bomb into the greens'. As a result, over two-thirds of the 231 attacking aircraft on the initial wave succeeded in bombing the correct aiming point or its immediate vicinity. WO Johnson's crew was the first in from 101 Squadron and they attacked from 20,500ft and at 140kts. 'Target identified and bombed on Green TI markers. HC and incendiary bursts very concentrated in target area and large fires seen on leaving target. One of the most concentrated attacks I have seen and Pathfinders were very accurate.'

The last aircraft of the first wave withdrew at 12min after zero hour, but only one out of the five 'Shifters' managed to place his red target indicator on the rocket factory which was the second aiming point. The backers-up naturally ignored the single red and went for the larger, but inaccurate concentration. This was where the master bomber, down at 8,000ft, earned his money, and Grp Capt Searby broadcast a warning that the first backers-up had overshot and that the remainder should not compound the error. He was just in time, and as 113 main force Lancasters thundered in he twice ordered them to ignore the green markers to the south and bomb only those to the north. It was advice well taken by many as witnessed by Sgt Jean-Jaques Minguy, a French-Canadian mid-upper gunner on 101:

'Peenemünde was growing very "lively". On the ground, everything was going up and burning as it isn't possible. This was a mixture of flashes from the ground defences, which seemed to increase their firing in the same measure as we were raining them with bombs, and of explosions which were all more spectacular one from the other. It looked like coal burning — an inferno! Flames were of every colour possible — red, orange, green, blue and what not! Explosions succeeded one another at a rate that surpasses imagination.' (Quoted from *The Peenemünde Raid* by Martin Middlebrook.)

The third and last attack was carried out by Halifaxes of 6 Group and Lancasters of 5 Group, and while they were bearing the brunt of the late attentions of the Luftwaffe fighter force, the 18 101 Squadron aircraft and crews that had successfully attacked were making their way home. Before the raid crews had been assured that if they did not make a good job of destroying the 'research station', they would be sent back night after night until the task was completed. This worried some returning aircrew like Sgt Geoffrey Whittle, the navigator on WO Walker's crew, because 'we did not think the raid had been very successful. The master bomber was not very encouraging'. But others had seen the damage inflicted on Peenemünde for themselves — 'Buildings seen to disintegrate' reported Flt Sgt Rays' crew on their return. It was a job well done, even if crews at the time did not appreciate the implications for Britain of delaying the arrival of German V-weapons. With hindsight, a 1 Group report in May 1945 was to describe this as 'the most telling single raid of the war'.

Nevertheless, if Bomber Command was becoming more proficient at precision as well as area bombing, the Luftwaffe air defences were also not backward in coming forward to defend their airspace. 'Since the disorganisation of the German night fighters caused by the introduction of Window in July,' wrote Bomber Command's Operational Research Section in the *Monthly Review of Losses and Interceptions of Bomber Command Aircraft in Night Operations — August 1943*, 'a considerable readjustment has apparently been made'. Previously, responsibility for the defence of Germany from air attack had rested with five fighter divisions which controlled a system of fighter 'boxes' running down from Denmark to the Swiss frontier. This was the Kammhüber Line, and any bomber approaching from Britain had to pass

96
Sgt Geoffrey Whittle DFM. *IWM*

through one of its 'boxes'. The underground operations room for each division was so well endowed with sophisticated communications and control systems fed from a bevy of advanced early warning and fighter control radars that it was known as a 'Battle Opera House', and from here many controllers could direct small groups of fighters or individual interceptors. This superb German ground-controlled interception system enabled a controller to talk a fighter round its appropriate 'box' until it was precisely into position behind the bomber such that the kill could be completed by reference to the fighter's own airborne radar and pilot's eyesight. Each division could fight its own air battle, and therefore German night fighter crews nearly always operated within a few miles of their own airfields and always under the control of the same ground station.

The drawback to the Kammhüber Line was that it depended for its success entirely on ground and airborne radar systems and once these were 'blinded' by 'Window', close control became impossible. Consequently a former bomber pilot, Major Hajo Herrmann, suggested to Goering that single-seater day fighters be brought into what had previously been a two-seater night fighter preserve. It had been noticed that when a city was being attacked a high flying German pilot could see

bombers below silhouetted against the glow of burning buildings or searchlights, so Herrmann advocated that the Luftwaffe set about the enemy over the targets themselves. All available fighters were to be assembled over radio beacons at the approach of bomber formations, and when the object of their attentions became clear, the fighter pack would be hurled en masse into the bomber stream over the target. They would then pursue and harry the intruders visually to the limit of their endurance and then refuel at the nearest airfield. This new tactic was code-named 'Wild Boar' and it was revolutionary in that it neutralised the effect of 'Window' at a stroke. One fighter control officer could now scramble the whole air defence force and assemble it over the radio beacons thought to be in the bombers' path. 'Enemy night fighters have been identified in groups en route to and over target areas at least 300 miles from their bases,' continued the *Bomber Command Monthly Review* with surprise, 'and during all operations subsequent to 9/10 August a part of the fighter force has been given general directions by a running commentary ... This running commentary gives the height and direction of the bomber stream and the areas over which it is passing. The probable target is frequently given as soon as the target is marked and bombs have

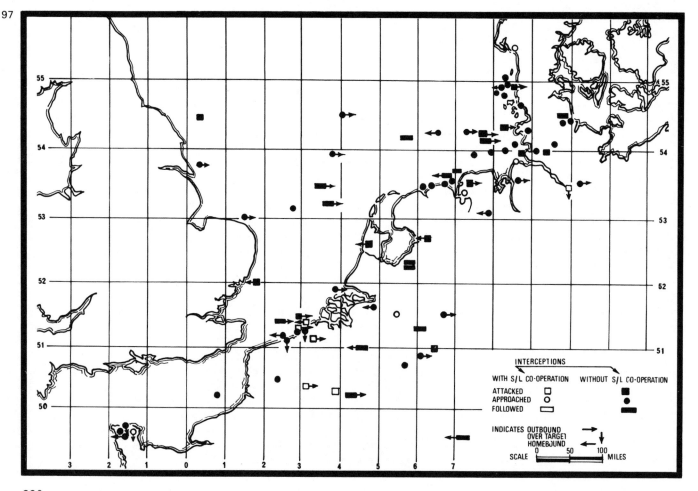

97

fallen, and the main object of this direction appears to get the fighters to the target rather than into the bomber stream'.

Herein lay the key to the success of Major Herrmann's 'Wild Boar' scheme. Ideally, the Luftwaffe hierarchy would have preferred to confront British bombers over the less politically sensitive approaches to the Reich, but if 'Window' rendered such hopes impossible, then the attacking force had to be hit where it was most vulnerable. Concentrating bombers in time and space, like concentrating merchantmen in convoys, made mutual protection much easier but it also gave the opposition much more to aim at. Over the target itself therefore, all means were employed to enable the fighter crews to find their opposite numbers by visual means. High flying German aircraft would drop flares to illuminate the incoming bombers while the masses of search lights would play evenly on the bottom of the cloud layer so that the bombers could be made out in silhouette, an effect that was further enhanced once the fires started below. Moreover, the bomber crews were at their most vulnerable on their bombing runs, and no amount of tin foil could protect them at such a time.

After overcoming much opposition, Major Herrmann was allowed to try out his theory for the first time against Bomber Command on 3 July. He and nine other 'Wild Boars' claimed 12 'kills' that night, and Herrmann further proved his point on 27 July over Hamburg, as described in Martin Middlebrook's *The Battle of Hamburg* (Allen Lane, 1980):

'The clouds of smoke over Hamburg were so dense that it made you shudder. I flew over the target several times, and then I saw this bomber in the searchlights. He had nearly reached the top of the smoke cloud at the time.

'The attack was very simple. I went into the searchlights. I was not very experienced; another pilot would have kept in the dark. I was almost level with him, probably just above the turbulence of his propellers. It was like daylight in those searchlights. I could see the rear gunner; he was only looking downwards, probably at the inferno below. There was no movement of his guns. You must remember that, at this time, the British were not generally warned to watch out for us over the target. I had seen other bombers over the target with the gunners looking down.

'I fired and he burned. He banked to the left and then through 180° to the right. As he fell, he turned and dropped away from the smoke cloud. I followed him a little but, as he

97, 98
The growth of the German night fighter threat was represented by the number of interceptions of Bomber Command aircraft plotted for November 1941 (**97**) and September 1942 (**98**).

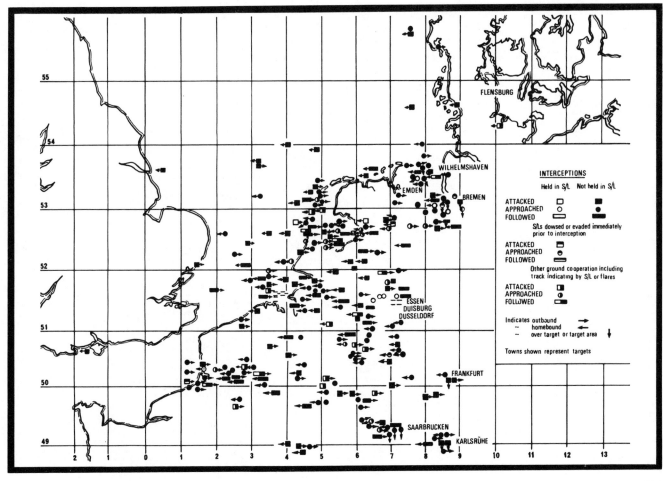

got lower and lower, I left him. I watched him burst on the ground. By the light of his explosion, I could see the "Knicks" — the small walls with bushes built on them against which the cattle found shelter from the sun and wind. That was my homeland — Schleswig-Holstein — as I knew it.'

Major Herrmann's victim crashed into Wellingsbüttel, a northern suburb of Hamburg. It is almost certain that it was Flt Sgt Hurst's crew from 101 Squadron who were then on their sixth mission — there were no survivors.

The Germans were not slow to allocate resources to 'Wild Boar' and the initial British reaction was to mount diversionary raids to protect the main force. 'The reversion to free-lance methods, which commenced at the end of July,' commented Bomber Command's *Monthly Review of Losses for September*, 'has continued on an intensified scale with large groups of fighters (probably as many as 200 on individual nights) being directed by running commentary alone... The policy followed has been to hold back the fighter force, orbiting beacons, until the target is known with certainty, the fear of attack on Berlin appearing to be the governing factor and foremost in the minds of the running commentary controllers'. Thus a purely diversionary raid by eight Mosquitos on Berlin coincidental with the attack on Peenemünde led to much confusion and the concentration of over 200 fighters near the German capital so that when the first target markers went down at Peenemünde, the night fighter crews had to transit 100 miles to the north and only got there in time to catch the final wave of attackers. Nevertheless, they still managed to dispose of 41 aircraft or 7% of the bomber force that night, which was a higher loss rate than that being inflicted before the introduction of 'Window'.

Diversionary raids therefore had their limitations, and the clear summer nights of 1943 compounded Bomber Command's problems. The only restriction on 'Wild Boar' missions, besides fuel, was weather conditions at the fighter landing grounds, as at the end of an attack on Berlin on 23/24 August when the fighters were forced down by fog. Not that this did Bomber Command and 101 Squadron much good. 101 lost Flg Off Mahoney's and Flt Sgt Naffir's crews that night, 'and it is estimated that roughly 10% of the force dispatched was attacked'. Moreover, Bomber Command noted with alarm that 'the proportion of total sorties returning damaged by fighter action is more than 50% greater than in the preceding seven months', and the situation was going to get worse. During the Peenemünde raid, Gefreiter Holker shot down two bombers using two cannons pointing obliquely upwards from his Bf110. This was *Schrage Musik* ('Slanting music' or jazz) and it was to enable many German crews to creep in below and into the Lancaster's blind spot. Here the fighter remained invisible unless the Lancaster pilot happened to be weaving at the time, and as *Schrage Musik* used non-tracer ammunition, in most cases the doomed bomber crews never knew what hit them.

To make life even more uncomfortable and nerve-wracking for the attackers, another night-fighter expert, Oberst von Lossberg, proposed that twin-seater night fighters infiltrate into the bomber stream on the approaches to Germany. Each fighter division retained the responsibility to launch its fighters when it saw a force coming — and a radar screen full of 'Window' was as good an indication as any — but once they were in the air, the best placed operations room would broadcast to all fighters. The subsequent running commentary would not give detailed orders but would rather provide a continuous broadcast of the bomber stream's progress and specifically any changes in its course. The night fighter crews would use this flow of information to find the stream and then use their airborne radars or eyes to strike down individual bombers. If a fighter crew lost the stream, they would return to the running commentary in an attempt to re-locate their quarry.

This technique was christened 'Tame Boar' and it used the RAF's own 'Window' to confirm the position and track of the bomber stream. Von Lossberg was in fact proposing a freelance running battle that might last for over 100 miles and, together

99
'Oor Wullie' as painted on Lancaster LL757 by Cpl Jock Steadman. Most 101 Squadron aircraft had gaily coloured mascots emblazoned on their flanks.

100
A hive of activity at 'Oor Wullie's' dispersal at Ludford. 'Wullie's' captain, Plt Off 'Rusty' Waughman, is looking out of the cockpit window and Cpl Jock Steadman is on the wing. The ABC aerials are clearly in evidence and the anonymous photographer must have known that it was forbidden to take pictures of such secret equipment because the photo was taken from inside a ground crew hut. *via Waughman*

with 'Wild Boar', it marked the virtual demise of totally controlled interceptions in neat little 'boxes'. Between them, the 'Boar' packs accounted for 123 RAF bombers and crews in three raids against Berlin at the end of August 1943, and brought an end to any peace of mind that Squadrons such as 101 might have enjoyed following Hamburg and the introduction of 'Window'.

In an effort to regain the initiative, Bomber Command looked for the means to exploit any loopholes that might be inherent in the Luftwaffe's new freelance tactics. Compressing the bomber force still further — and no raid in October 1943 lasted for more than 26min — gave diversionary raids a chance to throw German controllers off the scent until it was too late, but it was not always possible to fool the opposition in this fashion, especially as Bomber Command was increasingly attacking targets deep inside enemy airspace. So it was decided to concentrate on the major weakness of the freelance system, namely that 'while commentaries are still transmitted from several stations, they are now coordinated, authority frequently being delegated to one controller who deploys the whole available force to cover possible targets.' The German fighter crews relied completely on getting timely and accurate information on the position of the bomber stream otherwise they would stumble about all night, and if it had not been possible to stop 200 controllers talking to 200 fighters, it was surely not beyond British ingenuity to prevent the night fighter force from hearing a single controller's running commentary and thereby thwarting the whole freelance endeavour.

The VHF radios fitted to German night fighters covered the frequencies from 38 to 42 MHz, and the first British response was to erect 15 ground transmitters in England to put a barrage of noise over the whole band. This was known as 'Ground Cigar', but as it only had a range of about 140 miles, a similar jamming device had to be taken into the air on raids beyond the Low Countries. Fortunately the Telecommunications Research Establishment at Malvern had a suitable device in the pipeline which was originally named 'Jostle'. 'Jostle' was conceived in early 1943 to counter the fighter control frequencies in the Kammhüber boxes, and a letter from Air Cdre S. O. Bufton, Director of Bomber Operations, laid down the requirements for the 'Jostle' carrier on 23 April 1943:

'The aircraft required must be capable of proceeding with the main bomber force to the target in order to provide protection.

'As enemy aircraft may home on to the jammer, the aircraft must have the performance to give a sufficient degree of immunity from interception.

'It has to be a heavy aircraft to accommodate the equipment.'

The Lancaster was the obvious choice to carry 'Jostle' and by 30 May it had been agreed that 100 Squadron at Waltham would fit the bill. But then a complication arose. 100 Squadron aircraft were then earmarked for H2S installation, and as the Lancaster's power supplies could not cope with the demands of H2S and 'Jostle' together, 'it will be necessary to alter the H2S programme or alternatively fit "Jostle" into a different squadron'. The former was too difficult, so

101
Squadron Lancaster SR-B
dropping a stream of incendiaries
over Duisberg on 14 October
1944. The most interesting
features of this photograph
however are the two ABC aerials
on top of the fuselage. Such secret
sights were normally hidden from
the photographer's eye, and
whenever a crew landed away
from base the tell-tale masts were
covered and an armed guard
placed on the aircraft. Thereafter
only groundcrew from Ludford
were allowed to carry out aircraft
repairs. *IWM*

someone must have looked at the next
squadron on the list, for on 10 June 1943 it
was decided that 101 Squadron would carry
'Jostle' as it 'will not be fitted with H2S in the
initial programme'.

Having changed the Squadron, the RAF
then decided to change the name. The first
'Ground Cigar' station became operational
on 30/31 July 1943, and as 'Jostle' was only
an airborne version of 'Ground Cigar', it
came as no surprise when 'Jostle' was
rechristened 'Airborne Cigar'. However, this
was a bit of a mouthful, and 1 Group only
legalised common practice when it sent the
following telegram to Bomber Command
soon afterwards:

'In view of the brevity and simplicity of the
term, it is requested that you refer to "Airborne Cigar" aircraft as "A.B.C." aircraft in
all future communications.'

ABC equipment trials took place in a 101
Squadron Lancaster on 4-6 September 1943
under the guidance of Flt Lt F. Collins, a
radar specialist seconded from Bomber
Command. On 8 September a test flight was
made over the North Sea to within 10 miles
of the enemy coast, and this was so successful that the Squadron was ready to try out
the new jamming equipment operationally
against Hanover on 22 September. Eight
operators listened out that night, and the first
words they heard over the ABC were
'Achtung, English bastards coming!'. The
new, and highly secret, equipment had a
most successful baptism of fire on that
occasion, but ironically the only aircraft shot
down out of a Squadron complement of 18
dispatched to Mannheim on 23 September
was the sole Lancaster to carry ABC.

ABC had a range of approximately 50
miles, and the equipment, which was soon to
be fitted into every 101 Squadron aircraft,
was officially described in the following
terms: 'ABC is designed for use on bombing
raids over enemy territory to interrupt enemy
communications by jamming particular frequencies on which radio messages are being
sent to night fighters from ground control
stations. It comprises three 50-watt
transmitters each capable of sending out
frequency-modulated jamming signals covering narrow frequency bands selected within
the 38.3 to 42.5 MHz range by means of
manual tuning controls. A "panoramic"
receiver provides means of locating enemy
transmissions in this range of frequencies,
and setting jamming signals accurately upon
them.

'The total weight of the equipment is
604¾lb. When the equipment is switched on,
all three transmitters are suppressed
simultaneously while the panoramic receiver
sweeps over the 38.3 to 42.5 MHz band 25
times each second. Any signals picked up are

101

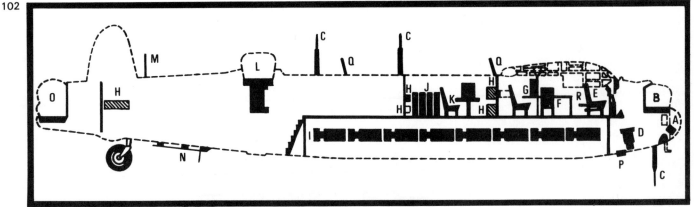

102
Interior view of a 101 Squadron
Lancaster.
    Key:
A: Bomb aimer's position,
B: Nose turret,
C: ABC transmission masts,
D: Camera,
E: Pilot's position,
F: Navigator's position,
G: Radio operator's position,
H: Wing and tail spars,
I: Bomb bay
J: ABC transmitters and receiver
    (mounted on the port side of the
    fuselage),
K: Spec Ops position,
L: Dorsal turret,
M: ABC reception aerial,
N: Beam approach aerial,
O: Rose Rice tail turret,
P: Window chute,
Q: Standard radio fit aerials,
R: Flight engineer's position.

103
View from the rear of a Lancaster
looking forward over the main
spar at the Spec Op's position.
via Waughman

104
Kassel cartoon.

displayed on a three-inch diameter cathode
ray tube. Here the frequencies are
represented as a horizontal line, and any
signals picked up are shown as vertical
"blips" which grow out of the base

'When a "blip" appears, the operator sets
a bright strobe spot to mark it, and "throws"
a switch which stops the panoramic sweep of
the receiver; he tunes it to the single frequency marked by the strobe and brings his
earphones into the receiver circuit so that he
can listen to the incoming signal. Having
identified this as an enemy ground transmission, he may then switch on a transmitter
and turn the tuning control until the jamming
signal, as displayed on the cathode ray tube,
covers the marker spot. The enemy signal is
then completely obliterated in his earphones
by the output of the jamming transmitter.
Whenever desirable, the operator may
suppress the transmitter in order to determine whether the enemy has changed to a
new frequency, and if so, readjust the
jamming signal. Three transmitters are provided so that three communication channels

in the enemy Ground Control Intercept band
may be simultaneously jammed.'

Such then was the theory, but what did it
mean in practice? For a start, 101 Squadron
Lancasters suddenly sprouted three 7ft-long
aerials, 'giving the appearance of three
telegraph poles which looked far from safe'.
Two were on the upper fuselage and the third
stuck out under the nose until it nearly
reached the ground — surprisingly, they had
very little effect on the Lancaster's performance.

Then there was the question of the ABC
operator, and for this purpose an eighth
member was added to the 101 Squadron
crews to be known as the 'Special Operator'
(one of the reasons for the abbreviation to
ABC was that Spec Ops naturally objected
to being called 'Cigar Operators'). 'Spec Ops'
were selected from all aircrew categories with
every man being a German-speaking
volunteer for unknown special duties. 'All
that was really necessary,' recalled Sgt H.
van Geffen, 'was the ability to recognise an
R/T transmission as definitely German
rather than Russian, Czech, or Polish, but
obviously some Spec Ops were more fluent in
German than others. (Spec Ops were also
taught some of the codewords that the
German controllers used, such as 'Kapelle'
for target altitude and 'Karussel' for fly an
orbit.) After a short course on set manipula-
tion, we were posted to Ludford where we
were given further training in searching on
our receiver for enemy R/T and back-tuning
three transmitters to that signal in order to
jam it. Once we were able to do this in 30sec
we were ready for business...'

101 crews were still expected to carry on
with their normal bombing duties while the
Spec Op jammed, but the weight of ABC and
the extra crew member reduced bomb loads
by about 1,000lb. Before flight, each Spec Op
was allocated his own section of the VHF
waveband that he was required to search and
jam. 'We were given a position, usually 6°
East,' explained a Spec Op quoted in *Instruments of Darkness* by Alfred Price
(Macdonald and Jane's, 1977), 'at which

point we would switch our receiver to "On" and commence to search the waveband for any German R/T. When we saw a signal on the cathode ray tube, we would tune our receiver in to it and listen. If we heard Jerry vectoring his fighters, we would turn on one of our jammers which showed as a blip on the screen base line. We then moved this blip along the line until it was on top of the German blip, and when they coincided, we started the jammer. We would then watch to see if he changed frequency and then carry out the same procedure with the second jammer (leaving the first still jamming), and so on with the third jammer if the German changed frequency again. Thus we could not only hear him but also see which frequency he had changed to so that we could jam him before he had a chance to send his instructions. I could also tune two or three of my jammers to a single frequency depending on the strength of signal I received.' Hopefully, the German fighter crews would then find that the reassuring voice of their running commentator had been replaced by what can best be described as a 'wig-wog' noise produced by a constantly varying audio note running up and down the scale. From then on it was just a matter of following the blips around the screen. 'If the jamming got too bad, the German controller would go off the air altogether. Later he would appear on a different frequency, but it only took a matter of seconds to cover the new blip. Often the German controller would get rather angry and I sometimes felt a little sorry for him, trying to get through while I was stopping him.'

All in all, ABC was a very ingenious piece of equipment. The ABC Spec Op and his black boxes were situated just aft of the main spar on the port side of the Lancaster fuselage, cut off from the rest of the crew except for the intercom. 'We sat in darkness and the nearest other crewman was the mid-upper gunner — his boots were at my level, about 4ft further down the aircraft. We were even more isolated when we operated our sets because we had to cut out the intercom circuit to prevent distraction. Thus we had no idea of what was going on around us, and the only link with reality was a little call light which the pilot could operate to attract our attention in a crisis.'

Over half the Squadron aircraft were fitted with ABC by 6 October 1943 — a modification which took about 3,000 man hours for each Lancaster — and the 101 personnel complement increased accordingly as one corporal and six aircraftmen wireless mechanics were posted in to 'maintain special duties signal equipment' together with an eventual total of 33 Spec Ops to use it. Many of the latter were Britons with a gift for languages, but others such as Sgts Shultz, Liersch, Engelhardt, and Herman probably had a head start in the business. But on a serious note, some of the Spec Ops were German-born, and they not only took a double risk whenever they flew over enemy territory but also those who were German Jews took a treble risk. They were very brave men.

On 4 October it was decreed that 'never less than eight ABC aircraft should operate on a raid, spaced at distances of not more than 10 miles apart'. Besides jamming, Spec Ops 'were required to record any German transmissions received in their logs, together with the times of transmission, and this information was handed in at the post-flight debriefing'. However it has to be emphasised that the ABC operators did not send spoof messages to confuse the German fighter force — they had to know enough German to recognise the language when they heard it, but thereafter their only task was to jam the control frequencies with noise. 'Most of our school German accents,' said one Spec Op, 'would not have fooled a deaf German in a thunderstorm'. Jamming the control frequencies was more than sufficient according to Bomber Command's *Monthly Review of Losses for November 1943*. 'Enemy freelance night fighters had an unsuccessful month, as reflected in the low casualty and attack rates. This was due in part to the weather, which was mainly unfavourable, and also to the continued use of the tactics developed with such success in October. Radio countermeasures, particularly Airborne Cigar, have also played a great part in interfering with the running commentary control.

'Airborne Cigar has fully justified expectations. Frequently the whole VHF band used by the night fighters has been obliterated and, on occasions when operation channels have been found clear of jamming, the ABC operators have found the frequencies concerned and effective jamming has followed

104

ANOTHER PATIENT SUCCESSFULLY TREATED

105
WO Jack Laurens stands in front of Lancaster K-King with his crew at Ludford in January 1944. Laurens, a South African, captained what was known on the Squadron as the 'League of Nations' crew because of the many and varied backgrounds of its members. L-R: WO Laurens (Pilot), Sgt Davies (Spec Op), Sgt 'Cass' Waight (W/Op) — note the new body armour being worn on test — Flt Sgt Les Burton (Nav), Sgt 'Wag' Kibble (Flt Eng), Sgt Don Bolt (Mid-Upper), Sgt Ted Royston (Rear Gunner), Sgt Chris Aitkin (Bomb-aimer).

106
Post-flight debriefing for those who returned from Berlin. 'The intelligence officers had to glean from us every last bit of information such as had we hit the target, had we been engaged by fighters, had we seen any aircraft hit, and were any parachutes seen to open afterwards? There were lots and lots of questions until they were satisfied that we could tell them no more.' L-R: Flt Lt Henderson (Int O), Plt Off R. A. Nightingale (Pilot), Sgt K. F. Scott (Nav), Sgt J. Muldowney (Rear Gunner), Plt Off A. McCartney (Bomb-aimer), Sgt L. Ley (Flt Eng). The Nightingale crew had just completed their 11th op to Berlin and their 27th mission.

immediately. The enemy has been forced to attempt the use of morse and of the higher-pitched female voice in order to minimise the effects of interference.'

The first raid on which all 101 Squadron Lancasters carried ABC was mounted against Kassel on 22 October, and the Spec Ops had a great time picturing the consternation they were causing on the ground. But the real aim of radio countermeasures was to afford a measure of protection for the main force during the forthcoming Battle of Berlin. 'We can wreck Berlin from end to end if the USAAF will come in on it,' wrote Sir Arthur Harris to the Prime Minster on 3 November 1943. 'It will cost between us 400-500 aircraft. It will cost Germany the war.' Such confidence, with its attendant promise of decisive results, impressed Churchill sufficiently to gain his approval, and although the Americans decided not to 'Come in on it' following a period of severe daylight losses, Harris was content to go it alone.

The Battle of Berlin was launched on 18 November by 444 heavy bombers, and although the round trip of over 1,100 miles necessitated a vulnerable 60min flying time over enemy territory, only nine bombers failed to return. It augured well, but unfortunately Flg Off McManus' aircraft from 101 was one of the nine shot down and its ABC equipment fell into German hands. It was sent to Telefunken for examination, and on 30 November Engineer-Colonel Schwenke (the Intelligence Officer in charge of the Luftwaffe sections dealing with captured enemy equipment) submitted the following report to Field-Marshal Milch quoted from *Instruments of Darkness*:

'I have some interesting foreign Intelligence concerning a number of new things that have come to light. Three transmitters have been found in the Lancaster aircraft — in fact it was flying not with the normal seven-man but with an eight-man crew, one of whom was an additional radio operator. This set is called T.3160 (the official RAF designation for the ABC transmitters) and is apparently there for the jamming of our VHF radio-telephone traffic. At present I cannot say how far this jamming can be defeated by appropriate counter-measures or frequency alteration.'

Nevertheless the Germans took an increasing toll of the British bomber force as the winter of 1943/44 progressed. Moreover, 101 Squadron suffered more than its fair share of these losses. It lost three crews on 26 November 1943 against Stuttgart and Berlin, 10 more crews over Berlin between 2 December 1943 and 2 January 1944, and eight more crews against Brunswick, Berlin, and Leipzig before the end of February. In all

the bomber squadron which was supposed to help protect everyone else lost no fewer than 176 aircrew killed or taken prisoner in the first three months of the Battle of Berlin.

What were the reasons for this apparent contradiction? The most obvious answer, and the one which most crews feared to be true, was that 101 Squadron Lancasters made themselves more vulnerable whenever they jammed. Any transmission from an aircraft could be homed on to once its frequency had been established, and the Luftwaffe certainly equipped their night fighters with the means to home on the H2S transmissions from the heavy bombers. But although the Germans considered using ABC transmissions to their own advantage, they dismissed the idea because 101 had foreseen the danger. 'Spec Ops are never to jam for more than a few seconds at a time,' wrote the Squadron orders, and as crews stuck scrupulously to this injunction in the beginning, Colonel Schwenke declared to higher authority that ABC jamming transmissions were of such a short duration that it was impracticable to think of homing on to them.

However, as time went on, and bomber losses grew, what if a frightened Spec Op kept his ABC jammers on for longer and longer? Homing on to the transmissions of another night fighter acting as *Fühlungshalter* (observer of the route of bomber streams) was common in the Luftwaffe, and it would not have taken a German genius to deduce that it was just as easy to home on to an airborne jammer. Certainly the equipment was available in the shape of the FuG 16ZY, a direction finding device which conveniently operated in the 38.5 to 42.3MHz band. FuG 16ZY gave no distance but it could display right or left, and up or down directions to an emitting source, and it is hard to believe that no German night fighter crew thought of using this equipment against ABC.

Nevertheless, there is no evidence that the Luftwaffe ever homed on to ABC in large numbers and therefore the reasons for 101's relatively high losses must be found elsewhere. Partly they may have been due to simple bad luck, for the Squadron's Lancasters were always distributed throughout the bomber stream at the same height and conforming in all respects to the main force attack plan so that they should never have been more vulnerable than anyone else. But the Squadron did have special circumstances of its own. Firstly, 'because of the cover 101's ABC was providing for other squadrons, we were called upon to fly on all major operations when other units in 1 Group might be resting'. From October 1943 onwards, 101 Squadron accompanied *all* main force attacks on German targets by night, the number of air-

craft operating varying from six to 27. Secondly, when 101 flew it sent a lot of men into the air. Some bomber squadrons only had an establishment of 20 aircraft and crews, whereas 101 was established for 30 and had an average of 33 aircraft on charge. It was merely routine to launch 26 aircraft and crews to attack Berlin on 22 November, and 21 eight-men crews were detailed to revisit the German capital on 2 December when Sqn Ldr Robertson's, Flt Lt Frazer-Hollins', and Sgt Murrell's crews failed to return. Yet whatever the reasons, such was the measure of the Squadron's apparent vulnerability that when Bomber Command requested more effective twin 0.5in Browning machine guns for the 'heavy' rear gunners in place of the standard quadruple 0.303s to improve 'under defence', 101 was placed at the top of the Lancaster squadron priority list. 101 Squadron were to win the hamper of 'grog' offered by the firm of Rose-Rice of Gainsborough, manufacturers of the new turret, for being the first unit to shoot down a night fighter with their improved armament.

By the beginning of 1944, Bomber Command possessed the ability to embark on a battle of wits with the enemy. The steady improvement of navigation equipment and techniques* allowed the planners to select routes with the greatest care to

hoodwink enemy fighters and prevent them finding the bomber stream. 'Dog-legs' were introduced to weave 500 bombers around the sky, and thrusts were made this way and that so that the ground controllers could never be sure where to concentrate their waiting fighters. ABC was further updated in January 1944 by fitting plug-in coils to allow unmonitored jammers to operate on 31.2MHz and thereby thwart the German Benito system of homing fighters on to British bombers. Yet despite such refine-

*To overcome the difficulties attendant on one man navigating safely, each bomber now had a 'Navigation Team' consisting of the navigator and two assistants, ie the air bomber was responsible for astro and drift observations, and the W/Op was responsible for Gee fixes and DF assistance.

107

After the Intelligence officer came the other specialists. In this picture Flt Lt Knute Brydon, the Canadian Bomber Leading (seated with greatcoat), is debriefing Flt Sgt Ross (far left, seated). At far left in the background is the Met Officer, Flg Off Stan Horrocks, who was interested in all the route weather information he could gain. At the extreme right, holding a cigarette, is Flg Off Arthur, the deputy Squadron Engineering Officer, who needed to know how the crew's aircraft had behaved and any damage it had sustained. The remaining aircrew members are from the Laurens crew.

108

Route of the Nuremburg raid.

109

Refuelling and bombing up. The standard 101 Squadron operational load on 31 March 1944 was either one 4,000lb bomb, 270 4lb incendiaries, and 168 30lb incendiaries, or one 2,000lb bomb, 1,650 4lb incendiaries, and 36 30lb incendiaries. The fuel bowser is in the process of filling the Lancaster with up to 2,154 gallons of 100-octane fuel at the rate of 30gal/min.

110

Members of the Adamson crew enjoy a 'cuppa' in their billet at Ludford before their fateful raid on Nuremburg. (L-R): R. Luffman (W/Op), Kippen (Nav), J. Goodall (RG), N. Bowyer (Flt Eng), W. Adamson (pilot). Don Brinkhurst was at the Sick Quarters when his photo was taken. He had been wounded in the right arm on the way back from Berlin on 2 December 1943, and Luffman had been awarded the DFM after taking over his turret. Jimmy Goodall shot down an Me110 that night.

ments and electronic wizardry, Bomber Command continued to have a rough passage during the Battle of Berlin. With hindsight, it is not surprising that the average German fighter pilot should defend his homeland and capital with the same degree of dedication and bravery as his opposite number displayed during the Battle of Britain. In addition, after years of fighting an offensive war, the Germans were only now getting to grips with a defensive strategy and this they did with their customary efficiency. For example, the Germans used a captured ABC transmitter to jam their own fighter control frequency, except that periodically they faded it out when orders had to be passed. This was undertaken in the mistaken notion that Spec Ops would not tune into another jammer when they heard it, whereas in fact they had instructions that if there were no signals on their screens, they were to reinforce any other jammer they could hear.

Another German ruse was greatly to speed-up their R/T, in the hope that they could pass their instructions before ABC could be brought to bear. Then again, the ground controllers would broadcast a continuous stream of music, break off to snap out an instruction, and then bring the music back on again. Such devices had their limitations — R/T instructions that were rattled out before the Spec Op could jam them were often too fast for a fighter pilot to catch — but there were always other loopholes to exploit in the electronic battle of wits. For instance the Germans discovered that the ABC operators stopped jamming for a short period every half hour so as not to interfere with the regular wind forecasts from

England. The running commentators used this respite to alter all their frequencies, so that when the Spec Ops switched on again they had to hunt afresh for the new frequencies to jam. It all took time, and gave the Germans several minutes of uninterrupted commentary every half hour. Subterfuges such as this, combined with increasing the power of German transmissions, ensured that although British radio countermeasures caused massive disruption of the enemy aerial defence system, they never succeeded in stopping all ground-to-air communications throughout a raid.

The limitations of the British strategic bomber offensive at the beginning of 1944 were vividly underlined by 101 Squadron's experiences on the night of 30 March. The target this time was Nuremberg, a city deep in southern Germany which housed one of the MAN heavy engineering works and played host to the great Nazi rallies. A force of 795 bombers was dispatched to attack it, of which the largest individual squadron effort came from 101 with 26 aircraft and crews.

Unfortunately the outbound leg not only took place in moonlight without protective cloud cover, but also the crews were briefed to fly in an almost dead straight line for 220 miles across enemy territory before the final turn towards Nuremberg. This prevented any changes of course to cause confusion, and even while the leading bombers were crossing the English coast the German listening service had determiend the stream's path very accurately from H2S transmissions.

The 101 Spec Ops warmed up their receivers before crossing the Belgian coast, and as they approached the first turning

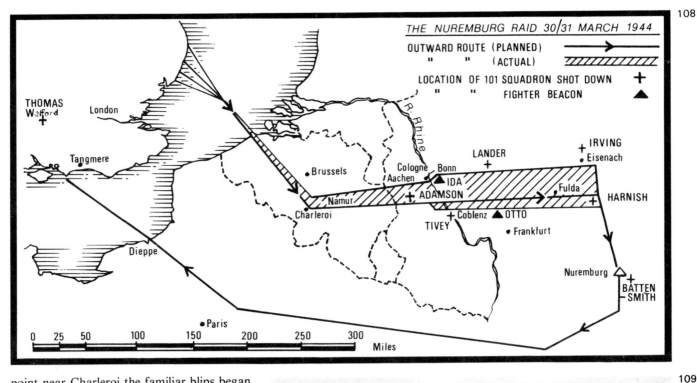

THE NUREMBURG RAID 30/31 MARCH 1944
OUTWARD ROUTE (PLANNED) ———▶
"   "   (ACTUAL) ▨▨▨▨▨▨
LOCATION OF 101 SQUADRON SHOT DOWN ✚
"   "   FIGHTER BEACON ▲

point near Charleroi the familiar blips began to appear on the cathode ray tubes indicating that the running commentary had started to the night fighter force which had already taken-off. It was the Third Fighter Division's controller ordering all Tame Boar crews to assemble over radio beacon 'Ida' SE of Cologne, and despite the attentions of 26 Spec Ops the running commentary continued to break through. This was crucial, for at Charleroi the bomber stream was to turn straight towards Ida.

The bomber crews had been nervous for some time that they might be caught in the bright moonlight, and these nerves took their toll. 'A Halifax came right over the top of us, about 300ft up,' recorded Sergeant Don Brinkhurst,* the mid-upper gunner on Plt Off Adamson's crew. 'He was roughly 10 o'clock from us when I last saw him and, just as he disappeared, I saw one long burst of tracer come down at us from that direction. German tracer was bluish but this was the pink and red that we used. It caught us down our port side and we were soon on fire. At the time we were weaving and I expect that to a gunner who was on edge and jumpy we could have looked like a fighter making an attack.

'I tried to contact the skipper on the inter-com but got no joy. I got out of my turret, got my parachute on and managed to reach the door by pulling myself upwards for we were going down steeply. I could feel the "Special" holding on to the back of my

*This quote, and some of the others, are taken from Martin Middlebrook's excellent book, *The Nuremburg Raid*, Allen Lane, 1980.

"ERRORS DUE TO ... WIND."

111
Wind cartoon.

ABC jamming was spread too thinly and the running commentary came through clearly on most occasions.

It was bad enough that the force had been routed just past 'Ida' and that it was now heading just to the north of 'Otto', the fates had conspired against the bombers in other ways as well. For a start the winds were much higher than had been forecast, so that the stream soon lost its protective cohesion. Then, on top of the moonlight, the night was so cold that long, white condensation trails issued out from behind the bombers, pointing them out for all to see. Finally, a Luftwaffe bomber unit deposited strings of parachute flares high over the bomber stream to unmask what-ever protective cover of darkness still remained.

The German night fighters were therefore able to harry and hunt the British bombers all the way from the Rhine to Nuremberg. Plt Off Lander's crew were the third from 101 to go down, this time at Dillenburg, followed by Plt Off Irving's crew 10 miles north of Eisenach. In all, 59 Bomber Command crews were lost on the long leg and the turn towards Nuremberg did little to halt the onslaught. Even though they twisted and turned and jammed, there was little that a 101 Squadron crew could do to shake off an interceptor that had them in his sights, especially if that interceptor carried Schräge Musik. Leutnant Wilhelm Suess had already dispatched two Lancasters with this lethal device when he came across a third. Once more he crept in underneath his prey and fired, only to see the bomber immediately go into a violent corkscrew. The German had to wait for three minutes while his radar operator changed the 'Schräge Musik' ammunition drum during which time Suess formated underneath the weaving Lancaster to remain unseen. When the cannons had been reloaded he fired again, setting the bomber's wings on fire and igniting the incendiaries in the bomb bay. The Lancaster pilot, Flt Sgt Clyde Harnish, a Canadian serving with 101 Squadron, made a last desperate attempt to extinguish the flames by diving down 7,000ft, but to no avail. Four of his crew got out but Flt Sgt Harnish was to perish as the fifth 101 aircraft and the 67th casualty of the bomber stream went down. Harnish's Lancaster crashed on the village of Simmershausen, some 12 miles east of Fulda. Its 4,000lb bomb exploded on impact causing considerable damage, and one of the crew was unfortunate enough to land by parachute immediately afterwards, whereupon he was attacked by irate German villagers. The mid-upper gunner, Sgt Mike Greer from Canada, had the presence of mind to hide in a nearby chicken house until the fury subsided.

harness and I felt sure he would follow me out.' The Spec Op did so, but he was found two days later hanging dead by his partially open parachute harness from a tree. Five men died on the first 101 Squadron aircraft to go down, and it was tragic that Plt Off Adamson DFC and his crew were on the penultimate mission of their tour that night.

Another Squadron crew, captained by Flt Sgt Tivey, strayed south and was promptly shot down by the flak batteries at Koblenz, so 101 had lost two Lancasters by the time the force reached the Rhine. But this was nothing to the welcome that the Luftwaffe was waiting to hand out at Ida. Not that they had any real idea of the rich pickings coming their way — the element of surprise, as loitering fighters suddenly found themselves inside a bomber stream, was mutual. But once they collected their wits the 'Tame Boar' fighters could make their final kills easily in the moonlight on the straight leg past 'Ida', and the Germans saught to throw every available fighter into the fray by means of the running commentary. The Second Fighter Division came down from northern Germany, Hajo Hermann's First came across from the Berlin area, while the Seventh Division hurried up from the south to wait for the stream by radio beacon 'Otto'. In the process the Germans rapidly switched between nine different speech channels and two Morse channels, and during the main air battle itself the running commentary was broadcast on five separate channels. The Spec Ops found and jammed all of these but the enemy transmissions were so powerful, and so many frequencies were used, that the

To crown it all, few bombs fell on Nuremberg that night. The first target markers were to fall at 0105hrs, five minutes ahead of the main force, but although the bombers were in clear skies themselves, the target was shrouded by ground haze. It was bad enough that the Pathfinders had to mark blindly when they had come prepared to bomb visually, but a sudden increase in wind strength blew some of the Pathfinders off course and they marked in the wrong place. Most main force bomb aimers were content to bomb into whatever markers they could see, but Sgt Alderson, the bomb aimer on Flt Sgt Davidson's crew from 101, refused to bomb on his first run because he was doubtful about the position of the target indiactors. Davidson hauled his Lancaster, together with its mainly Geordie crew, round in a wide orbit to try again, only to find on the second run that their heavy 2,000lb MC bomb had stuck and had to be taken back to Ludford.

The fact that the Germans did not definitely appreciate that Nuremberg was the target until 0113hrs was of little consequence. *'Nach Nürnberg, Nach Nürnberg'* came the invocation from the running commentator over the earphones of those Spec Ops still remaining, though for Plt Off Beer — one of the rare breed of pilot Spec Ops — on Plt Off Batten-Smith's crew, it was probably the last thing he did hear. 'Think of me at one o'clock, will you,' said Jimmy Batten-Smith to his WAAF girl friend as he went through his usual pre-flight routine of handing over his writing case containing farewell letters for his parents, who lived in India, which were to be sent if he went missing. Assistant Section Officer Patricia Bourne, an equipment officer at Ludford, dutifully set her alarm for that time, and approximately half an hour later Plt Off Batten-Smith's Lancaster was caught by a German fighter as it flew out of the target area. The wreckage of the Lancaster fell beside an autobahn junction six miles east of Nuremberg and all the crew died — theirs was the 86th bomber lost that night.

The only good thing about the Nuremberg raid from Bomber Command's point of view was that the single-seat 'Wild Boar' units were all too far away to see action, and that the bomber force was so dispersed by the time it left the target that the 'Tame Boar' crews lost is completely. Not that an unmolested return eased the strain on Flt Sgt Thomas' crew — at 0530hrs their Lancaster flew into the ground at Welford, Berkshire, as they tried to land at Newbury.

Back at Ludford, the impact of Nuremberg — 101 suffered the heaviest loss of any squadron taking part with seven of its aircraft and 56 of its aircrew missing — only came with the dawn. 'We waited and waited

112
Sgt Don Brinkhurst with members of the Resistance at Herstall near Liege. The man on the right is Robert Oliver who at their first meeting took Brinkhurst into a back room where his mother-in-law was frying mushrooms. 'What is she frying?' he asked Brinkhurst in perfect English. Brinkhurst gave an immediate answer whereupon Oliver uncocked the revolver he had in his hand and said that if Brinkhurst had stopped to think or hesitated, he would have been shot as a German imposter. The girl is Jenny Dubair. She got Brinkhurst across a guarded bridge over the Meuse by pretending to be his girl-friend. Such photographs are extremely uncommon because of the obvious risks to the brave people involved (see p 108).

113
Safe at last — a relieved Don Brinkhurst in friendly Swiss company.

113

and waited,' said E. T. 'Dutch' Holland, an Australian pilot on 101. 'We were accustomed to losing the odd one or two aircraft . . . but with nearly one-third of our Squadron missing, this was a big kick in the guts for us all. We waited up until nearly mid-day before going to our huts — stunned, shocked and silent, each crew member wrapped in his own mental anguish.'

Ludford Magna

Although 101 made the greatest contribution to the 96 Bomber Command aircraft which failed to return from Nuremberg, one man did eventually get back to Ludford and he was Sgt Don Brinkhurst. His crew had always agreed that if they were shot down the survivors would do their best to get home and contact the relatives of those who died or were prisoners of war. So when Sgt Brinkhurst found himself on solid ground some 10 miles inside Germany he started walking towards Belgium through the heavily wooded Eifel countryside. He travelled 40 miles over the next four days, skirting enemy patrols and living off raw potatoes when his survival rations ran out. The raw potatoes were a mistake and, wracked with stomach cramps, he eventually approached 'a very fat lady at an isolated farmhouse who was putting out her washing'. From then on he was given shelter by the Resistance at Visé just north of Liege, and during the next three weeks he was even given a grand 21st birthday party. Then his presence was betrayed by a young woman and Sgt Brinkhurst only just managed to evade the subsequent German search party. He eventually reached Switzerland, but he soon became bored with internment and recrossed the border to meet up with Allied troops who had just landed in the south of France. On his return to England, Don Brinkhurst was commissioned and sent back to 101 where, on 2 January 1945, he took-off at the start of another tour — ironically the target for that night was Nuremberg!

All Bomber Command aircrew carried survival aids such as compasses cleverly hidden in collar studs or tunic buttons to help them return home after baling out. There was even a pigeon loft, manned by one corporal and two aircraftmen pigeon keepers, at Binbrook to provide homing pigeons for crews at Ludford to carry on ops to bring messages back after a ditching at sea. (The RAF Pigeon Service was disbanded in January 1944.) But if most crews eschewed the company of feathered friends in the air, that

114
Ludford Magna at eventide.

did not stop one Squadron crew from carrying a rabbit mascot on all operations, complete with its own oxygen tube fed into its box, in an effort to bring them enough luck to avoid being shot down in the first place.

Perhaps it was due to lucky rabbit's feet, alive or otherwise, but other members of 101 besides Sgt Brinkhurst did live to tell the tale after being shot down. The unfortunate ones ended up behind barbed wire as 'Kriegies' where most survived to be repatriated after the war, unless they were unlucky like Flt Sgt Cook who was 'shot attempting to escape and died of wounds', or could not take the strain like a flying officer who was 'wounded on baling out over Berlin and committed suicide in PoW camp hospital'. Those with luck on their side came back with the help of the Resistance, to carry on the fight, but even then the ordeal was not over as Sgt Jack Worsfold discovered. On 3 May 1944, Sgt Worsfold was a 19-year old tail gunner who was the only member of his crew to survive when their Lancaster was shot up over France. On his return to England he visited some of the relations of his dead colleagues, 'But only once, it was awful. They tried to talk to me, but there was no communication really. I felt antagonism, as if they were saying, "Why him, and not our boy . . .?"'

Yet there was always 'home' at Ludford Magna to come back to, for although 101 Squadron lost 163 aircrew in the first three months of 1944 alone, in the midst of death there was always life. As 1 Group expanded in 1943, the Air Officer Commanding had found it increasingly difficult to exercise realistic operational control unaided over all his stations, so the Base Organisation was introduced. This sub-divided 1 Group airfields into geographical cells or Bases, each of which was commanded by an Air Commodore, and on 20 November 1943 approval was sought to create No 14 Base at Ludford with Grp Capt R. S. Blucke DSO, AFC as Base Commander. This request was passed by Bomber Command to the Under Secretary of State, Bush House, on 24 November, and the proposal was officially approved on Christmas Eve, 1943.

The newly promoted Air Cdre Blucke therefore found himself in control of a Base with its HQ and 101 Squadron at Ludford Magna, 12 and 626 Squadrons at Wickenby, and 1667 Heavy Conversion Unit at Faldingworth. Ludford itself was a standard heavy bomber station which had cost around £800,000 to build. Its runways were laid out in a triangular pattern, the main one being 5,850ft long and the intersecting ones 4,290ft and 3,600ft respectively. The usual perimeter track, 50ft wide, encircled the airfield, and branching off from this were the dispersal points for the aircraft. Dispersal was all important to minimise losses from air attack, with aircraft only being taken into hangars for major servicing; consequently, the completed airfield covered upwards of a thousand acres, the runways being built on Magna and the dispersal sites on Parva, adjacent to the village of 210 souls after which the airfield was named.

Like every other Bomber Command station was that thrown up in a hurry, Ludford was purpose-built, and that purpose was to fight a war rather than to live in

115
Ludford Operations Room. 2nd left, Grp Capt King (Station Commander); 3rd right, Air Cdre Blucke (Base Commander); Standing right, Sqn Ldr Thompson (Intelligence Officer).

115

235

116
'Right, let's get this lot loaded.'
Station armourers plus 4,000lb
'cookies', incendiary containers,
bomb trolleys, and tractors at
Ludford.

comfort. For a start it had none of the brick-built living quarters complete with central heating that characterised the 'permanent' stations — the only brick buildings at Ludford were the gymnasium, education block, and parachute store. 'We lived a life typical of many others in wartime airfields,' wrote a mid-upper gunner. 'Officers and men lived in the same Nissen huts dumped down on "communal" sites often with no such thing as water laid on, and with a mile or more of unmade roads separating us from our messes and working quarters which were just another patch of Nissen huts. The only solid features were the concrete runways, taxiways and dispersals. Everything else was either hard mud or soft mud depending on the weather conditions — no wonder gum boots were an essential item of equipment at Mudford Magna!'

But the bleakness of the Lincolnshire countryside and the periodic heavy rains did not dampen spirits. 'Here the simple necessities of life are catered for,' wrote Cecil Beaton in *Winged Squadrons* (Hutchinson & Co, 1942) — Cecil Beaton was only one of many artists who visited RAF stations during the war to capture the atmosphere for posterity — 'no concessions are made to sensuous comfort. Such a community creates, by its own fervour, the warmth and cosiness in which it lives.'

Another observer was Carl Olsson who visited the airfield for the benefit of *Illustrated* magazine, and his article which appeared on 25 March 1944 began by under-lining the fact that Ludford was far from small and that it took a lot more than the aircrew to keep 101 Squadron operational. 'This is one of the war-built stations. Its Lancasters cost £40,000 each and they were

delivered, slick and new from the factories. Its personnel strength is about 2,500 officers and men and WAAF. About one-tenth of that are aircrew.

'It costs £3,000 a week to feed the station, and to clothe the groundstaff and aircrew costs £40,000 or the cost of one Lancaster. The maintenance stores is a vast array of spare parts, enough to refit completely about half the aircraft on the station strength.

'The stock includes such items as spare engines (£2,500 each), tail planes (£300), parachutes (£35), turrets (£500), tyres (£50), wireless sets (£250) and countless other items down to rivets, screws, and aluminium sheet for patching flak damage.

'The station is equipped to defend itself with such items as searchlights, (£1,250 each), AA guns (£2,000), Bren guns (£35), ammunition (£7.10s for 1,000 rounds), grenades (4s each), etc, etc.

'It is a township, a factory, a battle head-quarters and a front-line assault point from which men sally forth to attack the enemy. It is never at complete rest — throughout the 24 hours of the day someone is working. Set down among the fields of home its 2,500 men and women can lead an entirely independent existence from the rest of the country for weeks on end.'

Cecil Beaton noticed the same thing. 'There is a timeless quality, exaggerated by the fact that the inhabitants of the station are constantly changing. The men know the date of the month from completing their forms and log books, but seldom are they conscious of the day of the week, for Sunday differs in no way from the other days. Their work is continuous . . . Former existence, with its ties and interests, is intentionally forgotten; family or fiancée must remain outside the

117
The Ludford Engineering Officers
in 1944. The Senior Engineering
Officer, Sqn Ldr Buckingham, is in
the centre of the front row.

118
Squadron groundcrew on
suitably inscribed 1,000lb
bombs.

118

barbed wires until the big job is over. The aerodrome is the orbit of these men.'

However, Carl Olsson was not there just to look at the station hospital or messes, and he went on to describe a typical day at Ludford as the station prepared to launch every 101 Squadron aircraft to take part in a 2,000-ton long-distance trip into Southern Germany. 'Take-off will be before dusk, say 5pm, so that the long journey out and home is completed before the moon rises or early morning fog settles down on the aerodrome.

'By eight am the handling crews will be hard at work down in the bomb dump at the far end of the aerodrome. Scores of men will be slithering about in the mud bringing 100lb cases of incendiaries to a central section where they will be packed into the special containers carried on the aircraft.

'The men advance from the bomb dump in lines of 10; with the exception of the two end men, each man holds in either hand one handle of the incendiary case. Thus at each journey the men are carrying 900lb of bombs to the packing section.

'In another part of the dump other men are rolling out the great 4,000lb high explosive "cookies" and mounting them on to low engine-driven bomb trolleys. Others are loading flares. All this work goes on without a pause or break till the early afternoon when the trolleys are driven out to the aircraft. Lunch is a hastily eaten sandwich and a cup of tea.

'Meanwhile in another section armament crews are working against time feeding tens of thousands of cartridges into the ammunition belts which will go to the gunners. Over the airfield at the tanks other men are filling the great 2,500 gallon capacity petrol

119

bowsers and the oil bowsers, each of which holds 450 gallons.

'One petrol bowser holds just enough petrol for filling one Lancaster if it is a long raiding journey. So many journeys must be made back and forth from the storage tanks to the aircraft waiting at the dispersal points. Again it is mid-afternoon before they are all filled.

'At the dispersal points ground crews are swarming over the bombers in their charge. Every point in the bomber is being checked and re-checked, engines, plugs, instruments, guns, turrets, undercarriages, tyre pressures, bomb door mechanism and the host of other things. Some "snag" to one part or another of the bomber is nearly always found, and it has to be set right, with the toiling men always working against time.

'If it is a fault connected with the flying ability of the aircraft it has to be set right in time for a test flight which must be made to make sure that the fault has been rectified long before take-off on the raid.

'It sometimes happens that two or three test flights are made before the sweating ground crews have completed the job to the satisfaction of the captain of the aircraft.

119
Mass briefing at a typical Bomber Command Station. *IWM*

120
Flt Sgt C. T. Akers, an Australian then on his first tour with 101, gets a helping hand to zip up his heated suit from his gunnery leader, Flt Lt Bill Hill. The gun turrets were the coldest place on the Lancaster, and when the centre panels were removed the temperature could fall as low as -40°C. 'In spite of our electrically heated suits,' wrote one gunner, 'which were made of kapok and had their own built-in Mae Wests, it tended to be a mite chilly at times. I recall one occasion when the boiling hot coffee I had poured froze in the cup while I was replacing the cork in the Thermos flask.' Other gunners, such as 'Mac' Mackay, refused to wear the electrical suit 'because I found it too bulky and restrictive even though the cold was paralysing and I once broke off a six inch icicle from below my oxygen mask. Even on warm nights, which were few and far between, I padded myself up as much as possible starting with ladies' silk stockings — they were popular among crews! — and finished with the ordinary Sidcot flying suit.'

121
Wrapping up the in-flight rations.

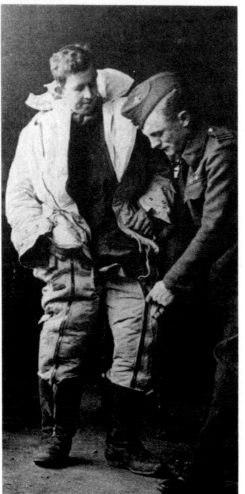

120

121

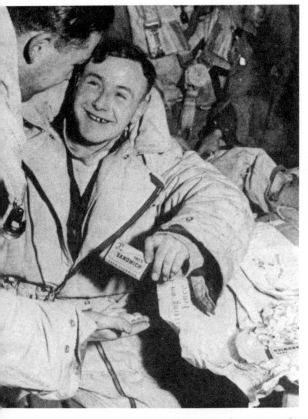

'Over at the sheds there are almost certain to be two or three bombers getting a special overhaul to put them into full serviceability at the hands of skilled maintenance crews and fitters. Perhaps whole engines may be changed, as a result of damage, patches fitted over flak holes, new instruments put in or pipe line and cables refitted.

'Test flights are made in these cases, of course, and not infrequently the maintenance crews are working on the aircraft right up to a few minutes before take-off. Skilled crews have been known to refit a new engine within less than an hour before take-off, which is certainly running it close.

'While all this sweat and toil is going on in many different parts of the airfield other special staffs are also working against time.

'The intelligence officers are sweating on their filing systems getting out data about the target, getting out target maps and photographs, collecting information from Group Headquarters and from the path-finder force engaged — all to be ready for the briefing of the crews which will take place by 2pm.

'The meteorological officers are collecting and revising up-to-the-minute weather information from their own central channels.

'In the locker rooms another staff is sorting out the items of clothing and equipment which will be issued to each member of the air crews as soon as the briefing is over. About 15 articles for each man ranging from life-saving waistcoats to socks.

'In the kitchens WAAFs are cutting sandwiches for nearly 200 aircrews and parcelling rations of chocolate, fruit, chewing gum and other items of refreshment.

'In the station offices the commander and other officers are selecting the crews and working out technical data for the journey. Sometimes new information comes through from Group Headquarters making a change of plan necessary.

'It may happen that this change has to be made and most of the morning's work altered within half an hour of the briefing.

'The only people who have no part in the unceasing labour are the flying crews who will go on the raid.

'Theirs, perhaps, is the worst part — the waiting from the time they are "warned" for a raid that night until the final take-off. A long wait which is broken only by the briefing and then by the dressing up in the crew room.

'But everybody else on the station goes unceasingly and doggedly on until the moment comes when the last aircraft is signalled down the runway and off on its journey.

'Then, and only then, do the tired ground crews, the bomb crews and the others stretch their aching limbs and take their ease in canteen or mess huts. But not for long; in an hour or so it is time for bed, to be ready for an early morning start and another long exhausting day . . .'

But even Olsson's descriptive powers did not do full justice to every link in the

122
Some couldn't wait to get at their rationed chocolate.

123
Groundcrew of one Lancaster with their mascot.

strategic bomber chain. Take something as small as a Lancaster spark plug for example. There were 96 of these in each bomber, and if they became oiled-up at the wrong moment it could prove catastrophic. So WAAF Group II Sparking Plug Testers had to undertake the filthy job of cleaning hundreds of the things in petrol at regular intervals.

Then there were the wireless mechanics. Marjorie Philips was a WAAF wireless mechanic on 101 in 1944 and her job was to test flying helmets after they had been used on several missions. One day a young aircrew member came to her to say that he couldn't hear the intercom properly in the air, and that he was afraid that he might miss an instruction to bale out. She could tell that he was frightened so she stripped the helmet again and again until she discovered different stores reference numbers on the respective earphones which meant that they were incompatible. 'After his next trip he was so pleased that he gave me his month's ration of sweets.'

It is possible to go and on in similar vein. 'Has it ever occurred to you,' wrote LACW A. M. Douglas in *Slipstream, A Royal Air*

Force Anthology (Eyre and Spottiswood, 1946), 'that aircrews would never win their battles had their nerves and sinews, their brains and muscles, their minds and hearts not owed their power to the backstairs service of the cooks'. Before the Battle of Berlin came the Battle for Breakfast, 'and he who has not frizzled 500 slices of bread, or turned out 500 fried eggs before 0700hrs, has yet to know the fullest content, that deepest satisfaction, which can only spring from great achievement!'

The efforts of the 2,250 on the ground at Ludford* were therefore much appreciated by the 250 who flew.

*Up to 1943 the Squadron was a self-contained unit and the Squadron Commander was in complete command of all 101 activities including maintenance. Then, for a variety of reasons it was decided that control of technical personnel should pass to technical officers. This resulted in the formation of separate servicing echelons for all Bomber Command units, and although the ties between aircrews and ground-crews remained as close as ever and the latter still regarded themselves as part of 101, in theory the Squadron's aircraft were maintained by No 9101 Servicing Echelon.

124
A last cigarette to calm the nerves while waiting to leave for Berlin on 20 January 1944.

125
Still more interminable waiting. Approximately one hour before take off, crews would proceed to their aircraft to carry out final checks while waiting for start-up time.

126
'Not a Flanders field but an aerodrome somewhere in England.' An evocative press description as crews paddle across 'Mudford Magna' to the transport which would ferry them to their Lancasters dispersed around the airfield.

127
Forced smiles before boarding the truck. All the crew members are carrying parachutes and escape packs — the latter were small packages containing French money, a map of northern Europe painted on a silk handkerchief, matches, a tiny compass, and other items including malted milk and water purification tablets. In the large canvas bags were Very pistol cartridges for firing the colours of the day in an emergency, together with logs, charts, and code-books.

127

There was certainly a glamorous side to aircrew life on a bomber squadron — discipline tended to be relaxed, there was extra flying pay and much leisure time on non-flying days to spend it, and anyone sporting an aircrew brevet had a head start with the girls at the local dance halls. But on the debit side, the crews lived a life of great stress. 'When at last I found myself in the Mess anteroom,' observed H. E. Bates shrewdly back in late 1941 when 101 was at Oakington (quoted from *The World in Ripeness*, Michael Joseph, 1972), 'it was to be assailed by the impression that I had somehow strayed into a gathering of Sixth Form school boys grown prematurely old. I think it true to say that of all the officers assembled there that evening scarcely more than a dozen were over 25 ... (However) it was the eyes of these young but prematurely aged officers that made a powerful and everlasting impact on me. Perhaps I can best illustrate it by telling of a young Australian pilot (of whom) I grew very attached before he was finally shot down and killed over Germany. After the war his parents came to see me — they showed me a photograph of him taken when he had first joined the Royal Australian Air Force: a mere boy, starry-eyed, proud too, the new entrant on his way to the big school.

'I did not recognise him. Nor, as I handed them my own photograph of him, the gaunt-faced, glassy-eyed, weary veteran of Heaven knew what Hell had been his lot over Germany, did they recognise him either. In silence, they were more shocked than I, we realised that we were speaking of two different men.'

'Foreigners,' wrote Cecil Beaton, 'often remark on the apparent lack of feeling in the British. They say that we British do not feel anything deeply. A casual visitor to a Royal Air Force station would certainly get this impression from the light-hearted way in which unpleasantness, danger, and the war itself, are banished from talk. Death is mentioned flippantly, if at all. Someone has "gone for a Burton" or has been "bumped off" ... But the feeling is there, controlled and smothered by a self-preservation instinct. The realisation of their proximity to danger is never far removed from the minds of the men, in spite of their easy grace of heart.'

Sgt Jack Morley, a W/Op, was just one man who appreciated this when he joined 101 with the Harris crew early in June 1944. 'Aboard the bus, which was taking us to our dispersal points, I experienced the feeling of excitement, wonder and apprehension before this first operational sortie. But among the joking and laughter I was amazed somewhat, this first time, at such comments like, "I hope you get yours", or "Can I have your watch if you don't come back?" These remarks seemed cruel but as we were to learn, they were not meant seriously and were only words to hide the seriousness of what was to lay ahead during the next few hours.'

Sgt Brian Hawkins was a Spec Op who flew with Flt Sgt Jenkins' crew until the night they were detailed to bomb Russelsheim. After the standard pre-flight meal of bacon and eggs that was eaten an hour before briefing, Hawkins experienced stomach pains and went to see the Medical Officer who put him straight into hospital in case it was appendicitis. But from that moment on, Hawkins knew that his crew were not coming back. He spent all night in the hospital toilets smoking cigarettes, and in the morning his

130

R.A.F., LUDFORD MAGNA
F 1250

Name... TURNER .... No. 575

Meal ..	BREAKFAST				DINNER				TEA				LATE SUPPER			
DAY	WEEK NO.				WEEK NO.				WEEK NO.				WEEK NO.			
	1	2	3	4	1	2	3	4	1	2	3	4	1	2	3	4
SAT.																
SUN.																
MON.																
TUES.																
WED.																
THUR.																
RI.																

Meal ..	BREAKFAST				DINNER				TEA				LATE SUPPER			
DAY	WEEK NO.				WEEK NO.				WEEK NO.				WEEK NO.			
	1	2	3	4	1	2	3	4	1	2	3	4	1	2	3	4
SAT.																
SUN.																
MON.																
TUES.																
WED.																
THUR.																
FRI.																

NOT TRANSFERABLE
DISCIPLINARY ACTION WILL FOLLOW LOSS OR MISUSE OF THIS CARD

41510/S637

131

R.A.F. STATION
LUDFORD MAGNA

*

Sergeants' Mess

*

CHRISTMAS DINNER
1943

SNCOs await this Yuletide fare,
25 December 1943.

fears were confirmed. It was no consolation to find that he only had an upset tummy after all.

Some men also knew themselves when it was their night for the 'chop'. 'After the bacon and eggs, we went by coach to the mass briefing,' continued Brian Hawkins. 'Everyone was always very serious then because we did not know what was in store for us, but once we entered the briefing room and saw the maps with the red lines on, the smiles and the chatter returned. We now knew what we were up against and the uncertainty was replaced by the bustle of planning. But on the coach out to the aircraft I knew exactly who was not coming back and they knew it themselves. I remember one man saying to me: "I wish I was flying in your aircraft."

' "Why?"

' "Because mine isn't coming back."

'And it didn't. Some men were dead even before they took-off.'

Having therefore flown hard, it was not surprising that the crews also played hard. To Carl Olsson, Ludford personnel lived 'a front-line existence almost as completely as if they were operating from newly conquered territory', but this was a little hard on those who tried to make the best of a bad job:

'25/8/43. Weather good. ENSA gave a play this evening, *Dangerous Corner* by J. B. Priestley. About 400 personnel were present. A car park is being constructed and the front of Station Headquarters and gardens are being laid out in front of this building and the Officers' Mess.'

'1/2/44. Weather today is again spring-like. A fifth session of the Discussion Group was held on the subject of "Emigration to and development of the Dominions".'

Nevertheless there were some who soon tired of a station that only possessed a solitary film projector, and who sought their entertainment farther afield.

Aircrew got six days' leave every six weeks, while on non-flying days 'the pubs in the area took a fair share of our pay of 13s 6d per day,' wrote Sgt Whittle, a mid-upper gunner. The 'Black Horse' and 'White Hart' at Ludford had a quiet time during a period of concentrated operations, but whenever circumstances allowed, the Senior Flying Control Officer, Sqn Ldr F. Tomlinson, would organise 'liaison visits' with the precision of a bomber raid. Primary 'targets' were the 'Ship' or 'Wheatsheaf' at Grimsby, with the 'King's Head' at Louth being the 'secondary objective', and although the outings provided moments of welcome rest and relaxation, they always had a serious side. 'Sqn Ldr Tomlinson — known to us as "The Squire" — always arranged for the bus to stop on the return journey opposite a wood yard to allow revellers to relieve themselves. This wood yard was guarded by alsatians, but the Squire would not allow anyone back on to the bus unless they brought a piece of wood with them — we were very short of fuel for the Nissen hut heating stoves at Ludford.'

This theme of living off-duty moments to the full was repeated over and over again during 101's wartime history. 'When we were at Holme,' said Sandy Greig, 'we usually flew two nights in a row. Sometimes we would hang around all day waiting for an op before we were told that it was off at the last moment because of weather. If we were stood down early, we went off in the Squadron bus to York. I personally didn't get much further than Betty's Bar — it was a

favourite haunt of bomber crews and you could hardly get into the place — and then maybe on to the de Grey Rooms for a dance. On the way home we would sing the Squadron Song — '101 Boys are Returning, 101 are Coming Home" — which we sang to the tune of *Clementine*.

'What did we do off duty?' mused 'Mac' Mackay. 'Drink — what else was there in war apart from the ubiquitous snooker? With nerves always taut like banjo strings, drink for us was a blessed salve. Strangely enough, almost all those unfortunates I knew who were grounded because they lost their nerve did not drink. We just lived from day to day.' Those men who lost their nerve and refused to carry on flying were classified as LMF — Lack of Moral Fibre. They were posted off the Squadron and station within 12hr so as not to demoralise others.

Nevertheless, although there were certainly some fatalists who drank because they feared that they would never survive a tour, it would be wrong to over-emphasise the negative aspect of the desire to get away from the war. For every tear there were gales of laughter and comradeship which forged links between men who had originally come from totally different backgrounds but who now faced the same dangers together. 'When a crew completed a tour successfully,' wrote Jack Morley, 'there were great celebrations, first in the village pubs and then in the Officers' and Sergeants' Messes. We sang many songs such as "101 are Operating" and "The Monk of Great Renown" but a favourite Squadron song was "The Muffin Man" during which the first man, with a chunky beer glass full of ale on his head, would bob up and down singing, "Do you know the Muffin Man, do you know his

name, do you know the Muffin Man, that lives down Drury Lane?" He would then point towards another man who would accordingly (he was jeered if he didn't) place his own glass on top of his head and reply, while bobbing up and down in similar fashion, "Yes I know the Muffin Man, yes I know his name, Yes I know the Muffin Man, that lives down Drury Lane." At which, the whole company, with glasses on heads, would join in with, "Two men know the Muffin Man, two men know his name, Two men know the Muffin Man, that lives down Drury Lane." So the ritual would continue, with the number of acquaintances of the Muffin Man increasing and the whole scene becoming uproarious, especially if someone declined to join in. Then the whole chorus would point at the unfortunate subject for derision and sing, "He don't know the Muffin Man, he don't know his name, He don't know the Muffin Man, that lives down Drury

134
Fog — that treacherous foe — drifts in towards Ludford from the East Coast. Fog had always been a problem for returning bomber crews, and on the night of 16/17 December 1943 alone, Bomber Command lost 131 aircrew in 29 crashes around fog-covered airfields. The Prime Minister had already instructed Geoffrey Lloyd, Minister in charge of the Petroleum Warfare Department, to find a means of dispersing fog at airfields, and his experts came up with FIDO (Fog Investigation Dispersal Operation, or as the RAF called it, Fog, Intensive, Dispersal of). As Ludford was the highest airfield in 1 Group and Lincolnshire, and therefore situated where the fog should be thinnest, it became one of 15 airfields that were eventually equipped with FIDO.

135

Lane." These, and many other songs and scenes, were our pastimes in the hours between the harrowing flights over enemy territory, contrary to the popular belief that we were always chasing after girls.'

Social life at Ludfrod was not all beer and skittles though. In nearby Tealby, one of the most beautiful villages of Lincolnshire and home of Lord Tennyson, there was an old tea shop full of 'olde Worlde charm' that was run by two dear old ladies. 'It was a regular haven of peace. We cherished those visits with the home-made scones and tea, which served to take us back to a calmer, saner world.'

There was a thriving newspaper called the *Base Bulletin* which was only one of the many examples of productive off-duty ingenuity and enthusiasm at Ludford. Perhaps it reflected the irreverence of the age — *'LOST*. One pair of battledress trousers, belonging to the Senior Intelligence Officer of

a certain Base Station, after a slight Bacchanalian orgy. Finder will be suitably rewarded.' — but the vitality of its contributions and the response to the Editor's plea for 'humorous items of gossip' gave the lie to any outward hint of fatalism or despondency.

'These men therefore create their own circumstances,' concluded Cecil Beaton. Their off duty moments were a time to recharge emotional batteries, but once back at work 'their absorbing enthusiasm towards their duty is like that of a scientist. Everyone is trying to learn more about his particular task. While waiting by their aircraft the pilots are forever exchanging experiences, suggesting new tactics. In the mess they are poring over aeronautic magazines of a highly scientific nature, or still talking the most exciting "shop" in the world. In the face of all difficulties and dangers these men are self-inspired to live up to an ideal. They are ever ready to sacrifice their personal interests and safety in the pursuit of their duty. They believe in the Force and their faith is the motive power behind their judgement and skill.'

101 Squadron's only respite during the Battle of Berlin came in February 1944 when the snows descended on the Lincolnshire Wolds. Nearby Binbrook was completely cut-off and had to rely on supplies dropped from the air, while the snow was 3ft deep with 16ft drifts at Ludford. So hundreds of men, working in shifts throughout the day and night with little more than shovels, set to work with a will to maintain the momentum of the bomber offensive. 'It looks like the Aleutians,' wrote one newspaper reporter visiting Ludford, 'but it is England. Flight mechanics, changing plugs on aircraft required for ops, worked while standing on high platforms in a horizontally driven storm of sleet. As one man turned the plug spanner, his comrade would be restoring circulation to his frozen fingers ready to take over when the first mechanic could no longer hold the spanner.'

The newspaper captions proclaimed that 'even heavy snow did not break their business appointment with Germany,' and if this was not quite true, Ludford was clear enough to launch part of 101 Squadron in just over a week. The Squadron Commander, Wg Cdr R. I. Alexander (who had taken over from Wg Cdr Carey-Foster on 18 January 1944), was very appreciative:

'To: All members of No 101 Squadron.
Date: 5th March 1944.

'During the recent state of emergency, special efforts were called for from all ranks. The response to that call was immediate and the special effort was forthcoming with a spirit which was a subject for admiration.

'We were able, thanks to your loyalty and devotion to duty, to operate six aircraft against Germany on the night of 1st March. That may appear to be a small number, but it was vital that we should operate, and the work required to get those aircraft off called for a maximum effort from all ranks.

'To me, it means more than the fact that six aircraft took off from this airfield. The routine and organisation required to operate under normal conditions calls for effort enough, but the true test of a Squadron is made when they are required to increase that effort to combat emergency conditions. You were tested and did not fail.

'I am indeed proud to serve with you.
Thank you.

R. I. Alexander,
Wing Commander, Commanding
No 101 Squadron, RAF'

135
Lancaster C-Charlie after Sgt Dixon had belly-landed at Ludford. Note the buckled FIDO pipelines. These were laid along each side of the main runway with two smaller pipes at each end. Small valves were set at intervals into these two miles of piping, through which jets of petrol were squirted and ignited. FIDO burnt 40,000 gallons of fuel at a time, but the heat generated was so intense that it could burn off the fog in 10 minutes. FIDO's only drawback at Ludford, apart from its cost, was revealed when a Lancaster approached the ring of fire with a fuel leak. After one unfortunate accident, FIDO was modified and the end bars were removed — they only made the approach bumpy anyway.

136
Sgt Sandy Sandford and his crew in Lancaster III G-George await a green from the caravan before taking off on 20 January 1944 from Ludford on their way to Berlin. A spare 'trolley acc' and standby groundcrew wait by the FIDO pipes in case the aircraft stalls and blocks the runway.

Of Valour, and of Victory

In company with many others at the beginning of 1944, Carl Olsson's imagination was fired by the Battle of Berlin. 'It is difficult for ordinary citizens to visualise the effect of concentrated *aerial* bombardment,' he wrote, 'but the following comparison may help. On the Sangro front in Italy, often spoken of as the biggest *land* bombardment of this war, 1,400 tons of shells came down in *eight hours*. Remember that this front was many miles in length and mostly open country, yet they smashed the German defence and prisoners spoke of the astounding paralysing effect of these heavy bombardments.

'And now compare the figures of air assault. To take an instance only, on the night of 20/21 January, 1944, 7,300 tons of bombs went down on Berlin in *thirty minutes*. Remember, too, that the bombs are falling into built-up areas on a shorter front than a land attack. Remember, too, that tonnage for tonnage, a bomb contains a much higher explosive charge than a shell.

'No city, no defence system, can stand up to such attacks, scientifically delivered, as Bomber Command is now making . . .

'Good-bye, Berlin!'

But as the long, protective winter nights drew to a close and the spring of 1944 dawned, it was clear that Berlin was still very much in existence. Moreover, back in November 1943 Sir Arthur Harris had prophesied that the Battle of Berlin would cost him and the Americans 400-500 aircraft — 35 major attacks later, his Command alone has lost 1,047 aircraft with a further 1,682 damaged, culminating in the Nuremburg raid which had accounted for a massive 13.6% of the force dispatched. To the critics of Nuremburg Harris gruffly retorted that if you launch a massive onslaught against an enemy night after night, you must expect a bloody nose once in a while, and certainly the Nuremburg losses were not typical. Nevertheless, the Battle of Berlin neither wrecked Berlin from end to end nor did it cost

137
A Squadron Lancaster sets out to bomb France.

137

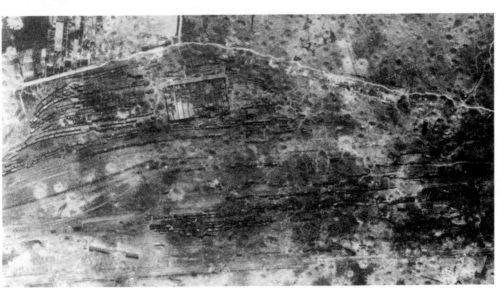

138, 139
During and after the bombing onslaught on the communications systems of France in preparation for D-Day. The Aulnoye marshalling yards after two attacks in March and April 1944 — each of the 32 tracks has been cut in several places and there are signs of scattered damage to sheds and rolling stock. However this damage was minor compared with that inflicted by the concentrated Bomber Command attack on 27/28 April. During the raid the site was completely obliterated. The road at the top of the picture is in use again but it has become a series of curves caused by vehicles and people trying to get to the scene of desolation. *IWM*

140
Wg Cdr Alexander stands before the Ludford Ops Board showing 101's contribution to the D-Day effort on 5/6 June 1944.

140

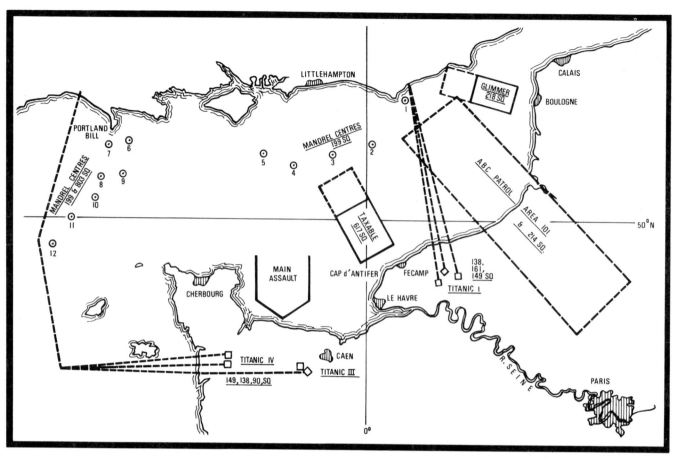

How the ABC jammers fitted into the Radio Countermeasures plan for Overlord. 'Taxable' aircraft covered the 'ghost' fleet supposedly aiming for Cap d'Antifer, and 'Glimmer' simulated an invasion force heading towards Boulogne. 'Titanic' consisted of 29 bombers simulating a fake airborne invasion in the Caen and Cap d'Antifer areas, and the 'Mandrel' aircraft jammed the German early warning radars.

Germany the war; it was time for a shift of emphasis.

Up to now Bomber Command had been employed almost exclusively against long-term strategic targets, 'but with the approach of D-Day we switched our attacks to targets of immediate tactical importance'. Anything which could reinforce the German forces of occupation west of the Rhine or hinder the invasion was to be attacked, and even though 101 had suffered terribly against Nuremburg, there could be no time for respite or the licking of wounds. The success of the invasion of Europe was vital, and so seven aircraft from Ludford were back in action against Villeneuve St Georges on 9 April.

Because such 'tactical' targets were relatively close at hand rather than in deepest Germany, Bomber Command decided that all raids on French targets should only count as 1/3 of an operational trip when it came to calculating tour lengths. 'But even on these short, and so-called easy ops,' wrote one W/Op, 'the enemy was not going to let us drop our "eggs" at will'. The proof came on the raid against the military depot at Mailly-le-Camp on 3 May, which 'was one of the most scaring raids that I did', recalled A. A. Castle who by then was a flight lieutenant. 'I can recall seeing more of our aircraft shot down than on any other trip. It started almost as soon as we crossed the French coast and continued until we crossed it again

on the way home.' Forty-two bombers, or 11.3% of the force, failed to return that night, with 101 losing five of them — fortunately the one-third ruling died at the same time.

The pinpoint bombing techniques demonstrated over Pennemünde were refined and put to even more good use in the run-up to D-Day. 1 Group dropped a total of 13,798 tons of bombs during June 1944, with 101 dropping 1,282 tons of them, yet being a radio countermeasures squadron as well, 101 was just as concerned with thwarting the enemy's aerial defences. It combined both functions admirably when it contributed 16 aircraft to the bombing of the Bruneval early warning radar station on 2 June.

Nevertheless the whole invasion plan could still flounder if the Luftwaffe got through to bomb the thousands of landing craft, or if it was let loose among the huge armada of gliders and heavily-laden troop transports that were to lumber across for a dawn drop on Normandy. Allied fighter escorts could not protect them all — the attentions of the Luftwaffe defences had to be totally distracted away from that crucial area.

Two diversion plans were therefore put into effect, aimed at deluding the enemy into thinking that the invasion was to take place on beaches around Cap d'Antifer and Boulogne. To lend realism to these feints, and to protect the Airborne Forces, a 'Special

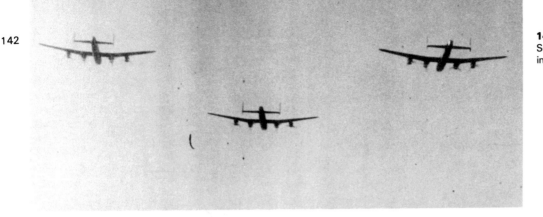

Squadron Lancasters over France
in formation.

142

143

Duties Patrol' was ordered to place a 'curtain of VHF jamming between the area of actual assault and the direction from which the enemy fighter reactions was expected'. This patrol consisted of 24 aircraft from 101 Squadron and five Flying Fortresses from 214 Squadron, and between them they were expected to simulate nothing less than a ghost 'bomber stream' along the line of the River Somme. On board each aircraft crew members tossed out bundles of 'Window' for all they were worth while the Spec Ops monitored the ABC screens, and the combination of 82 ABC transmitters and thousands of bundles of 'Window' were completely successful in their endeavour. 'All the German night fighters that operated were put up against the patrol of ABC aircraft,' wrote the official report, 'which was at first mistaken for "the spearhead of a main bomber force in the neighbourhood of Paris". On their arrival in the area, the fighters found that they were being subjected to serious jamming on the R/T communications channel; then the fighter control plotting became confused due to the presence of German fighters in among the jammers. The fighters returned towards their control points, but appear to have received instructions to go on hunting in the bomber stream as there was sporadic fighter activity in that area between 0105hr and 0355hr. The result of all this confusion was that the Airborne Forces

met no opposition in the air and landed with negligible casualties — a remarkable achievement when it is remembered that a casualty rate of at least 25% was expected.'

Six Squadron crews reported sightings of enemy aircraft and three combats ensued, the crew of Q-Queenie exchanging fire with a Ju88 which broke away emitting smoke. Otherwise it was 'a quiet trip' for all, apart from Plt Off M. J. Steele's crew who were on patrol at 0025hr when an inexplicable vibration began in the constant speed unit of the starboard outer engine. The New Zealander captain feathered this engine, but immediately afterwards both inners also went out in sympathy, forcing Lancaster L-Love and her crew to ditch in the sea at 0050hr some 25 miles south of Beachy Head. After an hour in the Channel they were picked up by HMS *Orwell*.

On 7 June, 101 was back in action against the marshalling yards at Acheres as Bomber Command strove to prevent the German Army from bringing up reinforcements. Other interesting post-invasion targets were the ports of Le Havre and Boulogne, which the Squadron attacked on 14 and 15 June to help sink or damage the entire German E-Boat fleet than threatening the cross-Channel supply lines. The Ludford Lancasters subsequently bombed everything from V-1 flying bomb sites to railway depots,

144

The flying-bomb site at Siracourt being plastered on 29 June 1944.

145

The flying-bomb site at Les Hayons coming in for some attention. Note the camouflaged Lancaster below.

but the most important mission for July was Caen.

For the direct assault on Caen, where the Germans had dug-in in strength, General Montgomery decided to seek the assistance of Bomber Command in a close support role on the battlefield. 'This was the first time that we had attempted a battle of this nature,' he wrote in *Normandy to the Baltic* (Hutchinson & Co Ltd, 1947), 'and it was jointly decided with Bomber Command that the bombline would not be brought nearer than 6,000 yards from our leading troops.' It was a precise objective, but the heavy bombers did not let the Army down — they dropped 2,350 tons of bombs in 40min on the evening of 7 July and, in addition to reducing the defences to rubble, some German defenders were found still stunned many hours after the attack had been carried out. The way was clear for the Army to advance at dawn.

'Having captured Caen,' wrote General Montgomery on 10 July, 'we must now gain depth and space... for manoeuvre, for administrative purposes, and for airfields'.

146
Plt Off Piprell's crew attack the oil storage depot at Blaye, just up from Bordeaux on the Gironde, on Saturday 5 August 1944. 'There were prying electronic eyes all along the coast,' said one W/Op, 'so we decided to fly the whole route a few miles off the French coast as low as possible to keep below enemy radar cover. We found out during training that when the Lancaster's trailing aerial was wound out to its full length, it would stream out some 50ft below the aircraft, so we used this aerial to maintain an accurate height of 50ft. I would watch the dials on my transmitter/receiver, and when they dipped I knew that the aerial had hit the water and earthed the set. I would yell out a warning to the pilot who would ease up until the dials indicated that the aerial was clear. This method enabled us to maintain a fairly constant 50ft until we were close enough to climb up and bomb the target.

147
Grp Capt King, Ludford's Station Commander, tries his hand at bombing the dykes at Westkapelle on 3 October 1944 in a 101 aircraft. The aim of this exercise was to flood the German defences and installations on Walcheren and thereby gain access to Antwerp.

147

Unfortunately for him, the enemy resolved to deny him this space, and although the Germans had fewer tanks they were dispersed in depth in advantageous positions and fortified by minefields and numerous long-range anti-tank guns and mortars. All these obstacles had to go if the British formations were to break out of Caen, so Montgomery sought the full assistance of the RAF to neutralise this formidable line of defence.

'We were therefore informed,' said Jack Morley, 'that from now on, all aircrew and maintenance personnel were to be on 24-hour standby, ready to be called at short notice for offensive duties to support Monty's forces around the Caen bridgehead. On the fifth day of this standby, we were called from our beds and taken, without a wash, shave or breakfast, to the briefing room; there we were told that a maximum effort was to be made at once on the German gun and mortar emplacements at Mondeville just outside Caen, and we were to reinforce aircraft that were already on their way to attack. As we went to change into flying gear, we received the information that the Lancasters were already "bombed up" with, not the usual load of a 4,000lb "cookie" plus high explosive and incendiary bombs, but just 16 1,000lb HE bombs. We hastily changed and made our way to dispersal, this time to fly in A-Able.

'Once airborne, we set course southwards, and as we climbed and maintained course,

148
Volkel airfield, Belgium, as seen by Plt Off Baker's crew on 15 August 1944.

149
The Bowater crew's post-flight observations on the Volkel raid.

CPA V LUD LUD36/15 P

FROM LUDFORD MAGNA 151455B
TO HQ NO 1 GROUP
INFO 14 BASE
SECRET QQX BT

RAID REPORT NO 119 15TH AUG 1944

SECTION A
1 GROUP INFO 14 BASE   101/T
15TH AUG 1944   LUDFORD 119
4 X 1000 MC TD 0.025   LANC III
4 X 1000 USA GP TD 0.025   LM472
3 X 1000 USA SAP TD 0.025   SGT BOWATER
4 X 500 GP TD 0.025   NIL
ABC API BOOZER I
VOLKEL A/F FIRST

SECTION C
1   VOLKEL A/F
2   NO CLOUD , GOOD VISIBILITY
3   VISUALLY BY RUNWAYS AND DISPERSAL HUTS
4   1204 HRS , 14,500 FT 086 T 170 MPH
6   DISPERSAL HUT SE OF RUNWAYS IN BOMB SIGHT
8   BOMBING WAS VERY CONCENTRATED AND MAIN WEIGHT OF ATTACK
     APPEARED TO FALL ON A/P
16   M/B HEARD DISTINCTLY SAYING
     '' VERY GOOD BOMBING WIZARD SHOW ''
     OTHER ATTACKS WHICH APPEARED CONCENTRATED SEEN IN
     VICINITY MUSTANG FIGHTER COVER SEEN EN ROUTE ALSO
     THUNDERBOLT AT LOW LEVEL IN TARGET AREA
17   JER

BT 151455B

HW B K O
          LUD R VIA OPS R.1723B/LHK K

149

we joined up with the greatest force of bombers that I had ever seen — all around, ahead, behind, and on both sides were aircraft, as far as the eye could see. A great column, of which we were part, headed south while at the same time another great column, seemingly never ending, was heading north after leaving the target. We were one continuous stream, to and from France — the scene must have been tremendous from below. Some of the sights we saw as the Lancasters and Halifaxes passed by on their return filled the heart with wonder, and foreboding, as signs that the enemy was grimly prepared to resist us to the best of his ability were plainly evident. There were some aircraft with tremendous damage — gaping holes in fuselage or wings, two in particular flying along minus one tailplane, others flying alone on three, two, or even one engine but still, somehow, managing to keep aloft. But our own effort was still to be made and we went across the Channel, into our bombing run, the flashes from below and the shell bursts around telling their own story. We still had to fight our way to the target — we were not being given a free run. Then "Bombs Gone" from Dai Jones, the bomb-aimer, and with a lurch we were free of our load and increasing speed as we flew out beyond the target area. As we looked back, we could see that the whole of the target area resembled one huge ploughed field and it seemed impossible for anyone to remain alive among that scene of desolation and destruction.

'Back home we heard the news that the effort had been a huge success and that our troops had begun to advance through the gap in the enemy fortifications as we came in to land. This was most heartening news for us all, for the British armies had been having a really hard time of it in the face of very fortified positions and we were glad to have helped in some small way to relieve the situation.' This was certainly confirmed by the AOC, No 83 Group, Tactical Air Force, who subsequently sent a message congratulating 101 Squadron on the part they had played in the Caen attack.

101 lost 12 crews in June and July 1944 because considerable demands were made on them as the Allies consolidated their foothold on the continent.

'POSTGRAM
To: Headquarters, No 1 Group
From: Headquarters, Bomber Command

BC/TS/31852/Air/Ops
Date: 1st July 1944
TOP SECRET
ABC, No 101 Squadron
'Whilst this Command is engaged on bombing both tactical and strategic targets, it is becoming increasingly difficult to forecast ABC requirements when the daily preliminary warning is passed. ABC is one of the most valuable radio countermeasures in use at the present time and in order therefore to ensure that ABC aircraft are available, it is

150
Flg Off Harris and his crew. (L-R): Sgt Jock Wood (Flt Eng), Sgt Don Dale (Mid-Upper), Sgt Jack Morley (W/Op), Flg Off John Arthur DFC (Nav), Flg Off George Harris DFC (Pilot), Flg Off Dai Jones DFC (Bomb-aimer), Sgt Vic Congerton (Rear Gunner), Sgt C. York (Spec Op).

150

requested that 10 aircraft of 101 Squadron are stood to daily. If these aircraft are not called for by 1600hrs on any day, they may, after checking with this Headquarters, be used for bombing operations which are being undertaken by your Group, provided that a further 10 ABC aircraft from 101 Squadron will be available if required the following day.'

Thus there were even more apprehensive faces in evidence when the Squadron crews found out that they were to combine their tactical duties with a return to the strategic fray. After a few hours of well-earned rest following Caen, it was back to the briefing room again on the afternoon of 18 July to be told that they were returning to the Ruhr Valley, and in particular to attack the giant synthetic oil plant at Scholven.

By now the Harris crew with Jack Morley had learned the operational ropes and had settled into a routine. 'While the skipper signed for the aircraft,' recalled Morley, 'we settled on the grass for a last smoke. I always took the third light as a sign to the gods of fate that I was not superstitious, but as this was to become a ritual of the tour, I suppose I was only underlining the belief that every-one is superstitious in one form or another.

'Then we taxied out to take-off. This was controlled by visual means because radio silence had to be maintained throughout the whole trip except for emergencies. Having been given the all clear by green Aldis lamp or flare, we would start to rev up the engines and there would be a growing sense of excite-ment amongst the crew. Then brakes were released and the whole aircraft shuddered — slowly, oh so slowly, we began to roll along the runway accompanied by the deafening roar of the engines as the great bird of war struggled to lift the massive load of some 16,000lb. The crew was full of apprehension as the runway in front of us got shorter and shorter, but then beneath us we sensed that the friction of the wheels on the ground had ceased. Struggling still, but gradually gaining height, the skipper called, "Undercarriage up", and we began to turn. As we climbed, the pitch of the engines changed from a might roar to a steady drone. "Rendezvous Beachy Head," said the navigator, a phrase we were to hear many times during the four-month tour, and I peered out of the astro dome. What a wonderful sight it was — Lancasters and Halifaxes arriving from all directions and taking their allotted places, based on time and height, to form a huge stream, some 2,000ft or so in depth and width. If you can imagine a cube of these dimensions, with an aircraft at each point of the cube and one in the centre, and the whole forming into a line, you will get some idea of

the sight. As the stream turned on course for the target area, our position was in the top layer and very near the front end.

'The plan once again consisted of many changes of course, plus our ABC working all out and Window drops, which were all designed to assist our safe passage to the target. But it was not to be on this fateful night. The enemy awaited our every move. At the point where the enemy coast was to be crossed, flares started to light up the sky and fighter attacks commenced immediately. Deadly and swift, no prolonged battles as depicted by films, these fighter pilots were masters of tactics. The attack would come in one swift burst, and the fighter would then disappear back into the darkness from whence he came. The ABC operator was busy doing his little thing while the others kept a special watch to the east, which was the darker side of the sky and the direction from which an attack was most likely to come. We did not open fire if the fighter did not see us — our mission was to deliver a load of high explosives to the target, not to play the hero by engaging in unnecessary fighter combat. Yet even if a fighter came in, the speed of the attacks was usually such that the gunners would scarcely have time to spot him before the attack was over and we were watching for others. Time and time again bombers were seen under attack, and some were seen to go down. Despite our many turns, the flares would also turn as if lighting up a path for us, which in fact they were — they were lighting up a trap to be sprung by the fighters.

'This was the pattern for the whole flight until the time came for the turn on to the final leg to the target area, where the flares died out and the fighter activity ceased. But it was only to be replaced by the expected continual heavy barrage of the fixed defences of this area. The Ruhr Valley in American terms would probably have been known as Hell Fire Valley. The whole sky, as we headed on this final leg towards Scholven, was one mass of exploding shells and coloured tracer, criss-crossing the sky across our path. In a seem-ingly impenetrable block of fire, our way ahead was made to seem almost impossible. How could anything get safely through this inferno of shellfire?

'Our mid-upper gunner, Don Dale, called out to me to have a look out of the astro dome. All around, as now we were running in towards the target, were the red and green tracers. Smoke from shells bursting in the distance, and red, or white flashes, followed by the ping of shrapnel as it hit us. I clung to the handrail attached to the astro dome mountings, absolutely terrified. I was not to leave this position until we had got out of the target area, and anyway I was so frightened that my legs would not have supported me had I let go of the hand rails. As a consequence, I missed one of the quarter hourly broadcasts, but fortunately, before going in for interrogation, I learned that it was just the normal check broadcast and got it copied down before my log was examined. At the time nothing seemed so important as seeing what was going on. If I was to die, I wanted to see how it happened. I can hear Dai's voice now as he gave his instructions, and the calm words from the skipper, "Steady Chaps", as right into the centre of this hell we went. Then, "Bombs Gone", and our Lancaster was relieved of its load and gave an upward lurch, as if it was a living thing and it too wanted to be away from this storm of destruction. We were suddenly away from it all, and heading for the safety of the dark sky beyond the target. The relief was almost too much for us, as, expecting vengeful fighters to be waiting, we turned on to a different heading for the journey homewards. But fortunately they ignored us and were still hunting the incoming force, in an attempt to prevent at least some of them from reaching the target. Despite all the setbacks we had succeeded in hitting the target, and as we turned we could see the smoke and flames of many fires, accompanied by intermittent explosions, as the giant oil plant was systematically being reduced to mounds of burning and exploding rubble. It was many many miles along our return journey before the glow of these great fires was eventually out of our line of vision.'

The homeward journey was uneventful but the arrival back over Lincolnshire after a night op exposed the Harris' crew to another perennial danger. Ludford lay between Binbrook, Kelstern, and Faldingworth airfields, and as their circuits crossed one another, the scope for collisions in the dark was considerable. The stations tried to solve this problem by flying designated clockwise and anti-clockwise circuits, but even so the Squadron Commander had the trailing aerial whipped away from his Lancaster by another aircraft one night. 'On approaching the airfield, therefore,' continued Jack Morley, 'our skipper transmitted, "Bookworm P for Peter calling Bookshop ('Bookshop' was Ludford's radio callsign and the Harris crew were flying in P-Peter that night), permission to join circuit". We would then be given a height to fly in the stack above Ludford, priority being accorded to badly damaged aircraft. But the close proximity of so many other aircraft meant that there could be no relaxation until we were safely down on the runway and back at dispersal. Yet, in spite of the danger, it was a really wonderful sight to see all the warbirds arriving back at base together'.

'It was always nice to come back from a trip and hear a friendly voice with a friendly joke from Air Traffic,' said one navigator. The flying control officers were a boon as well when it came to getting a host of bombers down — the average landing time for each aircraft in 1 Group was $4\frac{1}{4}$-min in July 1943, but by the end of 1944 this had been reduced to $1\frac{3}{4}$min. Nevertheless, it was never safe to trust completely the skies over Ludford — on 27 September 1943, after battling their way to and from Hanover, Plt Off Skipper and his crew were shot down over Wickenby by a German intruder lying in wait.

With pinpoint guidance from the Master Bomber, 101 could now place bombs to within an accuracy that could be measured in yards rather than in the miles of the bad old days. Such precision was greatly appreciated by the men on the ground. 'On 26 September,' wrote Jack Morley in his diary, 'we set off once more on a low-level daylight mission, but this time against the guns at Cap Griz Nez which since 1940 had been hurling daily devastation and death against the inhabitants of the Dover area. It was time to dispose of these guns, but the area around their emplacement was occupied by, amongst others, troops of the Canadian Scottish Regiment, so arrangements were made for them to mark the exact locations of the positions. As we approached the target a semi circle of colour could be seen — the Canadians had laid their kilts all around the perimeter of the coastal area still occupied by the Germans. Plt Off Dai Jones, our bomb aimer, once more did a very technical piece of bombing. We clearly saw our bombs hit the gun emplacements and soon afterwards the national papers published pictures of the huge gun barrels either broken in two or tilted over at the most crazy angles. This gave all of us who had been on the mission a great deal of satisfaction and pride in a job well performed'.

By 23 October the Harris crew had come through it all and were standing by for their 30th and last operational mission. As they trooped into the briefing room it must have seemed that the fates were having one last laugh at their expense. 'The target, in Happy Valley, was to be the giant Krupps works at Essen, still one of the hottest spots in the whole of Germany. It could not have been a more dangerous ending to our tour — they must have picked this one out for us. At least the planned route had many twists and turns, and we hoped to catch the enemy defences napping by coming in towards Essen from the south so that we could bomb from the "wrong" side.

'Then aboard the bus to our aircraft. At the dispersal we found a congolmeration of our comrades from 101 Squadron who were not flying that night and who had come to wish us good luck. To the accompaniment of their

153

153
The Rhine bridges at Cologne well and truly 'pranged'. 'Our own special target on our last mission,' wrote Jack Morley, 'was the bridge leading directly to the great Cathedral, which we had firm orders not to hit!'

cheers and waves from our groundcrew who had served us so well, we slowly taxied away from dispersal.

'Once airborne the tensions eased a little, but as we made landfall over Europe our port outer engine began to overheat. George Harris nursed it as much as possible but to no avail as flames started to flicker from this engine with increasing intensity. George hit the extinguisher button and feathered the engine. We were all ears now as the flames died out, and George trimmed the controls to keep us on an even keel. We lost a little height and George put it to the rest of us that, as we were so far along our journey, he thought we should press on to the target, to which we all agreed as this was our last trip, and we wanted to get it over. No distractions for now from enemy fighters, and shortly afterwards we approached the target area, bomb doors open, with Dai in his position in the nose, levelling out for our run in to the target. Then fate took a hand once more as the starboard outer received a hit. This engine provided most of the electrical power for various equipments in the aircraft, including the bomb release system, and consequently it left us with the problem of releasing the bombs manually by means of what was named the dead-man's lever. To achieve this, an implement similar to a car jack handle was inserted into a slot in the floor of the aircraft above the bomb bay, and then rocked back and forth. By this means the hooks on which the bombs were hung could, in theory, be opened to release the bombs. In fact, on this occasion at least, despite all the frantic pumping back and forth they remained firmly secure on their hanging hooks. Over the target, trying all the time to effect release of our load, but to no avail; doing a circuit of the target, then once more, through the barrage of fire and death, trying to unload our eggs. George threw the aircraft about to try to dislodge them, but still to no avail. With sinking hearts we finally turned for home, full of disappointment now, jinking about for the whole time to try to get rid of our load, even when far out across the sea, but fate was against us, and try as we did, they still hung there.

'Losing more and more height now, and with only two engines serviceable, George tried once more to re-start the port engine, but he could only re-start the flickers of flame. We tried again and again to rid ourselves of our load, to no effect, losing height all the time — we were in dire straits now, but every minute took us nearer and nearer to home. Then, at last within range of Ludford Magna, using battery power, the skipper informed them of our predicament, and after they received confirmation from us that we could make the trip, air traffic control told us to land at the crash land strip at Carnaby, a few miles south of Bridlington.

154

259

This place was a specially built huge concrete strip, used by aircraft in such a predicament as ourselves. With only two serviceable engines and a bomb-load which we could not be sure would stay fixed when we bumped on landing, it was a very apprehensive time for us all. Would we get down without crashing, and even if everything went right in this attempt would the bombs drop off and explode? We had done a great deal to make this a distinct possibility by the numerous efforts that we had made to dislodge them.

'The controller below gave us instructions to fly out to sea and approach as low as possible when we attempted to pancake. In giving us these instructions he then added to our misgivings by forgetting to switch off his microphone when he tannoyed to all personnel to clear the immediate surroundings of the airfield because a Lancaster with two engines out, and with a full bombload which was expected to explode on landing, was approaching the landing strip. What a time to let us hear his message, when we were the Lancaster involved.

'With the aid of the trailing aerial technique, George turned, and at a height of 50ft we flew towards the lights. Rising to clear the cliff-tops, the whole crew, except pilot and engineer, braced for crash landing; we waited and hoped, then, after what seemed an eternity, but was in fact only a few seconds, I said to the skipper, "Aren't we down yet?" to which the reply came that we were indeed down, and were just starting to come to a

stop. Engines off in the next minute, and to the scene of a greatly excited crowd of ground crew people, we climbed out, and kissed the earth, one and all.'

So the Harris crew returned to Ludford to receive the expected news that they had not yet finished their tour of ops because, although they had flown over the target at Essen, they had not dropped their bombs and therefore the mission was abortive. It was not until 28 October that they finally completed their tour by bombing the bridges over the Rhine at Cologne. 'As Dai Jones called "Bombs gone", the whole crew gave a great cheer. We then flew around Cologne as first one Squadron aircraft, then another, completed its bombing run and joined up with us to return to Ludford. After we switched off engines in dispersal we all shook hands before climbing down to meet the crowd of well-wishers who had come to congratulate us.

'After a night's hectic celebrations, we spent the next few days collecting our kit before going on leave. Then came the parting of the ways, some of us never to meet again.'

Given such experiences over Cologne, it might be assumed that Bomber Command had the skies of Germany to itself by late 1944. Certainly since D-Day Bomber Command had been operating by day as well as by night, and the ABC Lancasters went along dutifully on all occasions 'until some genius realised that the Germans could see us in daylight and there was little that ABC could do to stop them'. Thereafter 101 flew

155
Flt Lt Scrym Wedderburn with his crew in the autumn of 1944 after he had completed his second Lancaster tour and his third tour of ops on 101. Known as 'Wedderburn's Chindits' they were from L-R: Flt Sgt Schofield (Flt Eng), Flg Off Hunter (Bomb Aimer), Flg Off Patrick (W/Op), Scrym, Flg Off Sidwell (Nav), Flg Off Booth (Mid Upper), Flt Sgt Armishaw (Rear Gunner). Scrym was remembered with affection as a 'very colourful character who drove an ancient car, couldn't bear red tape, and who didn't give a damn for anyone. In the air he was superb.'

155

only by night, and at the Fourth Meeting on Radio Countermeasures Policy and Progress held at High Wycombe on 22 September 1944, it was agreed that '101 Squdaron should be relieved of its ABC commitment and become a main force squadron again'. This piece of reorganisation was designed to concentrate all radio countermeasures activities within 100 Group, and an existing Halifax unit was to be transferred to that Group for ABC duties to fill the gap left by 101 so that 1 Group did not lose a Lancaster squadron. However this tidy scheme foundered in the face of German opposition. Although the Allied armies were advancing on the Rhine and capturing many of the German early warning radar sites in the process, the Luftwaffe did not capitulate. In fact the German fighter crews only responded to the enemy at their gates with the sustained and tenacious vigour of men who had nothing to lose. For 101 this meant that although they could now fly a decreased proportion of ABC missions, the Command could not do without their services altogether, especially as the British bomber effort was being divided increasingly between a number of targets separated in time and space. Consequently, when 1 Group broke all previous records by launching a force of 292 aircraft on a most successful attack against Freiburg in October, eight ABC aircraft were also detailed to support another Group in an attack on Neuss. Certainly Bomber Command still needed all the defensive effort it could muster, and 101 was to lose 20 crews between 1 November 1944 and the end of the war in Europe.

Sgt H. van Geffen arrived on 101 as a Spec Op towards the end of the war. Born in Holland in 1917 to a Dutch father and an Irish mother, Van, as he was known to his friends, was brought up in France where he learned to speak both French and German. 'My family returned to England in 1931,' he explained, 'and by the time I found myself at Ludford Magna I was no longer at all fluent in German'. His operational experience makes fascinating reading. (Quoted from *Lincolnshire Life* by Bruce Barrymore Halpenny).

156

Sgt van Geffen outside the Sergeant's Mess while he was a member of the Lloyd crew. (L-R): Back row: Sgt 'Happy' Mummery (Mid-upper), Sgt 'Timber' Woods (Flt Eng), 'Van' (Spec Op), Flg Off 'Skip' Lloyd (Pilot), Sgt Wally Edwards (Nav). Front row: Sgt Phil Axford (W/Op), Sgt Des 'Blimp' Lamb (Bomb-aimer), Sgt 'Shorty' Satherley (Rear gunner), Sergeant Binder (Crew dog).

156

157

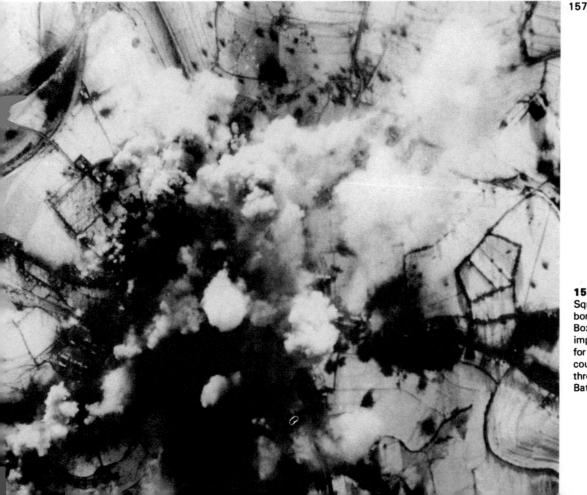

157

Sqn Ldr McLeod-Selkirk's crew bomb a snow-covered St Vith on Boxing Day, 1944. St Vith was an important road and rail junction for the Germans who were then counter-attacking and advancing through the Ardennes during the Battle of the Bulge.

261

158
Cartoon.

159
Lancaster SR-H 'How', together with her groundcrew who were known as the 'Naafi Gang'. There was an exciting race between H-How of 'A' Flight and S-Sugar of 'C' Flight to see which would complete 100 ops first. Sugar, with 'The Saint' as her crest, completed her 'ton' against Hanover on 5/6 January 1945, whereas How had to wait until 7/8 January when Plt Off J. A. Kurtzer RAAF and his crew attacked Munich. H-How survived the war to fly 121 operational missions not out, and although S-Sugar reputedly beat her by one op, 'The Saint' was finally shot down by a jet fighter on 23 March 1945 over Bremen Bridge after her crew 'pressed on' with three engines.

160
A load of 1,000lb bombs leave Z-Zebra for Bremen Bridge while S-Sugar was meeting her end. T-Tommy is the 101 Lancaster below which looks extremely vulnerable.

158

DOYNG!

N° 1 GRP

"1 GROUP DESPATCHED 312 SORTIES IN ONE EVENING."

'On my first three ops I flew with Flg Off Lloyd and his crew, who were then posted to a Pathfinder squadron, leaving me to find another crew. I joined up with the A Flight Commander, Sqn Ldr McLeod-Selkirk, and flew regularly with them until they were allotted a brand new aircraft which was not then fitted with ABC. This left me as a "spare bod" again, so I arranged to join up with Flt Lt McClenaghan, with whom I had flown previously on a couple of occasions.

'On the very next day, 23 February 1945, we were briefed to fly in an attack against Pforzheim, a town situated between two major targets of Karlsruhe and Stuttgart. It was now on the list of Bomber Command targets for the first time only because it was an important junction on the main line leading to the American Seven Army front. A force of 300 Lancasters took off in the late afternoon of the 23rd, but at the last moment our aircraft was U/S, so my crew flew without me in another, not fitted with ABC, while I stayed at home. Flt Lt McClenaghan and his crew did not return from this operation.

'7 March 1945 — Target: Dessau, a city situated south-west of Berlin and about halfway between Magdeburg and Leipzig, all former Bomber Command targets. It was a city with 120,000 inhabitants and an important target for it was the home for the Junkers jet-engine and main testing base,

though our main target was to disrupt the rail communications. These had been bombed by a small daylight force of the USAAF on 2 March and we were being sent in to finish the job. The pilot of the crew with whom I was to fly on this occasion was taken ill shortly before briefing. The "stand-by" crew were called upon to take his place and I joined them. Their own Spec Op Sgt Rudy Mahr, had on this occasion already been detailed to fly with Sqn Ldr Gibbons, and Rudy and I applied for permission to switch aircraft, so that he could join his regular crew for the trip. This application was not allowed. Sgt Rudy Mahr and the crew he flew with did not return from this operational mission.

'12 March 1945 — Daylight attack on Dortmund. Not being on the Battle Order for this raid, I arranged to fly as a "passenger", with Flt Lt Harrison, wishing to see for myself what a target under attack looked like. I obtained the necessary unofficial "permission", but being called a "bloody fool" and a "lunatic" in the process. We developed an oil-leak in the port-inner engine on take-off, and were compelled to feather the prop within a few minutes. We flew out over the North Sea, on three engines, in order to jettison our bomb-load, but were unable to climb to a safe height from which we could drop our "Cookie" 4,000lb bomb, without being caught ourselves in its blast when it exploded on hitting the sea, so we had to bring it back with us. However, we were unable to find our base at Ludford Magna, due to ground mist, and we were diverted to the emergency landing ground at Carnaby where we made a safe landing on our three good engines.

'Dressed in full flying-kit, we explored nearby Bridlington to pass the time away while awaiting engine repairs. Eventually, being without ready cash (not usually required over Germany), the skipper explained our situation to a friendly bank manager, and as a result we held an impromptu pay parade on the pavement outside the bank. In funds for one evening at least, we were able to visit the Dance Hall in Bridlington that evening and, in spite of (or was it because of?) our flying-kit, roll-neck sweaters and flying boots, we had no difficulty in finding dancing partners among the Bridlington girls, although we received a lot of black looks from the Bridlington boys! Four days later, our aircraft repaired, we hedge-hopped across Yorkshire and Lincolnshire, back to Ludford Magna.

'On landing there, I learned that Sqn Ldr McLeod-Selkirk, skipper of my former crew, whose new aircraft had eventually been fitted with ABC, had asked for me to re-join his crew. The target, during my absence, had been Gelsenkirchen, and another Spec Op

Sgt Johnny Toy, had volunteered to take my place. One thousand bombers flew to Gelsenkirchen that night — only one was lost, and returning crews reported seeing it blow up in the air above Germany. Sqn Ldr McLeod-Selkirk and his crew (whom I liked to consider as "my crew"), and Sgt Johnny Toy, were in that aircraft.

'I suppose one could truthfully say that I avoided death by "sticking my neck out" and tempting Providence, but after three narrow escapes in as many weeks I found myself wondering how long my luck would last.'

In the end, although bomber squadrons such as 101 never extinguished the Luftwaffe's will to resist — German night intruders had the nerve to shoot up Ludford airfield and village as late as 3 March 1945 with no opposition — Bomber Command eventually wore the German air force down to a state where the will could no longer inspire the deed. Luftwaffe fighter airframes certainly continued to roll off the production lines until the end, for German organisation and native cunning kept factories going in apparently shattered buildings and underground caves, but no amount of subterfuge could overcome bottlenecks inflicted by the bombers elsewhere. Completed engines and airframes often failed to mate as both lay stranded behind canals and railways smashed by the strategic offensive. Even if replacement aircraft did get to the front —

161

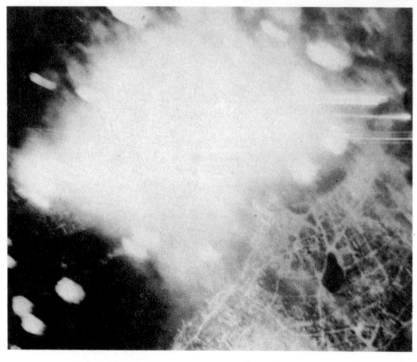

162

and some undoubtedly did as Sgt Ken O'Brien, a 101 rear gunner, discovered when he became one of the first bomber gunners to shoot down an Me262 jet fighter — there were less and less experienced pilots to fly them by early 1945 and minimal fuel to put in their tanks in the wake of the Allied onslaught on the Axis oil refineries. And even if the Luftwaffe did get airborne, the capture or dislocation of more and more of the German air defence system meant that the German controllers and their charges were often 'blind' until it was too late. So it came about that, less than a year after Nuremberg, 101 was able to contribute 21 aircraft and crews to the devastating attack on Dresden, a city much further inside the Reich. 'Adverse headwinds reaching 100mph extended the trip to a lengthy 10hr 25min and we heard the BBC giving out the news of the raid while we were still airborne.' Yet in spite of this increased vulnerability inside enemy airspace, all squadron crews bombed successfully and returned unscathed. Bomber Command had not knocked out the enemy so much as helped to choke him to death.

101 flew a mammoth 920 operational hours by day and 1,215 by night during March 1945 against targets as varied as Cologne, Mannheim, Chemnitz, Dessau, Kassel, Dortmund, and good old faithful Essen. The last Squadron crew to perish on ops was Flg Off Little's — they flew on a daylight raid against Bremen on 23 March and they went down in Lancaster III 'S' Sugar, an old warhorse which was then on its 119th sortie. Thereafter 101 had the German skies to themselves.

Thirty Squadron aircraft and crews attacked Kiel without incident on 9 April to help capsize the pocket battleship *Admiral Scheer*, but nothing underlined Bomber Command's final omnipotence more forceably than 101's last wartime operation on 25 April when it sent 24 crews to bomb

163

Hitler's redoubt at Berchtesgaden. 'It was a fitting climax to over five years of most strenuous endeavour,' and as the Lancasters streamed over this Bavarian bastion of the Thousand Year Reich in broad daylight, 'we demolished a great portion of that evil encampment in a brilliantly executed attack'. The lion in its turret had come a long way since he first looked out of an Overstrand.

Thereafter, 101 Squadron engaged in more humanitarian pursuits. On 27 April it began evacuating freed prisoners of war — 24 crammed into each Lancaster — back to the UK, and by the end of the month it was dropping up to 5,947 bags of food a day to the starving inhabitants of the Netherlands. It was rewarding work, though the conclusion of hostilities in Europe was greeted with equal enthusiasm:

'8/5/45. No operations are scheduled for today!

'All work on the station with the exception of essential servicing stopped today at midday. The Prime Minister announced the termination of the war in Europe to the whole country and his speech was broadcast over the station Tannoy system at 3pm. The afternoon was then mainly devoted to sports activities, the main feature being a football match between "England" and "The Rest". There were parties in all Messes during the evening.'

There must have been a lot of happy and contented men who rolled into bed that night, for at long last the war for them was over.

By what yardstick should we assess 101's achievements as a bomber squadron? Statistics can give some guide for 101 mounted 2,477 ABC sorties between October 1943 and the final raid on Berchtesgaden, and launched 6,740 Blenheim, Wellington and Lancaster missions during the war. Yet such bald figures mask the human dimension of the bomber offensive. 'Victory inclines to the force which is most thoroughly and efficiently organised,' quoted the AOC 1 Group to his men on 7 June 1945, and it was here that the success story of Bomber Command squadrons begins.

Back in 1940, the number of Blenheims dispatched by 101 on a typical night raid could be counted on one hand. Crews were 'advised' as to their route — it was up to them whether they took the advice or not — and the time on target for the 20 or so bombers which made up the 'mass' raid could be spread over an hour. Even if this less than formidable number reached the target area, which was by no means certain, the 1,000lb bomb load carried by each Blenheim was hardly likely to bring Germany to its knees.

The Wellington era was only superior in terms of numbers, but with the introduction of more suitable aircraft such as the Lancaster, improved aids such as Gee, Oboe, H2S, and ABC, and a Pathfinder Force to lead the way, a whole new era of aerial bombardment came into being. 'In the old days,' observed 'Mac' Mackay, 'we were very amateurish and slap-happy. We took off usually in our own time, flew our own routes, and bombed when we thought we were over the target, or on DR, or where the flak was. However, by the time I came back to do my second tour, it had all changed. Here was aerial marshalling at its most precise. Here was navigation with the minimum of error, and here was military discipline honed to a split second'. Thus aircraft from No 14 Base not only dropped 34,000 tons of bombs in 1944 alone, but they also dropped them with much greater effect. From being a clumsy blunderbuss, Bomber Command had become a surgical instrument capable of striking at the enemy's vitals with clinical precision. Its impact on the outcome of World War 2 was decisive.

Similarly the effect of radio counter-measures such as ABC in protecting the bomber force should never be under-estimated. By the beginning of 1944 the German bomber element, lacking effective jamming support, was losing an average of one aircraft and four trained crewmen for every five British civilians it managed to kill. Back over their Reich homeland, it was

161
No 101 Squadron, in all its sizeable glory, in 1945.

162
Kiel docks come in for plastering from 19,000ft on 9/10 April 1945.

163
The final Squadron operational mission of the war — Berchtesgaden on 25 April. This magnificent panorama of the Bavarian Alps was photographed by a flight engineer who had never used a camera before. The target itself is shrouded by the smoke of destruction in the centre.

164
Cartoon.

largely due to the distraction of jamming that the German defences could not deal as severely with their night raiders. As Alfred Price said in *Instruments of Darkness*: 'It is, therefore, no exaggeration to say that the radio countermeasures campaign played a major part in keeping Bomber Command's losses down to a level which the RAF could afford to countenance.'

Nevertheless, all this technological innovation relied for its success on the personnel to put it into effect. 'Instead of the usual game of snooker with some points after a raid,' said a pilot watching the Command improve as 1943 went by, 'I quietly said to the crew, "If we're going to survive this lot, everything has got to be right inside that kite of ours and that means all eight of us working together"'. So the various individuals who had previously filled a bomber were replaced by a *crew* who lived and worked together on a Lancaster. Surprisingly, in view of the strains and survival chances attendant on operations, there were remarkably few cases of 'Lack of Moral Fibre' on bomber squadrons. Perhaps it was because they were all volunteers from the start, and the training system certainly weeded out most weak links, but nevertheless there must have been many men who thought about opting out only to carry on through loyalty to their crew and squadron. 'I can do it alone,' said the injured pilot in *Fair Stood the Wind for France* as he tried to persuade his crew to leave him behind and save themselves. 'If I'd been a fighter boy, there'd have been no question of doing it otherwise.' 'You're not a fighter boy,' replied the WOp/AG firmly. 'You're part of us. We're a unit. We always have been.'

With a spirit such as this, 101 Squadron crews had the faith to move, and destroy, mountains.

The stories of bravery inspired by such dedication are legion, and none is more typical than the occasion at Holme when Sqn Ldr G. W. Fisher ignored the danger of exploding fuel tanks to enter the blazing wreckage of a crashed Lancaster in order to rescue the crew. In 1943, 101 recorded the award of three DSOs, 38 DFCs, seven CGMs, and 33 DFMs, while the following year Squadron personnel received a total of 98 DFCs, 49 DFMs, and one DSO. Yet if this was the profit side of 101's account, the loss side was grievous. Out of the total of 70,253 RAF casualties killed in action during World War 2, some 55,888 officers and other ranks died in action or on active service in Bomber Command. To put it another way, the British strategic air offensive over Western Europe cost 7% of the manpower directly absorbed by the fighting services during the war, but once again, although such statistics may be the only vehicle for conveying the magnitude of the loss, they only tell part of the story. This 7% was largely derived from the best sections of British youth because of the high degree of physical and mental skills needed to operate a heavy bomber. Bomber Command therefore lost over 55,000 men that the nation could ill afford to lose — such was the loss rate of educated men for instance, that by the end of February 1944 it was feared that 101 would soon run out of qualified Spec Ops and Bomber Command considered having to use men who could not even speak German. The bomber offensive therefore has rightly been described as the Passchendaele of World War 2, not simply because it was a war of attrition but also because both destroyed the flower of a whole generation.

These sentiments applied just as much to the groundcrew as to the men who flew, for even in the relatively unsophisticated days of 1941 it was estimated that approximately 35 people were needed on the ground to keep an operational bomber in the air. 'To aircrew is due the highest praise,' wrote Air Vice-Marshal Blucke in June 1945 after he became the last wartime Air Officer Commanding 1 Group, 'but let it not be forgotten that their feats of skill and gallantry were made possible only by the tireless energies and devotion to duty of each man and woman, no matter how great or how small their allotted task, throughout the months that are now past'. Certainly the 'chop rate' among the armourers who loaded the ammunition and armed the bombs was second only to that of aircrew. The maintenance of a squadron of heavy bombers night after night was no easy matter either, and no one needed unserviceable hydraulics or a sick engine to heighten the tension of a sortie, or carelessness by an electrician to cause a hang-up and thereby ruin an attack. 101 Squadron lived and worked as a team, and it only helped to win the war because it was a good team.

Not that the personnel of 101 would have wished to dwell on the dark side of Squadron life. 'I was 19 at the time,' recalled Sgt Geoffrey Whittle, 'and life was for living. We got on with the job — the higher direction of the war was for the older types, 25-year olds and above!! They were enjoyable days and of course we always expected to come back'. Suffice to say, therefore, that at least 277 aircraft went missing from 101 Squadron between 1939 and 1945, and that the Squadron lost a total of 1,094 men killed in action and 178 taken prisoner of war. It was the highest casualty rate of any RAF squadron in World War 2.

What of those left behind? Flt Lt Thomas Rowland was typical of the men who joined Bomber Command in their droves. 'My husband and I were married on 1 June 1938,' recalled his wife, Margaret. 'He was the village postman where I worked as a nanny to the three-year old child of the managing director of ICI, and I left only to marry my one and only love. We rented a small bungalow in the village and were very happy. In those days wages were not very high and my husband did part-time gardening to help-out. He was very well liked and we had our first child in September 1939. My husband volunteered for service in 1940 and did his initial training at Blackpool.

'After various postings he was sent to America to gain his wings. When he returned he was a proud man with his wings in place, and so were we. He looked so smart in his uniform as an officer, and all thought how well he had done even though he had acquired just an ordinary village school education with no scholarship to help him along. He had got on by his own merits.

'In December 1943 he came on what was to be his last leave. Because he had to go back to base for Christmas, we made our Christmas with him then. We had as happy a time as we could.'

On 14 January 1944, Flt Lt Rowland and his crew took-off from Ludford for Brunswick at the height of the Battle of Berlin. They never returned. The first news to arrive at Margaret's house 'was the dreaded telegram'.

'POST OFFICE
TELEGRAM
15 Jan 44

Priority CC

Regret to inform you that your husband 127942 F/Lt Rowland T. W. is reported missing from Air Operations on the night of 14/15 Jan 1944 stop Letter follows any further information received will be communicated to you immediately stop Pending receipt of written notification from the Air Ministry no information should be given to the Press
OC Squadron'

'His relatives and I were beside ourselves with shock and grief but we kept on hoping. The waiting continued, interrupted by official letters saying that they would let us know as soon as they heard something.'

'Dear Mrs Rowland,

'I am writing to offer you the sincere sympathy of myself and the entire Squadron in the anxiety you have experienced since hearing that your husband, Flt Lt Thomas Wilson Rowland (127942) is missing from Air Operations on the night of 14/15 - January 1944.

'Your husband and his crew took off on an operational sortie over enemy territory and I am sorry to say failed to return to base. No messages were received from the crew after take off and nothing has so far been heard of it or any member of the crew.

'There is always the possibility that they may have come down by parachute or made a forced landing in enemy territory, in which case news of this would take a considerable time to come through, but you will be immediately advised of any further information that is received.

'This is indeed a great loss to the Squadron for your husband was not only popular with all ranks but was also a most experienced and efficient pilot and captain of aircraft. His splendid record and the many operational sorties in which he has taken part fully testify to the courage and devotion to duty he has always displayed in the execution of his duties.

The personal effects of your husband are now in the custody of the "Committee of Adjustment Officer, RAF Station Ludford Magna", who will be writing to you shortly concerning their disposal.

'I can well appreciate your feelings at this anxious time, and we all join with you in hoping and praying that your husband is safe.

Yours sincerely,
R. I. Alexander,
Wing Commander, Commanding
No 101 Squadron, R.A.F.'

'Then we received notification that he had been awarded the DFC — more tears and heartbreak. My husband's mother and I went to Buckingham Palace to receive the decoration from the late King George. It was a very moving and proud moment. Back home the waiting and hoping recommenced and continued day after day, week after week.' But hope was finally extinguished on 24 July 1944.

AIR MINISTRY
(Casualty Branch)
73-77 OXFORD STREET,
W1.
24th July, 1944

'Madam,

'I am directed to refer to a letter from this department dated 6th March 1944 concerning your husband, Acting Flt Lt Thomas Wilson Rowland, Royal Air Force, and to inform you with regret that a further report has now been received from the International Red Cross Committee, Geneva, which states that Sgt Bateman, Sgt Cornwell, Sgt Clements, and the two unknown members of the crew of the aircraft in which your husband was flying on 14th January 1944, were buried on the 16th January 1944, in the Lower Cemetery, Lautenthal, about 25 miles south of Brunswick.

165
The Control Tower at Ludford in
1945, now brightened up for
peacetime use.

166
The final reckoning — a
devastated Krupps Works in
Essen in 1945. *IWM*

names were courage got nothing at all'. So it
must be left to an air gunner, R. W. Gilbert,
to write the epitaph for them all in his poem,
Requiem for a Rear Gunner:

'My brief sweet life is over, my eyes no
longer see,
No summer walks — no Christmas Trees —
no pretty girls for me,
I've got the chop, I've had it, my nightly ops
are done,
Yet in another hundred years, I'll still be
twenty-one.'

Yet in spite of the horrors and heartache of
war, the average man on 101 never lost his
human feelings. 'I remember one particular
night when the Squadron had been hit very
hard,' wrote Jack Morley, 'and while we were
resting from our labours we were awakened
by the sound of shouting and banging.
Coming slowly to our senses we perceived
the sight of the other occupants of our hut
stamping, banging, and dancing around as
though they had gone mad. But we were
soon to join in this strange ritual as we
realised that we had been invaded by
earwigs. The insects were everywhere, covering floors, beds, clothing, kit, walls, and
ceiling. After frenziedly shaking clothes and
boots we dressed and joined in the war
against these invaders. Beaten back by over-
whelming numbers, we finally evacuated our
hut and retired to the mess, leaving the battle
to the ground personnel who moved everything out and painted the whole place with
paraffin to clean out the creatures. Here we
were, having endured all that the enemy
could throw at us on upwards of 30 missions,
defeated by a swarm of earwigs.'

'People of the younger generation,' wrote
one flight commander, 'can get the impression
that Bomber Command was one big happy

'It is regretted that it is still not possible to
identify the two referred to as unknown but
nevertheless it is considered that you would
wish to be notified of this report.

'In conveying this information, I am again
to express the sincere sympathy of the
department with you in your anxiety, and to
assure you that you will be informed of any
further news that may come to hand.

I am, Madam,
Your obedient Servant,
for Director of Personal Services.'

'My son is now happily married,' concluded
Margaret Rowland, 'and my grandson is
very like his grand-dad who never came back
to know him.'

'Butch' Harris fought for everyone who
had taken part in the strategic offensive to be
awarded a special campaign medal after the
war, but he was over-ruled. 'This was a sore
point with a lot of us,' said 'Mac' Mackay,
'because so many of my good friends who
took the damnedest risks and whose middle

band of brothers. This was not so. Squadrons were very much individual entities — we didn't mix much with other squadrons — and they assumed the character and charisma of the people who were on the squadron at the time.'

As a result, few outsiders will ever appreciate what it was really like to serve on a bomber squadron. 'Is it any wonder that I avoid memorial services,' said an ex-flight sergeant, 'for I cry very easily and the sound of the Air Force March brings memories flooding back. Men are not supposed to cry but this one does mostly in private, for how many are there who can even begin to understand?'. Without in any way decrying the achievements of the more glamorous fighter squadrons, the classic dog-fight could never do more than prevent defeat. It was the largely unsung heroes on units such as 101 Squadron who took the battle to the enemy night after night for year after year when the other services were in no position to do so, and in so doing sacrificed their youth to sustain civilian morale and bring about eventual victory.

Nearly 40 years later, the scars have largely healed and the ravages inflicted by 101 Squadron have generally been obliterated. 14 Base HQ disbanded on 24 October 1945 and that same month 101 left for Binbrook. Ludford airfield was put on care and maintenance, much to the benefit of the locals. After countless generations of doing without basic amenities, the inhabitants of Ludford village had watched the electricity cables and water pipes being laid past their doorsteps with envious eyes in 1943, but the supplies were limited to the needs of the aerodrome. When it closed the villagers were able to tap the power, heat, water, and drainage for themselves.

The hangars at Ludford Magna were then used for storage, particularly during the ill-fated 'Ground Nuts Scheme', and the runways were removed in the early 1970s, some of the hard core being used in the construction of the Humber Bridge. Only the memories remain, and each year the survivors come back to Ludford where a Book of Remembrance in the village church pays tribute to their colleagues who never returned.

However, memories of 101 are also still vivid in less likely places. Plt Off T. A. Allen joined 101 at the beninning of May 1944, and after flying his 'second dickey' familiarisation trip with Plt Off Waughan against an ammunition factory at Augigne-Racan, he was ready to operate with a crew of his own. The Allen crew was typically cosmopolitan, with the Spec Op coming from as far away as Brisbane, Australia. On 28 May 1944, Bomber Command was briefed to attack a number of targets in Belgium, together with a 'spoof' on Dusseldorf, and 101 was spread among the stream. The Allen crew, in Lancaster K-King, were briefed to drop 18 500lb bombs on Bourg Leopold, a Belgian town in the province of Limburg noted for the manufacture of glass and explosives. Squadron crews were instructed to take-off at intervals from 0005hr on 28 May and the subsequent cryptic Squadron record in respect of the Allen crew was: 'No news after take-off.'

Their Lancaster crashed at Sommelsdijk on the island of Goeree-Overflakee off the Dutch coast in the early hours. The bomb load exploded on impact and there were no survivors; a local Dutchman who fought the flames stated that it was believed that the Lancaster was brought down by a night fighter. This was the only Squadron crew lost that night and they were buried in the civilian cemetery at Sommelsdijk. However the population of the area, who had suffered the traumas of enemy occupation which the British were spared, never forgot. Children at the Middelharnis Technical School made and erected a memorial to the crew in the form of an aircraft wing with the RAF roundel on a camouflaged background, and each year, on the anniversary of the crash, local school children place flowers on the grave in tribute to the men who died so that they might be free.

It is gratifying that the memories of such brave bomber crews will never die, but perhaps the last word should be left to Wg Cdr Tony Reddick who wrote the following message to his Squadron just before he departed in July 1943:

'In taking my leave of the Squadron I want to take this opportunity to express my appreciation and thanks to all ranks for the splendid co-operation and support you have given me.

'Since the Squadron converted to Lancaster aircraft it has gone from strength to strength, and it is now quite definitely the best Squadron in the Group. This is due entirely to the magnificent way in which you have all carried out your duties, under most arduous conditions.

'Very reluctantly I have to say goodbye . . . As some of you may know, my connection with the Squadron dates back to 1932 when I joined it as a very green NCO pilot. You can understand therefore my complete sincerity when I say that wherever I may be, my heart will always be with No 101 Squadron.' This feeling of belonging applied to everyone, no matter how much time they spent on 101, and because this everlasting spirit carried them through the dark times and was never to die, it epitomised everything that was great about a 'Bomber Squadron at War'.

167
The RAF Memorial at
Boxbergheide near Genke in
Belgium. This is just one of the
many memorials to fallen Bomber
Command aircrew in Europe and,
although it is dedicated to all the
airmen who died over the
province of Limburg, it was
erected on the spot were Pilot
Officer Ashton and his crew from
101 Squadron crashed on their
return from Cologne on
31 August 1941.